Effective Platform Engineering

Effective Platform Engineering

AJAY CHANKRAMATH
NIC CHENEWETH
BRYAN OLIVER
SEAN ALVAREZ

FOREWORD BY KIEF MORRIS

MANNING
SHELTER ISLAND

For online information and ordering of this and other Manning books, please visit www.manning.com. The publisher offers discounts on this book when ordered in quantity.

For more information, please contact

>Special Sales Department
>Manning Publications Co.
>20 Baldwin Road
>PO Box 761
>Shelter Island, NY 11964
>Email: orders@manning.com

Manning Publications Co.
20 Baldwin Road
PO Box 761
Shelter Island, NY 11964

Development editor:	Dustin Archibald
Technical editor:	Vikas Bijavara Narayanappa
Review editor:	Kishor Rit
Production editor:	Kathy Rossland
Copy editor:	Kari Lucke
Proofreader:	Jason Everett
Technical proofreader:	Borko Djurkovic
Typesetter:	Tamara Švelić Sabljić
Cover designer:	Marija Tudor

ISBN 9781633436497

To our families and friends: your patience, sacrifices, and steadfast encouragement gave us the strength to persevere through this journey. Your love and support made this work not only possible but also profoundly meaningful.

—Ajay Chankramath, Nic Cheneweth, Bryan Oliver, and Sean Alvarez

brief contents

contents

4 Governance, compliance, and trust   89

    4.1   Developer autonomy   90
          What does it mean to make a development team autonomous?   92

    4.2   Policy-as-code   96
          Introduction to policy-as-code using Open Policy Agent   96

    4.3   Platform-managed trust   102
          Software supply chain security   102 ▪ Zero-trust networking   105
          Separating platform customer identity from cloud infrastructure
          identity   108

5 Evolutionary observability   117

    5.1   Why observability matters   118
          Observability is more than metrics and alerts   119 ▪ Use cases for
          observability beyond basic monitoring of applications   121
          What does good look like?   123 ▪ Viewing observability through a
          single pane of glass   126

    5.2   Observability as a platform service   129
          The end-user access experience   129 ▪ Automatic collection of
          customer data   130 ▪ Who needs to respond when things need
          attention?   131

    5.3   Observability platform as a separate internal product   133
          Architecture of an observability platform   134 ▪ Should you build
          or buy?   136 ▪ Cross-platform observability   138 ▪ Strategies to
          drive adoption   139

    5.4   Observability of published service-level indicators, service-
          level objectives, and service-level agreements   142
          SLOs as code   143

6 Building a software-defined engineering platform   146

    6.1   Building our own example engineering platform   147

    6.2   Prerequisites to getting started   148
          Getting started with the example tools   150 ▪ Developer tools
          selection criteria   152

foreword

Over the past decade or so, business leaders have come to accept that they can't ignore, sideline, or outsource digital technology. This technology needs to be embedded in the core of business strategy to reach modern markets and deliver world-class services to customers. But environments and infrastructure have always been a bottleneck for developing and maintaining digital services.

The book you're about to read provides comprehensive guidance for an organization to plan, build, and run an engineering platform that fulfills the needs of its software delivery teams.

Leaders might wish that this was a solved problem, easily answered by choosing a cloud vendor for their developers. But the cloud is only the beginning of a platform strategy. A cloud provides low-level, general-purpose building blocks rather than an out-of-the-box solution. The parade of trends, including DevOps, PaaS, site reliability engineering, and now platform engineering is evidence of a persistent gap between raw cloud infrastructure and the needs of any given organization. The organization needs to use the cloud as the starting point for building capabilities tailored to the specific business needs, processes, and governance that will enable their developers.

Ajay, Nic, Bryan, and Sean have several decades of experience between them, at Thoughtworks and elsewhere, of helping organizations to define, shape, and implement platform engineering solutions. They have seen the pitfalls and challenges that teams face and are now sharing practical, pragmatic guidance for success.

The authors know that it's much harder to deliver the benefits of a well-managed, centralized development platform than it is to envision them. Too often, platforms are launched after many months of work only to meet with the profound disinterest of their intended users. Even when executives mandate platform usage, development teams easily find reasons to be given an exception. Any evidence of unreliability, learning curves, lack of features, and general low maturity shows that the platform is slowing development work and putting business-critical projects at risk. It's genuinely challenging to build a slick platform that accelerates development teams rather than creating friction.

Many engineers moving into platform work underestimate how much more difficult it is to build services for other people. Building a database for your application is one thing. Building a self-service database provisioning service that meets the needs of a dozen teams now, and more in the near future, is at least an order of magnitude more work.

The root cause of many platform engineering initiatives' problems is lack of engagement with their users. This book outlines an outcome-focused, product-thinking approach to designing and building an engineering platform. The authors answer questions about how to define measures of success and operational metrics for a platform. They provide detailed guidance for drawing on the disciplines of experience design and product management to ensure that a platform is built from day one to meet compelling user needs, generate feedback, and iterate and evolve along the way.

Here the authors provide concrete approaches to architecting and implementing an effective engineering platform. Lack of visibility into the workings of a platform, sometimes seen as a goal under the theory that developers should be "protected from the details," can make a platform unreliable and unusable in practice. Building observability into the platform is essential to ensuring that its users can not only develop and deploy applications for themselves but also troubleshoot, optimize, and improve their software.

Platform services should be built using modern, code-driven software-defined practices; control-plane architectural patterns; and automation to scale capacity to meet demand without exploding costs by overprovisioning. Above all, a platform, as with any modern software, should be designed and implemented from the ground up, knowing that it will need to change and evolve to avoid becoming obsolete in a few years' time.

The authors understand that the success of a platform is not in the platform itself but in the outcomes its users achieve. This book embodies what they've learned and will help your team help your users and your business excel.

—KIEF MORRIS
DISTINGUISHED ENGINEER AT THOUGHTWORKS
AUTHOR OF *Infrastructure as Code*

preface

I've been building software systems long before we called them "platforms." My earliest engineering memories are of wrangling SunOS/IBM AIX machines, running massive semiconductor simulations for programmable logic, and navigating system traffic spikes during primary compute needs, long before the era of ubiquitous computing power. None of us used the term "DevOps" back then; we were just figuring out how to keep things running. However, over the years, I realized that the scaffolding surrounding product teams encompassing invisible systems, abstractions, tooling, and culture was often the difference between sustainable progress and organizational entropy.

Platform engineering gave shape to that intuition. And, over time, I found myself drawn more to the enablers than the end products: CI/CD pipelines, developer portals, paved paths, golden templates, observability stacks. I've been fortunate enough to help shape platform strategy across large organizations and startups, from Silicon Valley to global digital firms, and have also been instrumental in setting up the platform engineering practice at Thoughtworks. With this book, I wanted us to distill the accumulated lessons, both technical and human, and offer a hands-on, opinionated, and deeply practical guide for anyone trying to build platforms that empower engineers rather than hinder them.

This isn't a book of platitudes or glossy visions. It's a manual forged from real-world constraints, tradeoffs, and context—what we learned the hard way so you don't have to.

—AJAY CHANKRAMATH

I have been captivated by complex systems since building my first Backus–Naur parser as part of a compiler design class back in college. Even though the path of my career has covered a lot of territory outside software engineering, for nearly two decades I've had the privilege, and the sheer fun (*most* of the time), of working alongside some amazing people across many sectors of the economy, with some of the largest stakes, to design and implement systems that enable the creation and support of software. This naturally involves not just infrastructure but also processes, organizational structures, and measures of outcomes—in other words, *systems.*

As Stafford Beer famously said, "The purpose of a system is what it does." The reason it takes days, weeks, and months of waiting or advance planning for developers to get access to the ordinary tools of their trade is that this is how the *system* (or process) was designed to function. The reason core technologies in even your most strategically important systems are multiple versions behind with upgrades happening painfully, if they happen at all, is because that is how those maintenance *systems* were designed to function. The reason there are five teams in the same company with five different approaches to the same architectural problem—I could go on, but I think you get my point.

It is absolutely possible to deliver on the goals of a modern engineering platform, but mere common sense or simple notions of management are not going to get you there. If they could, everyone who tries would succeed. Throughout this book, we capture the approaches, corporate cultural markers, measures, and engineering practices that have been part of the successful platforms we have encountered and helped create. Even when you're not building a platform, platform engineering practices are still a great way to improve your skills and bring more quality and value to any software-defined situation.

—Nic Cheneweth

When I first stumbled into platform engineering, it wasn't a defined role. I was the team member who enjoyed solving the annoying problems that no one else wanted to tackle, including dependency management, deployment automation, log aggregation, and internal documentation. Over time, I realized those problems weren't peripheral; they were foundational. They were the friction points holding everyone else back.

That's when it clicked: building a great product requires creating a great environment in which to build. And that's what platform engineering is all about.

My background is a blend of architecture, enablement, and leading large-scale transformations. I've seen how even the best technical ideas fail without developer empathy, good communication, and a relentless focus on solving real pain points. This book is our attempt to offer more than just advice; we want to provide you with a comprehensive working blueprint, from initial commit to adoption, that respects the complexity of your environment while guiding you toward simplicity and scalability.

—Bryan Oliver

I've always enjoyed learning how things work so they can be made more efficient, and a career in software engineering has only grown that passion. Finding the release process slow once software creation was complete, I dug into CI/CD, configuration management, and scaling DevOps practices to move away from deployment CDs stapled to paper checklists being sent from desk to desk for sign-off. As those practices evolved and new inefficiencies in the release process began to emerge, I discovered that the space between development, product teams, compliance, and leadership had real opportunities for improvement. That's where platform engineering thrives: at the intersection of delivery and enablement.

What I wanted from this book was something that developers could use—not a set of high-level principles but something they could learn practically, evolve incrementally, and adapt to their organization. I've seen too many platform projects fall into the trap of centralization without empathy or automation without trust. I wanted us to write the kind of book that platform teams could rally around: clear, grounded, and built for the real world.

If we've done this right, this book will meet you where you are and help you take the next step with confidence.

—SEAN ALVAREZ

acknowledgments

We would like to thank the many individuals and organizations who supported us on this journey, those who encouraged us in the authoring process, and those who gave us the time, space, and trust to bring this work to life.

We are especially thankful to Thoughtworks, whose bold support for our efforts, particularly in rechristening and evolving our internal digital infrastructure work into the broader platform engineering movement, laid the foundation for much of what's captured in this book. We also recognize Brillio for continuing to support and champion this initiative beyond our days at Thoughtworks, enabling a few of us to carry the torch forward and scale these ideas across industries.

Our profound gratitude goes to Ryan Murray, whose vision was the catalyst for bringing this group together in the first place, and to Brandon Byars, who was instrumental in helping us make the right connections. Martin Fowler pointed us in the right direction, while Neal Ford provided critical guidance in shaping our thinking. We are grateful to Kief Morris for writing the foreword and for being a strong, independent voice in the infrastructure-as-code movement. Sincere thanks to Kaspar von Grünberg, Manuel Pais, and Wesley Reisz for their timely support and ongoing inspiration based on their work. Special appreciation goes to Vikas Bijavara Narayanappa for his thoughtful and thorough work as the technical editor on the earlier versions of this manuscript. Vikas is the director of DevOps at Oracle, leading a global team of DevOps engineers. He has more than 20 years of industry experience with some of the leading technology companies in the world, including Yahoo and Oracle.

We would also like to extend our heartfelt thanks to the Manning team, whose support has been invaluable throughout this journey: to Brian Sawyer, our acquisitions editor, for his guidance and steady direction; to Dustin Archibald, whose editorial insights not only shaped the book but also taught us how to better teach our readers (a true learning experience for us as authors); to Melissa Ice, whose thoughtful guidance on structures, formats, and most importantly schedules kept us aligned and on track; to Courtney Kimball, whose marketing expertise opened doors to countless opportunities and amplified our reach; to Ana Romac, for her work on MEAP marketing and her steady guidance; and to the incredible production team, Aleksandar Dragosavljevic, Kathy Rossland, Kari Lucke, Jason Everett, and Tamara Švelić Sabljić, who helped transform our drafts into the polished work you see today. Your care, attention to detail, and dedication made all the difference.

In addition, thanks to all the reviewers who generously contributed their feedback across multiple revisions, helping refine the book into its final state: Adam Wan, Alexander Zenger, Alexey Artemov, Alireza Aghamohammadi, Amitabh Premraj Cheekoth, Andreas Polychronopoulos, Anil Pantangi, Anthony Nandaa, Anuj More, Asif Iqbal, Chris Kolosiwsky, Christopher Forbes, Divanshu Mittal, Elaine de Mattos Silva Bezerra, Emily Hansen, Erico Lendzian, Francis Setash, Henry Stamerjohann, Jérôme Meyer, Jim Welch, Jorge Ezequiel Bo, Jose San Leandro, Juan Gabriel, Kaushik Ramachandran, Kelvin D. Meeks, Kosmas Chatzimichalis, Leonardo Gomes da Silva, Michele Adduci, Mike Ensor, Milorad Imbra, Mohammed Salloom, Mostafa Negim, Nicolas Fantoni, Pedro Arthur P. R. Duarte, Raks Khare, Roman Zhuzha, Steve Goodman, Sue Pujdak, Yash Vanzara, Zach Peters, and Zachary M. Manning.

A heartfelt thank you as well to Ranbir Chawla, Zhamak Dehghani, Max Griffiths, Sridhar Kotagiri, and many of our past and present colleagues, whose insights have helped sharpen our vision over the years.

And finally, to our families and friends: thank you for your unwavering support and patience throughout this journey.

about this book

Effective Platform Engineering is a practical guide to building, scaling, and evolving internal platforms that developers love and organizations value. It introduces platform engineering as a modern discipline that empowers software delivery by reducing cognitive load, enabling self-service, and treating platforms as evolving products rather than static infrastructure. Rather than focusing purely on tools or frameworks, this book emphasizes product thinking, organizational alignment, and human-centered design, with a clear priority on outcomes. Whether you're leading a platform team or contributing as a builder, you'll walk away with patterns, practices, and mindset shifts needed to navigate the platform journey across various stages of maturity and scale.

Who should read this book

This book is intended for infrastructure engineers, DevOps practitioners, site reliability engineers, and even software developers who are responsible for enhancing software delivery and quality at scale. You'll benefit if you've ever faced friction building or operating internal platforms, struggled to improve developer experience, or wondered how to treat a platform as a product.

Several chapters will cover aspects that such practitioners face or interact with daily, even if they are not their primary responsibility. For example, we will spend time on product thinking and delivery. How an engineer envisions and shapes the architecture or operational life of a capability has a tremendous effect on the eventual results. You may not be the Product Owner, but we hope to provide an understanding of what you will need from these other and related roles to be *effective* in building platforms.

We assume that you have at least a moderate amount of prior experience with software development and the software delivery lifecycle, as well as the necessary infrastructure for running and operating software, including infrastructure-as-code (IaC). What does moderate mean in this case? For example, as part of the code-level platform building exercises in chapters 6 through 8, we will use the IaC framework Terraform. This will not include any introductory material as such but assumes you have worked with Terraform already, at least sufficiently to understand the general purposes and flows involved. One of the exercises will include building a CLI tool. The example solution is based on Go, although you are encouraged to use your preferred programming language to achieve a similar outcome. Regardless of the language, the exercise instructions assume that you are familiar enough with programming, using APIs, and software pipelines that those things alone won't create an insurmountable obstacle.

How this book is organized: A road map

The book is divided into three parts, comprising 10 chapters, that progressively guide you from core concepts to hands-on engineering practices, concluding with some thoughts on future roadmaps. By the end of part 1, you'll have a clear understanding of platform engineering fundamentals and how to begin building a capability-aligned, outcome-oriented internal platform.

Part 1 lays the groundwork for the rest of the book. It explains why platform engineering matters, what it is, and how to get started. You'll understand how platform thinking connects to developer productivity and delivery efficiency:

- Chapter 1 introduces platform engineering, provides a definition, and describes how it addresses modern delivery challenges and relates to the evolution of DevOps.
- Chapter 2 explores ownership models, product thinking, evolutionary architectures, and the software-defined principles that underpin effective platform teams.
- Chapter 3 shows how to measure platform effects through capability models, developer productivity, and organizational health.

Part 2 begins the practical application of the principles from part 1. We will build a working implementation of the foundational components of an engineering platform to better understand the relationship between the practices in part 1 and how these can be translated into actual implementation patterns and choices. By the end of part 2, you'll have a working model for the use and lifecycle experiences that a platform can deliver to both users and maintainers:

- Chapter 4 discusses how to design for control, trust, and compliance without slowing down developers.
- Chapter 5 introduces evolutionary observability and the signal-driven feedback loops that enable platforms to be resilient and able to evolve.
- Chapter 6 presents the applied patterns for software-defined infrastructure practices, domain boundaries in practice, and bootstrapping from a greenfield start.

- Chapter 7 builds on the initial structures in chapter 6, creating the networking foundations and control plane base that will host much of the primary engineering platform capabilities.

- Chapter 8 explores a scalable model for managing the platform services and extensions that will run on the control plane and how these can incorporate the capabilities defined in the minimum usable starting point for developers (the minimum viable product of the platform).

In the final part of the book, we turn our attention to what happens when your platform needs to support more teams, more technologies, and more ambitious goals. Scaling isn't just about adding capacity—it's about making deliberate architectural and organizational shifts so the platform remains a force multiplier rather than a bottleneck. We'll look at common growing pains and the patterns that help you navigate them, as well as how to prepare for a future where platforms are AI-augmented, product-driven, and capable of learning and adapting over time:

- Chapter 9 explores the architectural changes and operational patterns that allow a platform to scale across teams, domains, clusters, and regions without losing reliability or developer trust. This includes strategies like event-driven automation, federated control planes, and distributed orchestration—approaches that help you handle growth without collapsing under its weight.

- In chapter 10, the final chapter, the focus shifts to platform evolution as a continuous product journey. You'll learn how to build a roadmap that reflects both technical and business priorities, measure platform maturity in ways that resonate across the organization, and embed enduring site reliability engineering and developer experience principles that align with your engineering platform. We'll also discuss intelligent tooling and cultural practices that can keep your platform relevant, resilient, and ready for whatever comes next.

Solutions to the exercises

At the end of the book, you'll find an appendix that provides direct links to discussion, exercises, and solutions intended to provide the essential code elements for demonstrating the code-level platform engineering practices. Complete and working references can be downloaded from the Manning site at https://www.manning.com/books/effective-platform-engineering and are also maintained on GitHub at https://github.com/effective-platform-engineering/companion-code. Future updates may also be made available at one or both locations.

About the code

This book contains many examples of source code both in numbered listings and in line with normal text. In both cases, source code is formatted in a `fixed-width font like this` to separate it from ordinary text. Sometimes code is also in **bold** to highlight code that has changed from previous steps in the chapter, such as when a new feature adds to an existing line of code.

In many cases, the original source code has been reformatted; we've added line breaks and reworked indentation to accommodate the available page space in the book. In rare cases, even this was not enough, and listings include line-continuation markers (➥). Additionally, comments in the source code have often been removed from the listings when the code is described in the text. Code annotations accompany many of the listings, highlighting important concepts.

Generally, your laptop (Mac, Windows, or Linux) and an internet connection are all you will need to start working on the exercises. The additional tools and resources used along the way will be described in detail. In the middle sections, where you create some foundational components of a platform, the examples use AWS and assume you are working on a Mac or Linux operating system. Providing a working example means using specific tools and technologies, but the principles in the book are by no means limited to these selections. Though the implementation details will be different, you can achieve the same outcomes using a Windows computer and Google Cloud or many other combinations of resources. In many places, we will reference some of these alternatives.

You can get executable snippets of code from the liveBook (online) version of this book at https://livebook.manning.com/book/effective-platform-engineering. The complete code for the examples in the book is available for download from the Manning website at https://www.manning.com/books/effective-platform-engineering, and from GitHub at https://github.com/effective-platform-engineering.

liveBook discussion forum

Purchase of *Effective Platform Engineering* includes free access to liveBook, Manning's online reading platform. Using liveBook's exclusive discussion features, you can attach comments to the book globally or to specific sections or paragraphs. It's a snap to make notes for yourself, ask and answer technical questions, and receive help from the authors and other users. To access the forum, go to https://livebook.manning.com/book/effective-platform-engineering/discussion.

Manning's commitment to our readers is to provide a venue where a meaningful dialogue between individual readers and between readers and the authors can take place. It is not a commitment to any specific amount of participation on the part of the authors, whose contribution to the forum remains voluntary (and unpaid). We suggest you try asking the authors some challenging questions lest their interest stray! The forum and the archives of previous discussions will be accessible from the publisher's website as long as the book is in print.

about the authors

AJAY CHANKRAMATH is the founder and CEO of Platformetrics, a specialized consulting firm focused on platform engineering and developer experience. With over three decades of leadership experience as chief technology officer, senior vice president, and other senior technology roles at companies like Brillio, Thoughtworks, Oracle, Broadridge, and Xilinx, Ajay is widely recognized as a visionary technologist and has led large-scale digital transformations with a strong emphasis on platform thinking, team enablement, and engineering excellence. Ajay is also a platform engineering ambassador, team topologies advocate, and passionate educator, frequently speaking and teaching on platform strategy, modern software delivery, and technical leadership. He holds a bachelor's degree in computer science, multiple master's degrees in engineering management and computer science, and an MBA. Learn more about his work and insights at www.platformetrics.com.

NIC CHENEWETH is a principal consultant and strategist at ThoughtWorks and is the founding infrastructure contributor to ThoughtWorks Digital Platform Strategy. His undergraduate studies are in computer science, and he holds an MBA, a doctorate, and a postdoctorate degree. With 30 years of executive leadership, consulting, and engineering experience in roles ranging from the courtroom to the boardroom, as a former CEO, vice president, chief counsel, director, or entrepreneur in

startup, private, and publicly traded companies, Nic brings a unique perspective to technology strategy and implementation.

BRYAN OLIVER is an experienced engineer and leader who designs and builds distributed systems. He works on the platform engineering team at Thoughtworks, focusing on cloud-native platforms. He enjoys contributing to Open Source and speaking at technical conferences internationally.

SEAN ALVAREZ is the chief technology officer of the Life Sciences business at Brillio, advising clients and leading teams to drive digital transformations across business functions with pharmaceutical and biotechnology firms. Before that, he was a principal consultant at Thoughtworks, North America's head of business platforms. He has honed his skills with an MS in computer science and an MBA, and applied that to lead multiple enterprise-scale transformations using the principles of platform engineering across all cloud vendors. He is recognized for his industry presentations and roundtables in the practice.

about the cover illustration

The figure on the cover of *Effective Platform Engineering* is "Otaiti portant des présent au Roi," or "A Tahiti woman carrying presents to the King," taken from a collection by Jacques Grasset de Saint-Sauveur, published in 1788. Each illustration is finely drawn and colored by hand.

In those days, it was easy to identify where people lived and what their trade or station in life was just by their dress. Manning celebrates the inventiveness and initiative of the computer business with book covers based on the rich diversity of regional culture centuries ago, brought back to life by pictures from collections such as this one.

Part 1

Getting started with platform engineering

Have you ever wondered how high-performing companies manage to deliver software at scale with speed, consistency, and minimal developer friction? Behind the scenes, many of them rely on a powerful enabler: platform engineering. This modern engineering discipline is transforming how organizations build, operate, and evolve internal developer platforms, giving teams seamless access to the tools, services, and workflows they need to innovate without the usual overhead.

Platform engineering isn't about creating more tools; it's about building the right internal products to remove cognitive load, reduce duplication, and accelerate software delivery. Done right, it eliminates waste across the software development life cycle and allows developers to focus on what matters most: delivering business value.

The first part of the book lays the foundation. In chapter 1, you'll learn what platform engineering is; why it's not just another buzzword; and how it applies product thinking, domain-driven design, and developer empathy to solve engineering inefficiencies. Chapter 2 introduces foundational practices for building and delivering engineering platforms, from ownership models to software-defined principles. You'll explore how internal platforms can evolve to meet your organization's needs, utilizing flexible, cloud-native technologies.

In chapter 3, we dive into what success looks like. You'll discover how to measure platform effect beyond revenue. The three key considerations are developer productivity, cognitive load, and organizational health, which in turn can be achieved by building a capability model and measurement framework aligned with your platform's maturity.

By the end of part 1, you'll understand how platform engineering works, why it matters, and how to begin your journey, with real-world insights and lessons from organizations like Epetech that are already traveling this path.

What is platform engineering?

This chapter covers

- The definition of platform engineering
- Deciding when to apply platform engineering
- The mental models and core principles of platform engineering
- Comparing platform engineering with DevOps, site reliability engineering, and developer experience

An engineering platform is a system that brings together infrastructure, governance, and operational technologies into one place that internal development teams across a company can use.

The goal of platform engineering is to find a strategy for overcoming the fundamental challenges of creating custom software. We need to build software faster, but there are so many requirements and dependencies. Given constantly evolving technologies, extensive governance and operational requirements, and critical security challenges, how do we rapidly and sustainably deliver software experiences to customers?

The number of articles, posts, and conference tracks on platform engineering has increased dramatically over the last couple of years. Yet, these sources can have very different ideas about what it means, why it matters, or what *good* looks like.

Platform engineering is a craft which:

- Combines architectural, engineering, and product delivery expertise by dedicated teams who have complete ownership of their products
- Creates a shared engineering platform where internal development teams can directly access the tools and technologies needed to build, deploy, and operate their applications
- Enables development teams to work independently through self-service capabilities, eliminating dependencies on other teams
- Reduces administrative overhead by minimizing non-development tasks and cross-team coordination requirements
- Simplifies compliance by embedding security, governance, and regulatory requirements directly into the platform tools
- Tracks success through specific, measurable business objectives that can be monitored and reported on consistently

Platform engineering can transform the entire software development and operations experience [1]. Using a platform instead of traditional IT departments and ticket systems solves a major problem that slows down engineering work. Good engineering platforms boost productivity, software quality, and save money. This leads to faster product releases, better security, and less wasted effort. When developers have better tools and fewer obstacles, they're happier at work, which helps companies hire and keep skilled people [2].

You might think that these benefits are only found in large-scale organizations, but the effect can be felt in smaller companies and even startups. If you work at a large organization and are considering building a platform engineering practice, this book is for you. If you work at a tiny organization or startup, there are still lessons to be learned here that will make your life easier and help minimize costly rework as your organization grows.

1.1   *Platforms are more than just DevOps*

Most organizations have undergone some form of DevOps adoption or transformation that is heavy on DevOps tools and light on process or engineering culture change.

The definition of DevOps we most often hear is a development approach that emphasizes collaboration and communication between development (Dev) and operations (Ops) teams and values automating infrastructure configuration. This is a good value statement. Better collaboration has always been a goal (or a challenge). But what usually happens is shown in figure 1.1.

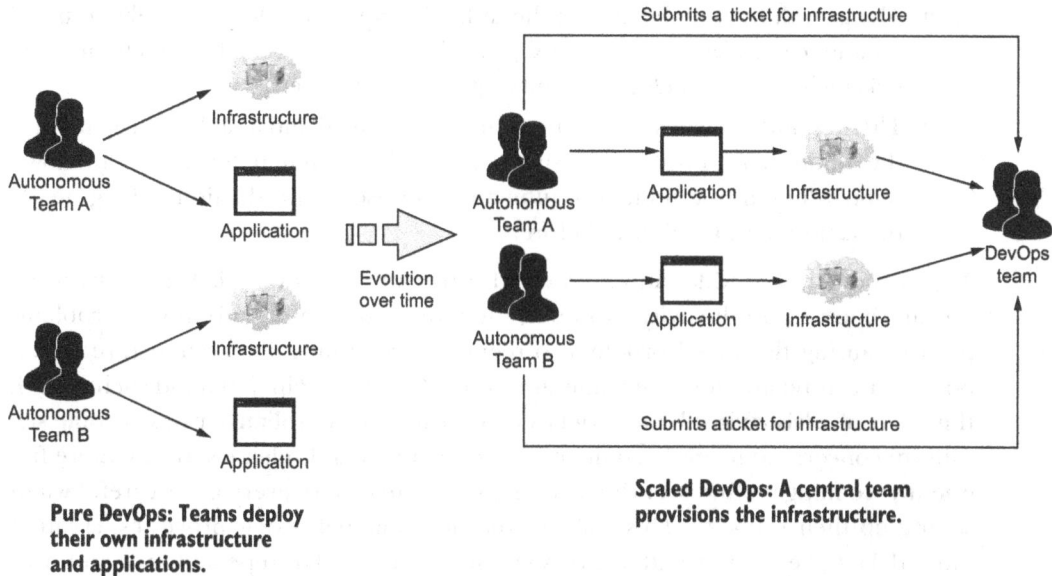

Pure DevOps: Teams deploy their own infrastructure and applications.

Scaled DevOps: A central team provisions the infrastructure.

Figure 1.1   Companies adopting a DevOps culture often start by enabling development teams to deploy their own infrastructure.

A repeating pattern begins to emerge:

- The responsibility for a portion of the infrastructure needs of development teams is moved to those teams, along with DevOps tools and probably a couple of people with experience using those tools. Usually, this *portion* refers to server configuration and nonproduction deployment activities. Many other dependencies continue to be managed in the same manner.

- A decent chunk of the infrastructure is now managed with greater speed and consistency. Still, since not much training is provided to developers and delivery pressure is always high, it is easier to let DevOps tasks go to the one or two DevOps people on the team. This doesn't scale well, so before long, a duplicated pattern emerges across the company, with clusters of two or three development teams sharing a dedicated DevOps team, which is now much busier.

- Soon, security or governance stakeholders in the company start co-opting the pipeline, causing the establishment of dedicated pipeline teams. This is the easiest way to demonstrate that various required tasks are happening within the pipeline automation. CI/CD changes are becoming growing bottlenecks.

- With multiple, perhaps dozens, of DevOps teams all devising their own solutions for many of the same needs, duplication and suboptimal solutions lead to increased costs, both in personnel and cloud resources.

- Required skill sets in cloud technologies, infrastructure as code, and networking requirements (among others) can be hard to find and staff across all teams.

- The growth in complexity and the difficulty in finding the right skills result in broader centralization, with DevOps work now being queued in much the same ticketed manner as before. (A pull request is still a ticket.)
- These *centralized* teams quickly become overwhelmed and unable to keep up with the volume of tickets sent in, resulting in lengthy fulfillment times that slow down onboarding, innovation, and, ultimately, releases to production, taking nearly the same amount of time as before.

The introduction or wider adoption of infrastructure as code initially provides a significant boost to productivity. However, the more effective organizational problems persist, causing the speed problem to reemerge. Solutions like architecture review boards or central architecture teams are formed to try to help, but amid such sprawl, the effect of advisors is still more delayed. Security and compliance rules become significant concerns as teams become more independent and release software more frequently. To mitigate this, security teams make lists to ensure everyone is careful when setting up their software. This leads to yet more manual review processes, creating more delays. We see this pattern, or something very similar, repeated over and over again.

We've also seen how organizations that are serious about tracking progress and broadening how they analyze to include the entire engineering and organizational process flow and are willing to change based on the results can achieve some pretty amazing results.

The initial platform engineering mindset

- Common sense won't get you there.
- Change will be required.
- It starts at the top.

Most of the time, it is ordinary, everyday common sense, working within the structures that exist and applying the successes that have worked in the past, that result in this pattern. Some outcomes require a new model—a new way of interpreting results and defining solutions. Platform engineering is about evolving beyond the goals of DevOps.

What if we reimagine how developers interact with all the other internal stakeholders who are responsible for infrastructure, security, compliance, finance, and other sources of dependencies and requirements? Figure 1.2 envisions a different outcome.

What if being onboarded to a development team automatically means having access to all the team's development, communication, and reporting tools? What if using this product provides development teams with a self-service means of obtaining infrastructure and other cross-functional dependencies? What if using these self-service capabilities meant developers could deploy software rapidly while also fully meeting all the internal security, governance, financial, or other institutional requirements

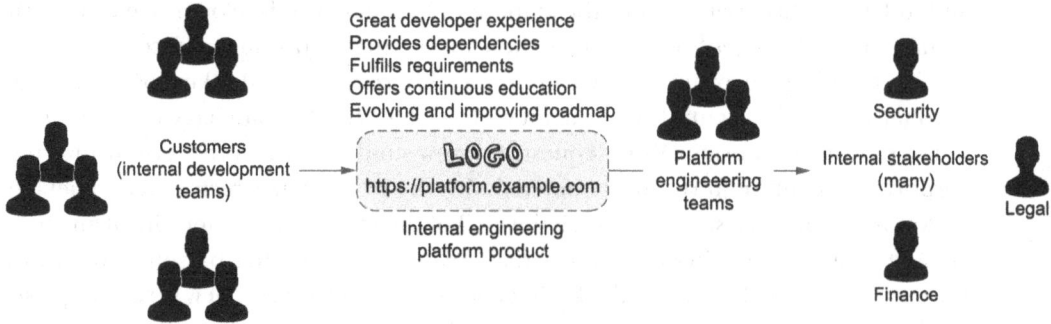

Figure 1.2 Platform engineers, working as unified product teams, build and deliver a product that provides internal development teams with the things they need to do their job.

without needing to first fully understand everything needed to achieve that level of compliance? Finally, what if this autonomy also included the ability to operate their software effectively and efficiently in highly resilient environments, where maintenance, upgrades, and the introduction of new technologies are frequent and stable?

The term for this development-oriented product is an *engineering platform*. Platform engineering involves the principles, practices, and measures for successfully delivering these platforms.

1.1.1 Why should I care about platform engineering?

Companies that successfully deliver an internal engineering platform report that 25% to 65% of a developer's time recovered by a platform can now be applied to strategically valuable work [3]—not to mention the dramatic increase in confidence in security and governance compliance. This also enables them to invest successfully in expanding their development capacity and take advantage of new opportunities if they arise.

Being successful at delivering on the potential of an engineering platform requires more than just deciding to do it. Your company may have such a strong product culture that the product thinking needed for success is a natural part of every delivery goal. We've seen companies like that, but not very often. It requires change and an understanding of how to be successful, which doesn't usually happen organically. So let's think differently about the outcome we want based on what began as a DevOps culture change.

Why is software as a service so successful? The market has demonstrated the value of business capabilities as software products made available through remote UIs and, more effectively, as APIs. Customers, internal developers, and third-party developers can independently use as much of or as little of these services as they need and when they need them.

Let's treat internal infrastructure and development technology teams as product teams that build and deliver products that internal developers use with the same ease and independence. Let's reduce the amount of knowledge a developer needs to learn (sometimes called *cognitive load*) to use these infrastructure products effectively.

The following are examples that capture the different ways of thinking. First, in a traditional approach, a centralized domain name system (DNS) team has exclusive access to the internal corporate DNS. Requests for new subdomain records for our internal corporate domain require a ticket opened with the DNS team, which assigns a person to do a manual, visual search through the GUI of the DNS tool to determine if an entry already exists before scheduling the actual creation with another person who creates the entry also directly through the DNS service GUI to ensure that new record requests don't result in conflicts with existing records. In a platform engineering approach, an API is provided that processes the ingress definition of every application deployment to consistently validate authorization and uniqueness and maintain actual DNS configuration, including cleanup when the deployment is deleted.

Second, a traditional approach requires that a centralized CI pipeline team have exclusive control over all CI automation to ensure that changes to software are scanned for known vulnerabilities. In a platform engineering approach, a pipeline step is published. Any team can include this in its CI pipeline that performs the scan and records the results; it can also deploy an admission controller to our Kubernetes clusters that confirms the required scan results exist for the commit secure hash algorithm (SHA) of any code deployed.

These are simplistic but real examples. But in each case, one decision creates friction (lead time planning requirements and waiting to make changes) while the other does not, even though both result in an underlying required outcome. There are thousands of such decisions scattered all across the landscape of the day-to-day experience of a software developer.

1.2   When to use platform engineering principles

We recommend introducing platform engineering concepts very early in an organization's journey. This might mean different things to different organizations.

For most organizations, the right time to begin intentionally incorporating platform engineering is after they first identify strategically valuable software development initiatives. Strategic value refers to how the organization can increase or protect its earnings.

Sure, you may say, "That day came and went a long time ago." However, enterprises often struggle to determine the value of their development efforts or identify which ones have the most significant potential for value versus those that are merely routine maintenance or, in fact, probably shouldn't be done at all. An example is if you use Salesforce to track and report on your direct sales activities, and the truth is that nothing about your *sales process* is itself the strategic differentiator between you and your competition. You should not be spending any material amount of money customizing your Salesforce implementation.

For an established organization without explicit product thinking, the challenges will be greater. Internal organizational structures can present barriers; the difficulty of change can be harder to predict, and the time needed before experiencing the benefits is likely to be longer. Large companies often create a separate digital division or even a new company to focus on important or new work. This lets them build new ways of working without having to change old, established systems.

As a startup, simply proving the value of your product by acquiring customers ASAP is the only thing anyone is willing to invest in, and every decision is made tactically. In this situation, you have to be more aggressive in the technical debt you take on. Make sure the result really is faster. Many aspects of platform engineering require no more initial investment than the alternative. When you do break the principles for speed, we strongly recommend tracking these decisions in detail. If the company succeeds, these decisions are almost certain to be among the changes you must make to sustain success.

1.2.1 When do these principles not apply?

Are there times when it is not worth broadly adopting platform engineering principles or making investments in an engineering platform? The answer is definitely yes. If very little of your organization's strategic revenue comes from custom software, then you probably don't have the internal users for a platform. For a governmental or nonprofit organization, this could be the strategic effect rather than revenue. In either case, if the organization's current health and future success aren't tied to custom software, then how valuable is maturing this capability?

Potential long-term savings from efficiency can be created with a platform. These come from the efficient use of technology resources and the acceleration of the broad adoption of critical security or governance concerns. If your investment time horizon is long, then this might also be an effective situation for applying platform engineering, even where time-to-market isn't as important.

> **NOTE** It's not all or nothing. Platform engineering brings together effective principles and strategies from multiple disciplines. Even in situations where the whole application may not be necessary or possible, we've seen individual principles still have a transformative and valuable effect.

1.3 Foundational concepts in platform engineering

As we dive into platform engineering, it's important to understand the key product principles driving this transformation. Like most products, software succeeds by meeting users' needs and expectations. How well it does this and for how long really depends on how well product management can understand and predict both current and future user needs. Users have numerous needs, and a product that solves just one of them might be enough to get people to start using it. However, if it doesn't address their other needs over time, they might stop. And needs aren't static—what's important today could be outdated tomorrow as new tech comes into play. Success also brings its own set of problems. As more users, features, and teams get involved, how do we stop the complexity from slowing things down or hurting product quality? Behaving like a product team means modeling how we function to become successful at delivering a product. Figure 1.3 introduces this model, called a *product delivery model.*

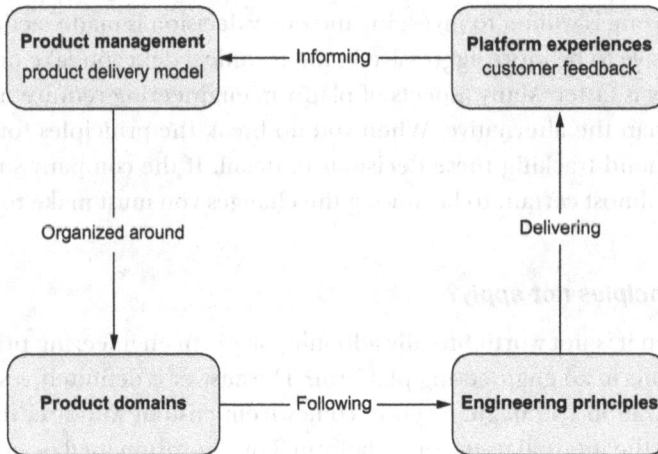

```
┌─────────────────────┐                        ┌─────────────────────┐
│ Product management  │ ◄──── Informing ────── │ Platform experiences│
│ product delivery    │                        │ customer feedback   │
│ model               │                        │                     │
└─────────────────────┘                        └─────────────────────┘
      │                                                    ▲
  Organized around                                     Delivering
      │                                                    │
      ▼                                                    │
┌─────────────────────┐                        ┌─────────────────────┐
│  Product domains    │ ──── Following ──────► │Engineering principles│
└─────────────────────┘                        └─────────────────────┘
```

Figure 1.3   Platform engineering depends on the disciplined application of a product delivery model. Product management drives decisions about the product's capabilities, features, and experiences. Effective platform engineering principles enable us to deliver these more successfully. Identifying and architecting around the internal product domains of our platform is how we successfully sustain the user experience as the product evolves and scales.

These concepts are interdependent. Developer needs and feedback inform the product roadmap. Over time, as the number of users and features in the platform grows, we must expand the team building the platform. We must organize these teams and their responsibilities in a way that supports our product experience goals and the pace at which we need to deliver them. If this sounds like a challenge that the rest of the software development teams have to manage, that's a good thing—it should.

Domain-driven design [4] provides a very effective way of measuring success by breaking up the delivery of a product into smaller parts delivered by multiple independent *domain* teams. Each domain team within the platform follows shared engineering principles to provide the capabilities in the roadmap to users, who, in turn, inform and influence the roadmap.

1.3.1   Product delivery model for platforms

Platforms work because they are products—managed with the same care, structure, and product thinking you'd expect from something customer-facing. Traditionally, though, infrastructure and developer tools haven't been built or delivered this way. Many companies contain a lot of stakeholders who haven't been encouraged to focus on the developer experience or to think about their work in terms of employee effect—and that's understandable. The way corporate IT has evolved, with its heavy capital costs and command-and-control view of user expectations, explains a lot of how we got here. But the value created by custom software and the cost-effect of these legacy assumptions have dramatically changed. What once made sense is now the cause of the problem. Treating your internal engineering platform like an actual product is the best way to meet developers' needs, drive adoption, and create lasting value.

1.3.2 *Platform product domains*

The idea of building a system based on a solid model of a domain isn't just found in software engineering—it's a core concept in engineering overall. In software, domain-driven design takes this idea further, and the serious application of domain design to engineering platforms was probably the key "breakthrough" we've seen for being successful at creating a valuable platform and maintaining this value over time. It gives us an effective framework for how teams working on different parts (or subdomains) of the platform should interact. Getting this right is crucial for creating a platform that can evolve on its own while keeping the user experience smooth and running efficiently.

What areas does an engineering platform cover? A domain succeeds when it's easy and pleasant to use. This user experience defines where one domain ends and another begins. Different platform teams can split up responsibilities in various ways, as long as the boundaries between domains work well together without being too tightly connected.

A reasonable domain boundary isn't just whatever you feel like—splitting things up based on traditional IT functional lines won't work. When teams are structured around real domain boundaries, they can truly operate independently, each with its backlog and priorities. From a larger product roadmap point of view, domains will still depend on each other. Coordination does happen but mainly between subdomain product owners and domain-level architects—not individual engineers. If developers from different teams routinely need to talk to each other, that's a sign that something's off. Frequent cross-team chatter is a bug, not a feature. We often use the term *smell* to refer to behaviors that should be considered a warning that something is happening that is unintended or undesired, like the smell of something burning to a chef. Occasionally, certain foods are supposed to smell burnt, but we tend to recognize that burning isn't a good sign universally. Similarly, domain-bounded teams should find the *need* to reach out to another team on Slack or email (or a Zoom meeting, God help us) to be a smell. Something has happened to foil the product engineering team's boundary goals. Many ways of breaking up responsibilities that seem logical at first turn out to be wrong, so we need to measure the results and adjust continually.

After years of trial and error at both large companies and well-funded startups, we've naturally figured out some boundaries that have worked well in various situations. While these might not be the only ways to do it, they've proven to be highly effective. Figure 1.4 shows eight domains that form an effective model for the internal domains of an engineering platform.

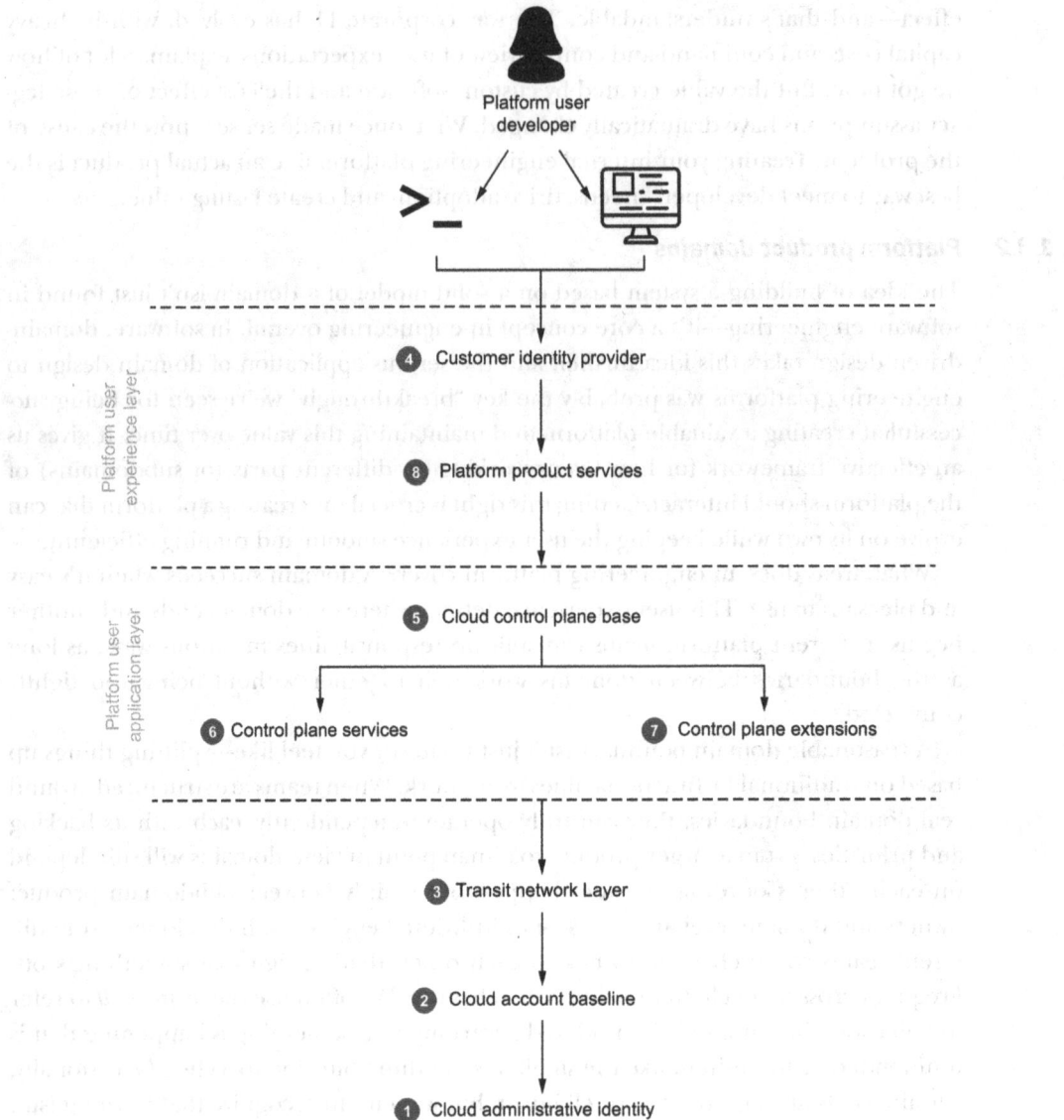

Figure 1.4 Eight principal product domains within an engineering platform. The numbers by the domain indicate an underlying dependency ordering when launching a new platform.

Self-serve, loosely coupled boundaries can be maintained where different domain teams are created among the top-level domains, as well as many effective subdomains within each. Each domain can be built to interact with others smoothly and with little friction, and there are high-quality Software as a Service (SaaS) options within almost every one that can be integrated in a clean, domain-focused way if you choose.

No matter where they are created, effective low-friction boundaries don't materialize by default. They must be carefully designed and maintained if the user experience is to be sustained.

We use the term *cloud* in several of these domains, since that is where most companies are building engineering platforms. Still, the domains are equally effective in a private data center context.

Eight domains don't require eight teams. Even starting from a single engineering platform product team, the platform can still be architected with these domains in mind. One should scale up the number of independent domain teams based on actual user demand and business value.

When building a platform from scratch, some domains must be built before others. For example, the control plane can't be deployed until a network is available. Once we get past that, however, each of these domains can evolve with the right amount of autonomy.

1.3.3   Platform engineering principles

The product delivery model and product domains focus on organizing teams and processes at the organizational level, not individual team practices. The results from doing those things well will appear in team topology, scope, and backlogs. Engineering principles, on the other hand, though they apply at every level, are often easier understood in terms of practices used at the delivery team level.

Figure 1.5 introduces seven engineering principles that shape the attributes of every capability or feature delivered by a platform engineering team.

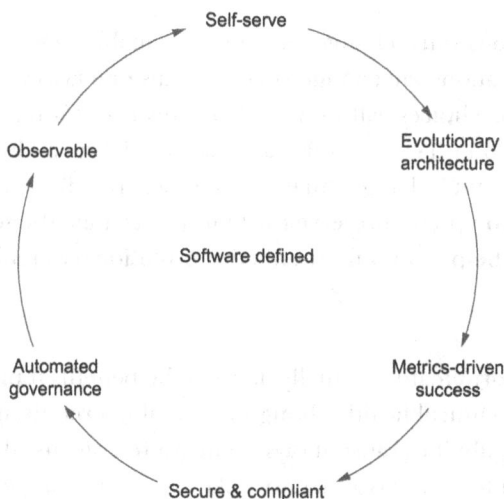

Figure 1.5   Software defined is placed in the middle because it is a core attribute of everything the platform engineer delivers. The rest of the principles share a connection because they continuously evolve, and decisions made in applying these surrounding principles can affect the requirements of the others.

What do we mean by a *shared connection*? Each of the principles is a requirement. Yet each can be applied in a way that will either enable or undermine the others. We could implement a security requirement in a way that cannot be effectively tested. This would defeat our principle of observability. We could implement a self-serve feature but without generating the usage data that tracks adoption or effect. This lacks the metrics-driven success required. Or what about the all-too-common situation where a compliance requirement is met without automation? Keep these principles at the heart of how a platform team works, and you'll dramatically boost the success of every initiative.

SOFTWARE DEFINED

A platform engineering team is a software team. Every aspect of the platform should be software-defined. The entire platform—every integration, feature, supporting automation, or technology—must be deployable from versioned source control and artifacts, managed by continuous integration and delivery pipeline coordination.

SELF-SERVE

Self-service functionality is built into every capability the platform offers. This begins with designing service interfaces first—meaning everything must have an API (application programming interface). Whether we purchase or build a capability, it needs an API. When we build capabilities ourselves, we create the API first, then add user interfaces or other developer tools on top of it.

This API-first architecture gives us the flexibility to create sustainable self-service experiences. It also creates clear working boundaries between different platform engineering teams, which is essential for collaboration. We recommend focusing on designs that prioritize the following elements.

EVOLUTIONARY ARCHITECTURE

Assume that architectural decisions must change over time. Valuable new technologies will appear. Customer expectations will change (platform customers as well as the end-users). Inefficiencies in prior choices will be revealed. This is just a reality. The architectures within a platform don't have an end-state. Instead, define architectural patterns based on small, incremental changes that can happen rapidly. With each functional attribute and integration point, preserve the ability to change the solution. Good resources are available to help map out an effective evolutionary architecture strategy [5].

METRICS-DRIVEN SUCCESS

Use data to prove that each platform feature actually delivers the benefits it promises. This means more than just the technical health, though that is also a requirement, of course. But technologies and capabilities must always be measured against the value they are expected to provide. If automation is added to make something happen faster, then we must be able to demonstrate that it is, in fact, happening more quickly. If a capability is added to improve quality, then we must be able to measure quality and the improvement. Cost optimization is an essential capability for a platform and must be measurable.

Most importantly, we need to measure all of this across the entire organizational delivery process. A change could be made that improves something at one stage for one team but has the unintended consequence of slowing things down for another team.

SECURE AND COMPLIANT

We tend to think of security and compliance in two contexts. First are the security or compliance requirements that the platform engineering team itself can (must) incorporate or demonstrate. Second, and separate from the security or compliance requirements for the users of the platform, are the security or compliance requirements for the users of the platform. The key difference between them is that the platform delivery team can assume direct responsibility for the first category. In contrast, they can only provide tools or technologies that *help* the platform users in the second.

An engineering platform creates a shared responsibility model. The platform team is responsible for the security of the platform, whereas developers using the platform are responsible for the application security *in* the platform. If the developers using a platform create insecure code, the platform can't magically remove the insecurities. The platform can provide capabilities that help users assess the security of their code and alert developers to known vulnerabilities. The platform team will use these same capabilities to determine its code.

Platform security includes protecting against data loss and service outages during failures like power outages or data center problems. Data center failures or regional power outages should not result in data loss or a prolonged disruption of services for a company's customers or employees. This means that the actual resiliency of the platform is a kind of security concern. Resiliency, which is different than availability in architectural terms, should be the primary architectural outcome goal. These can be almost interchangeable terms if you are just talking about uptime for an application. But in infrastructure architecture terms, there is an important distinction. Availability is historically a measure of redundancy and the ability of a system operator to redirect traffic to healthy infrastructure. Resiliency, on the other hand, is a measure of the ability of a system to self-correct from a failure event.

AUTOMATED GOVERNANCE

One of the goals of platform engineering is to enable teams to work autonomously so that other teams do not become a bottleneck on their ability to deliver software. This goal often appears to directly oppose the goals of your compliance, security, or governance team.

Rather than seeing compliance as a burden, we focus on making it seamless for developers while still meeting security requirements.

Developers need autonomy over the construction and evolution of the software build and delivery processes. Security and governance stakeholders need assurances as to the results of this development and delivery activity. How can we provide the security and governance stakeholders with the assurance that necessary activities took place and the state of the software environments is compliant, without turning over this responsibility entirely to some other team? We do this by separating the work of being compliant from the system of verifying that the work occurred. Through the platform features, developers are providing the self-service tools needed to become compliant. The confirmation of the compliance work is moved out of the pipeline and incorporated into the platform control plane, confirming compliance before any change is made. This strategy is known as *compliance at the point of change* and is a highly effective approach to automating governance.

OBSERVABLE

Observability measures how well you can understand what's happening inside your software systems by examining the data they output—logs, metrics, traces, and other information. People often confuse monitoring with observability, but they serve different purposes. *Monitoring* tracks specific, known system health indicators—like CPU usage or error rates—where you already know what "good" and "bad" look like. *Observability* goes broader, helping you understand the complete system state, including problems you didn't anticipate. Think of monitoring as checking your car's dashboard warning lights, while observability is like having a mechanic who can diagnose any unusual noise or behavior. Monitoring is actually part of observability, focused on the subset of issues you can predict. True observability helps you discover unknown problems by collecting comprehensive data about system behavior across all areas: your applications, infrastructure, cloud services, incidents, individual services, and most critically, how these technical metrics connect to actual business outcomes and user experience.

1.4   *Platform engineering enablers*

Several modern practices can be thought of as platform engineering enablers, or catalysts that make a platform more successful. Engineering platforms are more successful with the enablers shown in figure 1.6, to the point where they can almost be thought of as part of the platform.

We often hear dramatic and misleading claims that platform engineering will replace DevOps and site reliability engineering (SRE) in organizations. We need clearer definitions of these terms and how they're actually used in real situations.

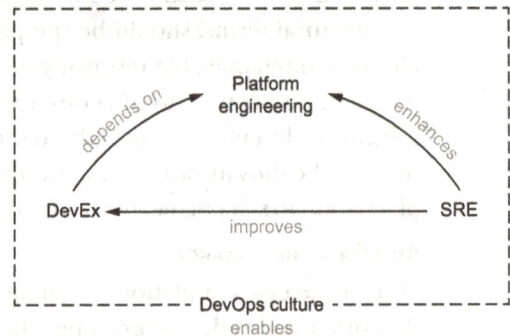

Figure 1.6   There is a direct connection between each of these enablers and the resulting quality and effect of a platform.

To help explain our perspective, we treat DevOps and SRE as practices that support platform engineering—each with specific, well-defined roles and responsibilities. Throughout this book, we'll use these more precise definitions to show how these practices work together.

1.4.1 Developer experience

In the past few years, the term *developer experience* (DevEx) has emerged as a significant area of focus in engineering. When you research the DevEx community, you will find an emphasis on centralized portals for development resources, such as Backstage (https://backstage.io). You will often see people talking about using such portals as ways developers are provided access to infrastructure and the things we've talked about here as part of an engineering platform. This can be confusing. Obviously, as the customer of an engineering platform, developer experience is what our entire platform product strategy is designed to improve.

There is overlap between the features of an engineering platform and the activities of development that can be treated as DevEx. Without clear boundaries, if you have simultaneously launched teams focused on DevEx, they will start conflicting with the engineering platform team. DevEx can be effectively treated as an internal subdomain of an engineering platform. In our platform product domains, DevEx falls into the ninth category: platform product services.

Product services focus on the developer tools and resources that help speed up and standardize software quality. This includes things like language starter kits, pipeline resources for cross-functional or nonfunctional requirements, contract testing automation, feature flag automation, and metrics that measure the value and effectiveness of these tools as they evolve.

1.4.2 DevOps

DevOps is most effective as a culture that brings together development and operational activities. DevOps should not be a team of people or a job description. After years of seeing this in action across many industries, we're convinced that the best DevOps cultural models include the requirement that the same set of developers who design the software, write the code, and build and test the code are also responsible for deploying, monitoring, and supporting the code. This principle also covers dependent systems like the engineering platform, where the engineers who build platform capabilities should also be responsible for running them in production. The platform engineers who build and deploy the platform capabilities also monitor and support these components throughout production.

1.4.3 SRE

SRE, on the other hand, lives outside of either the engineer platform, DexEv, or general development teams. The SRE value proposition lies in enhancing development teams that are already highly efficient in delivering and supporting their software lifecycle. Reliability engineering is applied as an end-to-end, continuous quality improvement discipline, not another operational silo and potential source of friction. SREs are allocated for a relatively limited period to product development teams (including the engineering platform team) who demonstrate a high enough level of maturity to be able to absorb SRE contributions into their everyday workflows, as well as offer learnings from their workflows that SRE can bring to other teams and introduce into the underlying platform itself. It is a continuous improvement activity. Here is a key question to ask: Does your SRE team have its codebase? If the answer is yes, this is a smell. It is not that they don't contribute to lifecycle code; they do. But they do this as a contributing member of the product development team to which they are temporarily assigned, which includes the engineering platform product teams as well as standard business capabilities. SREs enhance and improve other teams' code rather than their own.

1.4.4   *Impact of generative AI in the platform engineering space*

Given the tremendous growth in interest and innovation around large-language models (LLMs) and other forms of generative AI, it is important to note how this is currently affecting the approaches for platform engineering and building platform experiences.

The current forms of AI are most effective as a resource that can accelerate many of the repetitive and time-consuming tasks faced by platform engineers. LLMs can help engineers in analyzing observability data to find the causes behind service disruptions. They can also discover patterns in observability data that may indicate future problems. Integrating LLM tools such as Claude (https://www.claude.ai) into the platform engineering software development process can accelerate the pace of architectural implementation and experimentation.

The challenge in applying this type of AI to platform engineering is much the same as every form of software development. Generative AI is also prone to proposing solutions that are entirely wrong or even wholly unrelated to the actual problem described. Because there is no actual comprehension involved, AI tools must be wielded by people capable of discerning the seemingly brilliant responses from the hallucinations. This is a way of saying that AI can be very effective at helping a person be more productive at tasks that they are entirely capable of performing without the AI. This much potential value can't be ignored, and now is the time to start thinking about and experimenting with which aspects of platform engineering can be enhanced through the use of AI technologies.

1.5   *Let's get started*

Throughout this book, we imagine working for a company called Epetech, Inc., which is facing problems with inefficient practices in deploying and operating software to production. The challenges reflect situations we have seen recurring in actual companies. The problems at your company may be similar, and by following the journey of Epetech, hopefully, you will be able to see how platform engineering can improve things!

Epetech is a fictional healthcare technology company based in North America. In addition to actual medical hardware, they offer various mobile and web services that help people track their health vitals and share this information with their doctors when paired with consumer electronic devices. This approach is about providing doctors with better data and helping people achieve better health outcomes without frequent office visits. The company has experienced incredible success and growth, hiring more than 100 developers, and expects to have more than double that soon.

Epetech web services have always been open to third-party developers and business partners, and this is the area driving growth across their industry. The company needs to deliver better and newer customer experiences faster to capture as much of this growth sector as possible. Capabilities need to be composable and reusable so that they don't waste money on multiple redundant services. Epetech has adopted a distributed services architectural (microservices) strategy built around domain-driven software design principles.

But without a clear infrastructure lifecycle strategy beyond a mix of technology silos and DevOps teams, developers at Epetech are now spending half their time on lead-time planning and coordinating with other teams to get DNS entries, firewall rules, storage, compute capacity, monitors, alerts, pipeline changes, and everything else needed to build, deploy, and operate their software, often under tight deadlines. Maintenance and operational efforts take longer, are more frequent, and aren't seen as adding much value. Unsurprisingly, production incidents are rising, leading to frustrated customers and higher support costs. Figure 1.7 shows how many different teams and handoffs can go into even a simple change.

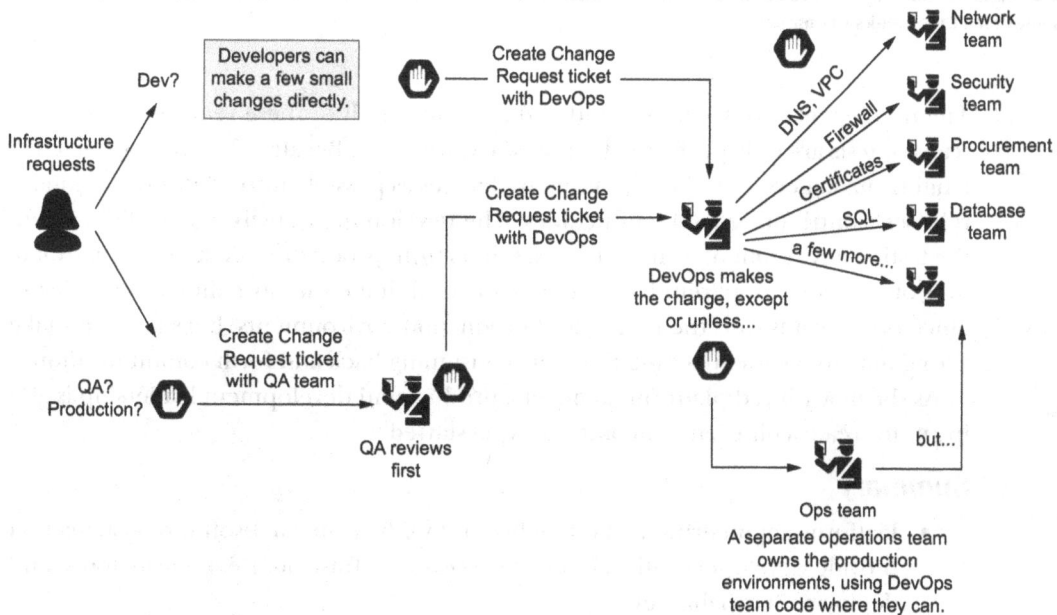

Figure 1.7 Infrastructure-oriented changes can go through as many as four handoffs by the time they reach the team that actually does the work. Each of these teams is only allowed to optimize a process within its own team's scope of responsibilities.

While, like most organizations, Epetech doesn't have as many teams managing infrastructure as creating custom software, the pace of change is just as high. The effect of all these handoffs and the process as a whole makes even routine changes slow and risky. The software release process is just as complex, as shown in figure 1.8.

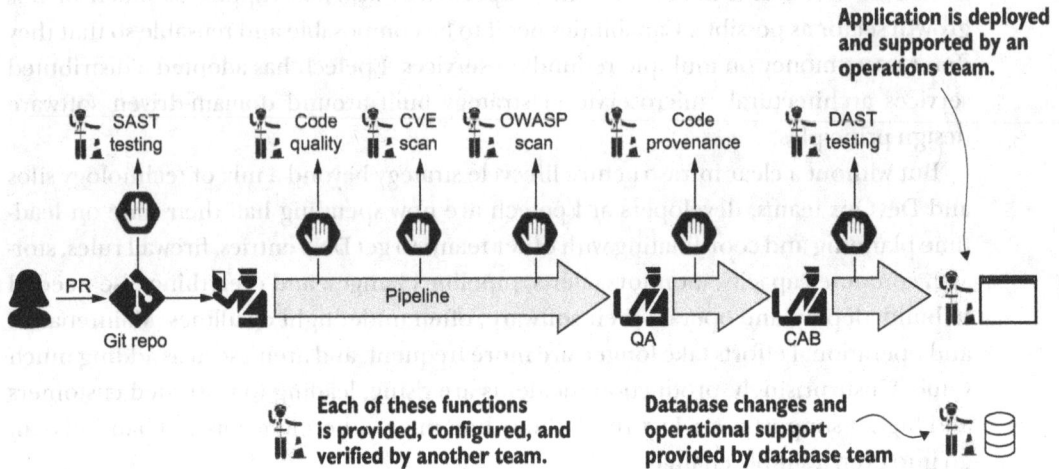

Figure 1.8 The application deployment process is fragmented, with multiple teams owning various requirements. A pipeline has been created to automate several steps, but a separate team also owns this process. A release can sometimes take weeks to complete.

The developers have to understand and account for all of these requirements. Many scans or tests are only performed on release candidates. Because the process is so challenging, managers try to bundle as many changes as possible into relatively infrequent releases, contributing to the difficulties. The development environment differs from the testing environment, which, in turn, differs from production. As a result, many failures only become apparent late in the process, adding even more time to the release. Since other teams own the testing and production environments, bugs and fixes take a long time to resolve, necessitating time-consuming back-and-forth communication.

As the newly hired platform engineers, product and development leadership is asking us to create a different outcome. Let's get started.

Summary

- Platform engineering is the practice of building internal software systems that provide developers with self-service access to infrastructure, security tools, and deployment capabilities.
- Effective platform engineering teams will work to deliver engineering platforms that provide internal software development teams with self-managed and seamless access to the tools and technologies they need to innovate, create, release,

and operate their software without the usual toil, delays, and the learning curve and mental overhead.

- Significant waste can be removed from the development lifecycle by providing developers with an effective engineering platform.

- Platform engineering principles and practices should be adopted as early as possible once an organization identifies strategic business value in custom software development.

- Platform engineering teams are software engineering teams that deliver internal products to stakeholders and users throughout the organization.

- Platform engineering requires a strategic approach with a product mindset to differentiate it from developing automation that can improve productivity.

- The development and delivery of engineering platforms should follow domain-driven design principles.

- Implemented correctly, platform engineering is neither a buzzword nor a replacement for the cultural paradigm of DevOps, the principles of DevEx, or the practice of SRE.

- Generative AI helps identify critical areas for platform strategy improvement (planning, design, testing, etc.) and accelerates these phases through automation and prediction.

Software-defined products and architectures

2

This chapter covers

- Differentiating between stakeholders and customers
- Optimizing engineering for the end-to-end lifecycle of the product
- Getting product features in front of users early
- Architecting for change

Companies that set out to apply platform engineering practices without including organizational structures, decision-making habits, and engineering culture in the strategy are destined for failure. It is that structure, decision-making, and culture that led them to where they are now in the first place. If your IT organization is already well suited to software product delivery, you will find it is already well on its way to delivering a platform product when you first realize you need it.

So what does the organizational structure need to reflect? What engineering practices and decision-making criteria have the kind of effect we want?

Measure organizational responsibilities and structures by how effectively internal products can implement a product delivery model. Reassign responsibilities, set new measures and expectations, and even change the structure if the current model prevents or detracts from the ability to deliver good internal products. Require the internal use of the output from each team or department to demonstrate that a good domain boundary exists and can be maintained.

Internal products are long-lasting. We know that requirements will constantly change, tools and technologies will become more valuable, and implementation methods will become more efficient. Evolution must be a visible attribute of every architecture.

Effective engineering quality that can deliver and maintain the product experience throughout all this evolution requires the entire engineering platform product to be software-defined. This means the entire product is created and maintained from versioned source control and artifacts using automated orchestration.

Let's expand on the product delivery model and the engineering principles of software-defined delivery, domain design, and evolutionary architecture.

2.1   *Product delivery model*

The default response in many enterprises when acquiring the infrastructure, developer tools, and other technologies needed to create and operate custom software is to treat each as a separate, one-off *project*. Usually, someone who isn't a software developer decides which tool or technology to purchase and which vendor to buy it from. They negotiate the purchase like it's a long-term capital investment, expecting it will be used essentially as-is for years to come, and then pass it off to another nonuser to set up, all accompanied by a detailed project plan that comes complete with a Gantt-style visualization of weekly, monthly, and quarterly milestones. Acquiring infrastructure and development technologies in this manner has become less and less effective over the past four decades. A large part of the success of the modern internet and SaaS-delivered business capabilities comes from letting companies escape the challenges of traditional IT. Every part of the delivery lifecycle of these software-provided capabilities is measured through the user experience.

Products are meant to last a long time, constantly improving and evolving to keep up with new conditions, technologies, and the features customers want. Change isn't just a one-time project; it's how software operates. A product delivery model is about the user experience and the continuous, ongoing development of that experience because this experience is what the customer values and why they use it. Adding features that aren't self-serve is missing the entire point of building a product. Building or implementing technologies in a way that makes change too expensive also breaks the product delivery model.

The third bullet in our definition of platform engineering from chapter 1 refers to this product by the name most commonly used: an *engineering platform*. A good start in defining the vision for any product is to come up with a brief description that helps people easily get the main idea. We could define our product as follows.

DEFINITION   An engineering platform enables software development teams to continuously create, test, deploy, and operate custom software with a self-serve experience, free from the usual engineering friction and delays, while still meeting all quality, security, and organizational compliance requirements.

The key to this is the definition of a product, which is the *self-serve experience*. Self-serve doesn't mean doing everything yourself. I can be sitting at my breakfast table, order a book, download it to my tablet, and start reading in just minutes. That is a self-serve experience. But behind the scenes, countless requirements are being met—contractual, regulatory, security, and financial requirements, just to name a few.

You might say, "Books aren't the same thing as developing software." Yet, a key part of how Amazon became the largest bookseller, and the largest in so many different commercial areas, is how it builds every internal capability as a product.

As an engineer on an engineering platform team, how can you tell if your organization is set up to deliver a product successfully? Consider the following questions:

- Is there technical *product ownership* of the platform?
- Are the architecture and engineering disciplines optimized for delivering and maintaining a product, or are they just provided as a professional service?
- Is the experience of using the platform the measure of success?
- Are stakeholders able to require implementations that defeat the product experience?
- Is the platform being delivered in rapid incremental steps, deeply relying on feedback from internal developers who actually use the features and the value of the subsequent results?

2.1.1   *Technical product ownership*

Creating a successful internal product will not come naturally for most companies. No matter how mature they may have become in understanding their external customers and creating value for those customers, internal ways of working that are not directly focused on external customers tend to be treated as simple cost centers. This means that just because we've successfully argued for the money-making effect on the bottom line from developers using an effective engineering platform doesn't mean the internal stakeholders assigned the task will recognize what is needed to be successful. Internal products, for all the same reasons as external-facing products, require the direction and focus provided by an empowered and accountable product owner. These relationships are shown in figure 2.1.

A true product team takes full ownership of what it delivers. It's the only team in the organization that provides a particular set of capabilities, and it's led by a product owner who has the responsibility and authority to set the team's product roadmap.

The product owner is often called a *technical product owner* (TPO) for an engineering platform. This can be a helpful distinction as it clarifies within the organization that an engineering product's users are skilled technologists with very different needs and

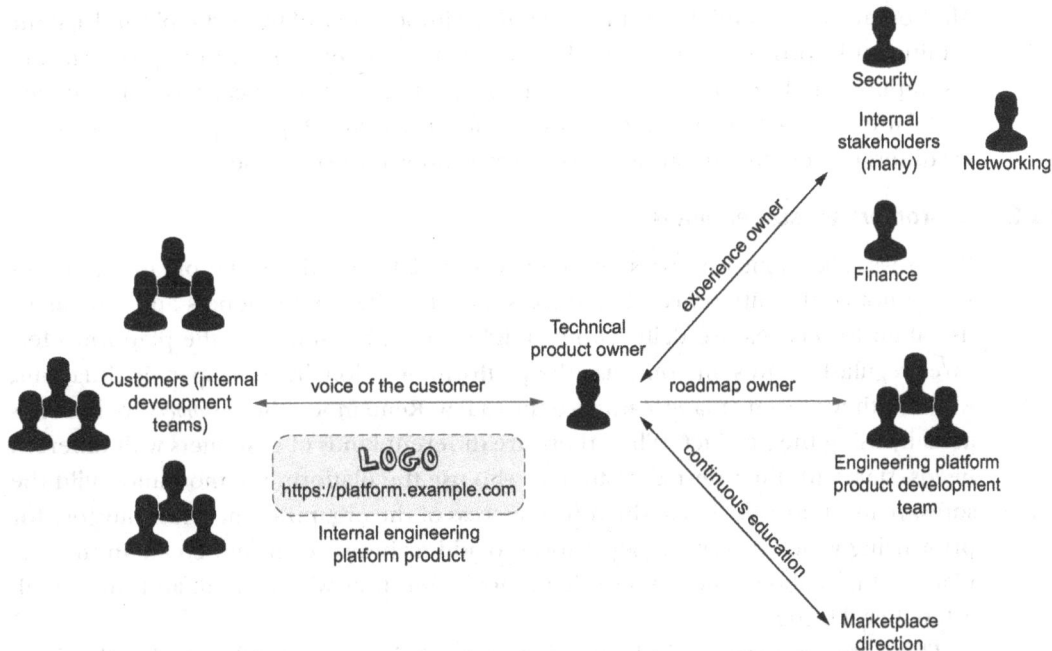

Figure 2.1 A technical product owner (who might be referred to as a technical product manager) serves as the voice of the customer, staying deeply connected to what the developers need and their experience in using the solution provided by the platform while constantly assessing the measurable value being provided.

expectations as compared to general consumer products. The users are internal, with different approaches needed for developing effective feedback loops. However, many of the fundamental activities remain the same regardless of the complexity or technical nature of the product.

The TPO's role involves the following:

- They are the voice of the customer. They deeply understand why customers use the product and what provides value. You might want to think of the customers in this scenario as your end-users.

- They find ways of meeting stakeholder needs without impairing the customer experience.

- They are responsible for knowing and understanding where the marketplace is heading.

- They prioritize the backlog, deciding on the order of release for platform capabilities, engineering improvements, or the refactoring of platform technical debt.

- They change the product roadmap when observations of actual usage or customer experiences indicate the expected value has not been obtained.

Most organizations initially misunderstand the importance of the TPO role and assume traditional IT processes can be used to deliver an engineering platform product. This assumption can lead to failure. Whether you are shipping skateboards or an engineering platform, a lack of actual, empowered product ownership will produce a product far different from the initial vision with significantly reduced value.

2.1.2   *Customers vs. stakeholders*

When we talk about who uses an engineering platform within the organization, it's key to notice the differences. Some folks, mostly software developers and engineers, use almost every feature daily. Others might only use a subset of the platform's features regularly. And some only use the platform occasionally or in specific situations, whether they're using many features or just a few. Remember: the *customers* are the ones actually using the product. When there are different kinds of customers with different needs, start with the internal customers who use the platform the most and build the software most directly tied to the future success of the organization. The same goes for prioritizing which features of a platform to add or improve (or not create in the first place)—think about who will use them, how often they will be used, and the overall value they'll bring.

There are also plenty of influencers. These people aren't actual users, but thanks to their roles as leaders or decision-makers in other parts of the company, they have significant influence in shaping or nudging the platform's requirements. They're invested in the outcome and influence things from the sidelines—they're not the customers: they are the stakeholders.

There are stakeholders both within and outside the organization. Think about the automotive industry as an example. Car companies start life building only a particular kind of vehicle. Initial success comes from offering a single category, such as a high-end performance sedan. Ford built their first passenger sedan in 1903 and iterated on the concept for five years before launching the Model T. They stuck to building only sedans until 1927, when they shipped their first truck. It was a few decades before specific categories of their light trucks became their biggest sellers.

Organizations also have many noncustomer interested parties. State and federal governments have a laundry list of requirements ranging from safety to taxation to insurance. Imagine if Ford had optimized the design and manufacturing of their cars to meet government expectations without regard for the effect on customer experience. They'd end up with a vehicle that nobody would want to buy. If the government set requirements that left no room for creativity or flexibility in car design, automakers would likely move their sales to markets free from those constraints.

In the context of engineering platforms, stakeholders often try to define how requirements are implemented in ways that undermine the usability of the platform. Yet, the actual outcome required can be achieved in many ways, including ways that don't break the product. Who are the noncustomer stakeholders when building an engineering platform? Figure 2.2 lists some of these sources of requirements.

Data
Subscriptions   Retention
Cost Localization   Regulations
Networking Legal Laws
Continuity Middleware   Contractual
Recovery Traditional IT Silos   Obligations   Protection
Storage DNS Compute Provenance   Change Management
Licenses Security Governance

Figure 2.2   Internal stakeholders have legitimate concerns. But these outcomes can be achieved without the stakeholders controlling the implementation.

Many enterprise stakeholders, including finance, security, legal, and project management, will expect to have a say in the platform's delivery. Traditional IT stakeholders may wish to own the technology capabilities found within an engineering platform through the siloes of networking, storage, computing, operating systems, middleware, Active Directory, and the like.

If the expectation is that the legacy silos can remain and behave in legacy ways while we somehow wrap an engineering platform around them, we will not succeed. If that were possible, adding the DevOps team would have been the solution.

> **NOTE**   Platform success is not about creating a wrapper; it's about introducing a whole new way of working.

For an engineering platform to achieve its potential, everyone involved needs to agree on how they think about and deliver products. All stakeholders must align around the model of product thinking and product delivery. We explain how his alignment happens through a simple scenario next.

What is the starting point for these stakeholders in this new product model? The most basic way to summarize this way of working is that stakeholders must provide either

- a service interface (API) to the capabilities they own that enables all internal customers who need the capability (or, at a minimum, the engineering platform product team) to obtain it in a self-serve and self-directed manner (e.g., as much of the service as they need, whenever they need it), or
- well-defined outcome standards that enable all affected teams across the enterprise to independently address their needs.

Take penetration testing as an example of a service interface. Typically, this falls under the security team's umbrella. To fulfill the minimum *service interface* requirement, the security team needs to set up a self-serve system. Any developer in the organization can get the credentials they need (if any), run scans on the endpoints they're working on, and assess their penetration-level compliance—all without having to sync up or even talk with the security team. One could correctly argue that this *minimal* outcome is less than ideal. An API available to everyone removes the usual friction, but how does the security team know what the scan revealed or what the response was to a negative scan? There are many ways. For example, security can automate the detection of every ingress point and perform recurring scans, comparing the list and results against the log history to determine who is using the scanner and which endpoints have vulnerabilities. Where such a scanner has a service interface and developers use an engineering platform, the platform product team can incorporate a high-quality experience and application of the control. It can be very costly to ignore these kinds of requirements in the scanning technology selection process.

The value of this service-interface-first architecture is one of the main reasons for building an engineering platform on a cloud infrastructure provider, such as AWS or Google Cloud, which is almost a requirement. Every service they offer is accessible via an API and designed to support independent, multitenant user patterns. While modern private data center vendors like VMware and Cisco offer products with comprehensive APIs, and there are open-source solutions like OpenStack for creating private clouds, most enterprises struggle to implement these to support this level of usability due to their traditional IT operating models.

Not all stakeholders will have the resources or expertise to provide a service interface to their domain. Fortunately, this is something that can be delegated to another team. Providing an API is the end goal, but this starts with well-defined outcomes. When stakeholders provide clear and testable outcome requirements, without implementation details, then the service interface can effectively be built by a different team.

Here is what we mean by defined outcomes: a security stakeholder defining corporate authentication standards as (1) requiring a single source of truth for internal authentication and (2) the internal implementations based on the Oauth2 framework (https://oauth.net/2/). An internal identity domain team could independently select and implement the single-source authentication service and provide self-service API access for teams building anything that requires internal authentication. If the identity team's solution can't meet the product requirement of a particular team, they can develop their implementation as long as it utilizes the single source of user identity and follows the OAuth2 standard.

As long as stakeholders follow one or both of these approaches, other internal teams are never blocked from waiting for the stakeholders to perform work on their behalf, nor do they have to create high-friction solutions for their customers.

When you're part of a platform engineering team, sketching out and maintaining a stakeholder map is a good idea. Track all the stakeholders who affect the platform to identify situations where a stakeholder's current or planned solutions or processes will not work with the platform. Use a diagram like the one shown in figure 2.3 to determine where the various stakeholders currently stand regarding their influence and alignment.

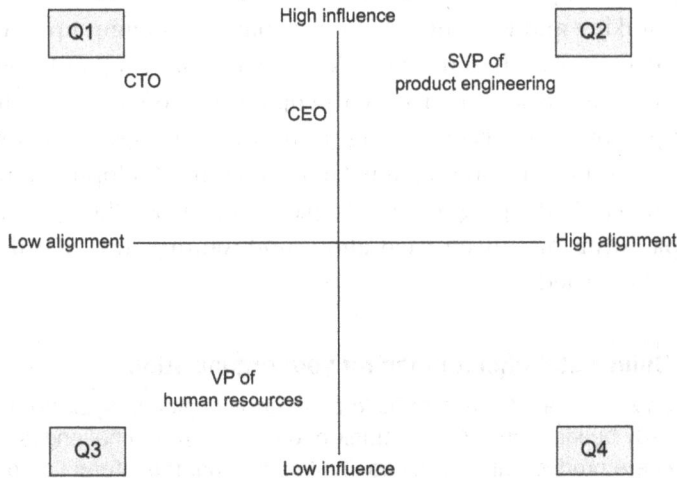

Q1

CTO

High influence

SVP of
product engineering

Q2

CEO

Low alignment ——————————————————————————— High alignment

VP of
human resources

Q3

Low influence

Q4

**Figure 2.3
A stakeholder
map visualizes a
stakeholder's influence
over the backlog against
their alignment to
platform objectives.
High-influence
stakeholders must be
highly aligned for a
platform to succeed.**

First, how much influence does the stakeholder have or want to have over the engineering platform? In the example diagram, the vice-president of human resources is neutral in aligning with the platform's goals and has meager influence, as you might expect. The CEO is highly influential, though they typically delegate their responsibility to others and attempt to reduce their direct influence beyond the broader corporate strategies. In both situations, the neutral alignment may have no negative effect. However, the CTO can be highly influential and is much more likely to be directly involved in setting operating models or budgets that directly influence an engineering platform.

Are the stakeholders highly aligned, providing the platform engineering team with API access or outcome requirements? Or are they unaligned, requiring the platform team to open tickets for needed configuration or conforming to existing operating models, regardless of whether they meet the engineering platform's needs?

People can disagree for all sorts of reasons. It could be due to a real difference in strategy, or someone may need more time or resources to align with the overall vision. An accurate and maintained stakeholder map effectively tracks delivery risk from internal stakeholders and processes. Focus on quadrant 1 (Q1). For each stakeholder in Q1, list their objections or constraints. Find the source of the constraints. Sometimes, a constraint imposed by one stakeholder results from a constraint placed on them by another stakeholder. At some point, a solution will be needed for each of these problems. Failing to provide these solutions will result in a *miss* in some aspect of the product vision. Each miss is a reduction of value, whether that be small or significant. If there are enough misses, the entire investment is at risk.

It's very important to spot and monitor any misalignments early on. This can save you from a lot of criticism later on, especially when you're diving into something as complex as an engineering platform. Introducing this platform means embracing a whole new way of thinking and working, which can sometimes bump up against the existing culture and processes. If you make clear what's changing and how much change is happening, there is less chance that people will wrongly blame the goals when things don't pan out as expected. Being upfront and transparent about these mismatches early on is crucial to sidestep any later criticisms of adopting a product-centric mindset in such a challenging project. To paraphrase G.K. Chesterton, it's not that engineering platforms have been tried and found wanting. It is that they have been found hard and not tried.

Exercise 2.1   Build a stakeholder map for your organization

Assume your organization has decided to build an internal engineering platform. Perhaps you are already building one. As you think about the current challenges, there are many areas where product thinking faces challenges from the interaction of various stakeholders within your company.

Create a stakeholder map and populate the map with several relevant stakeholders. Pick one stakeholder from Q1 and create a list of their objections or constraints.

Then describe how the capability owned by the stakeholder could either be

- provided as an API that provides the platform engineers with a self-serve experience *or*
- defined by a standard that would enable the platform engineers to solve for the desired product experience while meeting the needs of the stakeholders.

2.1.3   Optimize for a product

Deciding to build an internal engineering platform is, in large part, a response to the challenges and shortcomings of your enterprise's current setup. Your current setup results from your current organizational structures, how decisions are made, and the overall engineering culture.

As a platform engineer, how do you know which aspects of your organizational structures contribute to engineering and product quality and which detract? There isn't an easy answer. However, after building engineering platforms in dozens of national and multinational enterprises, we have found three key practices that have repeatedly been shown to be leading indicators:

- The entire end-to-end process for building, delivering, and operating software has been assessed and engineered for quality and success.

- All features or capabilities of the product have been delivered as a service interface first.
- Commitments to architectural and product experience decisions are made based on the results of actual implementations and observations of customer usage.

END-TO-END ENGINEERING OPTIMIZATION

Figure 2.4 illustrates an effective strategy for identifying all the factors that will affect the developer experience.

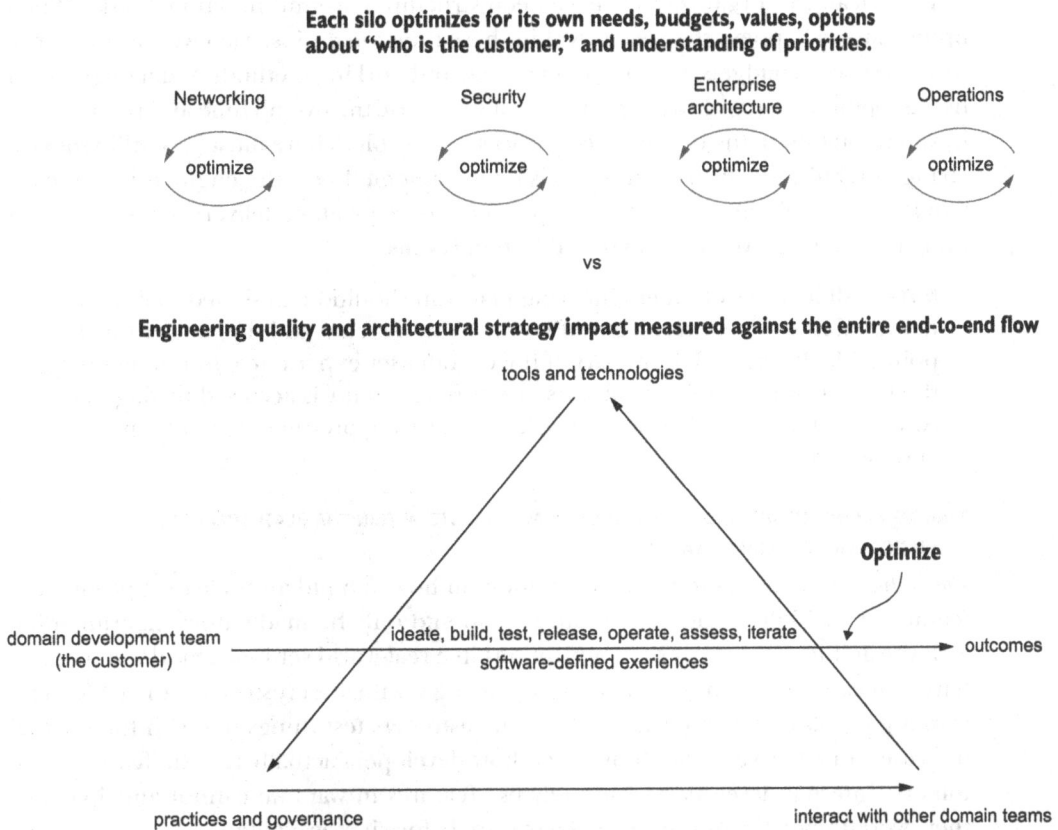

Each silo optimizes for its own needs, budgets, values, options about "who is the customer," and understanding of priorities.

Networking

optimize

Security

optimize

Enterprise architecture

optimize

Operations

optimize

vs

Engineering quality and architectural strategy impact measured against the entire end-to-end flow

tools and technologies

Optimize

domain development team (the customer)

ideate, build, test, release, operate, assess, iterate
software-defined exeriences

outcomes

practices and governance

interact with other domain teams

Figure 2.4   Look at all the activities, from ideation to operations, and assess engineering quality and effects from organizational or architectural decisions. Yrjö Engeström's human activity model inspires this developer activity model [1].

The developer activity model shown in figure 2.4 provides an effective means of determining the engineering platform's actual effect and, therefore, the scope of the assessment for end-to-end engineering effectiveness.

Success comes from independent, domain-focused development teams. These teams will experiment with ideas specific to their domain. They'll build and test software to create measurable experiences and value. Then they'll release the software to their customers and manage it, ensuring quality user experiences while keeping an eye on the results. Are customers using the product as expected? Is it delivering the intended value? Is it resilient and performant?

This range of activities outlines what the development teams need to do. They must be able to perform these tasks efficiently and without delays caused by cross-team dependencies. Regardless of how much of this scope the engineering platform supports at any given time, measure the experience against this outcome.

Historically, IT organizations have been structured around functional tasks. When optimizations happen, they occur within these functional silos, each with its own measures of success, budgets, management values, and working methods. What might seem like an optimization within a silo can actually increase the overall time and reduce quality when you look at the development process as a whole. There must be a willingness to change organizational structures, decision-making methods, the engineering culture, and any other relevant elements to support effective product delivery. If you do everything the same way, you can't expect different results.

NOTE   All features of an engineering platform should be designed, built, and delivered as service interfaces (APIs) first. You'll create additional user touchpoints, like CLIs and UIs, as part of the overall user experience. But no matter the type or number of touchpoints, the core capability is accessed through an API. This architectural choice is the key to ensuring product flexibility, quality, and longevity.

MAKING ARCHITECTURE AND TECHNOLOGY COMMITMENTS WITHIN THE PLATFORM ONLY AFTER REAL-LIFE EXPERIMENTATION

Commitment here refers to the final decision on how to build and release a production feature or capability. These commitments should only be made after experimenting with the architecture or technology options in a real-world setting. This doesn't always have to mean live-in production, although that gives the best results. It can be based on working proofs-of-concept where platform customers test things out with their actual use cases. In every case, carefully watch how developers actually use the feature. Customers (internal developers) routinely use features in ways we cannot anticipate, or they overestimate the importance of a feature before it is available.

WARNING   When deciding on the implementation of a durable message queue, an anti-pattern would be for the engineering platform team to independently assess available solutions and attempt to find something with the broadest range of features and capabilities, ostensibly to future-proof the decision against future requirements. However logical as this may sound, in practice, you simply cannot anticipate future requirements, and bloated, do-everything technologies underperform and are routinely more costly than a handful of smaller, optimized solutions

2.1.4   *The importance of a minimal valuable product and early adopters*

An engineering platform needs to evolve based on actual customer usage from the very start. In product development terms, this means figuring out the most basic implementation of a feature or capability and releasing it early. It's not always clear how much functionality the first version needs for customers to find it valuable, and opinions within your team or company will vary. Whatever you initially decide on, treat it like a hypothesis. Carefully analyze the behavior of early adopters, look for evidence that shows whether the initial features are effective, and be ready to change priorities if the evidence doesn't support your initial ideas. We commonly encounter deliveries where there seems to be consensus around a *long* list of features and capabilities that must be part of the initial use of a new technology. Yet, after taking sometimes months to ship it in that full-featured state, developers discover that in practice, only one or two basic configurations are valuable.

Everyone in or around software development is probably familiar with the minimum viable product (MVP) delivery diagram. It starts with a skateboard, which evolves into a bicycle, then to a motorcycle, and finally a car [2]. It is an effective analogy, but it is sometimes confusing, depending on the user's perspective. What if I'm right about needing transportation but wrong about needing it in the form of a car? Figure 2.5 shows an alternative way to think about it.

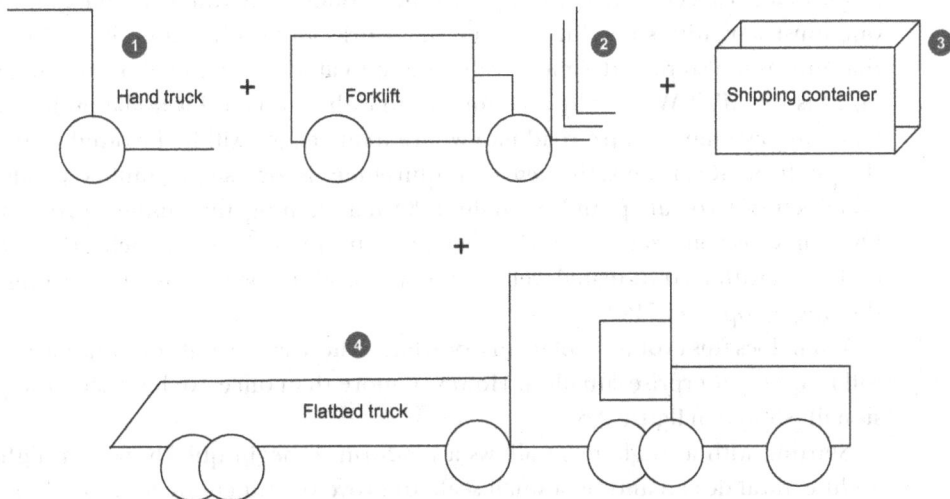

Figure 2.5   The progression of an MVP delivery process. A fully functional product does not need to be delivered at the start, but all phases should deliver some incremental value to the customer.

Imagine you need to move goods from your factory to your customers, but it's unclear how many customers you will have, what grouping of products they will use, how much volume there will be, and so on. Suppose the solution progresses from hand trucks to a forklift to loading cargo containers onto flatbed trucks, with each stage enhancing your delivery capability. In that case, you can see how each offers value and expands the capabilities. Throughout the process, you can assess the best *next step*. What if, during the phase where you use the forklift, you discover that most deliveries will be local and that loading the product directly on the truck will be more efficient without the intermediate shipping container? This model works well for platform engineers because the platform team isn't usually the creator of underlying platform capabilities. They often integrate open and vendor-sourced capabilities. Many evolutionary stages will be necessary to cover the full scope of developer activities. You can start with the smallest valuable element and keep expanding until you achieve complete coverage. Each new feature should undergo the same experimentation process, proof-of-concept, and real-world usage before it's fully implemented in the platform. The experiment will be far cheaper than the full implementation, and we need proof that it will deliver value before we incur the full cost.

BEGINNING DELIVERY WITH A SINGLE TEAM

> A complex system that works is invariably found to have evolved from a simple system that works.
>
> —John Gall [3]

Gall's insights hit home when we look at engineering platforms. He makes a crucial point that is especially true for a platform: to build something complex and mature, one must start with something simple that works and evolve from there. In our case, that means it also provides measurable value to at least the initial users. That starting point is the MVP. We usually recommend that this initial offering be built by a single team and assume a future roadmap where many teams will be involved in delivering the platform. Regardless, the *absolute* requirement is for a single, unified product (and architectural) roadmap and a single TPO maintaining this unified product vision. Over time, as you need to speed things up, you can go from one delivery team to several, each with its own team-level subdomain product owner but all reporting back to the single, top-level TPO.

What does this evolution of teams look like? There is no single evolutionary path that will fit every enterprise situation. However, more than once, we have seen the progression illustrated in figure 2.6.

Starting with a single team allows a platform to begin quickly, with a high-quality architectural design and on a small scale to prove the functionality and value that can be generated. Over time, specific capabilities are so heavily used and have such a broad effect that a dedicated team can be justified to manage them. Developer-experience teams are a common area, as is identity and DevSecOps. These areas quickly become essential enough that the initial single team cannot manage those areas and, at the same time, continue to develop new capabilities for the platform as a whole. Eventually, even the core engineering platform team begins to split as globalization is introduced,

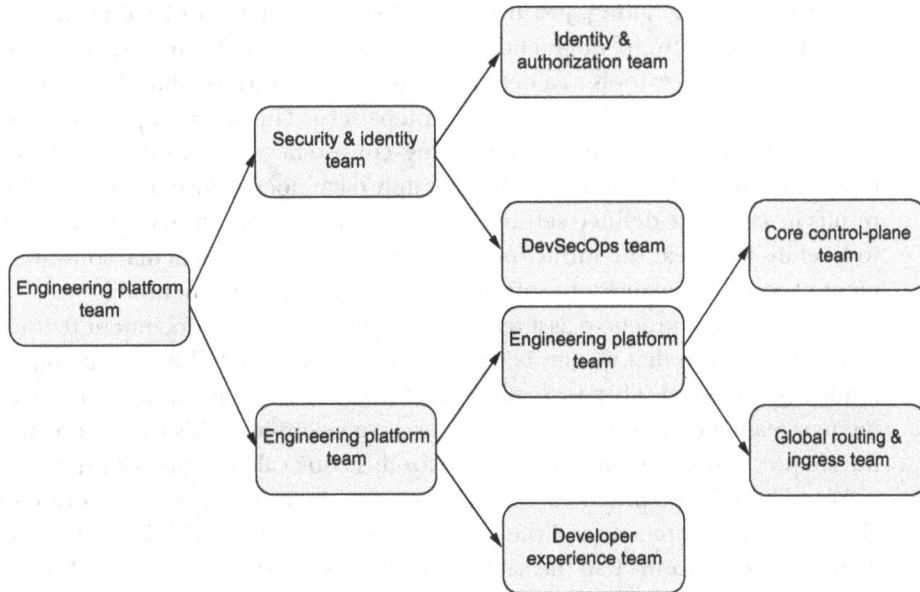

Figure 2.6   The evolutionary path of platform development teams. Often, while an engineering platform team starts as an effort driven by a single team, multiple teams spin up over time to handle specific aspects of platform functions, with all development efforts under a top-level product owner.

requiring dynamic routing between clusters to be supported by a dedicated effort. These splits could take the form of the capability simply moving to a legacy team if, during the intervening time, they demonstrate the same product delivery maturity.

> **Exercise 2.2   Define the feature set of an MVP engineering platform**
>
> Create a detailed list of the capabilities you believe are necessary to form the MVP for an engineering platform. For each, describe why the absence of the capability renders the MVP definition of the product unsuccessful.

2.2   Software-defined platform

Platform engineering is, at its core, a category of software engineering. When creating our platform, we must think about it like any other software product development and prioritize the same engineering practices. In our experience, many platform teams launch with engineers who have an operations background because they naturally have the most infrastructure experience. If we do this, we need to keep our eyes open for an anti-pattern we often encounter. Historically, managing infrastructure has meant following checklists, clicking through settings, manually uploading files, and racking and stacking physical hardware. Everything was verified by a human, step by step. When

DevOps tools came along, just dropping them into that world didn't magically turn operations into software engineering. The shift took time. Many traditional operations teams saw these new tools as a better way to run their scripts—but things stayed pretty manual overall. That's why we call it an anti-pattern. The manual approach made sense at the start—it was the only way to bring consistency and control. Understandably, that's the way things were done. But that approach doesn't give us the same beneficial results in a software-defined setting. As we move toward platform engineering, we need to level up and treat the infrastructure lifecycle more like an actual software development process, with consistent software engineering practices behind it.

Defining these practices as a team, it's helpful to create a document that the whole team agrees on so that we can be confident everyone will follow the standards consistently from the start. This document can also serve as a team charter to make onboarding new team members easier in the future. An example of this type of document is in the chapter 2 folder of the GitHub repo for this book called Team_Charter.md.

We will apply the practices we expect our engineering organization to require for all software development and the practices we intend to enable through the resulting engineering platform. Use the same supporting development tools and technologies that the platform will provide to platform users, a practice often called "dogfooding."

2.2.1   *The platform software delivery lifecycle*

The delivery lifecycle is a repeating process, illustrated in figure 2.7. We will add some detail to some of these processes in later sections, but for now, this serves as a base software delivery lifecycle process that we can document and expect the team to follow for every change made to the platform.

PLAN

All work is planned, whether a new feature, evolutions to existing features, or even recurring maintenance, to determine how it fits into the overall platform roadmap, what dependencies it may have, how to break down the work into small chunks that can be released in frequent and incremental change rather than a big-bang release, and most importantly, how to prioritize. This is the time for the TPO to define what success looks like and how it will be measured. These measures create the initial acceptance criteria for the platform engineers doing the work.

DESIGN

Before beginning development, address the architectural challenges and acceptance criteria. This is not to say that we expect the design to be final and unchangeable. We need to keep the ability to pivot as we learn new information. If the work is part of a completely new capability within the platform, this is where we define the experiments: small or incremental capabilities that can be released to provide actual data about usage and effectiveness. We need to find objective evidence supporting the value of the work before expending the resources for a complete and sustained implementation. This is also the right time to get general team feedback on the task breakdown's size and how well the work is understood based on the documentation or any other details.

1. Prioritize what comes next and the acceptance criteria of successful delivery.

Plan

8. Continuously assess the impact to overall operational health and the quality of predictive monitoring.

Operate

Design

2. Decide the architecture and implementation.

7. Carefully observe the developer and end-user experience impacted by the change, critically assessing both the user experience and the operational responsiveness.

Observe

Code

3. Write the automated tests that confirm code correctness and resiliency and that the acceptance criteria are met, then write the code.

6. Release the change to platform customer environments: first, to a preview environment not in the customer path to production, then to all nonproduction environments, and finally to production.

Release

Build

4. Incorporate the code and the texts into a CI/CD pipeline that orchestrates all actual change in a fixed path to production.

Test

5. Through the pipeline, thoroughly test in production-like environments outside of the platform user environments.

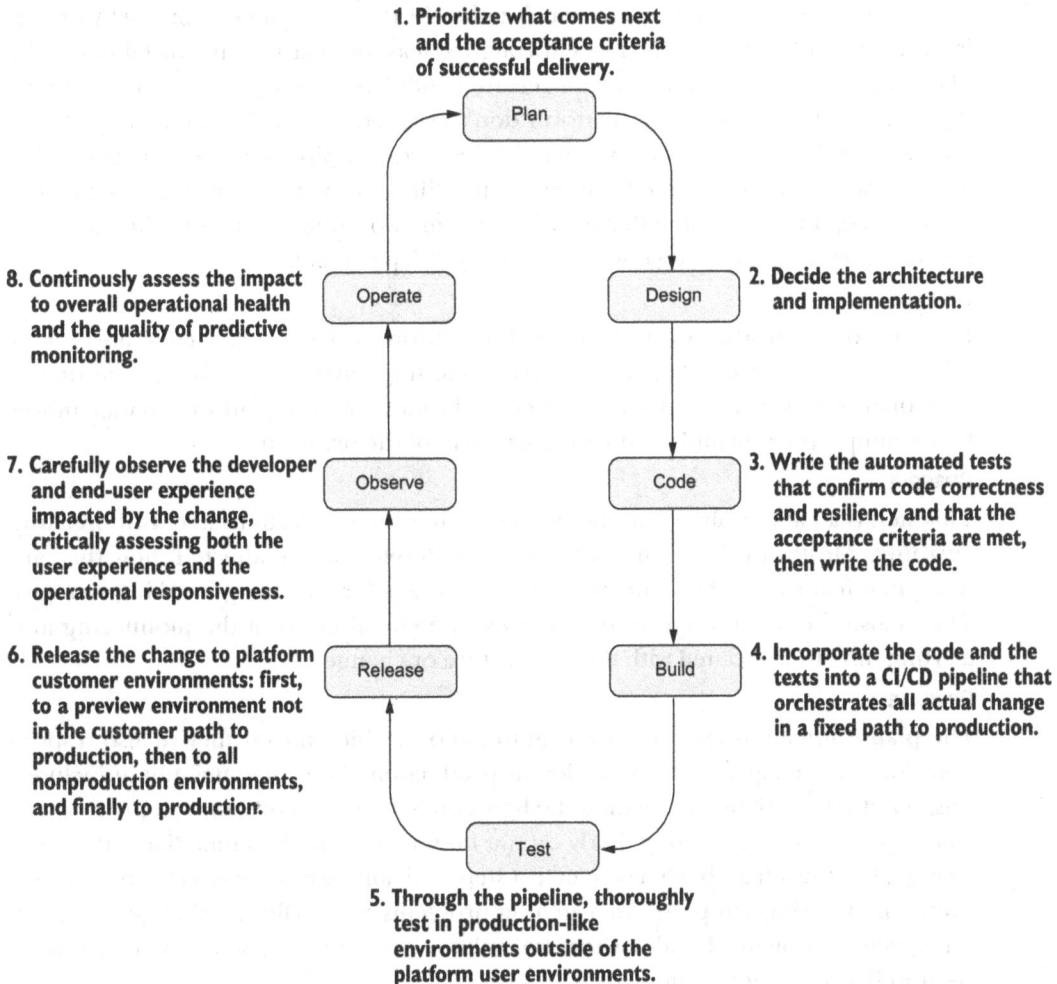

Figure 2.7 The software delivery lifecycle covers all stages from feature planning through running in production.

CODE

Once we have a design and understand the acceptance criteria, we can start code development. Step 1 is creating automated tests. Writing tests after principal development creates too significant a risk of confirmation bias, weakening the test quality. Creating the tests first is also the most effective way to uncover misunderstandings about the work before implementation starts.

BUILD -> TEST

Actual change happens only through an automated pipeline. This means going from the first cloud (or data center) environment to the last, including every integration, functional, and end-to-end test. For any change, every *environment* beyond the initial one must always be based on the same code—in this case, the commit SHA or tag. We recommend that a change move through at least two early testing instances of the platform before being considered a release candidate. These are test environments that the developers using the platform don't ever see. If you also want the platform engineers to have throw-away instances in the case of a pipeline that manages a platform infrastructure component, these should still be provisioned by triggering an on-demand step in the pipeline that assures the same workflow happens in the same way, including tests and anything else that is part of a deployment.

RELEASE

Releases to the production instance of the platform for developer code also follow a fixed release path that starts with a *preview* testing environment that is outside the developer team's typical path to production. From there, the platform change moves to the nonproduction and production instances of the platform.

OBSERVE

This step is all about observing the new code. It answers questions like: Is it breaking anything? Mostly, this is about observing how developers are affected, how they are using new features, or how effective our process was for managing breaking changes. This is also the initial opportunity to assess the effectiveness of the monitoring and alerting directly associated with the new feature or change.

OPERATE

The platform team is expected to be autonomous, which means they're also responsible for supporting what they deploy in production. The "operate" phase includes this, but it's more than just keeping the lights on—it's about constantly improving and learning from what's running. Early on, we might focus on the immediate effect of a change, but this phase is where we take a step back and assess the effectiveness of our overall monitoring setup. Are we catching problems early? Did the change cause any unexpected problems? It's also where we evaluate how good our predictive monitoring is—and figure out how to improve it.

REPEAT

The entire process is a never-ending loop: rinse and repeat.

We will go through several detailed examples in chapters 6 through 8. Note that, to be successful, you can't wait until the "observe" phase to create the code that automates the configuration of dashboards, monitors, or alerts. Remember: everything is code, including things that are more operational as they are used. Configuring observability is just part of the *definition of done* for every task.

2.2.2 *Observability-driven development*

This scenario is an example of something that happens all too frequently: A development team reports that some of their services have intermittent communication problems. They've tried to diagnose the problem by looking for unhandled exceptions and HTTP error codes, but they can't find any problems in their software, so they've become convinced it's a problem with the platform.

The platform engineering team spends a couple of hours trying to track down the problem and reviewing all the cluster logs and related service metrics, but they can't find anything either. Eventually, someone on the team suggests activating more granular network logs and trying to reproduce the problem once the new logging is in place. An analysis shows that a service mesh policy in the platform was throttling traffic because the throughput generated by the new services exceeded the threshold of a new traffic rate policy that was only expected to apply to external sources. A simple fix to the configuration is made and deployed to resolve the problem.

The teams lost a full day of work. Developers spent 3 hours unsuccessfully debugging, reported the bug, and waited for the platform team. The platform team spent 2 hours checking logs and another hour debugging the new services. Once network logs were activated, it took an hour to parse them, and the fix took just 10 minutes to code and deploy.

Observability-driven development (ODD) would have resulted in a very different outcome. ODD expands on the practice of test-driven development [4] by focusing on the observability data (and alerting) needed to enable platform engineers to know, at any point in time, what the new software is doing. Recall that observability is all about how effectively the data we collect about the system helps us understand system behavior. The easiest way to think about ODD is as an additional acceptance criterion applied to all work in the backlog, as shown in figure 2.8.

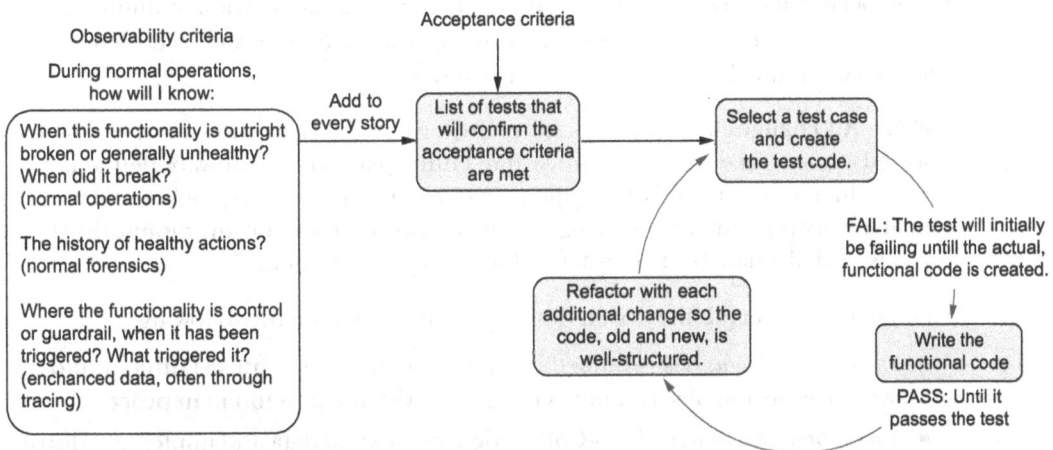

Figure 2.8 With every change you make to the platform, think about the kind of data you will need to understand how the new technology, service, or feature is behaving. Alerting from service failure is not enough. When we deploy automatic configuration behavior or control guardrails, even healthy behavior could be interpreted as failure.

EXTENDING THE DESIGN PHASE

Many of these observability questions can be boilerplate, and we should have a standard list that we automatically review. During the design phase, specifically ask yourself what observability data must be generated or accessible for this feature if we are to have confidence that we know exactly what it is doing or has done in the *operational* past. How can we prove that the features we release are functioning and performing as expected, including delivering the expected value?

Using our previous example, say we want to add a new control feature to the platform based on the distributed denial of service scenario. To prevent excess traffic volume by throttling traffic above 1,000 requests per second to a single service from the same source in addition to creating tests that send more than 1,000 requests per second to trigger the throttle and prove it works, we need to determine what observability data is required when this is working as intended. This includes the following:

- Source of the request
- Destination of the request
- An indicator of whether this is an internal source
- Historical volumes sorted by source and destination
- How often requests are blocked from a given source

Because this is a kind of control, we will need throttling events to be highly visible, perhaps even sending an alert.

We should include this with the general operational observability requirements in the acceptance criteria. Our automated tests will confirm that the control will trigger when expected and that general operational health logging, metrics, monitoring, and alerting are in place. Since this is a control, or guardrail, uniquely tagged event data is generated when the threshold throttle is triggered.

> **NOTE** All changes should generate event logs. A change causes most unexpected events (like outages). Since our entire platform is software-defined, every change we make will happen through a deployment pipeline. That means every pipeline needs to log change events so we can tie any monitoring or observability data back to exactly what changed and when.

At a high level, observability-driven design principles include the following:

- *Instrumentation as code*—Embed telemetry (metrics, logs, traces) directly into the system, ensuring observability is integrated with the development process.
- *Contextual data and tracing*—Collect rich, contextual data and implement distributed tracing to track system behavior across services, enabling quick identification of problems in complex architectures.
- *Actionable metrics and logs*—Define key, actionable metrics and structured logging that provide insights into system health, performance, and errors, making monitoring and troubleshooting efficient.
- *Automated alerts and self-service monitoring*—Enable teams to configure monitoring, dashboards, and proactive alerts, empowering quick responses to problems without centralized dependency.

- *Continuous improvement via feedback loops*—Use observability data to focus on root causes, drive continuous system improvement, and balance innovation with reliability through error budgets.

The twist here is that we go beyond writing tests to check if things work. We also ensure that data tracks healthy behavior and that we're getting the value we expect.

If we had delivered the control feature with the observability data we defined, it would have been much more likely that the internal versus external source error would not have escaped the development process. But even if it did, when the throttling scenario started to happen, the throttling event data would have been immediately visible in the operational data search for the service affected.

Exercise 2.3 Observability-driven design requirements

Practice defining the observability data needed for a feature using ODD principles listed in the previous section by considering the following feature of an engineering platform:

The platform provides many predefined ingress domains for Epetech API developers. For example, dev.api.epetech.io is an ingress URL reserved for all teams' initial testing environments, and a dedicated gateway has been defined that receives all traffic to this domain. Teams specify the dev gateway and the path for the dev instance of their API among the values passed during a deployment. Their Helm chart will include a VirtualService resource that includes these values, directing the service mesh to send such traffic to their API. Assuming the *customer* domain team deploys a *profile* service, their VirtualService definition would define and direct traffic:

```
apiVersion: networking.istio.io/v1alpha3
kind: VirtualService
metadata:
  name: profile
  namespace: customer-dev
spec:
  hosts:
    - "dev.api.epetech.io"
  gateways:
    - dev-api-epetech-io-gateway
  http:
    - name: profile-route
      match:
        - uri:
            prefix: /customers/profile
      route:
        - destination:
            host: profile.customer-dev.svc.cluster.local
            port:
              number: 8000
```

This results in the traffic direction of https://dev.api.epetech.io/customers/profile => profile.customer-dev.svc.cluster.local.

(continued)

As the platform engineering team responsible for maintaining this capability, what kinds of observability data will we need to be able to effectively operate, upgrade, and maintain this feature? Consider these questions:

- How do I know this is working correctly?
- What metrics, logs, traces, or event information would I need to diagnose success or failure?
- What kinds of behaviors do I want to be alerted about?

2.3 Evolutionary platform architecture

As we design our software-defined platform, we will face many design choices. Is the X tool or the Y tool better for security scans? Should we use an open-source tool or work with a vendor? Is using infra as code to self-manage our services and resources appropriate, or should we use a managed infrastructure service?

These are good questions, and they have different answers in different contexts. But if we want our platform to retain an evolutionary flexibility, we must include specific architectural requirements as part of every decision. For example, in chapter 6, we outline effective criteria in the software selection process. An important consideration that applies to all of these choices and the details of how they are implemented is that the reasons will change. When making design choices about our engineering platform, we can't possibly know how the platform will be used a year from now. Beyond that, we can't see how the available solutions will change. There will potentially be new options in the future that will create greater value than those currently available.

The result is that (routinely) capabilities that were considered essential turn out to be unnecessary. Highly valuable tools can come onto the market in a space that previously had few good options. Technologies that previously had to be self-managed can become available from cloud vendors.

How do we prioritize implementing capabilities and functionality to the needed degree? How can we implement in ways that make it less costly to change strategies in the future? In chapter 6, we will start building our Epetech engineering platform using several evolutionary implementation strategies. However, there are also product planning, user feedback, and even automated testing strategies that will make our platform easier to change.

2.3.1 Backlog management for incremental design

In practice, master plans fail—because they create totalitarian order, not organic order. They are too rigid; they cannot easily adapt to the natural and unpredictable changes that inevitably arise in the life of a community. As these changes occur . . . the master plan becomes obsolete.

—Eric Evans, *Domain-Driven Design* [5]

As we introduce the concepts of platform engineering to Epetech, the ideas start flowing. Everyone in product, operations, marketing, and leadership has an idea for the platform that we "simply must do." It's good to capture all those high-level ideas as large buckets, ideas, or epics in our iteration management tooling. However, as we gather the backlog and ideas from our stakeholders, leaders, and even our team and begin to analyze the requests, we make some observations—for example:

- *Someone on our team asked about the GUI for our platform APIs.* It's hard to know if we'll need a UI for the development teams interacting with custom platform APIs because we don't have any development teams using the platform yet! Most similar tools and technologies are typically used through a CLI.

- *The database team pointed out that all the custom applications use a particular brand of self-managed SQL database.* After talking with several teams, we discovered a database team that manages all the databases, not any of the development teams. None of the teams using the database was involved in the selection, and the few stored procedures used could easily be written in standard SQL. The database team considers the technology superior because it is faster at most internal database tasks than most of the more widely used SQL databases. It is, but there's no history of database performance ever causing problems. Very few custom Epetech systems even include synchronous database interactions.

- *There is a project underway to create a corporate data lake.* The team implementing the lake expects to use Kafka for some aspects, and there is a proposal to deploy a single corporate Kafka production instance and have all the existing event and message queues convert to this technology.

  The existing event streams use a basic pub/sub technology that our current cloud vendor provides. The cost is negligible, and the service is performant, supporting 100 times our most optimistic plans. Kafka would provide more queueing technology options, but there isn't presently any feature in the Epetech roadmap that requires additional features.

These examples point out an assumption probably being made in the feature request. But this is also a very typical pattern. How do we know we need the feature? How were the requirements determined? Have circumstances changed? Has it been tried in an actual working situation?

Rather than creating exhaustive and detailed feature lists extending years into the future, we should focus on proving value. We don't want to implement massively complex features that nobody uses. Getting the platform to a minimum viable usability allows us to quickly switch gears into a process of software development that enables the platform to grow based on the real needs of its users (see figure 2.9).

Once again, it's worth noting how important monitoring data is in this process. In step 2, "model the opportunity," we map out the requested change and check that we've got the correct data to support it. As we move forward and define the new capability, we'll also set up automated data collection so we can compare the real value delivered with what we initially estimated.

Model the idea. Can we assess the proposed value? Can we reasonably estimate the cost to implement and continue the feature? Could we gather the necessary data from actual use to compare the results against the model?

If the value can be modeled, does the potential value reach our product value threshold? If large and complex, is there a low-cost experiment to reduce risk?

Product owner identifies potential features or capabilities getting ideas from the industry, users, stakeholders, and even platform team members.

Identify opportunities

Model the opportunity

Qualify the opportunity

Delivery (backlog SDLC flow)

Estimate and prioritize

Define the implementation

Confirm / deny / adjust the model

Using the data gathered from actual use, confirm or deny the value assumptions of the model.

Create the detailed tasks (stories) that define all the work. Where the feature is large, the first iteration of this will be the validation experiment.

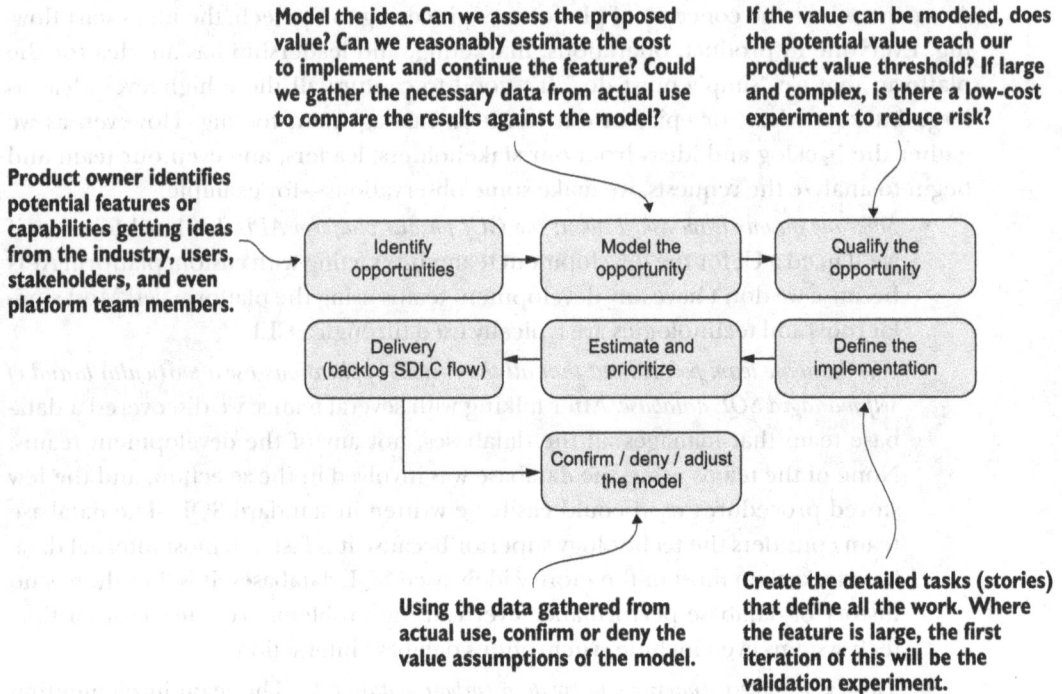

Figure 2.9   New features or changes should go through a value flow. Routine operations and refactoring will be happening simultaneously, and using this flow will help us stay clear on how our current work fits into the bigger picture.

What if a proposed change is related to a regulatory requirement? What would be the dollar value of implementing such a change, besides avoiding a penalty? If it is a change to meet an entirely new requirement, that would be an example of drawing the "feature" modeling scope around a description that is too narrow. A regulatory or security requirement is a cost of a larger feature, not a feature by itself. For new requirements, the price should be added to the overall cost of delivery of custom software. On the other hand, if the change is refactoring an existing regulatory control, we could rightly ask, "What does it cost us to meet this nonfunctional requirement now versus after the proposed change?"

What about that earlier idea we noted, the one about creating a graphical interface for a custom platform feature? This is a good example of where we need to step back and check whether we're framing the scope correctly. Is the graphical interface itself the "feature," or is it really just one part of a larger capability that delivers value? If we model it too narrowly, we risk overemphasizing the interface while underestimating the broader functionality and outcomes it enables. By treating it as part of the overall feature, we can more accurately assess its actual cost and value in relation to the bigger picture.

Exercise 2.4 Model the feature request for a browser-based means of integrating a new Git repo with the platform

Let's say a stakeholder comes and says, "My team wants a browser interface for integrating new git repositories with platform features. On our team, it is usually the analyst or the scrum master who creates a new repository, since we try to take care of as many things as possible for developers to save them time. These folks aren't as comfortable with the CLI you provided, and it causes stress and slows them down." Our Epetech platform team debates the idea internally. Using the CLI requires the user to install and maintain a sufficiently recent version of the tool on their laptop, ensuring it is in their terminal path. Integrating a repo requires the user to authenticate using the CLI and then run the repo integration command as follows:

```
$> <tool name> login
```

Your browser window will open (or click here) to complete the login:

```
$> <tool name> create repo <repo name>
```

Behind the scenes, the tool calls a custom platform API that will first check to see if the repo already exists for the team and, if it does not, will create it. Then, the API will add the repo to its internal reconciliation loop and maintain the integration between the repo and the software pipeline tool, along with a handful of other automated tasks provided by the platform to improve Git-related user experiences.

How might we model and qualify this feature request following our incremental change process? As a user of the Epetech engineering platform, I need a browser-based interface to create and integrate new GitHub repositories with the platform automation. What do we need to know to quantify the value of this feature? How can we obtain the information? How can we continue to track the value over time if we implement this feature?

When you're done with exercise 2.4, consider the following: over time, it costs more to operate software than to create it. That's not a bad thing by itself. The software generates value as it is used. But this should alter how we think about features in software that are not used (or rarely used), especially internal software systems like an engineering platform. What if, in researching a capability such as described in the previous exercise, we discover that the average team creates 12 new repos per year? Except for the team that made the request, the developers build the repos and spend barely 1 to 2 minutes doing it. If a GUI were made available, most developers would not use it, and anyone using the GUI would take more than 10 minutes to complete the same task. The team that requested it is expending several hours per year to save their developers just a few minutes. If that were the actual situation, we would lose money implementing such a feature.

Of course, it would be better to successfully figure this out before expending the time to implement a feature. But that isn't always possible. Sometimes, all the data suggests a feature is worth shipping, and only afterward do we discover that it will not generate the value we expected. It is better to remove the feature than incur the ongoing sustainment costs.

On the other hand, what if our investigation revealed that a 10-minute GUI experience would save 40 hours per quarter per team, and we have 100 teams using our platform? Implementing the feature would add back the equivalent of two full-time developers' time.

If we were to build this GUI for our users, what sort of data do we need to think about in our "define" stage? We'll want to ensure they have an excellent overall experience, including latency, low error percentages, and fast page load times. But more important than that will be confirming the time savings. Our GUI should provide the tracking data to verify the adoption rate and penetration. If users aren't adopting, we will need to figure out why. We will also need a few follow-up surveys to track the effect.

2.3.2   *Capturing user, stakeholder, and market feedback*

At this point, you might be wondering how to identify the opportunities you need to build a platform. There are several ways to measure the usage of our platform, discover what our customers need, and elicit feedback directly, as shown in figure 2.10.

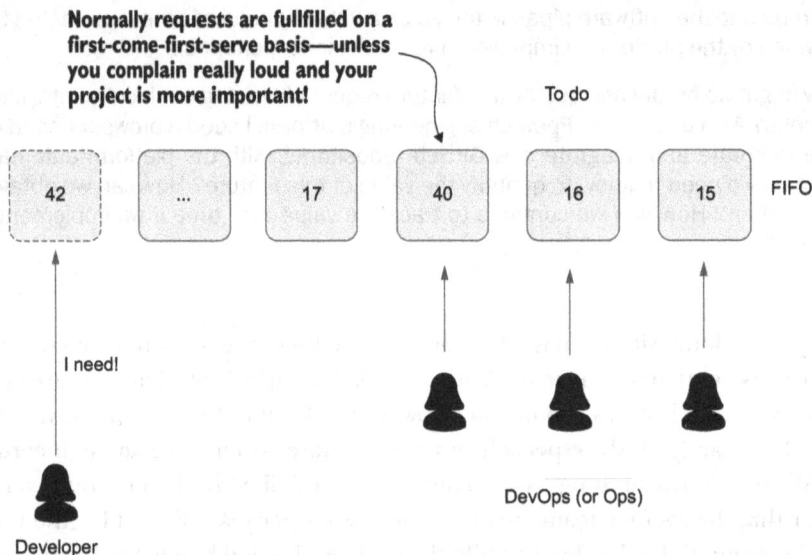

Figure 2.10   When we have a DevOps or traditional operations team, developers will be responsible for submitting requests for infrastructure or changes they need. The requests go into the queue.

Developers assume that when a ticket request is put in, there is an SLA on when it will be completed. (But there's an even bigger assumption we just glossed over. And that's the assumption that it will be done at all!)

Launching our engineering platform happens in parallel with this process. We'll start with a handful of the most commonly needed infrastructure features and rapidly grow from there. Developers will continue with the prior process when they need something that is not yet a part of the platform.

As a product team, the engineering platform team doesn't have this kind of queue. The platform's features are not built for individual team requests but are delivered as capabilities used by all development teams. However, these legacy work queues are an obvious source of data about the capabilities teams have historically needed. We can't rely only on this source. How do we source the features and technologies that should become part of our engineering platform?

Figure 2.11 highlights the primary sources of new ideas, such as stakeholders, industry trends, developers, and platform usage. Once these ideas are generated, they must still pass through the modeling and qualifying steps of the value flow (figure 2.9) before moving into delivery.

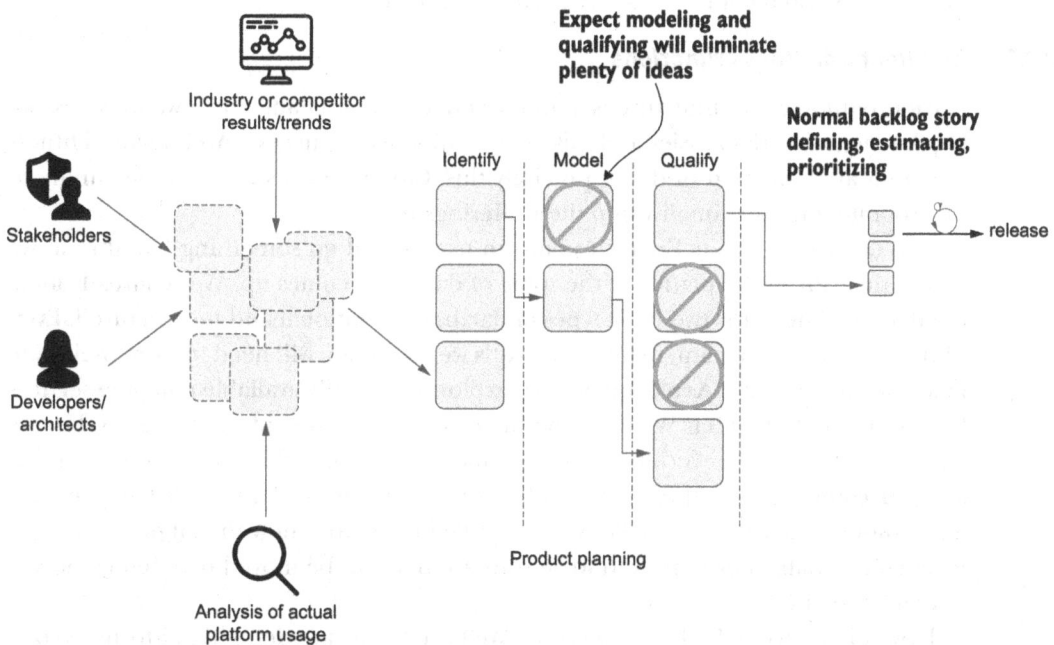

Figure 2.11 Ideas, improvements, and sometimes requirements will come from a variety of sources. These four are the most important. And everything needs to successfully make it through the top row of our value flow in figure 2.9, except for production outages, of course.

When building an engineering platform and using the product operating model, it's important to remember that all requests, except for outages (and nasty bugs), are treated as product requests. This means that product owners need to review and analyze each one carefully.

This doesn't mean we don't want a request queue. Applying a bit of marketing, instead of calling it a request or demand queue, call it a platform "idea" queue or platform "Feature Request" board. By changing the wording, we change its meaning, and teams will understand that requests can (and will) be denied if they don't fit within the platform as determined by the product team building it.

How else might we capture product ideas for the platform?

Stakeholders are a natural source for requirements, but their unique priorities can also be a good source of outside-the-box thinking. Feedback from users on existing platform capabilities is the best source for continuous improvement feedback. It is not just about the intentional feedback; it also looks for differences between how users claim they will use a feature versus how they actually use it. We'll talk much more about measurement in the next chapter.

Don't forget to pay close attention to where the platform community is headed. We don't want to have to learn every lesson on our own. People routinely blog and podcast their successes and failures. Watch the competition too.

2.3.3   *Architectural fitness functions*

Since evolutionary architecture is about architecting for change, can we make assessing the migration risks easier and raise our confidence in success? Architectural fitness functions are a method of doing precisely this. Cloud vendors are even beginning to incorporate this functionality into their offerings [6].

The discussion in our Epetech platform team could go something like this: as we define the APIs of the platform, the topic of databases comes up. We've already identified a broad need for two basic types of databases: relational and unstructured. Even without the platform team, many of the APIs we will create will need to store their state in a resilient database. As a team, we are exploring globally available database services from our cloud provider. What will be the challenges to providing this as a self-serve feature to developers? Another team member pointed out that Epetech just bought another company, and their entire infrastructure is on GCP. Epetech has plans for many more such acquisitions. We've been asked to explore how the engineering platform could enable developers to write software that can be moved between cloud services more easily.

How do we reconcile these concerns? We have a software-defined platform. A common software architecture pattern is abstracting dependencies, such as a particular database technology. The broader Epetech engineering organization will require a standardized abstraction layer as a part of any service development that includes a datastore. Let's say they decide on the repository pattern. With each database option we support, our platform can consist of the datastore layer and perhaps the repository layer of this abstraction. The repository layer will use a datastore interface, which will work with whatever database technologies the platform supports. As long as these databases use the same functions, we won't need to change the code in the repository or service layers.

Suppose, as in figure 2.12, our platform team created a custom *Teams* API to automate onboarding new internal development teams.

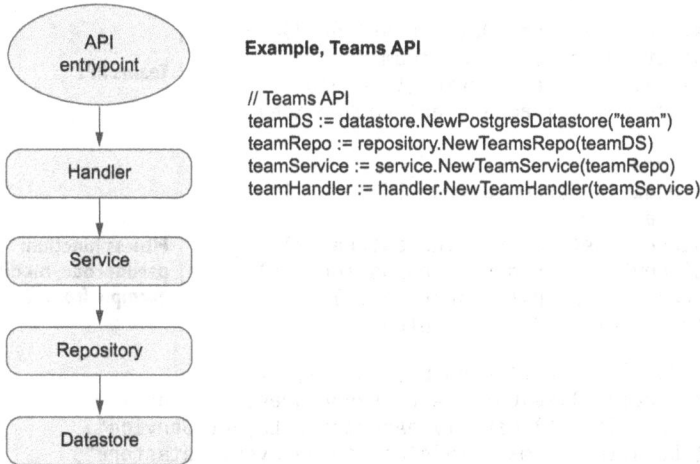

Example, Teams API

```
// Teams API
teamDS := datastore.NewPostgresDatastore("team")
teamRepo := repository.NewTeamsRepo(teamDS)
teamService := service.NewTeamService(teamRepo)
teamHandler := handler.NewTeamHandler(teamService)
```

(API entrypoint → Handler → Service → Repository → Datastore)

Figure 2.12 When a particular service within the API needs to interact with the API database, it calls a repository function that provides all the normal database methods. The repository function would call the datastore functions for the type of database the API needs to use (relational or unstructured, in our case).

The platform datastore library could determine and utilize the correct database interface based on the cloud and database technology support for the database type. Now the software can be migrated to another cloud without needing to be rewritten to support a new cloud-specific technology. Or, within the same cloud vendor, we could change the relational solution, such as moving from traditional AWS RDS for PostgreSQL to Aurora Serverless for MySQL, again without needing to rewrite the software. The code would only need to be rebuilt with the new datastore library.

Assuming we adopted this type of strategy, we could write automated tests that would assess the ongoing adherence to the architecture as well as the outcome when a change is made. You might have heard about fitness functions before. They're well explained in many books. Simply put, an architecture fitness function is a tool that helps objectively measure how well certain aspects of a software's architecture are performing. This concept is neatly summed up in *Fundamentals of Software Architecture* [7] by Richards and Ford.

To ensure we continually meet this pattern and keep these layers decoupled, we would write a fitness function that verifies the service layer only ever imports the repository layer and that the repository layer only ever imports an implemented datastore. We'd write another fitness function that ensures all our datastore implementations adhere to the standard datastore interface. These fitness functions ensure our control plane API logic doesn't ever change when we decide to implement a new database. They are a unit test that asserts that architectural patterns and decisions remain intact as we make changes.

```
Listing 2.1   Fitness functions
```

```
teamDS := datastore.NewPostgresDatastore("team")
teamRepo := repository.NewTeamsRepo(teamDS)                Teams API
teamService := service.NewTeamService(teamRepo)
teamHandler := handler.NewTeamHandler(teamService)
...
// Fitness Functions
// pseudocode - Modified example from [7]
layeredArchitecture()
    .layer("Datastore").definedBy("..datastore..")         Fitness function;
    .layer("Repository").definedBy("..repository..")       pseudocode, modified
    .layer("Service").definedBy("..service..")             example from [7]
    .layer("Handler").definedBy("..handler..")

    .assertLayer("Handler").notAccessibleByAnyLayer()
    .assertLayer("Service").mayOnlyBeAccessedByLayer("Handler")
    .assertLayer("Repository").mayOnlyBeAccessedByLayer("Service")
    .assertLayer("Datastore").mayOnlyBeAccessedByLayer("Datastore")
```

Here we can see that each layer is only consumed by the next, and we enforce this with a fitness function. This ensures that if we try to skip creating a datastore layer for a new database (choosing instead to call datastore functions from our service layer), our fitness function will fail, stating that we must use the repository layer to interact with our new database. You can see another example of this pattern in action in the companion code for the book.

When, in addition to providing a self-serve means of creating the data store itself, the platform also provides the software abstraction access layer and fitness functions, we have effectively given the platform team and the platform users the contract tests needed to feel confident that the future evolution of the database service will have predictable results.

For every feature we add to our platform, we should consider how it can be used and the sort of tests we could create to help users know whether they are using the feature correctly.

Exercise 2.5   Fitness functions

At Epetech, while we are going to build the engineering platform on AWS, we know that a merger with Alltech is about to happen. AllTech is 100% on Google Cloud. We know that when we build the platform for Epetech, we have to focus on our immediate customers but make architectural decisions that allow us to change and adapt the platform, such as supporting other clouds in the future. One area of high importance is our custom platform APIs:

1 Using the sample API provided in the chapter 2 GitHub repository (https://github.com/effective-platform-engineering/companion-code), write a fitness function that ensures our API keeps cloud-specific features and operations in isolated interfaces that don't affect our service logic.

What if we expand this fitness function to work for all of our platform APIs, not just this one?

After some debate among the team, we've decided that test-driven development is a rule we want to adopt and use across all of our platform's custom software:

2 Write an architectural decision record (ADR) that captures this decision. Include reasons, alternatives, and details.

3 Write a fitness function that will fail if someone checks in a new service layer without tests associated with it.

As we've seen throughout this chapter, observability and monitoring data are at the core of every decision we make. Consider how we might write ADRs and fitness functions that capture this:

4 Write a fitness function that would fail if a new API feature gets checked in without any monitors. Feel free to use a specific observability tool to write your answer and then compare it against the answer in the back for similarities.

5 Consider how a data-driven approach might change the dynamics of the team's interactions with other stakeholders and executives at the company. What tactics can you use to debate the merits of a new feature request using our ADRs, fitness functions, and observation-driven decision-making? Consider how these techniques remove emotions and assumptions from these sorts of debates.

2.3.4 *Domain-driven platform design*

Thousands of decisions will be made every year in your engineering organization, some big and most small, that will affect the experience of using a platform. The result of not having *standards* of platform engineering practice to inform decision-making is that expediency will become the de facto standard. Traditional IT, usually treated as just a cost center, has often fallen into this trap. How do we solve the immediate problem in a way that has the least effect on this quarter's budget? That sounds overly simplified. In reality, that is often exactly how things play out when we don't have a tested method for assessing the effect of our decisions. While the effects from using simple expediency will become apparent, even in small organizations, at scale, they can become crippling.

We routinely walk into organizations and find that it can take weeks—or even months—just to get access to the tools and infrastructure needed for development. More often than not, *product thinking* isn't seen as valuable—or sometimes, it's not even seen as an option, due to the following rationales:

- It will cost too much.
- Security says we can't do that.
- We don't know how (another way of saying it costs too much).
- Developers won't go any faster just because they aren't waiting on us.

Yet, when analyzing the amount of wasted time, the cost of not creating this experience is usually enormous, far exceeding the estimated cost to develop and maintain it.

It is easy to blame a source that feels out of our control. Probably every employee has heard the "This is a security requirement" explanation for some long and manual process. If this explanation is the *simple* truth, how is it that many companies are so successful at preventing this from being their external customers' experience? Even organizations with the highest levels of regulation or the lowest level of risk tolerance—government, finance, research—have been successful at creating pleasing and low-friction experiences for users when they believe it is necessary for their success (or survival).

In most situations, it isn't inspired creativity or innovation that is required to change the outcomes. It is more about measuring the real cost, changing expectations, and setting the internal structures and ways of working that allow teams to be successful at delivering a different kind of experience.

It's valuable to have a standard way of talking about and thinking through decisions around what the experience should be like—whether we're building or using business or tech capabilities. *Product* organizations have the following characteristics:

- They know they are delivering a product. This is meant to capture the idea that there are users who expect to be able to use the product independently, without needing to ask or coordinate with others to perform tasks on their behalf.
- All the capabilities of our product are broken down into domains and subdomains.
- The teams of developers building and operating the product are grouped around these domains or subdomains.
- The central characteristic for identifying these domains is that a domain team can effectively deliver the domain's roadmap while remaining only loosely coupled to the other domain teams within the product or larger organization. Loose coupling means
  - Teams can complete work without fine-grained coordination or communication with people outside the team.
  - Teams can deploy and release their capabilities independent of any services that depend on them or that they depend on, including data.
  - Teams can deploy at any time with negligible downtime.

This description uses the language of domain-driven design [4], which is focused on software development. This is important since everything we *deliver* as platform engineering is through software. But the underlying philosophy is about creating value and eliminating waste and the recognition that organizational and architectural decisions have far-reaching effects.

DEFINING THE BOUNDARY

When we talk about creating a team's domain boundary, we are referring to the experience when using a capability within a domain. You know you have identified an effective domain for a team when every feature or ability of a domain is usable by the consumer without needing to open tickets or engage in other synchronous or asynchronous interactions with that team. Consumers can use as much or as little as they need, whenever they need it.

At Epetech, we are familiar with domain-driven design. Our CTO handed out the book [8] to everyone at the company four years ago, during the "transformation," and popped around the office with random quizzes to ensure everyone read it. But in thinking about platforms, you start to wonder, "What are the domains of an engineering platform?" Recall that in section 1.3 we talked about eight effective domains of an engineering platform (see figure 2.13, a duplicate of figure 1.4).

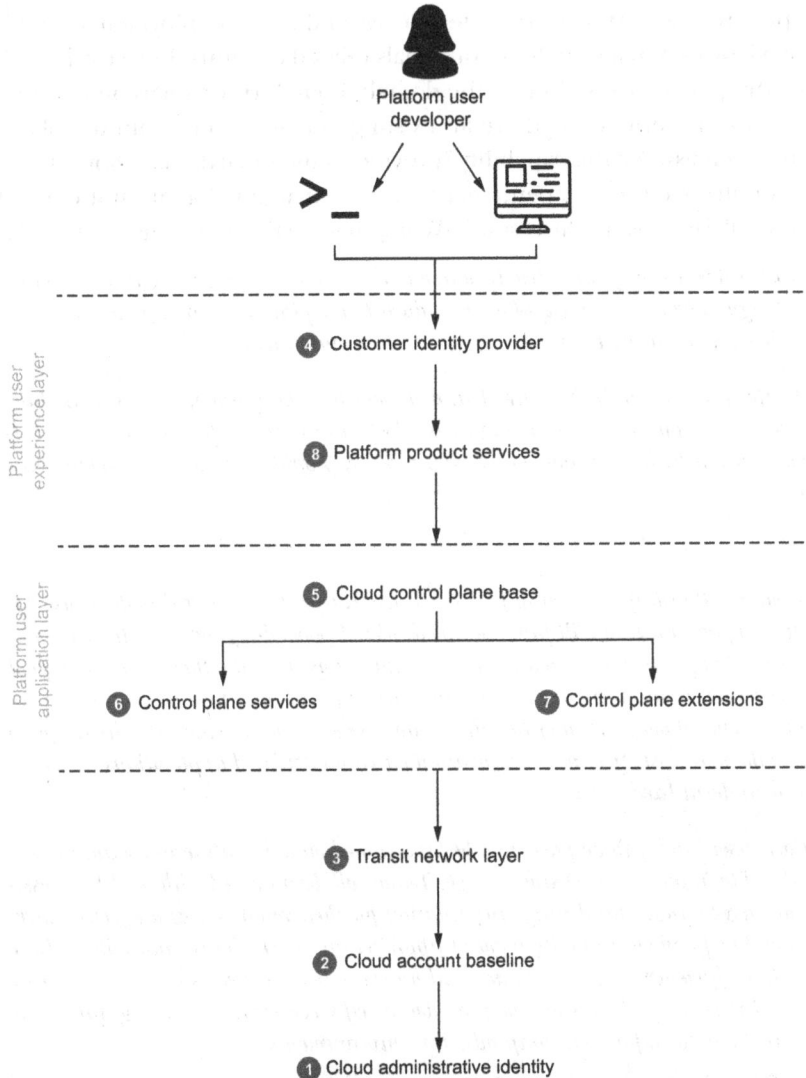

Figure 2.13 Primary domains in an engineering platform

By using these domains in our software practices, as described in this chapter, they become part of our planning and incremental design. Consider this example: Imagine that you are having a strategy session at Epetech, and one of the platform stakeholders says they think things are getting too expensive. One stakeholder states that the company should use cost-tracking software like IBM Apptio. Another suggests it tags and annotates the tooling and creates automated alerts. A third says it should implement a cost-approval process every time a developer uses a platform feature that provisions infrastructure.

The tricky part about these wide-ranging discussions is that everyone is focused on cost control without considering the potential offsetting cost increases from the solution. A process that results in repeated delays and failed deployments will likely cost more than it saves. What exactly are our goals related to controlling costs?

By focusing the conversation on the domain boundary, we focus on the desired outcome: the user experience. Is there an existing domain team within the platform that could effectively assume this capability (provide a functional domain boundary) and has the bandwidth? Are there dependencies to this capability that are not currently available? How will we measure the results? We might write the following (partial) ADR [9]:

> *The cost-efficient use of infrastructure resources is required for our engineering platform design. The following capabilities, added to the platform, are expected to create this efficiency according to the respective outcomes and measures:*

> *All platform costs should be tracked and allocated to platform user teams, including accurately apportioned overhead costs. Cost information reporting will be available continuously, in real-time, or where limited by provider restrictions, no less than monthly.*

> . . .

> *For compute, the platform control plane will use Karpenter-managed node pools. An effective implementation will provide standardized pools designed to fit the common use cases along with the means for individual teams to create their own node pool definitions where the standard definition is less effective or efficient. The node pool definition will allow Karpenter to balance node size among a wide capacity range to achieve the most cost-effective configuration based on deployed applications and consolidate underutilized nodes.*

> *Platform user teams' namespaces will be provisioned with default resource limitation, calculated to fit the average team's usage. Teams will be provided with readily accessible and easy-to-understand usage information for their resources, and effective early alerts will be provided to notify them of approaching limits. This data will include utilization efficiency statistics. Teams will have a self-serve means of adjusting their resource limits freely. Teams will be provided a self-serve means of setting automatic off-hours turn-down for their nonproduction environments.*

In figure 2.14, the Epetech example, we assume that we will have two delivery teams at the start: a developer experience team that owns the customer identity and platform product services product domains, and a platform cloud infrastructure team that is responsible for the rest of the product domains.

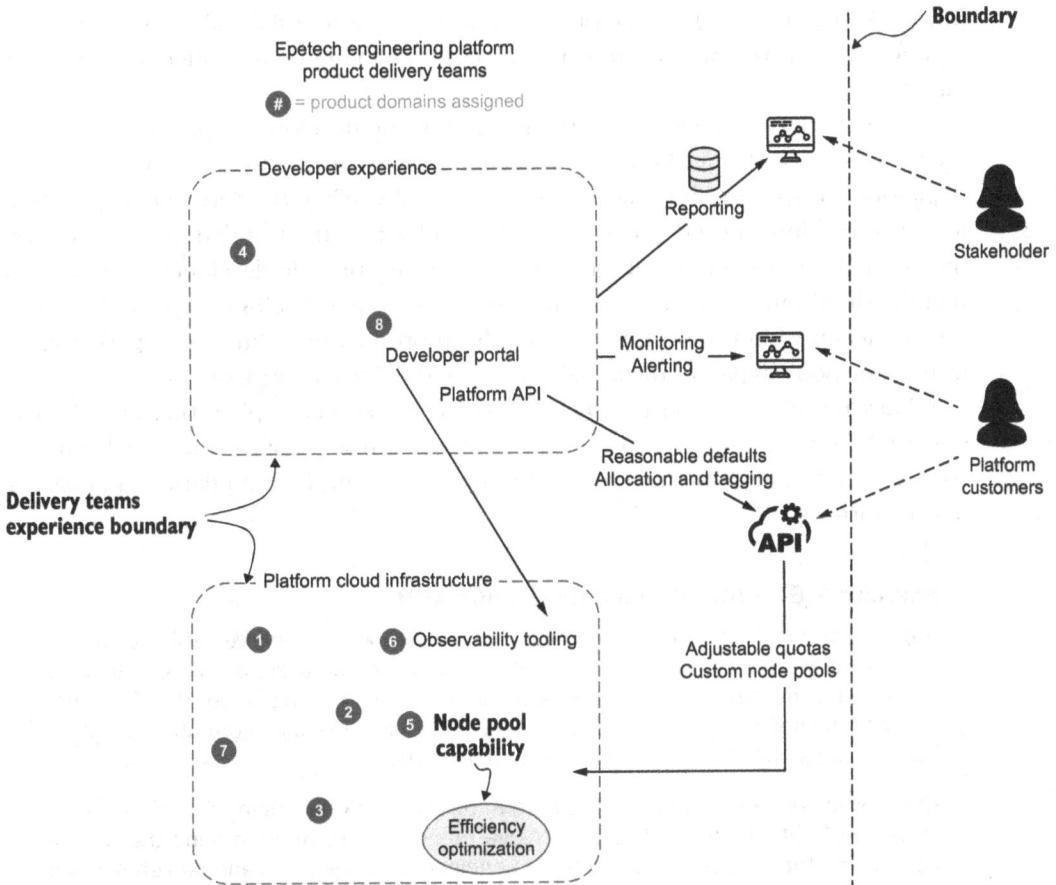

Figure 2.14 Start by defining the primary boundary experience, which is our platform customers. Then, figure out where the underlying changes or capabilities lie and when more than one team is involved, does an effective boundary experience exist between them?

In our ADR, we described the efficiency target we want for compute provisioning and the user experience that should go along with that. In this case, that means that new teams onboarded to the platform automatically have namespace resource quotas in place at levels expected to support everything the typical team will need, as well as an API they can use to customize the quota setting should they ever find the need. The same is true for general compute provisioning. We will provide default node pools that developers can use, optimized for most teams' usage, and a team can create their node pool configuration whenever they need.

We also describe a capability that enables teams to self-manage their compute *hours of operation*. If the team is sufficiently co-located to turn off their nonproduction environments for large blocks of time each day, they can use this feature to set an automated pattern that will further save on compute costs (kube-green is one example approach; https://kube-green.dev). Development teams or any interested stakeholder will have easy access to current and historical usage costs, enabling them to meet their budget targets.

In the course of implementing these features, the developer experience team will use the custom platform API they built to configure resource settings automatically and to provide the self-serve interface for teams to modify. When the developer experience team needs to interact with the platform cloud infrastructure team's domain resources, they should find the same self-serve experience they provide developers. This means that the cloud infrastructure team will have implemented a self-serve means for other domain teams within the engineering platform product to create new experiences of using node pools as part of the initial delivery of the Karpenter capability.

What's important about this ADR is the focus on cost-related platform capabilities in domain-boundary terms with the primary customer. Instead of focusing solely on cost reduction in isolation, we focus on cost reduction within the boundaries and goals of our platform.

Exercise 2.6   Writing a domain-specific ADR

Suppose the security team at Epetech establishes a new requirement that all the custom software we deploy must provide an associated software bill of materials. For the first year, developers can comply with the policy by providing materials information covering the software's contents at the time of release, leaving information about the build process and responsible parties for a later stage.

Using what we have learned so far, write a top-level ADR describing the primary components of automation that could achieve this outcome. Keep in mind the domain boundaries that will enable the platform engineers, developers, and stakeholders to achieve this outcome without introducing breaking product changes. The appendix provides an example answer, but there are definitely many different and creative ways to achieve the desired outcomes.

What if our analysis doesn't support automating a rarely used but necessary capability?

What if, during our cost-effect analysis, it becomes clear that a particular feature will never be used more than a handful of times in a year—for example, fewer than five times? If an honest analysis indicates that the cost of delay from a non-self-serve experience is less than the cost to maintain self-serve, does that mean we don't automate? Maybe. The additional questions to ask are

- Will the platform team be responsible for maintaining the manual process?
- How will the cumulative cost for these decisions be tracked?

If the platform team runs the manual process, you have to include the opportunity cost of the team's time being taken away from delivering additional platform capabilities. Allowing one or two of even the most seemingly infrequent and inconsequential manual processes in a platform product delivery team's responsibilities will completely overwhelm their delivery capacity at scale. You will nearly always regret making decisions like this for a product team. And, in practice, trying to walk that line is nearly impossible. The better rule is: where a manual process is added to a platform, it must be maintained by consumer support staff who are not part of the platform product development and delivery.

Not only does this avoid the unintended (probably unaccounted for) cost effects of increasingly diverting product backlog time to support, but it also provides a straightforward means of tracking the cost of these decisions, which is the second bullet point.

Can we accurately track the cost of breaking our boundary experience requirement? If we cannot, we are better off paying the self-serve implementation costs. Using separate staff to provide the manual support keeps us from derailing the product teams and lets us track the cumulative cost when making these decisions. Over time, these cumulative costs will reveal where scale is creating costs that will justify automation.

2.3.5 Evolutionary impact of cloud-native technologies

A good design is easier to change than a bad design.

—Thomas and Hunt, *The Pragmatic Programmer* [10]

The key difference between the ability to build platforms now versus 15 years ago is that now we have access to a full range of infrastructure capabilities behind exactly the API-first, self-serve experience we've been describing throughout this book. A large portion of the capabilities provided by these vendors fall under the banner of cloud native. We could probably debate exactly what cloud native means. Still, for our purposes, we can think of this as the fact that in building engineering platforms, a large number, not the majority, of the technologies that make up the list of need-to-have for distributed service architecture platforms are available from the top cloud vendors and include community-based standards.

All of the underlying technologies of an engineering platform, while being necessary to building, releasing, and operating customer software, are not strategic differentiators to your business. You need them, but having them doesn't give you an advantage over your competition. This means that time and money spent operating, upgrading, and maintaining such systems is time and money not spent on strategically valuable work. Any time you can shift this work to a capable cloud vendor, you are recovering valuable opportunity costs.

Having these technologies available behind an API, at the moment we need them and in whatever quantity we need, makes it much faster and cheaper to experiment with the capability before we commit effectively and much easier to maintain without taking time away from more valuable strategic work. This is a key part of why new capabilities should start from the API.

Much of the example implementation portion of this book centers around Kubernetes. Why is Kubernetes so important to platform engineering? The answer is standardization.

CLOUD-NATIVE CONTROL PLANE

Kubernetes creates standardization around two critical components of an engineering platform: distributed service compute orchestration and extensibility of that orchestration model. It was a response to the increased complexity and networking challenges of distributed system architectures [11, 12]. This architecture isn't a one-size-fits-all solution, but the explosive growth in SaaS and similar internet-oriented software has pushed it to the forefront, and most of what has happened in the last decade regarding corporate software development is centered around distributed services. The orchestration engine inside Kubernetes is designed to create resiliency in one of the most scaled systems in the world: Google. I define what constitutes the healthy state of my application, and the orchestration engine attempts to continuously keep the application healthy in the face of the unavoidable challenges of a distributed architecture.

Kubernetes is an orchestration engine for applications. However, Kubernetes also represents a standardized and agreed-upon set of APIs. No single cloud vendor is controlling this project. Many committees and special interest groups govern it with rotating chair policies to prevent leadership decay. They have vetting processes for new APIs and features, code reviews for changes to the project, proposal standards to make changes, and lively debates and discussions surrounding the project's future that any member may participate in. Much of the cloud-native ecosystem is built around Kubernetes. Figure 2.15 shows the basic components of a Kubernetes cluster.

In brief, a Kubernetes cluster will have a control plane containing the services used for cluster operation and management and a set of worker nodes used to run applications. The control plane includes the services to perform CRUD operations on cluster resources, manage service discovery, orchestrate scaling operations, and more. The worker nodes are used to run user services and applications. These include the applications and runtime services deployed to the cluster by both the platform engineering team and the development teams using the runtime.

Since I can extend this API, I have a built-in means of adding functionality, whether that functionality is to support regulations, compliance, development quality, or anything else. That standard allows me to move those organizationally specific capabilities anywhere I need them, without having to build the most challenging part (the orchestrator) from scratch or support a different orchestrator in every location.

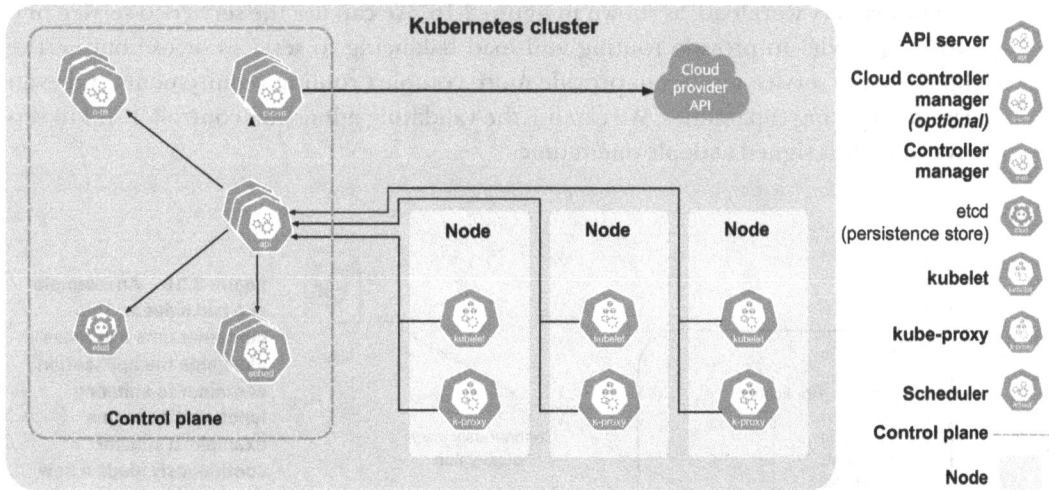

Figure 2.15   The components of a Kubernetes Cluster (Courtesy of https://kubernetes.io/docs/concepts/ overview/components/)

WHAT ABOUT CLOUD-NATIVE TECHNOLOGIES THAT REPLACE THIS CONTROL PLANE?

Most cloud vendors provide competing technologies for application orchestration. These completely abstract the orchestration process. Serverless is an example of this. Obviously, orchestration is happening, but we don't have any control over it, and it is not extensible.

Given that we expect our control plane to be responsible for all governance enforcement, removing the cloud control plane from the mix is a significant concern.

To understand how vital governed extensibility can be, consider the tradeoffs of serverless versus managed Kubernetes as a case study. Serverless platforms are generally defined as vendor-provided and managed offerings that allow one to deploy lightweight functions (usually written in JavaScript, Golang, Python, or Java) that do one or two things well and fast. Similar to managed Kubernetes, this allows developers to deploy a function to the cloud quickly. Unlike Kubernetes, there is nothing to first set up, nor is there extensibility to implement extended functionality, apply security controls, or any other custom behavior.

For a specific situation, that may be acceptable. But let's consider a few (not all) requirements of an engineering platform. We'll need secret injection, code signing verification, static code analysis verification, traffic routing, and identity verification, just to name a few.

In the Kubernetes context, most of these requirements are straightforward. We can use the mutating admission controller API to automatically add capabilities to every service when deployed, such as adding sidecar processes for retrieving secrets or performing authentication and authorization decisions before the request is passed along to our primary workload, as shown in figure 2.16. We can use the service-to-service networking model to provide routing and load balancing to services or use one of the open-source service meshes to provide more complex routing requirements and even circuit-breaking capabilities. We can use the validating admission controller API to verify our code is signed at deployment time.

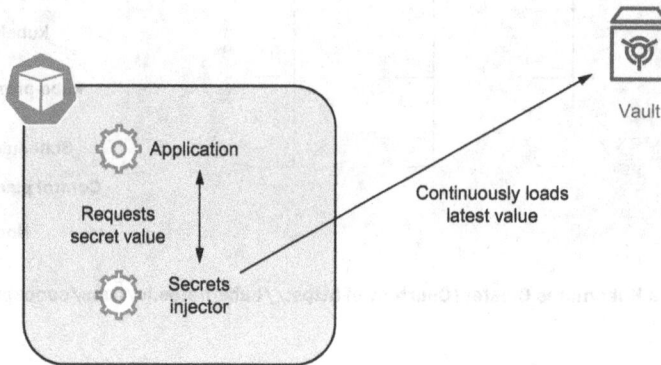

Figure 2.16   An example of a pod sidecar. This container runs a process alongside the application container to enhance functionality. In this example, a sidecar continuously loads a new secret value from a vault so that the application will always get the latest updates when secrets are requested.

In the serverless context, these extensible APIs do not exist—by design. All those additional capabilities are the developer's direct responsibility and must be managed during the deployment. For some of these requirements, we could use the build and release pipeline to substitute for actual compliance checks. But that would mean taking control of the pipeline away from the development teams, significantly slowing the overall process. And it is still just a substitute, not an automated check.

Remember that most observability, compliance, and quality requirements that we use a control plane to meet will be requirements regardless of the technology used. Be sure when assessing control plane alternatives that you have an equally low-friction means of extending the control plane.

BUILD VS. BUY IN-CLOUD NATIVE

In platform engineering, remember that the goal of a successful platform is to provide a product offering to your users. Product offerings require the ability to change and evolve dynamically and rapidly. When considering whether you should build or buy a capability within your engineering platform, keep these two considerations at the top of the assessment list:

- Is there a quality SaaS or cloud vendor-supported version of a technology?
- It is very unlikely that operating and maintaining the technology is itself a competitive advantage to our company, so we should seriously figure out the total cost of ownership. Include opportunity costs, the costs of delay, and every other real effect. Most of the time, the margin-cost-based vendor option makes more time and money available to invest in our strategically important work.

Summary

- Differentiate between stakeholders and customers and shape the customers' experience:
  - Stakeholders have significantly different success criteria than customers do.
  - Shape the experience of using an engineering platform for customers of the platform.
  - Stakeholder needs can be met without destroying the customer experience.
  - Don't underestimate the importance of tracking stakeholder impact on platform delivery. It can mean the difference between success and failure for the platform to provide a return on investment.
- Optimize engineering for the end-to-end lifecycle of the product:
  - Optimize the product team's engineering practices and the organizational support for delivering a product.
  - Optimize the engineering process from ideation to platform operation, not around individual teams, technologies, or departments.
  - Features and capabilities should be delivered as service interfaces first.
  - Make final architecture and technology decisions only after realistic experimentation that measures the expected value.
- Test experiences and implementation with alpha-users early. Find ways to introduce the fundamental aspects of new features before more complex implementations, using the feedback to influence next steps.
- Architect for change:
  - Try to start with a single engineering platform delivery team, with the initial squad setting the architectural foundations. Grow the number of delivery teams within the platform product based on the most needed capabilities.
  - Adjacent teams within the organization can provide capabilities to the engineering platform only if they can also provide their service-as-a-product and support the product roadmap of the platform.
  - The idea of a software-defined platform introduces more rigor into the software delivery lifecycle process, using software engineering principles to increase the product's stability, scalability, extensibility, and maintainability.
  - Observability is an integral part of each story in the product delivery backlog, not something added on afterward. Both the healthy and unhealthy behavior of each feature, capability, or technology of the platform should be easily observable.
  - Plan for evolutionary change, even in the way you manage the platform product backlog. Team engineering standards, such as test-driven development, include architecture fitness testing to support easier evolution.

Measuring your way to platform engineering success

> **This chapter covers**
> - Using data and measurements to determine success
> - Assessing engineering practice and quality over the entire end-to-end delivery lifecycle
> - Acting on platform product key performance indicators and developer experience effects
> - Planning for maturing capabilities

So far in our journey at Epetech, we have established a vision and strategy based on the business need for building an engineering platform, and we have put together the foundational engineering practices to create it. We have also looked at software-defined platforms and the cloud-native approach, which simplifies the process. Now it's time for the last critical element of our planning process: measuring what we will build. This chapter will round out all the pieces required to ensure we are setting up the platform engineering journey to succeed—not just in the short term but for scaling.

Measuring what we are going to build has several aspects. At Epetech, we have confirmed that leadership has understood the vision and worked with us to establish a strategy. We now know that the conversations with the chief technology officer (CTO) and the senior vice-president (SVP) of engineering have given us many insights into mapping this strategy to their overall business strategy. Then, as part of establishing an operating model, we talked about working with the product managers of each product domain and creating a prioritized set of capabilities required to build the engineering platform. So far, so good. We are now ready to produce the capabilities. But wait: there is one problem. How do we know that what we are building meets the success criteria? What exactly are the success criteria here? Is it just revenue maximization? What are the specific approaches that we should consistently consider in this journey?

There are five areas where we can plan from the start to track for success and maturity:

- Have we made the organizational adjustments necessary for success?
- Are we measuring our engineering effectiveness and quality through an end-to-end lens?
- Do we provide the quality documentation, self-serve capabilities, and complexity accelerators that minimize cognitive load, allowing new developers to rapidly begin adding value while also fostering the mechanical sympathy needed for seasoned developers to do their best work?
- Does our platform roadmap manage scope in a way that provides value early while evolving to cover the actual scope of ideation through operation?
- If skills and expertise must be acquired, do we have a strategy for building and measuring capabilities to achieve the required level?

To measure the business value enabled by this, we should examine how accelerated delivery of business features unlocks increased revenue potential. These are achieved by faster onboarding, improved deployment frequency, higher adoption of platform capabilities, reduced incident recovery time, and, of course, improved developer satisfaction and productivity.

3.1   Organizational aspects of platform engineering success

While working with a large banking client, which was one of the pioneers of platform engineering in the 2020–2021 timeframe, we encountered a situation where the grassroots-level buy-in was missing. We were brought in by executive leadership to build the platform-centric solutions. Organizationally, this company had some problems with a siloed structure. The platform, application development, and infrastructure teams operated in isolation, which meant that the hand-offs and the contract testing between the teams always led to finger-pointing. Moreover, we started noticing that the "not in my backyard" attitude of the application development teams made the adoption of the platform capabilities supremely difficult. Because the embedded enablement was missing and internal evangelism was nonexistent, we were the ones trying to evangelize to a team suspicious of our motives. The situation went from bad to worse, as demonstrated by our collectively missing our adoption key performance indicators (KPIs) quarter after quarter. The approach taken by the leadership was to penalize the development teams by reducing their budgets and forcing them to start adopting. By the end of 2021, after 18 months of efforts, the organization abandoned its engineering platform journey and went back to a siloed DevOps culture.

In hindsight, we now know that understanding the needs of the engineers and co-creating the solutions with them, while applying concepts of team topologies, mentioned in the next section, would have been the right approach to the transformation journey.

3.1.1   Changes needed for an organization to prepare for platform engineering

In the early part of the book, we called out the need for strong, team domain bounding. People within a team know this is happening when they can readily access the capabilities of other teams through an API or by self-solutioning to well-documented standards. Intrateam communication merely to be productive should not be necessary. This focus on the culture goes to the core message of *Team Topologies* [1], which refers to creating four distinct types of team topologies, as shown in figure 3.1.

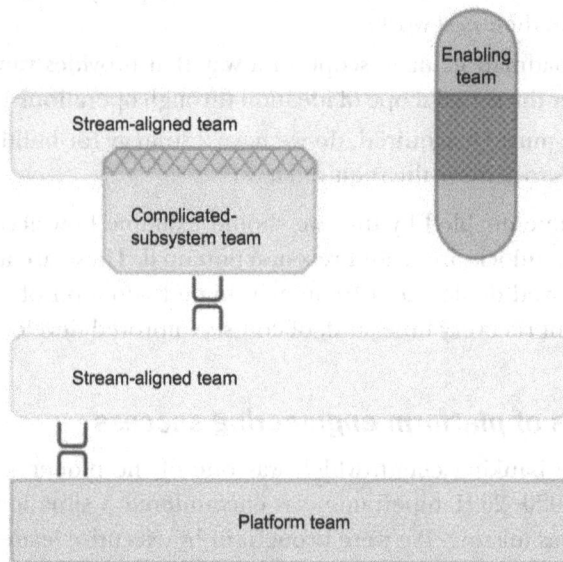

Figure 3.1   The stream-aligned teams are domain-bounded, but so are the platform team and subsystem team. (Image taken from [1]. Used with permission.)

Highlighting the regular business capability teams alongside the platform team helps emphasize that the platform's capabilities are inward-facing, designed to serve internal teams rather than external customers:

- *Stream-aligned teams*—These teams are organized around a continuous flow of work aligned with a specific business or customer value stream—a domain they have end-to-end responsibility for delivering and maintaining. Depending on the nature of the capability, this may be through an API or a UI; in either case, it is self-managed by the end user in the effective and expected format.

- *Platform teams*—They are like the stream-aligned teams, but, for the platform team, the customers are the other stream-aligned teams.
- *Complicated subsystem teams*—These teams focus on highly specialized or technically complex areas of a system, requiring deep expertise that is difficult to distribute among other teams. Typically, though, this is about the overall breadth of the capabilities they provide and not about the experience for dependent users. The rare exception is a technology used only by a single stream-aligned team, where the working relationship is closer to that of the subsystem team being part of the stream team.
- *Enabling teams*—These are the one team type that is different from the other three in the boundary relationship. These teams provide expertise and guidance in specialized areas like automated testing, site reliability, and architecture. They work temporarily with stream-aligned teams to build capabilities. This does not involve an enabler showing up whenever *their* skills are needed but is instead a means of upskilling and sharing knowledge across the organization.

If our organization currently has endless queues in front of infrastructure service or developer tool silos, then organizational change will be necessary for the platform team to succeed.

3.1.2 Prerequisites for the change

Not all organizations need to have a platform engineering team or to build engineering platforms. We use the following decision tree to determine whether you should be building engineering platforms. Most vendors of platform engineering solutions recommend ways to decide whether you are an ideal candidate to start building your engineering platform. We recommend using a simple decision tree, as shown in figure 3.2.

The decision tree guides organizations on whether they should build an engineering platform. It starts by identifying the type of organization, such as an early-stage startup, a scaling company, or an established organization. If the organization is scaling or established, has multiple development teams, or faces cognitive load challenges (e.g., overwhelmed teams), we recommend that it build an engineering platform. Additionally, the decision tree considers if developer experience metrics suggest building a platform; if not, it suggests waiting. The flow aims to help organizations evaluate whether investing in an engineering platform is appropriate based on their growth stage, team structure, and developer experience needs.

Our recommendation is simple. If you are a startup trying to get your first product out to your first customers, you should not worry about building an engineering platform. But once you start scaling out, or if you are an established organization, then confirm that custom software is a critical part of your strategic success. If it is, once you hit

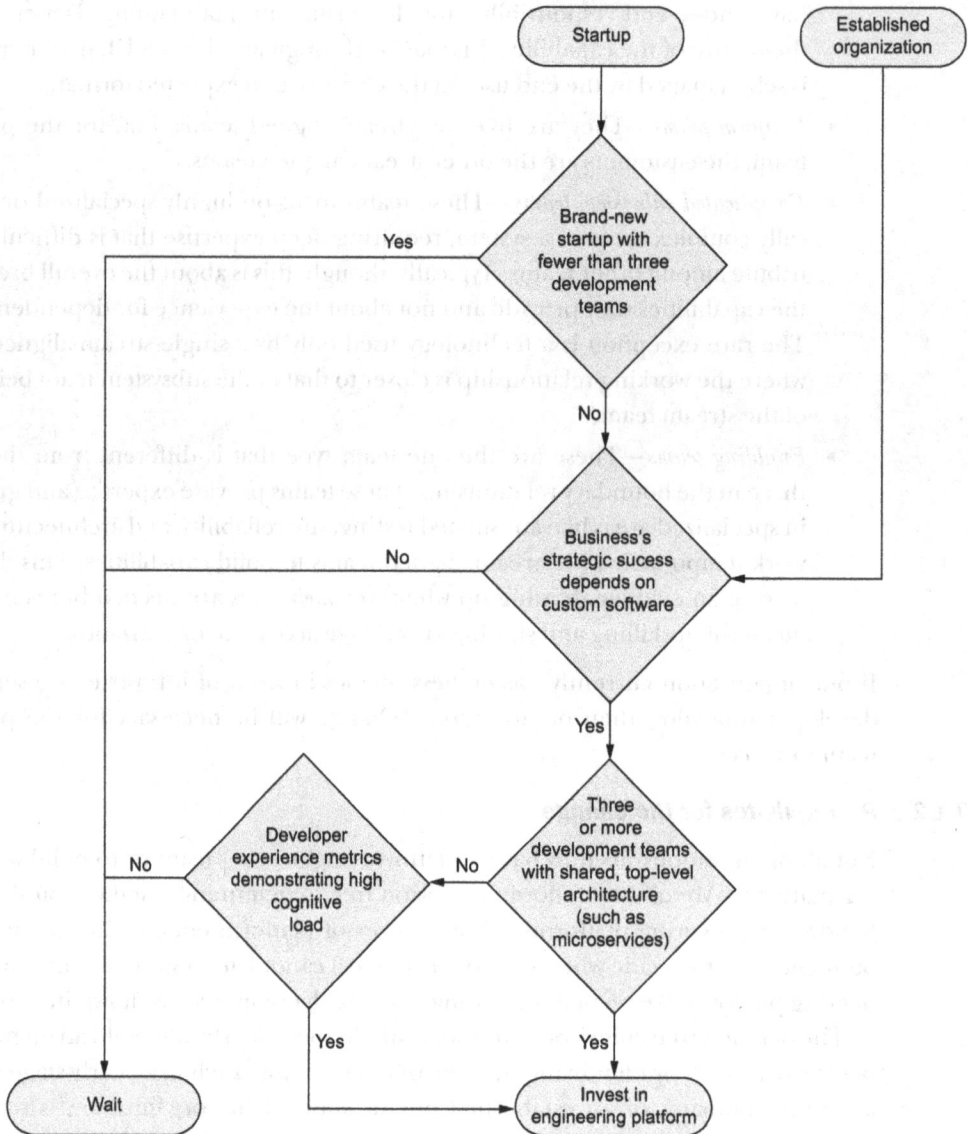

Figure 3.2   A decision tree for engineering platform buildout

three or four teams with a shared architecture, then the engineering quality effect and economies of scale will make investing in a platform valuable. Even if the software created by your teams is not cloud-native or otherwise cannot share a typical architecture, if your developers are experiencing high cognitive load, then there are aspects of platform engineering, with a strong developer experience focus, that can still offer value.

3.1.3 Implementing organizational changes

Making the right changes across your organization starts with building awareness and being open to input—especially when bringing together teams across different departments. Culture plays a significant role here; resistance to change or expecting processes and skill sets to remain static will not get it done.

The prior DevOps movement came about as a response to traditional IT operations being slow to change. As software teams started demonstrating the quality effects from releasing frequent, small changes, the legacy processes built around large, infrequent changes broke down.

Over the past 15 years, high-performing organizations have dramatically changed. It is not just IT that can do better—security, legal, compliance, engineering governance, and testing strategies have all improved, and we can do much better still.

The reality is that many IT operations teams are still stuck in ways of thinking that date back to the 1960s and 1970s: heavy upfront investments, project-oriented implementation, avoiding change, and keeping teams siloed by function and budget. These cultural and structural challenges are why DevOps efforts often fail to sustain the expected improvements. You might see some early wins, but they don't last. The same goes for platform engineering. It's essentially another push from software development, trying to drive maturity across the entire software delivery chain. It's about bringing solid engineering practices to every part of the process, not just development.

3.1.4 Building platforms in organizations

As discussed earlier in this section, leadership support and alignment are vital to enabling the platform engineering practice. Not all organizations are ready for platform engineering.

Let's look at the initial assessment areas we can measure before we start, which can tell us where we will face the initial challenges:

- *Stakeholders*—Whether through budgets or priorities, if stakeholders are unable to provide either service interfaces to the capabilities needed to meet their requirements, or testable standards the platform team can use to self-solve, then no better experience can be created. This will require an openness to think about how requirements can be met in automated or low-friction ways.
- *Platform dependencies provided by existing silos*—When platform teams don't directly own a necessary domain capability, then the providing team must have the same level of boundary maturity and stream alignment as the platform team itself or any of the business capability teams using the platform. It can certainly be the case that there are existing teams providing capabilities (such as developer tools or observability) whose user base is broader than the expected users of the platform. In those cases, it can make sense for those teams to remain independent. But if their services are to be incorporated into the platform, they must be able

to provide the same boundary experience as the platform itself, which may be an entirely new requirement for such a team. The platform team, as an integrator, is likely to need what has previously been categorized as admin-level access to the tool or technology. This might not be something the currently owning team has accounted for, and a change in process, capabilities, budgets, or perhaps all three will be needed.

- *Self-serve experience*—This is yet another of the basic tenets of platform thinking. Any expectation of achieving materially different and better results has to be preceded by an understanding of the effect of intrateam coordination and communication—certainly for users of the platform but also for any teams the platform delivery team depends on. Self-serving is challenging and requires empathy and an understanding of the user base with a clear product mindset. Over time, the lack of this within the platform and platform dependencies will result in platform teams having no time to deliver platform features, and developers will still be waiting in queues to get work done.

- *Developing requirements out of the current platform product scope*—An almost universally fatal mistake (fatal to a platform's success, that is) that many organizations make is to staff engineers to the platform team while making them simultaneously responsible for maintaining and even provisioning infrastructure or developer requirements through the legacy processes. A platform can't be built in an engineer's spare time, nor can an existing DevOps-style team simultaneously maintain its current responsibilities while creating a platform. That ongoing work must be done. Existing systems must be supported—even ones that will be migrated. And platforms are not a replacement or complete wrapper for cloud providers or all-things-infrastructure. There will always be pockets of technologies that are not part of strategic development or that won't be added to the platform product for an extended period. But a platform product is a full-time engagement for the team that delivers it. This is another reason we advocate for starting with a single team and scaling the platform delivery team as adoption of the platform grows. This can be an effective way to constrain labor costs in the early months and years of platform maturity.

- *Leadership*—Leadership that understands and supports these goals is necessary. Support means changing the structures and processes when needed to enable the platform engineers. Widespread adoption and support of engineering platforms, once they have demonstrated their potential, will happen easily. Getting alignment at the start to begin building a platform is rarely possible without direct leadership intervention and a strategic mandate. For most large companies, this will mean C-suite direction.

These aspects are illustrated in figure 3.3.

It is now time for us to revisit our favorite organization and look at a case study.

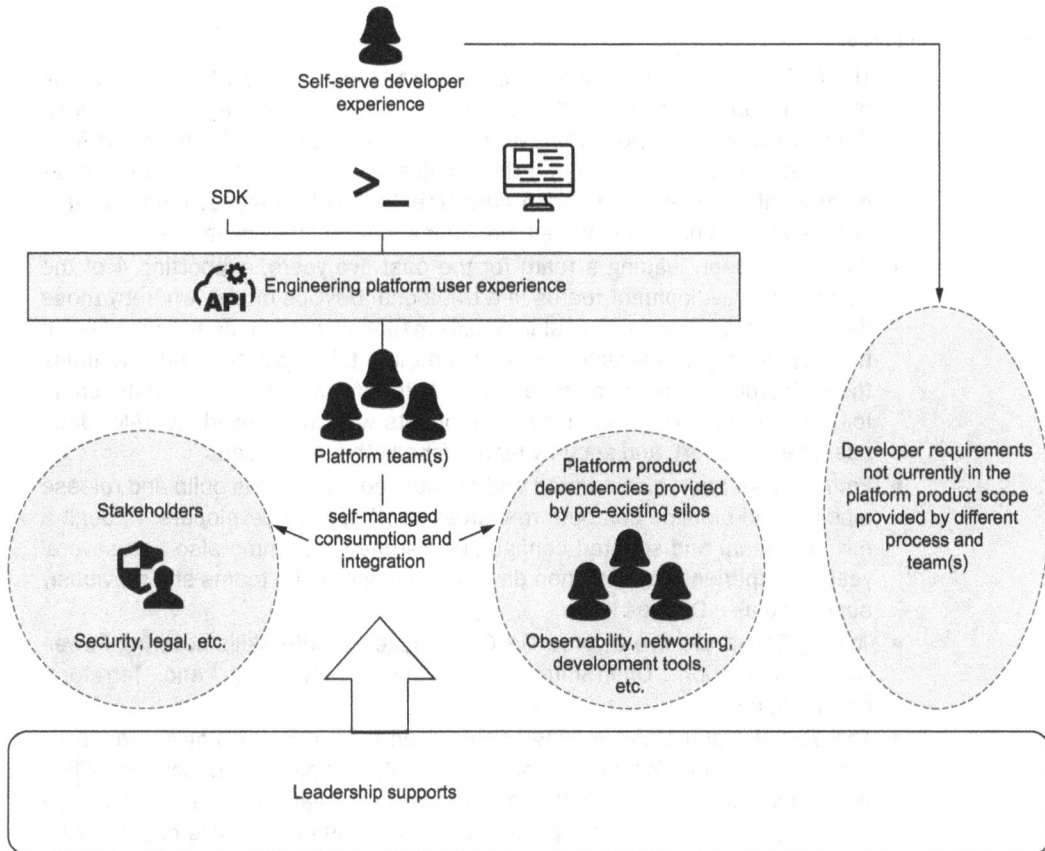

Figure 3.3 Key organizational prerequisites for building platforms

Exercise 3.1 Organizational review: Starting platform team at Epetech

With 23 eager teams awaiting the benefits of these platform capabilities, the Epetech SVP of product engineering has launched the initial platform team with the following characteristics:

- The SVP of product engineering supports the Epetech chief product officer in the architecture and delivery of Epetech customer-facing software but is a direct report to the chief information officer (CIO). The CIO reports to the chief executive officer (CEO).
- Together, the SVP and CIO have made the case that the delivery and use of an engineering platform is the best way forward in achieving Epetech's product goals.
- The CTO, who also reports to the CEO, has pulled together a dedicated team of six engineers from across various DevOps teams to form the initial platform team, led by one of the more senior DevOps engineers at Epetech, Emma.

(continued)

- The CTO has asked his various department leads to support Emma and the platform team to the best of their ability. This platform team will have allocated the funds also to support whatever they need to use on AWS. Still, apart from that and their payroll, this is all the funding available for the next four to six months, after which any needed adjustments could be made. Emma's team can also have a part-time project manager if they feel they need one.
- Emma has been leading a team for the past five years, supporting 4 of the 23 existing development teams in a traditional DevOps model, whereby those development teams have regular, weekly meetings with Emma to make known their upcoming infrastructure needs. Emma's team creates and maintains these resources through a combination of Terraform and custom bash scripts for servers and by opening ticketed requests with the networking, IAM, database, tech support, and security teams for all other resources.
- Emma's prior team also created and maintained the Jenkins build and release pipeline and pipeline compute resources used by their developers, through a mix of manual and scripted configuration strategies. Emma also has several years of experience as a Python developer on one of the teams she previously supported as a DevOps lead.
- Joining Emma are five diverse DevOps engineers, with skills covering Power-Shell automation, OpenShift administration, networking, and Terraform configuration.
- The SVP of product engineering has pledged the customer profile domain as the early adopters for the platform. The customer profile product owner has two subdomain teams of eight people each. These teams build and operate six individual APIs that together provide the entire customer profile capability for all Epetech software products. These product teams will provide early feedback to the platform engineering product team.

Based on everything we have discussed so far, pretend you are Emma: what are the positives or negatives about this launch strategy? Assume the CIO described the expected engineering platform product outcomes and user experiences in the same way we have been in the book. How likely are you to succeed in delivering a platform? What did the Epetech leadership do right? What could they have done differently? (Hint: Success measurements should always be aligned with the overall business success. Engineering success is the leading indicator—which means hardly anything if the eventual business outcomes are not achieved.)

3.2 *Path-to-production and platform value metrics*

A key attribute of engineering platform success is the focus on the end-to-end lifecycle of building and operating software. There's simply too little chance of material change in quality and velocity when Conway's law determines the analysis boundaries. Analyzing effectiveness only within the traditional functional silos is similarly one of the key practices that leads to high-friction engineering and operations.

Real improvements come when we analyze and measure the complete path to production.

3.2.1 How do you identify the scope of your engineering platform?

Value stream mapping (VSM) [2] is a popular process-mapping technique that originated in manufacturing to understand the current state and to design a future state that eliminates waste and improves quality. The fundamental idea behind VSM in software originated with lean software principles, as the complexity of the software development process increased and the need to improve efficiency became paramount. To be most effective, within software development, VSM must include the scope of the overall software development life cycle (SDLC), which consists of all of the processes, people, tools, and technologies used to build and operate the software.

In the context of platform engineering, VSM begins with analyzing the path to production for the software that the platform is meant to support. It then extends that analysis inward, examining the platform's own internal processes and value streams. There is a massive overlap. You might argue that the VSM of the platform is just a subset of the VSM of our customer software in general. There is some literal truth to this, but we rarely encounter organizations with the strength of an internal product culture to organize and measure this way. They will easily recognize wasteful processes or dependencies when analyzing the traditional software development teams yet repeatedly create and ignore the same problems when addressing infrastructure, DevOps, operations, and perhaps all of the nonfunctional requirement teams.

Figure 3.4 shows the steps of a simple path-to-production flow (https://flowengineering.org/) along with associated areas of a VSM.

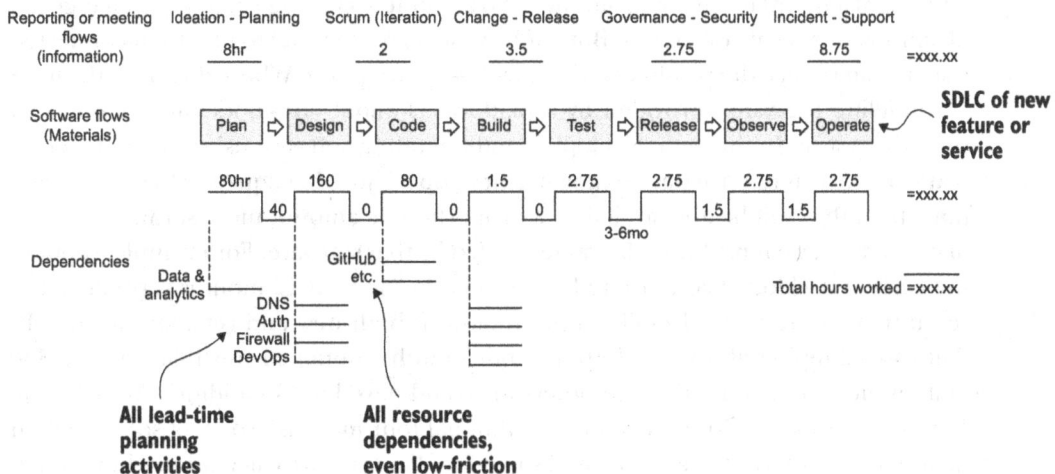

Figure 3.4 A sample VSM for software delivery, mapping steps from planning to support and highlighting delays or bottlenecks. The times shown should account for all tasks or meetings, using averages for recurring items such as quarterly reviews.

Dependencies should account for the full lead time if one exists. Even when you have successfully requested infrastructure that requires 30 days to obtain, 30 days before you need it, you still need to account for the planning overhead and (usual, frequent) times when knowing far in advance isn't possible.

The outcome goal for this map is to estimate the full scope of work involved in the complete SDLC. This is the actual scope that exists for an engineering platform, even when we start with features that target only certain areas.

This is also the scope required for end-to-end engineering optimization. We need a process, both at the materials level and the information level, that is designed to eliminate waste and create quality.

3.2.2 *Platform value modeling and metrics*

How can we measure the value of investing in platform engineering and providing developers with an engineering platform? We need an objective and quantitative approach to show the return on investment (ROI). Projected ROI helps secure investment, and assessing actual value helps us decide where to continue or stop investing.

Platforms create value through removing waste. Waste comes in multiple forms. The largest category is wasted time. Developer time is wasted by extraneous load (which we will discuss in section 3.3), working on lower-value tasks due to being blocked by dependencies, and dealing with poor quality. Waste comes in the form of inefficient spending on infrastructure. But the returns from removing wasted time are vastly greater and start returning value much sooner. Governance and security risks create waste in dealing with failures in these systems. This risk category is like buying insurance, though. You could have poor security practices in certain areas but, by chance, never be subject to a breach. This makes justifying spending on security more of a challenge. How much is the right amount for my car insurance? No amount of coverage is going to change the likelihood or severity of a crash. But applying stronger security to my cloud-connected systems can reduce the possibility of a breach—up to a point. Where do I draw the line?

Modeling the value provided by a platform is about cost-modeling the effect of removing waste. If, through developing and operating software using an engineering platform, we can remove wasted time in a developer's job that equals 33% of their total time, then they will be able to deliver a proportionate amount more software. To estimate its value, we must know the value created by that software. For example, suppose the current backlog of software to be delivered in the next 12 months is predicted to result in an average of $10 million per month in both new and retained income. In that case, shipping all of that software four months sooner means that we have $40 million more in income than we otherwise would have had. In addition, in the same 12-month period, we will now ship an additional four months' worth of software than we otherwise would not have had, and so on for all our future calculations. But even if, for some reason, we believe developing faster won't create greater income, then saving one-third of the time means that at least we could achieve the same results with one-third less of the cost. The key takeaway here is not to consider software development as a manufacturing pipeline but rather to look at the output. What we are measuring is, indeed, the ideal outcomes.

Once we identify the waste to be removed by a platform capability, we need a way to measure the effect continually. For example, imagine a particular manual process that requires one full-time person to maintain and results in 1,000 wasted developer hours per quarter that we can currently track using metrics pulled from our ticketing system. Let's replace the process with a self-serve interface. In that case, we will need a way to measure how long it will take to orient developers to the new process, and the new service should generate similar metrics on how long the automation takes to complete the task.

Defining platform value metrics helps decision-makers prioritize investments and determine when to build new capabilities. There is a six-step process for platform value modeling and metrics:

1 Identify inefficiencies and potential improvements.
2 Calculate the current cost of the inefficiency.
3 Simulate potential ROI through accelerated throughput or reduced cost.
4 Secure investment based on projected ROI.
5 Compare actual results against projections.
6 Adjust investments based on actual value delivered.

Figure 3.5 shows the critical elements of building a platform value model.

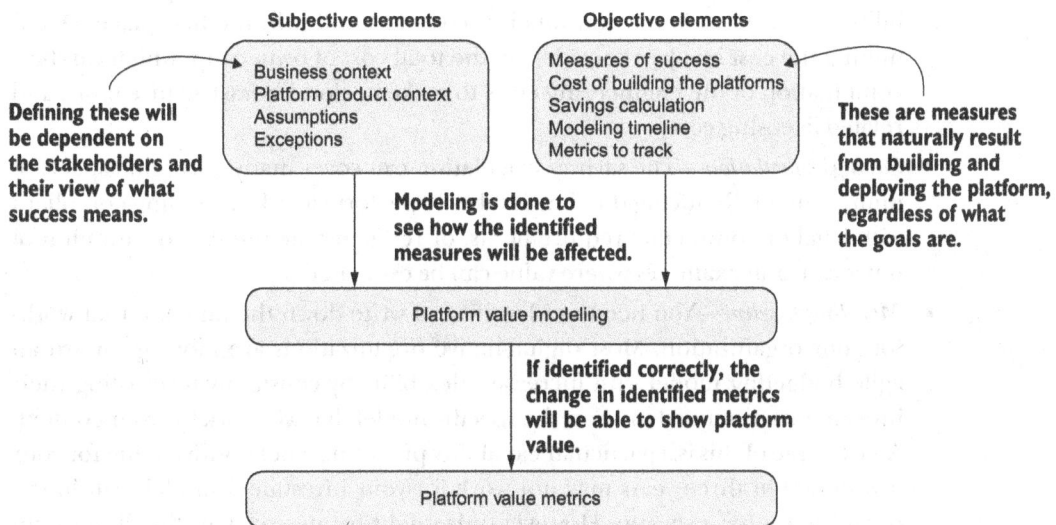

Figure 3.5 Components of value modeling process. These are both subjective and objective measurements that a technical product owner should identify by working with stakeholders and engineers, which will be used to show platform value.

Here is a list of critical elements—both subjective and objective—of building a platform value model:

- *Business context*—Working with stakeholders to understand the business context is critical to determining the overall platform strategy. Writing it down explicitly helps you describe your business goals and the problem you are trying to solve with a platform-centric approach. It will be the first step in modeling the value that the process can generate.

- *Platform product context*—This is where you will discuss the platform product capability you want to build and the expected value generated from this effort. You need to have a clear vision that clearly articulates the specific outcomes and the adoption of the capability built by multiple development teams within your organization. For example, an organization might be saying that it wants to develop a standardized container orchestration platform that makes the adoption of Kubernetes easier for at least 90% of the development teams, with a 10% increase in cognitive load or less, measured through feature development velocity.

- *Assumptions*—The decision-makers should agree on the assumptions being made about the business context and the outcome goals for the platform feature. These should continually be accessed for accuracy. Assumptions can easily change.

- *Measures of success*—This is the most crucial part of the value modeling process, where you identify how to measure the product's success. A sample success measure might be a 30% reduction in the average time it takes for new code to go from the first environment to production, resulting in the intended outcomes.

- *Cost of building platforms*—To understand the value of a particular platform capability, you need to know how much it costs to build it in the first place. Determining the cost involves considering the total cost of ownership, which can be a combination of the engineering costs to make it, cloud infrastructure costs, and related licensing costs.

- *Savings calculation*—The savings calculation can cover many different aspects of improvement. Reducing the time it takes to perform a task, becoming compliant with legal or contractual requirements, or reducing the number or duration of outages are all examples where value can be estimated.

- *Modeling timeline*—You need to identify and write down the timeline that works for your organization. Most digital-native organizations are moving toward an agile budgeting model with increased flexibility by constantly forecasting their investments. You need to know the specific model that will work for your context. An example of this is a particular capability providing a net positive value for your investment in three years may not work for your investment models within the organization for a startup. However, this might be an excellent timeline for an established organization to build a capability to scale its product line.

- *Metrics to track*—Which metrics to track at the investment level will depend on how your organization makes investment decisions. Most companies use some form of ROI calculation, in which the value returned over a specified period is compared to the cost of delivery [3].

Exercise 3.2   Develop a platform value model

Develop a platform value model for Epetech that can help communicate the value of your intended platform capability to decision-makers. There are no right or wrong answers for this exercise, as the outcome you seek is a value-driven response to whether you should invest in building a particular platform capability.

To complete this exercise, follow these steps:

1 Create a value stream map that reflects the current situation at Epetech.
2 Identify the specific platform product capability you want to build to address a problem on the value stream map.
3 Describe the business context that could capture what has been said about Epetech so far.
4 Identify the costs to implement and maintain the capability.
5 List any assumptions.
6 Describe the value that will come from removing the waste.
7 Identify the measures of success and the metrics you want to track.

3.3   Cognitive load and mechanical sympathy for developers and platform engineers

In cognitive psychology, cognitive load refers to the total amount of mental effort being used in one's working memory at any given time. Even from the earliest days of computing and software development, researchers started thinking about the psychological aspects of development. Arguably, one of the earliest works in this space came from Gerald M. Weinberg in his book, *The Psychology of Computer Programming*, published in 1971.

3.3.1   What is cognitive load for developers, and how do we measure it?

Cognitive load for software developers refers to the mental resources required to do their jobs. How much information do they need to process to understand the outcome goals, acceptance criteria, and resources available to them in performing their day-to-day tasks? This includes the kinds of problems that must be solved, the organizational processes that must be followed, and the new things that must be learned.

In addition, while engineers or developers have to do all of these things, they do them each with varying degrees of skill and familiarity. Things that take a significant amount of time when new to them can later require a trivial amount of time when they become second nature. They may find new things that they must learn to be difficult or fairly easy, depending on their prior experiences and aptitudes or the quality of learning material available.

Cognitive load is unavoidable. We want to minimize the cognitive load required for a developer to reach their full potential at their current skill, experience, and aptitude level. And then, over time, we want to constrain the load required for developers to progress in their journey of acquiring the knowledge, skills, and experiences that make them more effective as developers. It will always be the case that some of the problems to be solved are hard. But most of the load on developers comes from things that we have made hard, either by accident or design.

We can measure cognitive load in two ways:

- *Subjectively*—Developers self-report their mental state.
- *Quantitatively*—There are structured measurements to assess the effect of cognitive load.

Cognitive load comes in two forms:

- *Intrinsic load*—This is the mental effort required to understand and perform a task, based on its inherent complexity.

  Examples of this for developers are (1) creating a new algorithm to reflect the business logic of a new feature, (2) understanding how recursion works, (3) deploying an application on Kubernetes, and (4) provisioning a new message queue within an event-driven architecture.

- *Extraneous load*—This is the mental effort imposed by the way information or tasks are presented, rather than by the task itself.

  Examples of this for developers are (1) unclear error messages; (2) confusing and incomplete documentation; (3) cryptic, unreadable code; (4) poor or absent naming conventions; and (5) repetitive and redundant manual tasks.

Intrinsic load cannot be eliminated, but there are very effective strategies for breaking down the amount of learning that must take place before a tool or system can be effectively used. Automated onboarding and language starter kits are good examples of this. Say a developer is added to a GitHub team, and, behind the scenes, every configuration needed to correct team-level access is automatically performed, as opposed to pages of checklists; asking for help; or hidden tribal knowledge in a lengthy, manual onboarding process. The developer calls a Python starter kit API, and a complete working repository of code is automatically generated that includes the CI/CD pipeline. The developer can immediately start adding business logic with changes triggering a pipeline that performs all the CI and CD tasks without needing to understand Helm, Kubernetes, and OpenAPI specifications to build and deploy applications effectively.

A platform provides similar opportunities for provisioning databases, durable message queues, managing ingress, and more.

Extraneous load can be eliminated at least within the context of the platform product itself. Each development team has to do the same with the resources they create. But providing standards, conventions, and automated enforcement of the same can make this much more successful.

3.3.2   Why reduce cognitive load?

Unaddressed extraneous load is just waste. It is ignored technical debt, the lack of engineering leadership, or poor architectural (and framework, tool, process selection, etc.) decision-making.

Intrinsic load can come from some of those same behaviors, but often this is less about direct waste and more about the failure to optimize or mature. It is usually the right choice to wait to optimize and mature architectures and systems until we have the data to demonstrate the financial value. But we often see organizations that never mature once there is an established practice while also never honestly addressing the cost of doing so.

In addition to the end-to-end engineering analysis we discussed in the section on the path to production, research in the developer experience field has identified two additional key areas to focus on: feedback loops and flow state. The first is feedback loops. Feedback loops in software development are essential for quick and high-quality responses to actions taken. They help developers get input, evaluate it, and adjust their work accordingly. These loops include not just functional testing of code but also code reviews, performance feedback, stakeholder input, and retrospectives at the end of each sprint. Efficient development depends on fast feedback loops, which allow tasks to be completed smoothly and quickly. Slow feedback loops can disrupt the development cycle, leading to frustration and delays. To improve efficiency, organizations should shorten feedback loops by optimizing development tools and processes, such as build and test procedures or the development environment.

The second is flow state, which refers to a developer's complete absorption and enthusiasm in their work, resulting in intense focus and enjoyment. Experiencing flow regularly enhances productivity, innovation, and personal growth. Studies show that happy developers often produce higher-quality outcomes. Therefore, fostering conditions that promote flow is crucial for improving employee well-being and performance.

The concept of flow state can be compatible with pair programming and mob programming, though achieving flow in a collaborative setting might look different than in solo work. In pair or mob programming, flow can emerge when the team achieves a shared rhythm, clear communication, and mutual understanding of the task. When done effectively, these collaborative methods can foster deep focus and engagement as long as the team members are synchronized and distractions are minimized.

While flow in solo work is often about individual immersion, in pair or mob programming, it becomes about group cohesion and collective problem-solving, which can also enhance productivity, innovation, and personal growth. Creating an environment where team members can support one another and stay focused on their shared goals allows for the benefits of flow in a team context.

Developers are the primary users of engineering platforms and often know best what they need to work on. While this can be debated, platform engineers should not dictate a single way to use platform capabilities.

3.3.3   Techniques for reducing cognitive load

An engineering platform, as a self-serve product, is the fundamental starting point. Techniques for reducing cognitive load include the following:

- *Accelerators for platform architectures or dependencies*—These are the automated onboarding or starter kits we discussed earlier. Making the standard ways of using platform resources available as fully preconfigured, automated actions is the most effective way to accelerate developers' effectiveness. At the same time, they learn about the underlying technologies.
- *Centralized source for documentation, resources, and feedback*—This centralizes documentation for all developer resources, including the engineering platform, which means we have the opportunity to create standards and encourage continuous feedback on the quality of documentation and automation. Using developer portals such as Backstage from Spotify can add structure and acceleration to the process if done well.
- *Data democratization*—We cannot overemphasize the importance of having access to the same data across your whole software development lifecycle. Observability is the first approach that provides actionable insights to fix these problems before they reach the end-user. Suppose you are building a set of containerized microservices orchestrated in your Kubernetes cluster. By using a platform capability that can incorporate a distributed tracing tool into your service mesh, you can now see how the requests are flowing between services, and any bottlenecks can be identified programmatically and addressed.

3.3.4   The need for mechanical sympathy

This term was coined by Jackie Steward, a Formula 1 driver, to describe how great drivers can perform at such a high level. To become a better driver, you have to have mechanical sympathy–a high and increasing understanding of how the mechanical systems of the car work to drive in a way that maximizes the effectiveness of those systems. This is not the same thing as being an engineer who could design and build these systems. *Mechanical sympathy* for software developers refers to the understanding and awareness of how the underlying hardware and system architecture behave to achieve performance, reliability, and efficiency.

Developers can use Kubernetes with zero understanding, but no amount of abstraction or site reliability engineering (SRE)-style improvement can be as successful as those things combined with developers who create software with an experienced and meaningful knowledge of the underlying systems they use. This means that any paved roads or guardrails that we make in the platform user experience that truly act as shields, preventing the developer from gaining this mechanical sympathy, will result in lower-quality code with lower performance, reliability, and sustainability.

Exercise 3.3   Identify and set up measurement techniques for reducing cognitive load

For this exercise, you will create a backlog of 10 potential platform capabilities that can help reduce cognitive load. To do this, create a table using the following format.

Sample table to be used for tracking the cognitive load problems and the platform capabilities that can fix the problem

Cognitive load problem	A platform capability that can fix the problem	How will it solve the problem?	Effort in person-weeks
......	....	....	....
......	....	....	....

3.4   *Common platform performance metrics*

Regardless of the ways a platform is a reflection on each organization where it is built, there are some common performance indicators that we should always consider. Understanding and tracking these KPIs is valuable because they help measure the platform's adoption, efficiency, and effect on business outcomes, ensuring the platform delivers its intended value. Figure 3.6 shows three common groups of metrics that are typically KPIs of platform value.

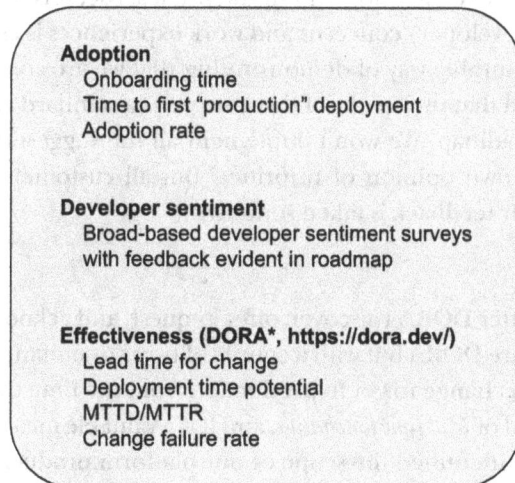

Adoption
    Onboarding time
    Time to first "production" deployment
    Adoption rate

Developer sentiment
    Broad-based developer sentiment surveys
    with feedback evident in roadmap

Effectiveness (DORA*, https://dora.dev/)
    Lead time for change
    Deployment time potential
    MTTD/MTTR
    Change failure rate

Figure 3.6   Shared measures for any platform

3.4.1   Adoption

Onboarding time for teams and individual team members must be instant. This doesn't mean developers instantly know how to use all platform features. Authorized individuals who can subscribe a team to the platform should be able to do so with a single command or from a single web form. Managers or leads who add or remove individual developers to teams should equally find this self-serve and instant. And from the moment a team is onboarded, all members of that team, and those who come and go in the future, should find that they have the correct access permissions to all platform features and capabilities. This includes the core platform technologies but also all of the developers' tools and services that are used in their jobs.

Time to first production deployment is an individual developer metric designed to track the cognitive load of using the platform. Of course, this timing isn't entirely under the control of the platform engineering team. A more consistent way of measuring this aspect of using the platform is to include an exercise that involves moving a demo program from creation in Git to running in production in the orientation documentation. This does not measure how effectively individual teams are at introducing new team members to their code base and getting them deployed to production. Those metrics can also be calculated and provided to each team for their self-assessment purposes.

Once migration timelines are established, tracking the *adoption rate* for teams using the platform is also an effective means of uncovering problems in onboarding and platform usage.

3.4.2   Developer sentiment

This may sound like a fairly subjective measure, and in the usual sense, it is, but effectively responding to customer (developer) concerns and work experiences is critical to product success. We need a measurable way of demonstrating that we are consistently gauging developer sentiment and that the results of these surveys (a standard method) can be found in the platform roadmap. We won't implement all the suggestions, and each developer may have their own opinion of priorities. But all customers should have a visible indication that their feedback is taken seriously.

3.4.3   Effectiveness

In figure 3.6, we put an asterisk after DORA (discover, offer, request, and acknowledge) to indicate that these indicators are DORA but with a couple of twists or enhancements.

The average time it takes for a change to get to production from the time the developer picks up the story is one kind of *lead time for change*, and it is a valuable measure. But in addition to this, once we have identified the scope of our platform product, we will capture how developers have to plan to request dependencies from other teams. This, too, is all lead time planning time. It's also *wasted time* that the platform will recover. Hopefully, this can amount to detailed information within the roadmap that can be checked off as capabilities and features are rolled out within the platform. We want this to be visible throughout the lifetime of the platform.

Deployment time means how long it takes for starter kit pipelines to move a change from initially pushed to Git to running in production. This is what the platform is capable of in a general way. Deployment frequency is the DORA measure, and for individual development teams, this may be a good way for them to assess their own sizing and velocity goals, but by itself, it is a poor measure for the platform. Only the things that are tested through our "potential" measure could be influenced by our platform product. That test tells us how the platform affects deployment frequency. Everything else is about team behaviors or challenges.

The *mean time to detect* a failure within any platform technology or capability should be looking for two things. First, of course, is that an actual automated system is configured to watch for some metric, log, or trace and trigger an alert. But at any given time, there is only a certain number of known health indicators. So, specific problem monitoring is only part of the solution to managing failure incidents. What we want to know is: how long does it take from the time a problem is discovered until the team with the most context, meaning the team that can fix the problem, is notified and able to engage?

The *mean time to recover* is the combination of mean time to detect plus the time from detection to resolution. The goal for the platform is that all platform features are both resilient and highly available, as well as able to self-correct at a pace that prevents customer effects.

Finally, we need to know how often a change results in a failure; this is called the *change failure rate*. Within the measure, though, we have to calculate this in terms of change failure between environments. Every change that is made, both by platform engineers within the context of platform features or capabilities and by developers within their specific applications and services, goes through multiple identical environments before production. In the case of the platform itself, we will have our own development and quality assurance instance of the platform where things are tested before being released to developer environments. Even then, we will push things first through a preview environment that is part of the developers' release pipeline but not necessary for release. All of this is about minimizing or preventing failures that affect end users. We expect a change in the development environment to break things. That's why it is there. We want to measure the number of breaking changes in development, nonetheless. We follow that up with the next environment and the next, up to and including the production context. What we want to see is nearly all the failures happening in development and a few appearing in QA but zero from there on out.

There are many other ways that we will measure and monitor the platform and the product roadmap. Most of these will reflect our organization's priorities and problems, which, of course, can be different from company to company. But in platform engineering, this list of common indicators is almost universal as measures of real value.

3.5   Evolving measures

Beyond the shared measures, there are many other areas that we will focus on as the platform evolves. An effective practice is to use our development lifecycle and our product domains as an analysis model, considering all aspects of the domain or a given step in our SDLC. How can we measure for improvement or health?

3.5.1   Cost planning

Total cost of ownership in software product development means all costs involved in acquiring, deploying, operating, and maintaining the product throughout its lifecycle. Consider the following for creating continuous measurements or monitoring:

- *Cost models for cloud infrastructure provisioning and usage*—While infrastructure provisioning may not always be on the cloud, standardizing on the baselines requires a set of services that can provide a relative view of infrastructure availability. Public cloud providers do a great job of this.

- *Licensing models and agreements around the third-party tools*—Third-party tools can be SaaS, PaaS, or IaaS, depending on the organization's needs. Establishing standards, guardrails, and the acceptable numbers of the total cost of ownership will include not just the licensing costs but also maintenance activities such as administration, installation, and upgrades, as well as the time saved by using these third-party tools.

- *Buy versus build analysis*—The planning process should include planning for the capabilities to be built as part of a shared services stack. These should start with a buy versus build analysis that will again consider the total cost of ownership. Engineering platform capabilities that look like a fascinating solution implementation may be better candidates to build at times if you can buy components and integrate them well with yet another basic tenet of platforms: replaceability. Just like improving the code base with changing client requirements, you will also see drastic improvements in the capabilities of the tools you might buy. Instead of having a vendor lock-in during such a time, which we see in every organization, by using a composable architecture, you will find it easier to replace them en masse without significant retraining, redesign, or replatforming.

- *Performance and scalability metrics*—Establishing these during the planning phase is critical. This is where your business strategy alignment, as discussed earlier, will come in handy. For example, if one of Epetech's business goals includes streaming training video content globally, have we accounted for the expected cost at this scale, and how effectively can we predict these costs?

3.5.2   Risk assessment

Based on all the security requirements that the security stakeholders in our company establish, what things need to be continuously measured? When thinking of the answer, go beyond the literal security requirements and include all governance and compliance requirements required from stakeholders. How will we measure or *score* our desired risk profile against the actual state?

3.5.3 *Mapping measurement to core platform principles*

Let's look again at our SDLC from earlier. The lifecycle is a continuous process of improvement that is based on the feedback from the previous steps in the lifecycle (see figure 3.7). In tables 3.1 and 3.2, we list several different areas within the stage that are commonly suitable for continuous measurements and reporting.

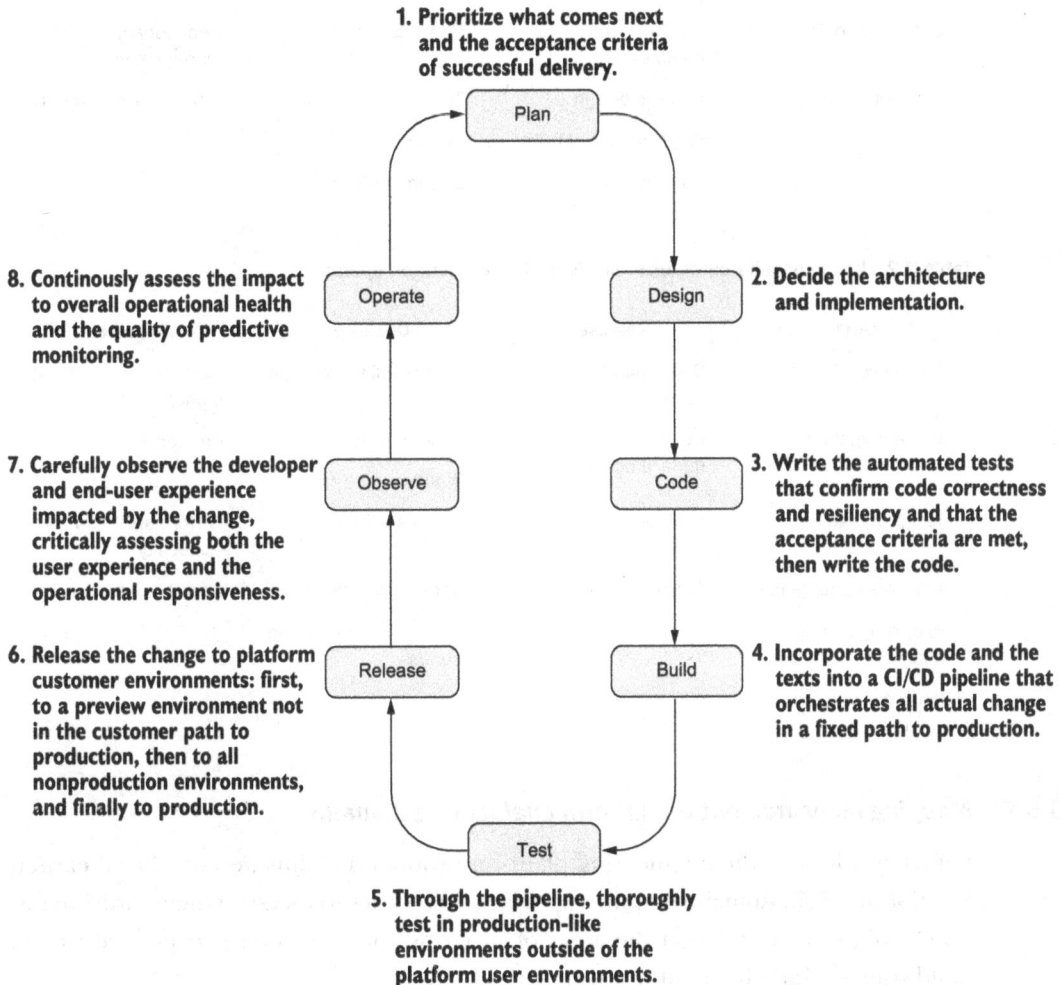

1. Prioritize what comes next and the acceptance criteria of successful delivery.

Plan

8. Continuously assess the impact to overall operational health and the quality of predictive monitoring.

Operate

Design

2. Decide the architecture and implementation.

7. Carefully observe the developer and end-user experience impacted by the change, critically assessing both the user experience and the operational responsiveness.

Observe

Code

3. Write the automated tests that confirm code correctness and resiliency and that the acceptance criteria are met, then write the code.

6. Release the change to platform customer environments: first, to a preview environment not in the customer path to production, then to all nonproduction environments, and finally to production.

Release

Build

4. Incorporate the code and the texts into a CI/CD pipeline that orchestrates all actual change in a fixed path to production.

Test

5. Through the pipeline, thoroughly test in production-like environments outside of the platform user environments.

Figure 3.7 Analyze each step and how it feeds into the next for the measures of success or improvement.

Table 3.1   Key capability categorization: Plan, design, code, build

Plan	Design	Code	Build
Developer involvement	Loosely coupled architecture	Maintainability	Continuous integration
Customer feedback loops	High cohesion	Complexity	Continuous delivery
VSM	Appropriate design patterns	AI assist effect	Provenance
Work sizing	SOLID principles	Readability	Environment configuration
Organizational support	Constrained complexity	Consistency	Dependency management
User centricity	Intuitive design	Testability	Artifact management
	Single source of truth	Security	
	Consistency	Documentation	

Table 3.2   Key capability categorization: Test, deploy, monitor, operate

Test	Release	Observe	Operate
Test types	Deployment automation	Observability coverage	Incident response and management
Test automation	Deployment patterns (blue/green, canary)	Observability	Resiliency
		Quality	
Test coverage	Scalability	VSM visibility	Performance and scalability
Test data management	Feature flagging	Data aggregation	Anomaly detection
Reporting and analytics		Predictive analysis and trends	
Security			

3.5.4   *Mapping measurement to platform engineering domains*

Let us now look at the engineering platform product domains we introduced earlier. Each of the eight domains requires appropriate metrics to measure them individually, which will, in turn, tell you the areas of progress and improvements needed as you build your engineering platform (see figure 3.8).

No matter how we define the domains of our platform, we should continuously assess whether the domain remains valid by measuring against the attributes of a successful domain:

- Loose coupling
- Service interface first design
- Evolutionary architecture and preserved domains of change
- Precise and ubiquitous language for terms and meanings
- Release independence
- Accessible domain events

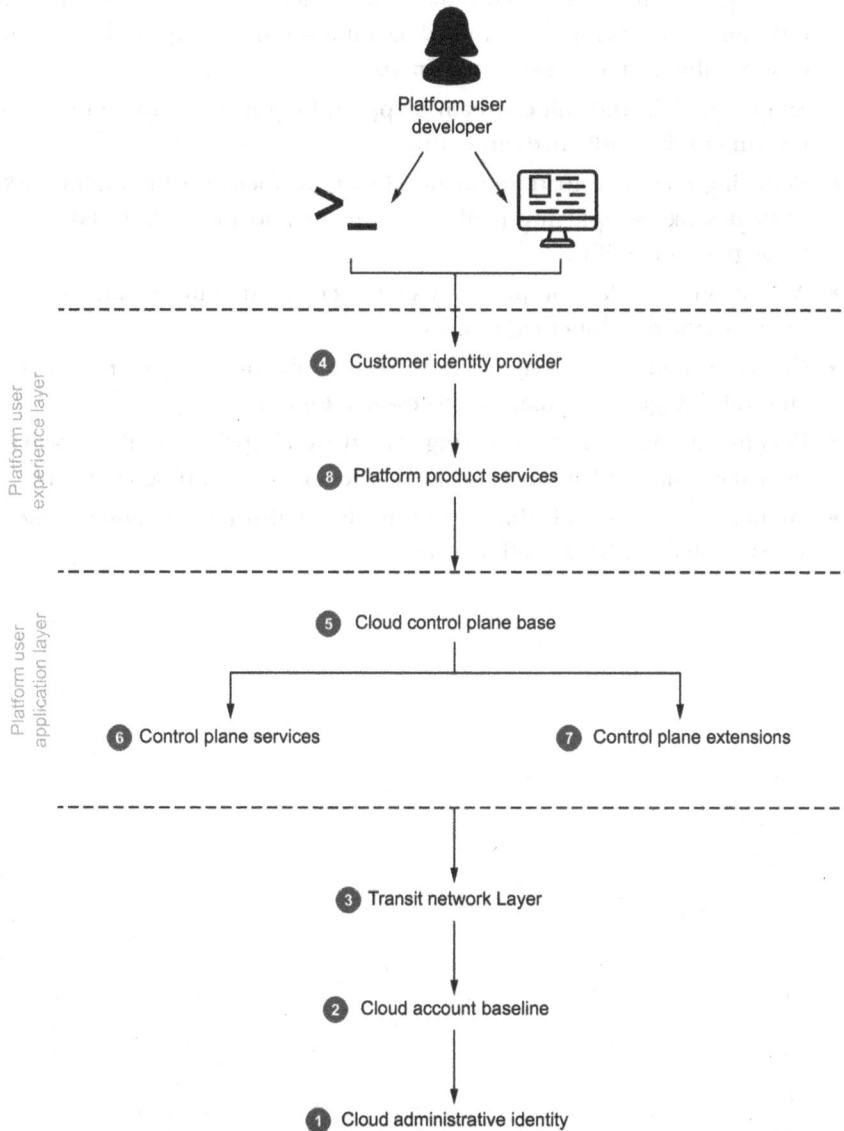

Figure 3.8 Engineering platform product domains

Summary

- We should look beyond just revenue as a success metric and also consider employee morale and other factors in platform engineering.
- To determine whether our initiatives are effective, we need both objective and subjective assessments, as proven results show the value of our investments.
- We need to set measurement criteria at both the domain level and throughout the SDLC process to get a detailed view of platform engineering metrics.
- By tying measurements to core platform principles, we can assess success across different areas, promoting a product mindset and using tools like end-to-end observability and self-healing mechanisms.
- Simple models and value stream mapping help us quantify returns and justify investments in platform engineering.
- Reducing cognitive load allows developers to focus on high-value tasks, using strategies like simplifying problem domains and promoting data accessibility through observability.
- A capability model for platform engineering streamlines measurement and improves the developer experience.
- Corporate culture has a significant effect on platform engineering, so managing cultural change is essential for successful adoption.
- For effective platform engineering, data-driven improvements and scalable practices like structured automation and cloud-native technologies are crucial.
- We need to define KPIs that align with the platform's operating model to measure the platform's value effectively.

Part 2

Building engineering platforms

Modern software delivery demands more than speed. It requires consistency, security, and reliability at scale. As organizations embrace cloud-native development, the need for engineering platforms that enforce standards, automate compliance, and provide actionable visibility has never been greater. The shift from ad hoc automation to software-defined platforms is not just a technical evolution; it's a fundamental rethinking of how internal software systems are built and governed.

Behind every successful platform lies a robust foundation of governance, observability, and control. These capabilities ensure that platforms are not only usable and extensible but also secure, compliant, and aligned with organizational priorities. From defining guardrails to offering self-service capabilities, platform engineering teams must design for both control and developer autonomy.

This part of the book will guide you through building the next level of your engineering platform: a secure, observable, and extensible internal product. Chapter 4 begins by exploring how governance, compliance, and trust can be integrated into platform workflows without compromising delivery speed. Chapter 5 introduces the concept of evolutionary observability, explaining how to make platforms introspectable and resilient through the use of feedback loops and signal analysis. By the end of this chapter, you will have been exposed to all the foundational and building blocks of an engineering platform. The following three chapters in this section teach you how to build an engineering platform.

In chapter 6, you'll learn how to architect a software-defined engineering platform from the ground up, applying modular design, domain boundaries, and composability principles. Chapter 7 introduces the core foundations of a control plane: a centralized interface that exposes platform capabilities in a consistent and discoverable way. Finally, chapter 8 expands on this control plane with value-added services and extensibility patterns that elevate platform usability across teams.

By the end of part 2, you'll be equipped to confidently build platforms that address the requirements of developers, govern responsibly for the industry standards, and deliver organizational value continuously.

Governance, compliance, and trust

4

One of the assumptions we often see organizations make is that they can be successful at platform engineering without changing how they think about governance, compliance, and other forms of internal trust. They assume that underlying all the talk about *platforms,* there is just a new tool to buy and a one-time project to fund, all of which can be implemented through the existing organizational structures and leaders.

The reality is quite different. It is those very structures and leaders that brought about the existing situation. Unless the company is a startup, the engineering culture, with its priorities and decision-making incentives, is established to a degree that has likely survived multiple leadership and directional changes at many levels. Change will not come easily, and it won't happen by default. Governance and compliance cover a wide range of topics. Collectively, these are in a tie, if not the lead, among all the causes of the engineering friction that an engineering platform seeks to change.

Delivering software requires adherence to the domains of compliance, audit, security, and data. Teams like Infosec, Security, Legal, and Governance are not going to disappear. Each of them has different requirements:

- Our security team requires that there are no known, exploitable vulnerabilities rated critical accessible to potential attackers.
- The audit team wants nonterminable evidence of every deployment to meet SOX compliance.
- Infosec has stated there must be controls on sensitive dataset APIs to ensure only authorized users have access.

These example requirements are similar to those you will find in any organization. Let's assign the implementation responsibilities for each of these to the stakeholder teams without platform engineering standards. In that case, we will continue to face the same roadblocks and friction for our developers, defeating the entire purpose of the platform.

We'll need to apply some new patterns and ways of thinking to change this dynamic. Much of this chapter deals with enabling development teams to retain complete functional control of their CI/CD pipelines. Software continuous integration and deployment pipelines are a core development tool. Developers created this orchestration strategy to build quality into the software development process. It's like a scalpel to a surgeon. We've co-opted this tool and turned it into a command and control gate because doing so was an easy way for stakeholders to feel confident. By easy, we mean the least cost and effort for the stakeholder. But centralized pipeline teams or the operational abstraction of CI/CD from development represent one of the most significant sources of friction and waste.

People often think separating pipelines brings benefits like better compliance and reduced complexity—and by *complexity*, they usually mean that dealing with pipeline tools and orchestration feels like a time-consuming distraction. The idea is that developers shouldn't have to worry about building pipelines, and instead, a small dedicated team can handle it for everyone. But that kind of thinking misses—or misunderstands—the real purpose and value of having pipelines in the first place. So how do we retain developer autonomy while managing complexity and maintaining compliance?

4.1   *Developer autonomy*

Autonomy doesn't mean there are no controls or that developers are left to create pipelines all by themselves—it just means we have the flexibility to tackle the pain points that come with rigid control processes. We've seen this approach work well time and time again. And beyond the clear wins in a platform setting, there's some solid science behind why autonomy is such a key part of successful platform engineering.

In 1979, two brothers named Stuart and Hubert Dreyfus conducted a study of mastery on airline pilots, as described in *Medical Education Online* [1] and well documented elsewhere. They had a set of expert and instructor pilots make a checklist for novice pilots to follow in an emergency simulation. When the novices used the checklist, their performance was markedly improved. When the experts used their checklist, their performance suffered when compared to simulating with no limits and complete autonomy.

The brothers were able to show that the experts had reached a level of mastery that can be thought of as intuition. Using their findings, they defined the Dreyfus Skill Model as shown in figure 4.1. You'll notice that at the levels of *Expert* and *Master,* the Decision Making function has moved to *Intuitive.* This is similar to how a master chef can make a dish from scratch without a recipe. And when asked to explain it step by step, they can't; they made it on intuition alone. Another example is when a doctor walks into the room and accurately predicts the diagnosis within 5 minutes of seeing the patient.

TABLE 1

Skill Level / Mental Function	NOVICE	COMPETENT	PROFICIENT	EXPERT	MASTER
Recollection	Non-situational	Situational	Situational	Situational	Situational
Recognition	Decomposed	Decomposed	Holistic	Holistic	Holistic
Decision	Analytical	Analytical	Analytical	Intuitive	Intuitive
Awareness	Monitoring	Monitoring	Monitoring	Monitoring	Absorbed

Figure 4.1   The original table from Dreyfus and Dreyfus's paper [2]

As humans, we develop intuition in directed skills over time. We pick up on very subtle cues (many of which we aren't directly aware of; it's subconscious thinking) that tip us off to the task at hand.

As another example, a master hockey player skating down the ice sees very tiny movements and minuscule shifts in weight from the defenders in front of him, and he instinctively knows which movement to make to counter them. A novice or intermediate player barely has time to look up, let alone analyze the movements of the players in front of him. But when given a set play or pattern, novices are often taught to "skate to the outside and then cut inward," and they have increased success. The best players are usually defined by their hockey IQ. This comes down to their ability to make swift decisions in fractions of a second, being in the right place at the right time, or placing the puck in the perfect spot. Novice players are taught a simple checklist: Scan, Ask, Act. They *scan* the ice, they *ask* themselves what is about to happen and how they should respond, and they *act* on their questions. Over years of training, this list becomes instinctual. Master players don't use the checklist in their head because they are doing it constantly in their subconscious; every moment is analyzed and actioned on. If placed on the same sheet of ice, the master intuitively knows where to be at all times, while the novice is still on step 1. If we forced master players to follow the list audibly (or mentally), it would slow them down tremendously.

The purpose of outlining this study and the examples is to show that forcing experts and masters to follow a script will lead to reduced performance (or worse, they'll just find a new place to work). We have to provide a platform that helps the novices get off the ground (for example, with starter kits) and allows the experts to quickly make design decisions without the need to coordinate communication and change requests through a centralized pipeline team. This example does not imply that the checklists are a waste of time for every context and every user persona. Overreliance on checks and balances, instead of intuitive expertise that developers have garnered over the years, is counterproductive, especially when we can ensure higher levels of confidence in adherence due to recent advances in autonomous agents doing their job. We are not advocating a free-for-all approach by the experts but emphasizing that one needs to balance enforcing governance and creativity in equal measures. In our experience, with our long history in the software industry, this is also the reality of how things will work, whether or not we agree with it. Thus, providing a structure to operate is critical.

We need our developers to understand exactly how the build and release pipelines work. As they grow more experienced, they will intuitively know what changes and design decisions will make the pipeline effective and efficient. Often, our senior-most experts move around from project to project, helping teams improve their codebase (i.e., SREs). Giving them the freedom to make those changes without hundreds of hurdles from policy-focused teams has a significant effect on the organization.

4.1.1   *What does it mean to make a development team autonomous?*

In the legacy environment of Epetech, teams that needed simple things like an S3 bucket, database access, and even deploying their application to production faced a mountain of tickets, manual requests, phone calls, and maybe a smoke signal. So we've decided to take this journey to remove much of that friction for our development teams. To do this, we must analyze what areas affect our teams the most in their day-to-day engineering processes.

> **NOTE**   The example we are using here to explain the concept is pipeline control. Still, the autonomy is applicable across all aspects of platform engineering, such as infrastructure provisioning, service scaffolding, access control and IAM requests, secrets and configuration management, observability setup, and feature flag rollout and experimentation, to name a few.

The most utilized point between engineering and the platform is the development pipeline. As we pointed out in the previous section, taking control of the pipeline away from the development teams is a bad idea. We want to give teams complete control over their own pipeline with necessary guardrails. Remember the Epetech pipeline we introduced earlier? This is a reasonably common pipeline experience. A different team often controls each step of the pipeline. This leads to bottlenecks and friction between our development and security, audit, and compliance teams (see figure 4.2).

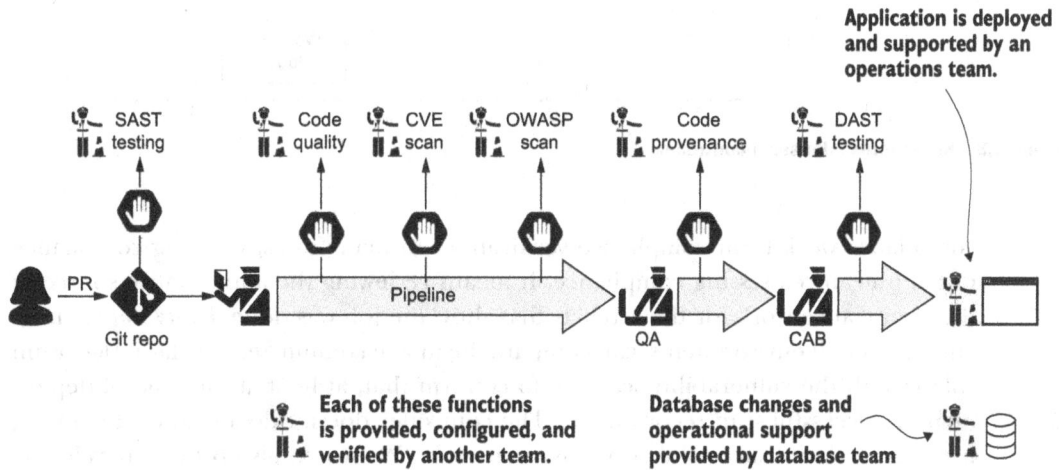

Figure 4.2 The all too common pipeline

To remove this friction, we need to divide the governance and compliance work into two distinct events:

1 Doing the work of becoming compliant
2 Verifying that the work of compliance was done

To accomplish this, we move #2 to the moment when the resulting change to an environment occurs; for software, this is at the point of deployment. We often call this the *point of change,* and it starts with the very first environment, usually referred to as "all the way left." Up to this point, the change is only happening on the developer's laptop. Beginning with the first environment and continuing with every deployment thereafter, including, most importantly, production, the verification occurs.

To move verification to the point of change, we'll need a way to intercept the deployment and verify that the compliance work has been completed. Kubernetes has a very mature way of handling this, called an admission controller (see figure 4.3).

The admission controller lets us create validating webhooks that can perform any task we want before deployment. This is how we can meet our criteria of decoupling

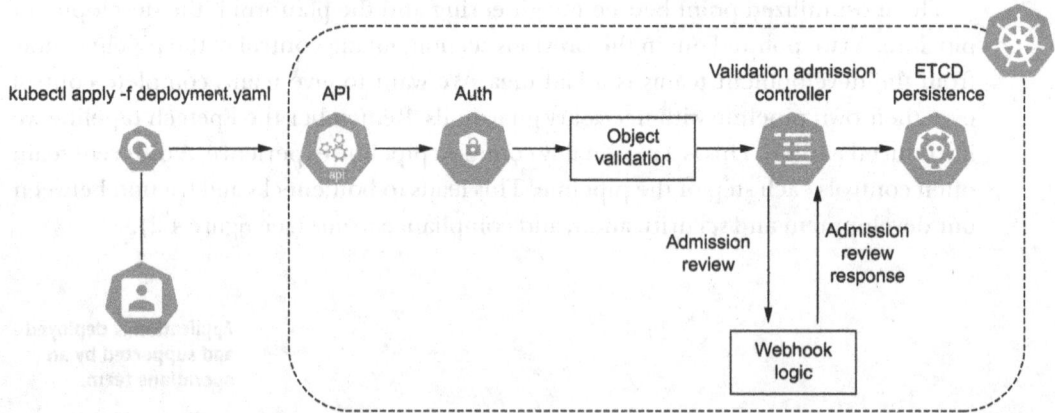

Figure 4.3   Kubernetes admission controller

compliance work from compliance verification. In many cases, verifying compliance doesn't mean reassessing compliance. It means reviewing the authoritative source of the compliance work for the artifacts that show the job was done. Every deployment attempt, for all environments, can compare the image commit Secure Hash Algorithm (SHA) with the vulnerability scan log to confirm that, at least at the time of deployment, a successful scan record exists. The controller doesn't do a scan of the image; it confirms that a successful scan has been done. We would also provide developers with a reusable, versioned piece of pipeline code that can be included in any pipeline to perform this scan. Of course, this is included in the preconfigured pipelines that developers use to set up a new project. But whether they used a project starter kit or just refactored their existing pipeline, they would always have a means of performing any compliance requirements. In theory, our security team can even own the reusable pipeline code and the policies can be deployed to the admission controller.

In other situations, verification only makes sense as a direct check that a particular configuration exists. Consider figure 4.4 as an example, where we are enforcing the presence of specific labels on all deployments. This is a critical control. Most cost-optimization and tracking software depend on specific tags to perform their functions.

Here we are going to accept or deny the deployment based on the presence of the labels object in a Kubernetes deployment. We might further enhance this policy by specifying which labels are required in the labels object.

Note that Gatekeeper is an open-source admission controller based on Open Policy Agent (OPA) and the Rego policy language and includes excellent resources for getting started. We talk about OPA in the next section. As we do, you will notice that the previous Gatekeeper example is similar but also different, formatted more like a Kubernetes resource than as a general policy language. This is a unique feature of Gatekeeper. OPA has a much broader application than just as an admission controller enforcing Kubernetes compliance policies, which is something to keep in mind. Suppose your

```
apiVersion: templates.gatekeeper.sh/v1beta1
kind: ConstraintTemplate
metadata:
  name: k8srequiredlabels
spec:
  crd:
    spec:
      names:
        kind: K8sRequiredLabels
        listKind: K8sRequiredLabelsList
        plural: k8srequiredlabels
        singular: k8srequiredlabels
      validation:
        # Schema for the `parameters` field
        openAPIV3Schema:
          properties:
            labels:
              type: array
              items: string
  targets:
    - target: admission.k8s.gatekeeper.sh
      rego: |
        package k8srequiredlabels

        deny[{"msg": msg, "details": {"missing_labels": missing}}] {
          provided := {label | input.review.object.metadata.labels[label]}
          required := {label | label := input.parameters.labels[_]}
          missing := required - provided
          count(missing) > 0
          msg := sprintf("you must provide labels: %v", [missing])
        }
```

Figure 4.4 Admission controller built using Gatekeeper (https://github.com/open-policy-agent/gatekeeper), which checks for labels on the deployment

organization will be adopting policy-as-code practices across multiple disciplines using a standard policy language such as Rego. What will be the effect of one particular implementation (the compliance checks on Kubernetes) uniquely structuring its policy language? There are some other differences, such as assumptions about policy distribution. The long-term effect of the differences can become a source of friction. Adopting a shared standard is a trivial exercise at the start and should be considered.

Using Kubernetes as our platform control plane makes deploying point-of-change logic for most activities easy, as this is a built-in capability. But we can still implement this strategy in other settings. There are vendor solutions such as Hashicorp Sentinel for Terraform-managed environments. And when using a cloud vendor for infrastructure, we always have the option of requiring the use of a reverse proxy in front of the vendor API, where we can add verification logic before passing the call.

This strategy can still be effective even after using after-the-fact scans. Rather than intercepting change events, we could have compliance scans occur as a result of the change, with immediate reporting and alerting on compliance violations. Whether it is a precheck or a postcheck, by separating the event from the work of compliance, we eliminate the need to remove pipelines and other development orchestration from developer control.

4.2 Policy-as-code

Let's say that the head of engineering has declared all deployed code must now have 90% or higher test coverage. In the old way of doing things, the DevOps team would code up a script or pipeline orb and add it to the standard development pipeline. But no DevOps team owns the pipelines in our new world of platform engineering. Instead, every development team owns its pipeline. And while our CTO trusts his development organization, he wants to keep everyone honest without taking control of their pipelines. We do this with our compliance at the point of change admission controllers, which we discussed in the previous section. But to implement our admission controllers, we'll need a policy engine.

One popular option for this type of policy engine is written in a language called Rego. It is the language used to interact with Open Policy Agent, a graduated Cloud Native Computing Foundation project that provides a declarative policy engine. We will use OPA in all of our examples. It is mature and has a broad ecosystem beyond Kubernetes. There are other options in this field (such as Kyverno: https://kyverno.io/).

4.2.1 Introduction to policy-as-code using Open Policy Agent

Open Policy Agent can be deployed as an admission controller that will apply any compliance or governance requirement policies we provide. The technical details of deploying the OPA agent and publishing policy sources are relatively simple. The valuable part of OPA, but also much more challenging, is the Rego policy language.

The OPA agent is a highly tuned data comparison engine. We invoke the engine by providing it a chunk of data, large or small, as JSON and then a list of requirements. The engine will very rapidly compare the data to the requirements and return a Yes or No.

The data can be built into the OPA deployment or fetched *just in time,* and it can be anything needed for the policy requirement to be able to return an answer successfully.

The *requirements* are written in the Rego language. Rather than being a programming language, Rego has more in common with query languages like GraphQL or SQL; it is designed to interact with data. (Rego was inspired by Datalog, which is an early declarative logic programming language in the Prolog family. Logica by Google is a more exact modern example.) It also has some similarities to Terraform in that it is declarative. In Terraform, we define precisely what we want our infrastructure to be, and the Terraform API will interact with our infrastructure API, requesting the necessary individual components and dependencies, comparing our definition to the result. If the results match, then Terraform returns success; otherwise, it fails. Rego has a similar declarative approach. This means that, using the policy language, we describe a fixed structure to say, in effect, that data that looks like this is *approved*. These policy statements are referred to as assertions.

We make assertions in the form of predicates: statements about data. This vocabulary comes from the history of the science behind data query and logic languages and is still the way data scientists and language developers talk about these ideas—in much the same way we use terms like "object-oriented" or "ternary operators" in procedural languages. Assume that at Epetech, this is a true statement:

Bryan is writing a book.

In this sentence, "Bryan" is the subject and "is writing a book" is the predicate. Predicates are properties or descriptions of what their subject are or do (in grammatical terms). If we know that in total there are four people at Epetech writing a book, we could say:

Bryan, Ajay, Sean, and Nic are writing a book.

In this case, the list of four people is the *extension* of the predicate: the list of all subjects that satisfy the predicate. Imagine that the list of all people working at Epetech is

Bryan, Ajay, Sean, Nic, Brandon

This is our data domain, which is the set of all possible subjects that our predicate *could* refer to.

Going back to the original statement, if we replace the subjects with X, we would have

X is writing a book.

What is X? It's a subject variable. The statement as a whole is the assertion. Recall that assertions are either true or false. Given some value for X, is the assertion that *X is writing a book* true?

For all values X where X is the list of all people working at Epetech

X is writing a book.

The output of this last assertion is false! Nic, Ajay, Bryan, and Sean are writing a book. Brandon is not. So, given that the data we fed into the equation—the domain against which the assertion is applied—included everyone at Epetech, our assertion is false. If we input a domain of only Bryan, then the assertion would be true.

This helps us arrive at a helpful definition for a predicate: it is a statement that contains variables, and it may be true or false depending on the values (also known as the *domain*) of these variables. Suppose Epetech wanted a policy that allowed only employees who were writing books to see information about other employees who were also writing books. In that case, you can see how we might go about describing the assertions and defining the data extensions we need to evaluate the assertions.

Let's look at another example, but now we use our actual policy language, Rego. We can use the Rego Playground (https://play.openpolicyagent.org) to work through this example.

First, let's describe our predicate in English:

Users must be older than 12 to access our site.

Users on the site must create a login and provide their date of birth. We require users to be at least 13 years old to use our site.

Over the past few days, three users have created logins, and we now have the following information in our data domain. Put this data into the DATA area in the Rego Playground. It must be noted that the Rego Playground opens by default in the Examples mode, and gaining access to the DATA area requires changing to access control or some other predefined template:

```
{
    "user_attributes": {
        "ama": {
            "age": 20
        },
        "darryl": {
            "age": 35
        },
        "ling": {
            "age": 11
        }
    }
}
```

This is a straightforward example of the information we are likely storing about users. We would typically have additional information such as last name and email, and we would ask for their date of birth to then calculate their age. But you get the point.

When Ling tries to use our site, her input data is

```
"user": "ling"
```

Enter this info into the INPUT area in Rego Playground. In a real setting, this could contain all kinds of information, such as the web token that the user's successful login provided them, their IP address, and any information they provide or that we have saved.

Now we need a policy that asserts a user's age. By default, we could set our policy to deny access and then add assertions that grant permission:

Syntactically, policies are part of a package. We can just name ours a test.

We decided to use policies kind of like firewall rules. We will allow it to be false by default.

```
package test
default allow := false
allow if user_is_over_12

user_is_over_12 if {
    data.user_attributes[input.user].age > 12
}
```

Here is our bare assertion. Allow will be set to true if the result of a rule called user_is_over_12 returns true.

Our function uses the input information to find a matching user in our data and then compares the age information in our data with our age policy requirement of greater than 12.

Enter the policy into the POLICY area on the right side of the Rego Playground. Check the LINT area and correct any typos.

If everything is entered correctly, you can hit the Evaluate button at the top of the page, and you should see the following in the output area:

```
{
    "allow": false
}
```

Ling is only 11 years old, so the assertion about age is not true. If you change the name of the user to Ama and reevaluate, the result will be

```
{
    "allow": true,
    "user_is_over_12": true
}
```

Allow is now true because Ama is over 12. And, in terms of our entire policy language text, the assertion (or rule) that was evaluated as true was `user_is_over_12`.

Now let's work on an example closer to the kind of policies we might apply in our Kubernetes control plane. Suppose Epetech engineering leadership established a policy that custom code needed to have at least 80% code coverage. Development teams posted their coverage results to our reporting tool, which we will assume in this case is Codacy. We will deploy an OPA-based admission controller. Because we will need coverage data from our coverage data reporting tool, we create an API that OPA will call to fetch this data (see figure 4.5).

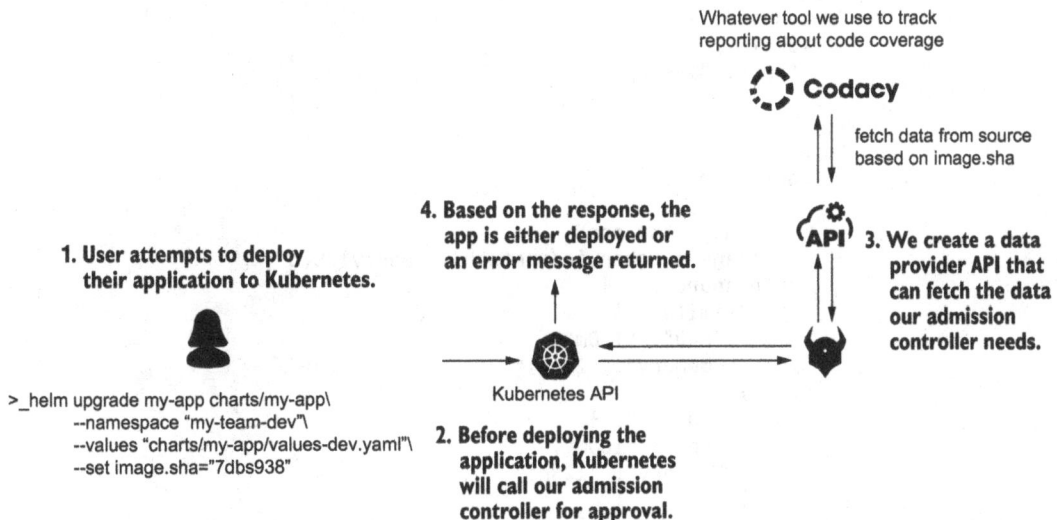

Whatever tool we use to track reporting about code coverage

Codacy

fetch data from source based on image.sha

4. Based on the response, the app is either deployed or an error message returned.

API **3. We create a data provider API that can fetch the data our admission controller needs.**

1. User attempts to deploy their application to Kubernetes.

```
>_helm upgrade my-app charts/my-app\
    --namespace "my-team-dev"\
    --values "charts/my-app/values-dev.yaml"\
    --set image.sha="7dbs938"
```

Kubernetes API

2. Before deploying the application, Kubernetes will call our admission controller for approval.

Figure 4.5 Before completing a deployment request, the Kubernetes API will call any admission controllers that we have defined.

The input data that will be passed to our policy will look something like this:

```json
{
  "kind": "AdmissionReview",
  "apiVersion": "admission.k8s.io/v1",
  "request": {
    "kind": {
      "group": "apps",
      "version": "v1",
      "kind": "Deployment"
    },
    "name": "my-app",
    "namespace": "my-team-dev",
    "operation": "CREATE",
    "object": {
      "apiVersion": "apps/v1",
      "kind": "Deployment",
      "metadata": {
        "name": "my-app",
        "namespace": "my-team-dev",
        "source-sha": "bc183a62",
        "labels": {
          "app": "my-app"
        }
      },
      "spec": {
        "replicas": 3,
        "selector": {
          "matchLabels": {
            "app": "my-app"
          }
        },
        "template": {
          "metadata": {
            "labels": {
              "app": "my-app"
            }
          },
          "spec": {
            "containers": [
              {
                "name": "my-app",
                "image": "ghcr.io/epetech/my-app:v1.8.3",
                "resources": {
                  "limits": {
                    "cpu": "100m",
                    "memory": "256Mi"
                  },
                  "requests": {
                    "cpu": "100m",
                    "memory": "128Mi"
                  }
                }
              }
            ]
          }
        }
      }
    }
  }
}
```

```
          }
        },
        "strategy": {
          "type": "RollingUpdate",
          "rollingUpdate": {
            "maxUnavailable": "25%",
            "maxSurge": "25%"
          }
        }
      }
    }
  }
}
```

This has been abbreviated, but it was taken from the actual input data the Kubernetes API sends. It will include all the details in the Helm charts (Kubernetes resources), along with detailed information about the caller ID and so on.

Now let's assume that we will add an HTTP request [3] at the start of our policy that will use the source-sha deployment metadata value to fetch values from our reporting tool and return a dataset that has the following format if the request is found and no SHA records if not:

```
{
  "code_quality_attributes": {
    "bc183a62": {              ◄──┐ This matches the commit value
      "issues": "4",              │ that was taken from the input data.
      "coverage": 98,
      "complexity": 5,
      "lines_of_code": 3769
    }
  }
}
```

Let's assume that we want to permit deployment to occur by default, but then we will deny the deploy request unless our policy requirement is met:

```
package test

# http.send request passing our input data could go here

default deny := false

deny if code_coverage_lt_required

code_coverage_lt_required if {
  data.code_quality_attributes[input.request.object.metadata.sha].coverage < 80
}
```

In this policy example, we compare the data returned from our code quality API for the commit of the code to be deployed with the required value. The deployment is denied if the actual test coverage is less than the policy.

Exercise 4.1   Create policies that require deployments to include availability and resource management requirements

In the previous example, our code coverage requirements are being verified with each deployment. Now let's expand on that policy. Assume that two more requirements have been identified:

- Deployments must have more than a single replica defined to provide availability.
- Deployments must have resource limits and requests defined to support improved resource management.

Using all the elements from the code coverage example (data, input, and policy), add the additional policy language that will apply these additional requirements. You can include statements like the following print statement within Rego rule statements (the body of the *if* {...statements} function-like definitions). The output will appear in the browser developer's console window.

4.3   Platform-managed trust

Trust is becoming increasingly important in how technology is managed overall. For custom software, using an engineering platform to support development is the most efficient way to build and keep that trust. In this section, we break down two fundamental trust factors and see how our ideas about software-defined product delivery and point-of-change compliance can make things easier and establish digital trust. Plus, we'll talk about how our recommended identity strategy for managing platform users (also a kind of trust) can give us the flexibility we'll need for future trust requirements.

4.3.1   Software supply chain security

Around the end of 2020, you may recall a little attack named Solarwinds (also Sunburst) [4]. If you aren't familiar with it, it was one of history's most significant cybersecurity breaches. Thousands of organizations were affected, and the breach ran undetected for over a year. While the attackers ran all sorts of attacks and used many methods after a breach, the initial way that they got in was by finding a way to make changes to SolarWinds' source code, via the build servers, so that the pull requests failed and appeared as if these were changes and commits that SolarWinds itself had made. Every Solarwinds customer then installed the malicious code during regular updates and patching, and the changes were trusted because the Solarwinds CI/CD process had signed them.

This breach sparked a massive industry-focused effort in software supply chain security. It also prompted the involvement of high-level government officials, including the president, who released executive orders and funded over $1 billion in state and local cybersecurity programs.

Software provenance has always been an important topic, but after this attack, the reality struck our entire industry deeply. It's essential to understand how much easier it is to protect yourself from an attack than to root out an attack that has already occurred.

One of the most effective methods to provide software supply chain security is to apply some of the principles we have already learned about. Combining supply chain audit principles with our policy-as-code and point-of-change compliance automation gives us a powerful and effective means to deliver supply chain security to our development teams without creating friction.

Let's talk about this in the context of our engineering platform (see figure 4.6).

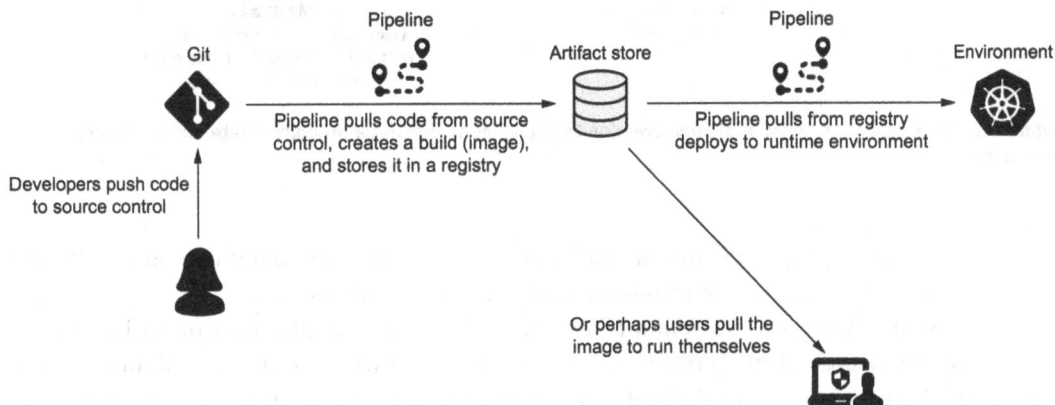

Figure 4.6 Software created by users of our platform follows a known path. Developers create code, the pipeline creates an executable version and stores it, and then the pipeline deploys the executable to the target environment. Depending on the type of application, end-users may get a copy to run themselves.

How can we be confident that we know about everything that happened to the software between its development and deployment? What can we tell users of the software that will offer them this same confidence? How can we do this without creating all kinds of time-consuming manual processes along the way? See figure 4.7.

We should require all our development teams to sign their commits with a valid, personal identifying key. Repositories in our platform-provided source control should be configured to allow only signed commits. When the CI/CD pipeline accesses any artifact store, source control, or image registries, the authentication and authorization mechanism should identify the pipeline source and maintain an audible log. Our image registry should be configured to require content trust (signed images). Images deployed to the registry should include a signed software bill of materials (SBOM) that documents all the packages that are included in the build from outside the original source code of the build repository. The SBOM should consist of a cryptographic means of verifying the integrity of the image and incorporated packages.

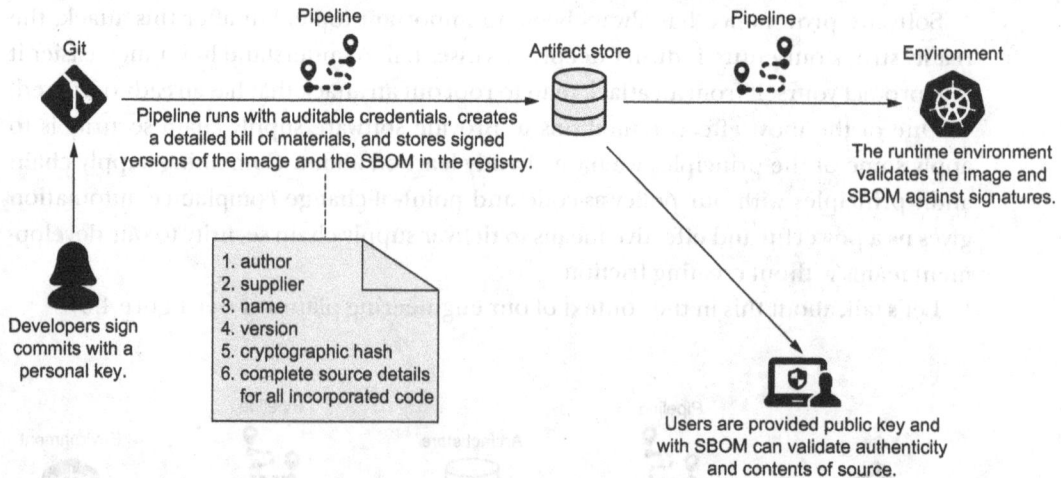

Figure 4.7   Steps along the way, from code creation to deployment, can automatically create the necessary provenance.

Our engineering platform can make all of these things happen both automatically and through easily accessible resources to all users of the platform.

Some of these requirements are created in the configuration of an integrated tool such as GitHub. Repositories can be set to require commits to be signed. Access to GitHub can be configured to enforce auditable authentication and authorization. Because our entire platform will be software-defined, all of these kinds of configurations will be managed through a delivery pipeline that will include continuous testing, with the test results available to any audit system. When development teams sign up to use the platform, which will be self-serve, if they don't already have personal signing keys, they can automatically be generated for them. Continuous automation in the platform can automatically configure repositories to require signed commits.

Some of the requirements are met by steps that take place within the CI/CD pipeline. We can provide versioned, reusable pipeline code (including complete starter kits) that developers can easily include in their pipelines to perform the necessary steps.

At the end, using our point-of-change compliance strategy, we can add verification steps to our control plane that confirm these requirements before code is deployed. This could be limited to requiring all images to be signed, to be pulled from a trusted registry, and to include SBOMs. Or, if our risk profile requires it, we could further validate the results of the nightly security configuration tests of all artifact stores to confirm integration requirements are still in force.

Let us now look at two exercises back-to-back that will solidify your understanding of this space.

Exercise 4.2 Create a bash script that signs a Docker image and then verifies the results

Cosign is an excellent option for signing images in a pipeline. Generate a signing key using Cosign and then create a script that could be used to sign an image and validate the signature. Cosign works with any Docker Trusted Registry-compatible image store.

Note: You can learn about software supply chain security in greater detail by learning more about the projects within Sigstore and the OpenSSF.

Exercise 4.3 Create an admission controller policy to allow only images from our registry and organization

Let's try another admission policy. In the earlier example, the input data from the deployment shows that we are using the GitHub container registry. Create a Rego policy that only allows deployments from our organization (ghcr.io/epetech).

4.3.2 Zero-trust networking

Zero-trust networking is a security assessment strategy that says, "We don't trust systems just because they are running on our network." There are several ways to tackle this architecture, and it is an excellent approach with much business value. One of the most effective ways to frame the implementation strategy is to exclude network security configuration from our threat assessment. This is not to say that we build insecure networks, but rather every system we connect to our network, large or small, is assessed and maintained as secure, without including any analysis of our network in the assessment or testing. Any system could, if desired, be confidently connected to the public internet from a security perspective. This means that whatever forms of security we apply to a system to make it secure, none should rely on purely network settings for security, regardless of whether those settings exist. One of the most significant business value effects of this is that it is far easier to decide to make internal services available externally when those services are already implemented to be secure on insecure networks. This strategy also provides greater flexibility in creating network designs intended for scaling.

Let's imagine a situation at Epetech where we have implemented a zero-trust network architecture. Even though most of our Epetech APIs are intended to be available to our customers and third-party developers, we have some APIs that should never be accessed from outside our environment. Our chief information security officer is concerned about accidental exposure. Only requests coming directly from other Epetech services should be to talk to those APIs.

There are several ways our engineering platform team can approach this. We could start at the network layer 3/4 level and create explicit network rules or define firewall or load balancer rules about allowed IP ranges. At this same layer, we could move over to the container network interface (CNI) and create network rules within the pod IP network that the CNI creates. But what would this mean for zero-trust network architecture? If we do this, then we are using our network to create a security posture around these APIs. In companies adopting zero trust, if they allow any connected system's security assessment to overlap with the general network security, then inevitably, all systems on their network must include the network in the threat assessment. Since Epetech has adopted zero trust, we should consider using network configuration to achieve this goal. However, it may have costly side effects, precluded by existing, valuable architectural decisions.

This is a layer 7 problem, and the application developers should be responsible for these kinds of authorization concerns. Historically, this approach has been quite common, and many mainframes and other monoliths have this architecture. But of course, this comes with lots of friction in a distributed service setting, as now all teams have to be more or less concerned with all the general access problems, not just those associated with their services. Indeed, we can do better than this.

Since our platform is based on a control plane, we can provide a couple of different, transparent implementations at layer 5/6. One of the most effective ways is to include a service mesh in our control plane definition. We will talk in more detail later about what a service mesh is, but in this context, we will say that, with a mesh, we could solve this access concern in at least two ways.

We could return to OPA and our previous policy-as-code example. We can use the service mesh to force all traffic to all services first to have OPA perform a policy assessment. With this approach, not only could general corporate decisions be included in the policies but our product organization in general would have the freedom to use policy-as-code to define and apply the authorization controls for all software deployed on the platform.

In the OPA-enabled context, the service mesh proxy directs the call through OPA before it ever reaches the destination. Policies can be pulled from a remote location (or can be cached and refreshed asynchronously) and have a software-defined lifecycle. If our applications use web tokens, the policy can validate the token, decode it, and use the token payload for verifying the request. The attributes of the request (in the token payload) provide information about the caller, and OPA can use this to verify whether that application is allowed to make the call.

We can do a variety of other things through a service mesh. Suppose security mandated that all external requests must be blocked, unless they are approved vendor URLs. This is simple enough:

```
meshCongif.outboundTrafficPolicy.mode = REGISTRY_ONLY
```

This setting is a simple default deny, which effectively means that unless a service is registered with our service mesh, we will block it by default.

To then add an *approved* service to our mesh, we create a ServiceEntry. We can make a simple ServiceEntry for google.com, which allows any workload to access google.com as if it were just another service in our service mesh.

You have probably noticed another growing trend: L7-aware CNIs. While cloud providers have built-in CNI support, there are also many other CNIs available, such as Calico, Cilium, and Flannel, to name a few. CNIs that enable domain name system (DNS)-based policies are typically extended Berkeley Packet Filter (eBPF)-based CNIs. These CNIs allow us to write DNS-based policies that block all requests to DNS entries, except for explicitly allowed DNS entries. Some, like Cilium, are working to provide a combination of service-mesh features with CNI. Why not use those?

We've already talked about the general zero-trust problem when using our network to create a security policy. There is also a pragmatic aspect to this. Our Kubernetes pod network does not make a strategic advantage for our business, unless our company's product is selling CNIs. We need a pod network. It is necessary, but the time and money we spend managing the pod network is time and money taken away from strategically valuable work, which is how our company will survive and grow. So if my cloud provider will give me this network basically for free, I'd better have a good reason for taking on the risk and expense of doing it myself.

By using a dedicated service mesh (and we're not saying a CNI provider might not offer mesh capabilities that can stand alone) that can be deployed to any Kubernetes cluster, we preserve our ability to change cloud vendors or equally to use additional cloud vendors for Kubernetes services without the added cost of having to self-manage our pod network.

The final thing to mention here is that Kubernetes itself is continuing to evolve in this domain. A new capability coming to Kubernetes is the AdminNetworkPolicy API. People involved in the historical development of Kubernetes network policy capabilities will tell you that this was not meant as a security policy engine or a replacement for general network security. There has been some discussion that the AdminNetworkPolicy API could become the future for Kubernetes.

Whether you are applying zero trust with layer 7 or layer 4 policies, make sure the tradeoffs are considered before doing so.

A note on network performance

It is surprising how often an organization will opt to self-manage its Kubernetes pod/service network for performance reasons without first having proven (e.g., with data) that better performance is a requirement or that their vendor's performance options aren't sufficient. The true table stakes here should be demonstrated, customer-facing performance problems that can be traced directly to the pod network itself. But when this is shown to be valuable, and you're interested in lower-level networking concepts, you may be wondering about the performance differences with IPTABLES, NFTables, and eBPF, and more importantly, how each fits within the cloud-native ecosystem.

(continued)

Generally speaking, most network interface specifications for cloud-native platforms are moving toward NFTables-based technologies as the standard. This requires significant work (cncf/k8s link) to move toward, but it is making progress.

Notably, however, eBPF-based interfaces and proxies are beginning to gain popularity. The advent of the eBPD *data plane* has reduced the number of network protocol steps a request has to take, which increases performance and reduces overall latency. That said, without significant experience in eBPF, we recommend going with the more widely used NFtables approach unless a specific need for eBPF arises (such as the layer 7 and DNS-based policies).

4.3.3   *Separating platform customer identity from cloud infrastructure identity*

We could have named this section "Implementing Customer Identity" since the challenge to be solved spans more than just our platform's customer identity in the context of the infrastructure resources the platform will provide. But the cloud infrastructure layer is usually the place where organizations outright fail to make the mental *product* connection between outcome and architecture.

WHAT IS THE CHALLENGE?

Consider the access situation facing a developer at most companies. Teams need access to a wide range of systems. At most organizations, this process is excruciating. To define our team, we need a defined identity group in the company's user identity system, such as Active Directory (Entra ID) or a similar system. This will require a ticket. Then, once we have our identity, we need to get our code repositories, Jira board, cloud file share, cloud platform namespaces, pipelines, etc. A different team often manages each of these artifacts. The IT operations team maintains the source control system, the Jira projects by the project management office, the security team owns some of the code scanners but not others, our storage team shares the files—and on and on we go.

This problem is so common and so painful (costly) that there are even industry metrics to measure it, like *developer onboarding* or *time to first production deployment*. These metrics aren't exclusively about obtaining access permissions, but the people, processes, and technology delays in obtaining necessary access make up a wildly disproportionate part of the problem. There is a large marketplace for Single-Sign-On products, and in the context of managing access across multiple SaaS developer tools, these can be very effective if implemented well. However, most organizations start seriously underfunding their integration automation and vastly underestimating the cumulative cost effects from doing so. But at least in the case of integrating a SaaS tool, most companies are framing the idea well:

> *We have all these products, and they each have their own access controls, but what we need is a central authentication and authorization service so that a person can be*

added once to the central location and then automatically have the proper access to all the products.

Correct! But what if we leave out 80% of the things a developer needs access to because we either identified the product incorrectly or ignored it altogether? Here is where infrastructure-oriented capabilities fail.

To be successful at delivering a self-serve, product-like experience using our engineering platform, we will need a customer-identity abstraction layer for the same reasons the SaaS tools we mentioned earlier need it. If GitHub had to directly map all of its users' authentication and authorization identifiers in a one-to-one implementation with all of the underlying infrastructure components (servers, storage, etc), imagine how inflexible their solution options would be. It is doubtful they could have ever arrived at the experience provided today. As builders of an engineering platform *product*, we will need that same level of flexibility. So much of what we do as platform engineers will be integrating systems—far more than in most other kinds of product development. The following architectural decisions can make us more successful and more likely to maintain this success as the platform continuously changes.

MAKING THE DEVELOPMENT TEAM THE CENTRAL AUTHORIZATION ROLE

Although it is individuals who authenticate, the principal authorization model should be built around the team. Domain-bounded teams are a topology that goes hand in hand with successful and sustained distributed service architectures. It requires discipline to maintain this structure over time, as there will constantly be temptations to compromise in minor ways. Enough of those compromises, and the structure will cease to deliver value. Anything we can do to make it easier to maintain should be considered. Making the default authorization model based on the team member will pay long-term dividends.

When a developer is added to a team, they should automatically have access to all platform and developer resources of that team with the necessary access control and governance around it.

USING A DEDICATED IDENTITY PROVIDER SOLUTION

As we said earlier, one of the main platform engineering activities is integrating systems. We need a mature, stand-alone identity provider (IDP) capability—one that will exclusively act as a kind of intermediary, with the source of authentication and authorization coming from other systems. We suggest using a qualified SaaS solution. Later in the book, we will go into more detail about the value and opportunity cost of SaaS.

As shown in figure 4.8, the IDP should act as the intermediary between authentication and authorization rather than serving as the sole source of truth. This allows the platform to use external systems of record while still customizing the results from the authorization service to fit organizational needs.

What will be the source of the authorization data? That will depend on how we implement the self-managed team membership experience. Companies that use Entra ID (Azure AD) as their source of truth for authentication might set up Entra ID to provide

The single source-of-truth for individual identity
(perhaps Azure Active Directory or Google
Cloud Identity)

For an engineering platform this is usually based on
team membership. What is the source of this information
and how do teams self-manage membership?

Authentication

Authorization

Are you who you say
you are?

Are you allowed to
take this action?

IDP

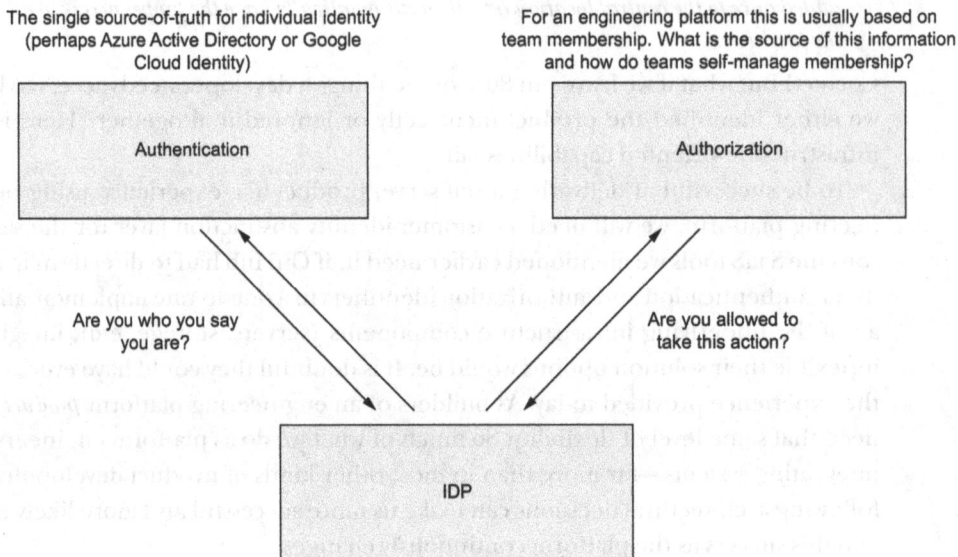

Figure 4.8   We want the IDP to be the go-between rather than the source of truth, and we will need to be able to customize the results from the authorization service.

a self-managed solution. Integrating GitHub and enabling self-serve team management is a fairly standard approach, and we will do this in a subsequent exercise to demonstrate. But there are many ways this can be done. Companies should consider having additional types of permission boundaries besides team membership.

Regardless of how team membership and other user attributes are stored, our IDP will need to allow us to include this information with the returned identity data. This will likely be a JSON web token, and we will need the token to include the user's claims.

CONVERGE AROUND A COMMON STANDARD SUCH AS OPENID CONNECT

Choose a broadly used standard and implement it wherever possible. This won't be possible 100% of the time, and that should be expected. But don't deviate from the standard casually. Avoid adopting development or operational systems that don't support automated integration. Watch out for stakeholder effects here. Sometimes a stakeholder, like security or governance, will find a tool that helps them do their job that has a developer use aspect to it, but cannot be integrated into an automated authorization configuration. Users are required to open tickets and have a human add them to the system and set up their role. This breaks the product experience requirements of our platform, and this threshold is actually pretty low. If we're willing to leave friction and waste in our process for convenience in a case like this, then we will repeat this decision in many other places.

OpenID Connect (OIDC)

At the heart of the OIDC functionality, we need the ability to configure the authorization server from our IDP. We need to be able to configure the authorization server to interact with our source of authorization data and include those authorization claims in the information returned from a successful user login.

To make effective use of an IDP within our platform, it's essential to understand the core concepts that underpin OIDC and how authentication, authorization, and token issuance work together to securely manage access as described here:

Entity—An entity is any distinct user or system interacting with the platform. It could be an individual user, an application, or a service.

Identity—An identity is a collection of attributes uniquely identifying an entity within a particular context. For instance, a user's identity might include their username, email address, and other attributes specific to the platform.

Authentication—Authentication is the process of verifying an entity's identity. Our IDP must be able to integrate without a source of truth for individual identity to confirm that the entity is who it claims to be. This step usually involves username/password verification, multifactor authentication, or biometric checks.

Authorization—Authorization determines what an authenticated entity can do within the platform. While some situations will require authorization checks at the time of use, there are many others where we expect the entity's principal permissions (claims) to be included in the tokens issued by the authorization server.

Token issuance—While many types of single sign-on (SSO) IDP integrations are among the included features of IDP plugins, we will also create custom services that will require the same authentication and authorization controls. We also need our IDP to support workflows that return tokens that can be verified and contain the claims provided by the authorization server. These claims provide the necessary context for making authorization decisions based on the entity's identity and role within the platform, which provides a great deal of flexibility for custom services and integrations.

CONTROL PLANE ACCESS IS INTEGRATED WITH THE IDP

The developer (user) control plane access will be through this same IDP resource. We need the permission policies within the cluster to be based on the team *claims*. Kubernetes directly supports this, and cloud providers typically also integrate their own custom IDP capabilities, so there are multiple ways this might be achieved. We will demonstrate one method in the exercises in chapter 7.

INFRASTRUCTURE PROVIDED BY THE ENGINEERING PLATFORM IS PROVISIONED AND MAINTAINED ON BEHALF OF THE USER

An engineering platform is not a simple wrapper for all of our vendors' cloud infrastructure capabilities. However, we still want to provide the standard technologies that most development teams use within the direct platform-managed capabilities. When we do this, it will be more manageable (and secure) and more sustainable for our implementation to be based on automation that does this for users on their behalf and does not simply grant the users permission within the cloud infrastructure provider's IAM system for users to provision and maintain themselves directly.

BUILD YOUR OWN PLATFORM INTEGRATION ORCHESTRATOR

Here we come full circle: back to the fundamental problem we called out at the start of this section. We've made these architectural decisions about the capabilities we need to manage our platform users' identity, but how do we use this to make sure that when a new team joins the platform, everyone on the team has access to everything? How do we make sure that when a new team joins the platform, there are the correct team resources in the control plane? (e.g., standard team namespaces and resource allocations, etc.) Even if we automate setting some permissions in a service that developers use, many of these are managed by other teams and have different sorts of users, which means settings I make today might get changed tomorrow; how do I manage that? What if we use a SaaS tool in which our IDP SSO feature has authentication support but not authorization?

You will face every one of those situations and probably a few more. This is why we will need to build our own integration orchestration API. The function of this API is straightforward: what does it mean for a team to be enabled on the engineering platform? See figure 4.9.

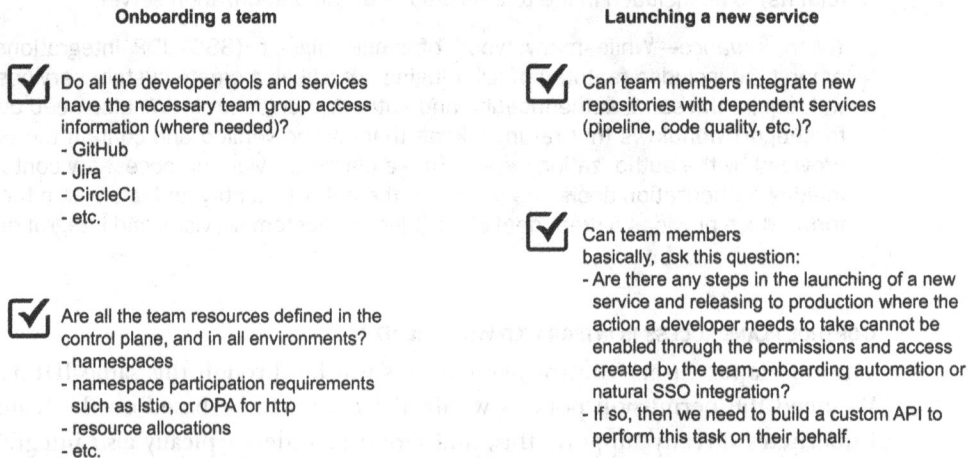

Onboarding a team	Launching a new service
☑ Do all the developer tools and services have the necessary team group access information (where needed)? - GitHub - Jira - CircleCI - etc.	☑ Can team members integrate new repositories with dependent services (pipeline, code quality, etc.)?
☑ Are all the team resources defined in the control plane, and in all environments? - namespaces - namespace participation requirements such as Istio, or OPA for http - resource allocations - etc.	☑ Can team members basically, ask this question: - Are there any steps in the launching of a new service and releasing to production where the action a developer needs to take cannot be enabled through the permissions and access created by the team-onboarding automation or natural SSO integration? - If so, then we need to build a custom API to perform this task on their behalf.

Figure 4.9   The result is something that is already happening. The problem is that developers are generally left on their own to figure out what these things are and then follow a manual process to obtain the result.

In practice, the technical aspects of this are much more straightforward than the internal organizational challenges of enabling the platform team to have the access they need to make it a reality.

We could make the engineering platform team the administrative owner of all the developer tools. But that isn't likely to be the correct answer. Many of the affected systems will have users and use cases in places outside the engineering platform that still need to be served. We can achieve this without removing control of these systems from the teams we mentioned earlier. The security team can still have administrative rights to CI systems, the project management office can maintain Jira, and the IT operations team can still manage GitHub. We *must* provide the platform engineers the API access they need to automate an outcome like the one in figure 4.10 for our organization.

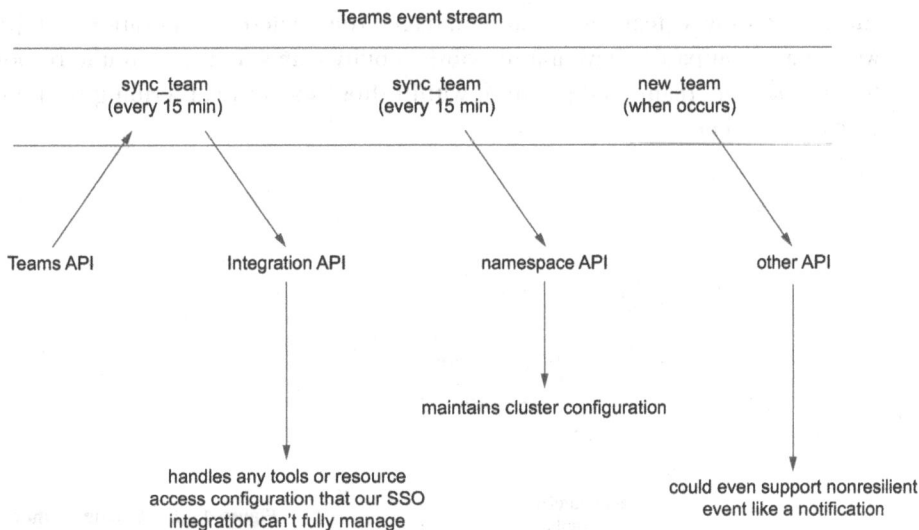

Teams event stream

sync_team
(every 15 min)

sync_team
(every 15 min)

new_team
(when occurs)

Teams API

Integration API

namespace API

other API

maintains cluster configuration

handles any tools or resource
access configuration that our SSO
integration can't fully manage

could even support nonresilient
event like a notification

Figure 4.10 Our integration orchestrator will be the authoritative source for teams that have onboarded to the engineering platform. By adopting an event-driven architecture in which each of the specific integration or configuration resources responds to, we make it easy to shift and scale the responsible teams as well.

Authorized users call the Teams API to onboard or modify Team information. The Teams API produces various events to which other orchestrator API respond. When the Teams API generates a sync-team-blue event, the integration API can fetch any details about the team it needs and then go out and idempotently run a configuration for any other integrated tool or resource that our standard SSO integration doesn't handle exactly as required. For instance, what if we were using Terraform Cloud but only the authentication piece was supported by our SSO tool? The integrations API would create and maintain the team configuration through the Terraform Cloud API.

Likewise, we could have a namespace API that, with each sync event, made sure the correct team namespaces exist in nonproduction and production clusters, with the proper resource allocations and Istio annotations, and so on. Generally, all need to be resilient configurations. This means the API will continuously check and, if needed, reset the actual configuration to match the desired configuration as defined by policy or the team information. But we can also populate the event stream with other kinds of events, so different parts of the organization can subscribe to other events of interest.

The engineering platform product team is responsible for all of this configuration. They could choose to put all these API resources into a single deployed service. But by adopting this event-driven architecture, we've made it easy to move any of these responsibilities to other teams, whether they are teams within the platform product domain or outside. For example, if the Project Management Department were responsible for the Jira configuration and they had the resources, they could create an integration API that subscribed to sync_team events and managed the related configuration with Jira. Likewise, many companies have mature observability teams that can assume responsibility for the needed Team configuration within those tools by subscribing to these events (see figure 4.11).

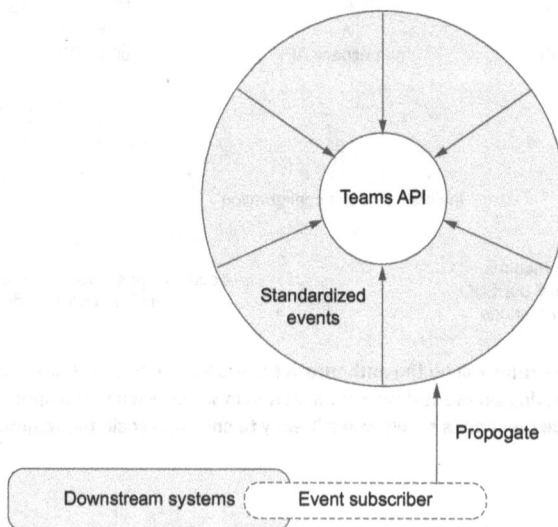

Figure 4.11   As long as there is a single, primary platform integration orchestrator modeled around the primary customer persona (the team) that maintains and populates this standard event stream, it is easy for these integration activities to evolve with our platform.

Exercise 4.4   Write a claims-based user authorization policy

We are implementing this architecture at Epetech. Imagine that we are at the point of building our Teams API authorization policy. When someone accesses the Teams API to create a new team (onboarding), we will need a policy that ensures only authorized users can create teams.

Let's also suppose that we are going to use the GitHub teams capability so that we provide users with a self-serve experience in managing their team memberships.

When a user wants to access the control plane or one of the custom platform APIs, they log in through our IDP and receive a JSON Web Token (JWT) that includes the GitHub teams in the Epetech organization to which they belong. Anyone on the Managers team is authorized to onboard a team using the Teams API.

Create a Rego policy that will verify the JWT has been signed by and permit someone calling POST v1/platforms/teams who is in the Managers GitHub team.

To tackle this exercise, use what you have learned about Rego already. Think about how you might apply this policy in the real world; what identity systems might you use to authenticate your users? What authorization servers work with your identity system? For an added challenge, test your policy with real tokens; you can generate them at https://jwt.io, which is an open, industry-standard way of developing secure web tokens.

Summary

- Governance, compliance, security, and audit must be integrated into both the platform and development processes.
- Overcontrolling approaches to governance and compliance lead to inferior results.
- We can create effective governance and compliance while still letting developers be responsible for the things that make them effective and better at their jobs.
- Compliance at the point-of-change decouples compliance work from its verification, enabling self-service deployments while maintaining security standards.
- A service that can validate or even change code right before the moment it is deployed is called an *admission controller.*
- The Kubernetes API includes support for admission controllers that can be used to enforce compliance at the deployment environment boundary.
- An admission controller enables governance, compliance, or security requirements to be verified before code is deployed without the need to control the development process itself.
- With so many different stakeholder disciplines making up governance requirements, it is effective to use a standard policy language to describe requirements.
- OPA and the Rego policy language offer a widely used and broadly applicable example of a common policy-as-code implementation strategy.
- Rego and OPA are designed to enable ingesting data from any source to make policy decisions.
- An engineering platform can reduce the complexity involved in implementing modern trust architectures.
- A built-in policy-as-code capability in a platform can be used to create enforcement gates for most trust concerns.

- Using a standardized control plane in a platform provides a mechanism for making zero-trust network controls portable.
- Trust around the platform user identity can be architected to create flexibility.
- Distinguishing between platform customer identity and the default cloud infrastructure identity system helps manage access and responsibilities efficiently.
- User access to infrastructure is through the control plane, and access to the control plane goes through the dedicated platform user identity data provider solution.
- Infrastructure available through the platform is provisioned by the platform on the development team's behalf rather than merely granting the team permissions to do it themselves.
- Decoupling customer identity from infrastructure is essential for managing access without overwhelming central teams.
- One of the first and central features of an engineering platform is in fully automating the development team (and individual developer) onboarding experience.
- SSO features in IDP solutions, when implemented well, are an essential part of creating the onboarding experience.
- To effectively maintain platform customer access automation, we need to build our own integration orchestrator API(s) to deal with the integration details not managed by our SSO service.
- Building the integration API around an event stream makes the solution much easier to adopt throughout the enterprise.

Evolutionary observability

This chapter covers

- Why observability is critical for both a platform and its users
- Providing observability as a service to platform users
- Understanding how observability platforms work and when they are needed
- Using service level objectives to gain user confidence

Imagine that work on the platform starts at Epetech with a backlog of stories, and things are going well. Prioritization of stories is leading to a steady stream of delivery, and with the observability-driven development practices that have been evangelized across the team, plenty of telemetry data can be used to diagnose and uncover problems. More importantly, the business has a great idea of the value that platform efforts are returning right from the start. Across the engineering department, we are improving observability and seeing the benefits! Beyond quickly diagnosing

117

and troubleshooting problems, leaders at the organization are starting to see that data can be correlated across applications and services to show how systems are performing across a whole portfolio, and they want to know more. They want to be able to quickly and easily define new queries that can be used to spot trends for areas that are succeeding and those that are failing.

The easiest way to do this quickly is by using spreadsheets. *Shadow IT* practices start popping up all over the organization as business leaders, finance, and even operations maintain their spreadsheets that are ingesting data into tables and charts. Teams are getting complaints that every time a data structure is modified, someone's spreadsheet breaks, and they need time from the developers to understand why and how to fix it. The more spreadsheets that are built, the more these support complaints grow with every release, because everyone has their own version. Leaders have come to rely on these spreadsheets, so it's always a high priority. Development starts to slow down because of the number of people who need to understand the changes. This is precisely the problem the platform and observability-driven design practices were supposed to solve. Is it becoming a victim of its success?

5.1 *Why observability matters*

As we have seen, good observability practices can increase the stability of a system by allowing the team supporting it to become aware of, diagnose, and fix problems quickly. It is also a powerful way to show value, proving to business stakeholders that investment in an engineering team can return value, whether customer-facing or not. This is because *data* can trump *opinions* on what is going well and what is not. True observability is more than just data and telemetry; it provides *insights*. Let's get specific about what we mean when we say *observability* in a platform product context.

> **DEFINITION** Observability is determining and explaining a software system's internal state and usefulness by gaining insight from its output data.

Observability

To understand why observability matters, let us look at 10 key principles in the context of Epetech.

Observability is foundational to modern software delivery. When a new feature you added to your commerce product at Epetech causes increased latency during checkouts, the team should be able to roll back before letting your customers be affected by it.

Increased visibility will lead to increased developer autonomy. Developers building the product features should be able to use observability as part of their design and development process to identify the root cause of the problem.

Observability makes the data a product in itself. If Epetech's finance team is requesting a monthly report on infrastructure costs per application, observability dashboards can automatically point them to those dashboards built on a Grafana/Prometheus stack instead of having to make developers pull this data together.

Shared data between development and business brings better outcomes. When the development team claims through data that the build times improved by 40% compared to historical trends, which has helped the company respond to customer problems faster, trust between the two teams builds.

Observability helps keep shadow IT out. Before the self-serve dashboard at Epetech, the marketing team, business operations, site reliability engineering (SRE), and stream-aligned teams all had their dashboards, which required them to invest their valuable time building different views of the same data, creating more confusion.

Observability helps avoid telemetry debt. When your baseline and measurement methods are nonstandardized, you are hurting not only the collaboration with the teams but also how your customers and markets perceive you. This is avoided by using a standardized observability dashboard.

Observability fosters sustainable platform evolution. When Epetch introduced a Kubernetes-based control plane, they used telemetry to monitor the adoption. It became easier for them to understand the adoption challenges and focus on fixing them.

Observability increases operational transparency. During major outages, Epetech leadership didn't have to ask the uncomfortable questions, leading to inevitable cultural breakdown of finger-pointing. The dashboards provided them with the answers to the questions to take a healthy approach to fixing them.

Observability is an evolution. Just like the rest of the components of an engineering platform, observability is also an evolutionary paradigm where the value can be realized from day 1, constantly increasing as the platform matures.

Observability is a feedback loop. At first, Epetech, like many organizations, looked at observability as a dashboard (after the fact), as opposed to a feedback loop that helped them improve customer value, which changed as the platform thinking evolved.

5.1.1 *Observability is more than metrics and alerts*

To gain quality insight from the observability data from any software system, we need more than just the default metrics coming from the infrastructure and apps. Most people are familiar with metrics and logs. We need to make sure that every tool or technology we integrate into our platform can support the extraction of the necessary metrics and logs. Beyond that, we want to collect traces. To use this data effectively, it helps to have a shared definition of what each type means and how they work together. Figure 5.1 shows how these three core parts of observability connect and support each other.

METRICS

Metrics are the point-in-time telemetry points typically aggregated over time and produced in high volume. When diagnosing a problem, the metrics will tell you *what* happened. This can be very useful for generating alerts if an unexpected event happens, such as an overloaded server or exceeding capacity. Common examples include

- CPU and memory usage
- HTTP errors
- Disk capacity

LOGS

Once you know about an event, you'll likely need to find out *how* the system got into that state. This is where logs become helpful. Logs are discrete events that happen as a process is executed and can be queried individually or as a set over time, and while aggregating logs into a single location is quite valuable, summaries or time-series style analysis typically are not. This means that combining

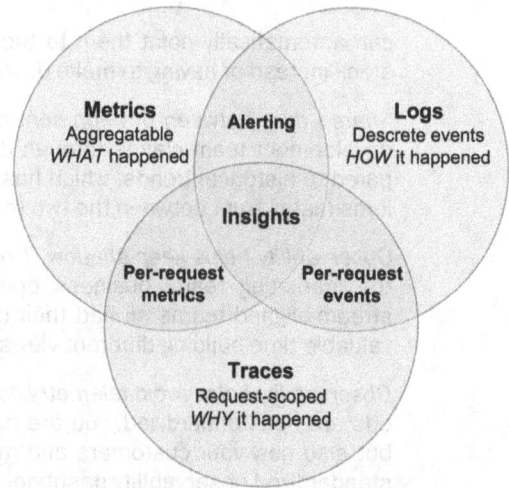

Figure 5.1 Components of observability go beyond metrics to include logs and traces. These can be used to show what is happening in the system, why it happened, and how it got into its current state. Metrics and logs are typically used to trigger alerts, but correlating all three types can result in powerful insights into the system state.

the logs from multiple events in a summarized form is not as useful as just looking at the detailed logs themselves. Data in logs can also be used for alerting when combined with metrics. Some examples include

- A function was entered or completed.
- A request was sent to an external API, and a result was received.
- The firewall blocked a network packet because of the source IP address.

TRACES

Knowing how a system got into a particular state is sometimes enough. Still, in modern systems, processes will usually cross multiple boundaries of applications and APIs as they are executed. When something happens there, we often need to know why an event occurred, and traces can help. Traces are events scoped to an individual request across multiple processes, and a correlation ID is used to join trace information across systems. An example trace could be

Request received by the web server -> authentication token verified -> request made to API -> event sent to message bus -> etc.

INSIGHTS

To get meaningful insights from a system, we need to connect all three types of telemetry data—metrics, logs, and traces. Consider this example: you get an alert saying multiple users have been seeing HTTP errors during checkout for the past 20 minutes.

Since you're responsible for that feature, you jump in to investigate. First, you check the logs for that time period and spot that the checkout service received an invalid response from the tax calculation system. That's a clue but not the whole picture. So you grab the correlation ID from one of those failing requests and use it to trace the full request path. That trace shows that, six functions deep in the tax service call stack, something ran out of memory because the node it was running on didn't scale up as expected. Adjusting the scaling configuration of that node pool and then playing back a similar load test prevented the problem from occurring again—the tax service itself did not need to be changed, just the scaling performance. Without being able to tie together logs, traces, and metrics, you could've spent hours chasing the wrong problem—only to find out it was an infrastructure problem all along.

5.1.2 Use cases for observability beyond basic monitoring of applications

As an engineer, it's easy to get stuck thinking about observability just in terms of maintaining the operational health of infrastructure or applications. However, we should also recognize that this data and the insights it can produce are helpful to many stakeholders across the business.

Let's now look at how we could expand this focus in the context of our imaginary company Epetech. Our initial focus, like many of the other organizations we know, was singularly on application performance. This helped our engineering teams troubleshoot the application problems, but pretty soon we realized this wasn't enough. The customer complaints continued, and the executive leadership was baffled to see that the much vaunted observability approach did not yield the results they were looking for—customer satisfaction with their products. After a deeper dive, the team recognized some critical gaps in our approach. We found the following problems:

- Third-party tools used across the development and delivery ecosystem are not adequately monitored.
- There is overnight processing of operational tasks that run as scheduled tasks. These tasks can fail, and the consequences significantly affect the customer's experiences.
- There is a silly problem of some disks filling up on two of the production servers, which the monitoring always caught after the fact, creating an annoying customer experience.
- The cybersecurity team has an entirely different process that is not integrated into the central observability framework, where the release management and senior leadership would hear about the security breaches. This is starting to have a reputation and credibility effects on the senior leadership.
- Conversion rates from first-time users to repeat users were dropping significantly. However, conversion data is two weeks old by the time it is made available, by which time we've lost half the battle.

- By standard practice, the CFO receives cloud usage reports every month and 30 days after the close of the monthly period. There are routinely significant overruns, but the data is so old that it isn't clear what can be done about it.
- As Epetech is expanding to a European region, obtaining specific feedback on how GDPR privacy is reported daily and ensuring compliance with this is becoming a critical requirement for which there is no automated mechanism.

One of the common anti-patterns we have seen in the industry is the singular focus on application observability. This is a significant reason why the end-user experience is often not great. Instead, we recommend looking at observability through eight distinct but related lenses to ensure a better outcome.

This list gives seven examples of the eight lenses shown in figure 5.2. Suppose you confine your observability efforts to just the applications and the infrastructure on which the applications run. In that case, you will miss the big-picture view of your eventual goal: an ideal customer experience while running your systems in the most cost-optimal manner.

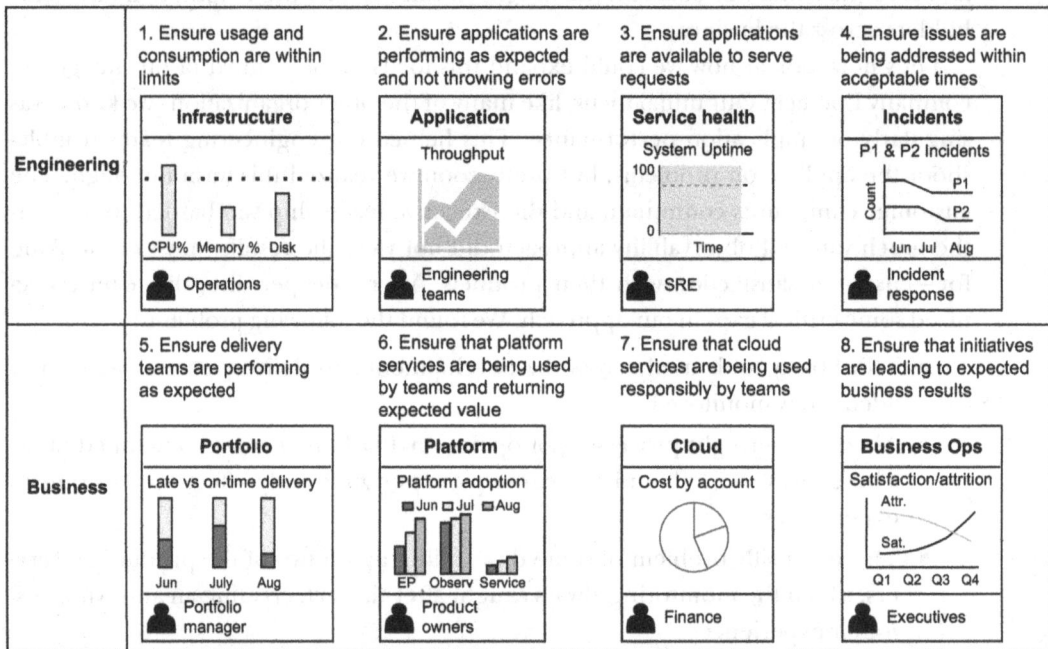

Figure 5.2   Observability data can be described across multiple engineering and business operations facets. Users and use cases are more than developers and operations personnel responsible for running the system. Stakeholders, security, and governance also have questions that the data can answer.

Observability can be broken down into these eight key areas, and understanding each one helps us figure out what kind of telemetry we should be collecting. Once we've got that data, we can slice and dice it across those areas to uncover insights that guide both engineering decisions and business strategy. Here are some examples of how engineering and business stakeholders can use each aspect of observability; you can likely think of many more:

- *Infrastructure*—Telemetry on the hardware (physical or virtual) that runs the systems can generate insights such as usage, consumption, and failures. It is typically used by operations and DevOps personnel but is also helpful to system architects to ensure right-sizing.
- *Application*—Telemetry on running applications. Engineering teams can use this to ensure the health of software systems and diagnose problems. Still, it is also valuable for product managers to determine whether new features are being used as expected or if a feature should be prioritized to enhance the user experience.
- *Service health*—Data that indicates whether a service (which may consist of many applications and infrastructure resources) is running well. Platform or SRE teams typically use it to optimize runtimes and ensure stability. Product owners can also use it to prioritize stability problems on a backlog over new feature development.
- *Incidents*—Data from ticketing systems or incident response workflows. Incident response usually uses incidents to measure team effectiveness. Engineering leaders can also use incidents to evaluate the success of a platform's capabilities designed to decrease incident response times.
- *Portfolio*—Data to measure the effectiveness of portfolio delivery across an engineering function. This could include telemetry around deployment frequency, on-time feature delivery, or user story cycle times aggregated across teams. Team leads use this data to monitor effectiveness, and managers use it to identify bottlenecks and cross-team dependencies to inform team structure decisions.
- *Platform*—Data indicating the platform's usage and health. This could include team adoption rates or how often platform services are used. Product managers use it to determine backlog priorities, and the business can also use it to value the return on investment (ROI) of a platform initiative.
- *Cloud*—Data on cloud usage and cost. Architects use it to meet runtime cost targets, and finance departments can also use it to calculate ROI on cloud costs across teams and environments.
- *Business operations*—Data on systems that indicate business value. Used by product owners to ensure that newly released features return expected ROI and also used by leaders to monitor the health of the business.

5.1.3 What does good look like?

As we start putting this kind of data together at Epetech, how do we prioritize which data to observe and why? This section will discuss a simple technique to look at the three potential data states and how these states can inform our decision on actions to take.

Data by itself has no meaning. If you were told that CPU usage on a critical server runs at 75%, is that good or bad? It is impossible to know the answer to that question without *context*, meaning we need to understand what that server is doing and what we expect the meaningful load to be. If we have a Kubernetes-based platform, we may want to take advantage of scheduling to ensure each node runs at a high capacity to maximize the value of our infrastructure investment. In this case, it would be okay if the CPU was at or even above 90%, as long as additional nodes become available as the system exceeds 95%. In another case, we may have a workload that experiences regular bursts of high activity, and we need to ensure that, on average, the CPU is below 60%. In other words, we need to know more than whether a system is healthy and running; we need to understand what it means to *run well* and *as expected*. Figure 5.3 shows three categories of operating states that help us determine whether the system has all the necessary signals to operate efficiently and correctly.

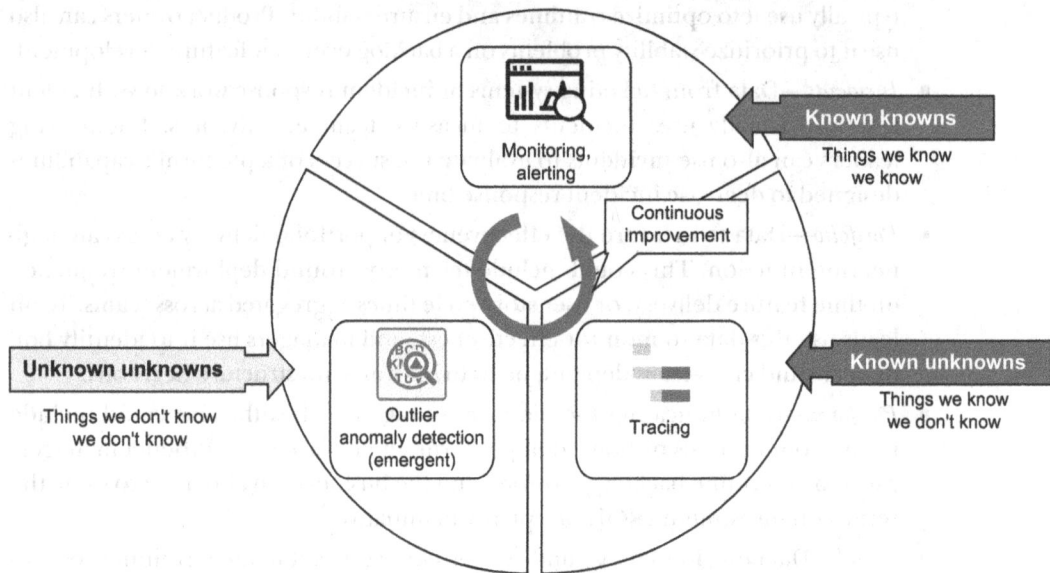

Figure 5.3   Knowing what to look for when querying observability data is an evolving process.

Executive leaders in a company think the achievable minimum requirement is setting monitors for exactly the healthy state and being alerted when something goes wrong. The reality is different. There will be some metrics we know our system should generate when healthy. We can build tracing data output into code to accelerate understanding when problems still occur. But we need different kinds of tools if we want to anticipate the potential problems before they happen effectively.

So, when defining what good looks like for a system, these are the three states that we need to be aware of to ensure we have the correct observability data to diagnose them.

KNOWN-KNOWNS

These are the things we know can go wrong and exactly how they go wrong. In the previous case, we might understand that sustained CPU activity above 90% indicates that our Kubernetes cluster isn't scaling as expected. Based on load testing, we may also know that an API designed to automate the creation of new team projects in source control can only handle 10 requests simultaneously. For the business, we may have defined that at least six teams must adopt a new platform service in the first month of release to consider it successful. In all these cases, we can and should define telemetry, queries, and alerts to indicate when a known good state is violated. These are the situations where we can develop self-healing strategies to remedy the system state quickly.

KNOWN-UNKNOWNS

There are known healthy states that we didn't know about until they failed for the first time. Here are some examples. We understand that a Kubernetes pod can fail to be rescheduled at an expected time because of an incorrectly defined pod disruption budget. We likely know a few more similar situations where the expected pod rescheduled can fail. But we don't know every possible situation. We may see how a call to a specific API with a particular kind of malformed data will respond, but we do not know all the ways data can be unexpected or the response to such data by every API to which it may be passed. Even existing systems that are thought to be well-known can act in unknown ways. We plan for this by instrumenting our software and systems with telemetry to help observe processes as they flow from one system to the next or one state to another. In a real-time service problem event, tracing is one of the best ways for us to quickly follow the flow of information through a system and identify problems as they arise.

UNKNOWN-UNKNOWNS

If you've ever been on an operations team—or been part of a development team that owns its software in production—then you know systems can fail in ways that you never saw coming. Some outages can be hard to unravel even when we have well-instrumented systems and all of the metrics, logs, and traces right in front of us.

For many years, our only real recourse was building highly flexible dashboards. We have to overlap time-series data from multiple systems until a human investigator recognizes an anomaly that leads to the root cause. Because of this, more vendors have been including trend and outlier analysis with their standard time-series tools. There is great potential here for large language models and other current AI-oriented technologies to help us find problems that we weren't even aware of or that we could have predicted with a simpler analysis.

In all of these cases, the goal is to continuously move what can be known about our systems into the known-knowns category. The better the quality of our tracing strategy, the faster we can resolve and then prevent problems that are discoverable through tracing. The broader the scope and the higher the quality of the observability data we can feed into our *predictive* analysis engine (whatever the technology used), the more likely it is that the analysis will find a weakness if it exists.

5.1.4   *Viewing observability through a single pane of glass*

As we have seen, the true power of observability data is unlocked when different data types can be correlated, both within and across systems. Let's use Epetech as an example again. Epetech uses several different tools, like many of the organizations we have seen, across different aspects of observability (hint: the eight axes), as shown in table 5.1.

Table 5.1   Tools used by Epetech across the eight different axes of observability

Axis	Tool Used
Infrastructure	Prometheus (metrics collection) + Grafana (Dashboarding)
Application	DataDog
Service Health	Pingdom
Incident Response	PagerDuty
Portfolio	JIRA
Platform	DataDog
Cloud Costs	IBM Kubecost
Business	Tableau

Now think about the effect on productivity if different stakeholders, such as developers, SREs, business owners, and others, have to look at multiple dashboards to understand their overall ecosystem. What opportunities do we have to create a single visualizer—a single pane of glass (SPOG)? By providing an easy experience to join these available data sources in a SPOG, observability practices will give a more significant benefit faster, making it much more likely your teams will be excited to adopt observability practices. This system will allow querying, correlation, and visualization of any observability data available from a central system, regardless of user persona. This does not mean all your observability data must be stored in a central, monolithic datastore. We can provide the data using multiple methods based on the data update type, volume, and frequency.

Figure 5.4 shows a high-level solution architecture for building a SPOG. It shows the solution components, the data sources, and how to bring the data together meaningfully.

At the base of the architecture are the sources of static data, which include cloud services, applications, infrastructure components, and monitoring services. These sources generate static data like system metrics, application logs, and traces that provide insight into the system's operational state. This data is sent to the observability system API endpoints. In scenarios where specific data endpoints cannot directly send their data to the observability system due to security restrictions or network configurations, they are periodically pulled and even scrubbed, allowing data to be collected securely. This polling mechanism is illustrated with a firewall and protected data sources, indicating that the observability system is designed to handle secure and protected environments.

Real-time queries of high-volume data are issued directly to the original data sources.

Dashboards

Execute queries

Users

Static data queries are resolved via API endpoints.

Query API endpoint

Query API endpoint

Query API endpoint

Metrics

Logs

Traces

Ingested data are stored to allow for aggregated queries over time.

Ingestion API

Ingestion API

Ingestion API

Static data is emitted to the observability system via API endpoints.

Data endpoints that cannot send to the observability system directly are polled periodically and data is sent.

f_n

Cloud services   Applications

Infrastructure   Monitoring services

Sources of static data

Firewall

Protected data sources

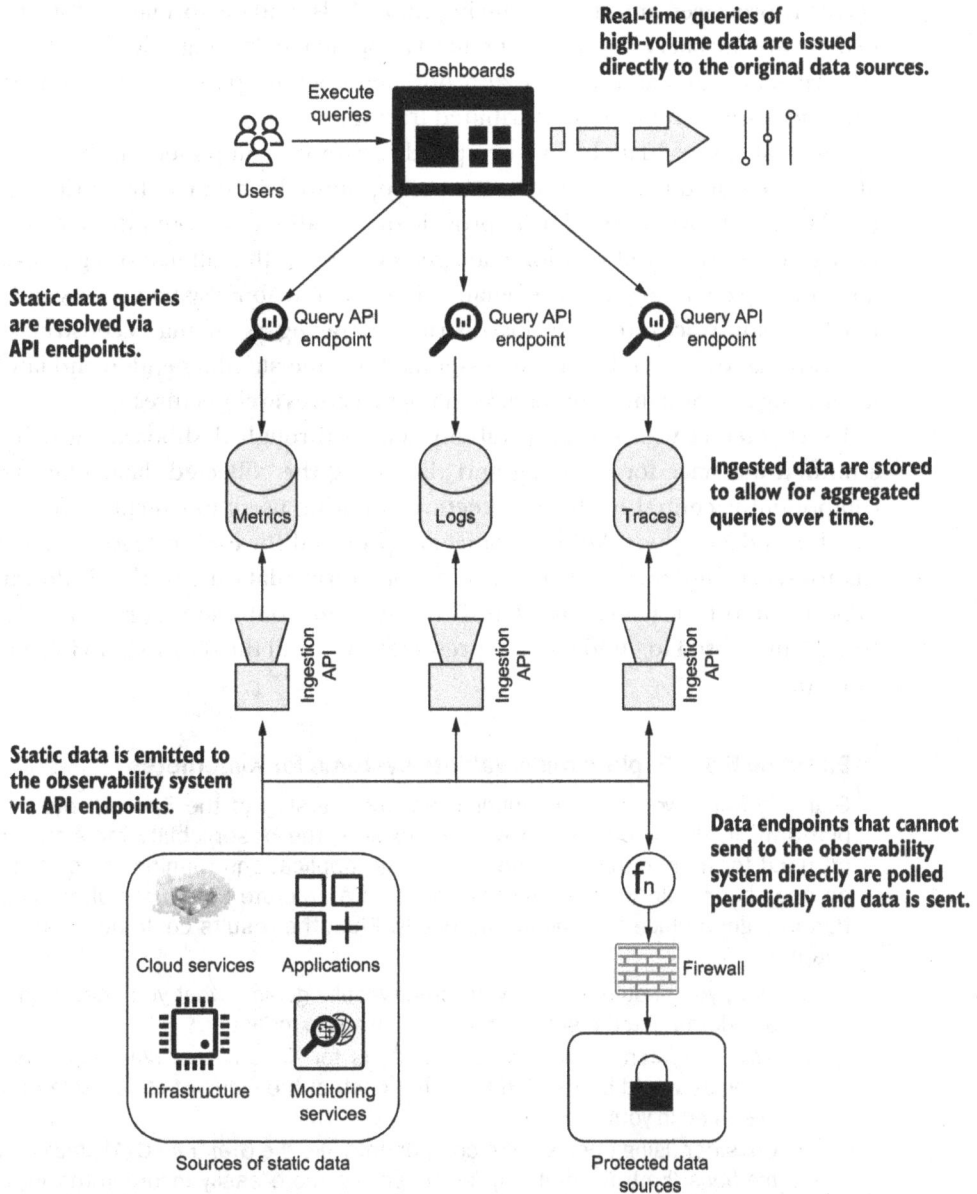

Figure 5.4 By allowing observability data to be queried across data sources in a single place, generating insights across the entire business is much easier. Users can create dashboards and alerts based on these insights, allowing them to see the business's health and individual systems.

The data sent by these sources is processed through ingestion APIs. These APIs serve as the gateways for data entering the observability system. There is a dedicated ingestion pipeline for each type of data—metrics, logs, and traces—to ensure the data is correctly processed and stored. The ingestion APIs validate, format, and store the data in their storage backends. This structured approach to data ingestion ensures that metrics are aggregated and indexed appropriately, logs are parsed and stored efficiently, and traces are correlated for distributed tracing.

Each category of data has a corresponding storage component in the architecture. Metrics are stored in a time-series database optimized for efficiently retrieving numerical data points over time. Metrics provide quantitative data about the system's performance. Logs are stored in a log management system that allows for aggregating and querying log data. Logs capture detailed information about system events and application behavior. Traces are stored in a distributed tracing system that reconstructs transaction flows across multiple services, essential for understanding end-to-end latency and identifying performance bottlenecks in microservices architectures.

Users interact with the observability system through dashboards, which provide a unified interface for querying and visualizing the collected data. The dashboard component is central to the architecture, allowing users to execute queries against the stored data. Query API endpoints are provided for each category for static data (metrics, logs, and traces). These APIs enable storing data and retrieval, allowing users to perform historical analysis, identify trends, and troubleshoot problems. The dashboard can be used to build visual representations of all the data to help fit a particular situation.

Exercise 5.1   Explore observability systems for Kubernetes

Going forward, we will start building an MVP version of the Epetech engineering platform. In this exercise, we want to explore the observability tools that could be used for monitoring Kubernetes and the applications running there. Naturally, an engineering platform will involve more infrastructure than just Kubernetes, but this is a good place to experiment locally. Plus, the results could be used in later chapters.

1 First, you should identify your observability goals—what you need to monitor and determine the scope of what you want to measure.
2 Next, research the widely used options for Kubernetes. What types of technologies would be needed to gather each of the kinds of observable data you identified in your goals?
3 Consider using open-source components like *the Grafana LGTM stack and Prometheus* (both for metrics), as these are more easily incorporated into later exercises.
4 Once you decide on the stack, if it is open source or offers a free trial, install it on a local Kubernetes instance. Make a list of the problems you think will need to be solved if this were part of our Epetech platform implementation.

As an optional step, take a look at how we could capture traces within Kubernetes if our applications were correctly instrumented. OpenTelemetry (https://opentelemetry .io/docs/) is a good place to start. What did you learn here that could influence a decision in the previous tasks?

5.2   *Observability as a platform service*

More companies (and vendors) are treating observability itself as a category for deploying a complete platform. This is very effective, and the best observability platforms offer robust integration capabilities, comprehensive data aggregation, and a user-friendly experience that simplifies the complexity of monitoring and troubleshooting distributed systems. Whether managed as its product or included as part of the engineering platform, there are key things to keep in mind.

5.2.1   *The end-user access experience*

Like any developer-facing technology, the platform requires an observability platform that can integrate effortlessly with the platform's existing authorization architecture. This typically involves integrating with our identity provider for single sign-on and role-based access control. End users need a frictionless experience when accessing the observability platform, using the same credentials and automatically having the correct permissions.

An essential aspect of the user experience in observability platforms is supporting platform-wide aggregation of metrics, logs, traces, and other telemetry data. Providing isolated observability per team can be tempting in complex, distributed service architectures. However, this approach carries significant risks. Isolated observability can lead to fragmented system views, where each team has visibility only into its services. This fragmentation makes understanding the overall system behavior challenging and increases the mean time to recover from problems. When incidents occur in a distributed environment, the root cause often involves multiple services interacting unexpectedly. Without a holistic view of the system, pinpointing the exact cause of a problem will be very time-consuming.

A key aspect of an effective observability platform is pulling together metrics, logs, traces, and other telemetry data across the whole system. It might seem like a good idea to give each team its isolated observability setup—especially in complex, distributed architectures—but that can create some serious problems. When each team can only see its services, it's hard to get a clear picture of how the whole system is behaving. That kind of fragmentation makes it harder to spot problems and slows down recovery when things go wrong. In distributed systems, problems often come from unexpected interactions between services, and without a complete, end-to-end view, tracking down the root cause will take a lot longer than it should.

Your users' experience is also influenced by how well the observability platform can scale to accommodate the organization's growing needs. As the platform evolves and more services are added, the observability solution must continue to provide a unified and responsive experience. As the volume of metrics, logs, and traces increases, the platform should still be able to quickly process and present this data to users in an actionable format. Slow or fragmented observability tools can frustrate users and hinder their ability to maintain system health, especially during critical incidents.

Features such as customizable dashboards, automated alerts, and intuitive querying interfaces must all be capable of being created and maintained in code, like the rest of our infrastructure. Platform accelerators should be able to fully incorporate baseline observability configuration as part of the starter kit code. Likewise, users need to be able to customize the automated management of dashboards, monitors, and alerts that manage relevant data in a way that is meaningful to them, whether it's high-level system health indicators for executives or detailed service-level metrics for engineers.

5.2.2 *Automatic collection of customer data*

Collecting telemetry data—metrics, logs, and traces—from user applications in a platform environment is a well-understood area with standard architectural patterns. Collecting telemetry data such as metrics, logs, and traces, from user applications in a platform environment follows well-established architectural patterns. As illustrated in figure 5.5, the collection system should automatically scrape metrics and logs from applications as they are deployed, while also allowing applications to publish telemetry and trace data directly to known platform endpoints. This dual approach ensures that data can be gathered both passively (through scraping) and actively (through developer-published endpoints), with all information ultimately forwarded to a centralized observability datastore.

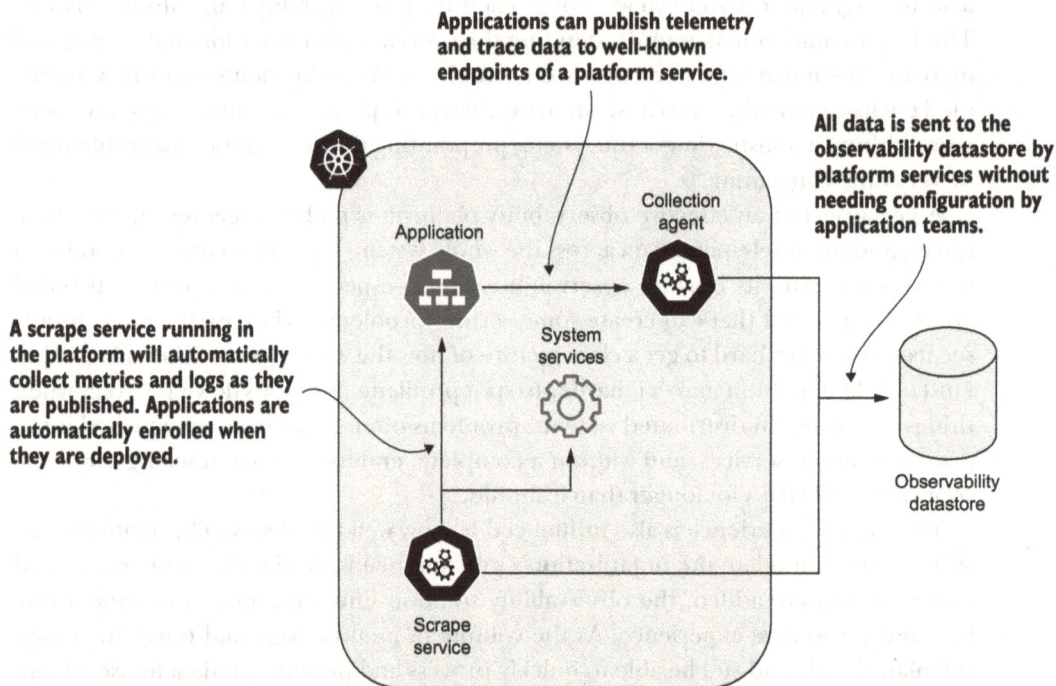

Figure 5.5   There are three primary forms of telemetry that user applications will produce and need to be ingested: metrics, logs, and traces. By collecting these automatically via well-known endpoints, your users will have a much easier onboarding experience when getting started. They will be unaffected as the backend technologies change over time.

The platform employs a collection agent and a scrape service to make this process seamless. This means that as soon as an application is deployed, it can automatically start sending its telemetry data to these endpoints without requiring additional configuration by the application teams. This immediate integration dramatically simplifies the onboarding process for new applications, reducing the friction that developers often face when setting up observability.

All collected data is then sent to a centralized observability datastore. This centralization allows the platform to aggregate, store, and analyze telemetry data in a unified way. Because the platform handles the collection and routing of telemetry data, it abstracts away the complexities for application teams. They don't need to worry about the underlying mechanisms of how their data is gathered and stored. Furthermore, if the backend technologies evolve or change over time, this setup ensures that applications remain unaffected as they interface with the same well-known endpoints.

5.2.3 *Who needs to respond when things need attention?*

Figure 5.6 illustrates a shared responsibility model that Epetech will adopt to implement and manage an observability platform. We want to set clear and well-known boundaries for who is responsible. By defining these roles, we reduce friction between regular development teams, the platform team, and external vendors, ensuring a more seamless and efficient observability experience.

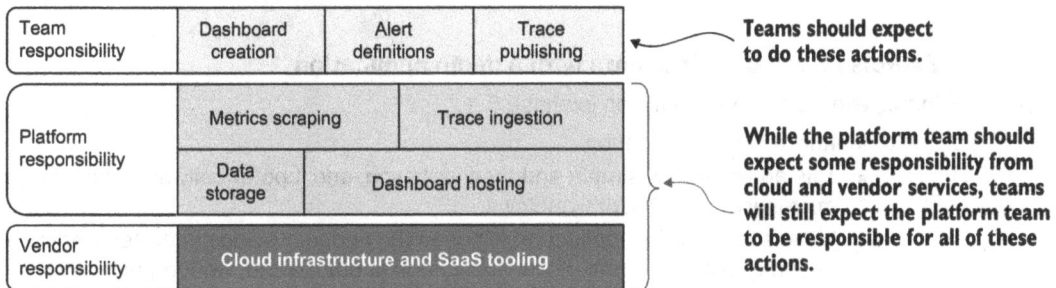

Figure 5.6 A shared responsibility model is critical to reducing friction when teams adopt any platform service.

Let us look at the layers in the shared responsibility model. While in this chapter we are talking about observability and the resulting operational health, this is also the shared responsibility model for security and governance.

At the top layer, the development team's responsibility includes tasks like dashboard creation, alert definitions, and trace publishing. This means that individual application or service teams within Epetech will be responsible for setting up the specific dashboards they need to monitor their services. They should also define alerts relevant to their operational context—such as setting thresholds for response times or error rates—and publish traces to track the flow of requests through their services. While the platform provides the tools and frameworks for observability, it is up to each team to utilize these tools effectively to gain insights into their applications. By making this a team responsibility, we ensure that the people closest to the services are configuring the monitoring and alerting, resulting in more meaningful and actionable insights.

The platform responsibility layer is where our Epetech platform engineering team comes into play. We will be responsible for managing the core aspects of the observability infrastructure, including metrics scraping, trace ingestion, data storage, and dashboard hosting. In practice, the platform team sets up and maintains the mechanisms that collect metrics and traces from various applications and services. They ensure this data is ingested into a centralized data store, which can be aggregated, queried, and analyzed. Additionally, the platform team might host and manage the observability tools, such as Grafana or Prometheus. Even if we integrate with a SaaS observability tool like Datadog, the platform team will still own the lifecycle of the integration and platform user experience. By handling these responsibilities, the platform team abstracts much of the complexity involved in gathering and storing telemetry data, allowing service teams to focus on interpreting and acting on the data rather than worrying about the mechanics of how it is collected and stored.

The bottom layer is vendor responsibility, which includes cloud infrastructure and SaaS tooling. This reflects the reliance on external vendors for foundational services such as cloud infrastructure (e.g., AWS, Azure, Google Cloud) and SaaS observability tools (e.g., Datadog, New Relic).

Exercise 5.2   Correlate data with a demo application

In this exercise, you will build on exercise 5.1.

1   Identify a demo application.
   a   This application is simple and familiar to you, and it potentially has multiple microservices, APIs, or workflows.
   b   Make sure that the application exposes the endpoints and generates traffic or some level of logging. If the application is not mature, work on extending this part.
   c   If you have access to an application that has built-in instrumentation with something like OpenTelemetry, we recommend choosing that.
2   Start your observability stack.
   a   You should pick a ready-to-run observability stack, like a combination of OpenTelemetry Collector with Prometheus and Grafana.
   b   Consider running this locally using Docker Compose, or as an alternative option, use a SaaS version.
3   Send the data from your demo application.
   a   If the application you picked already has instrumentation, configure it to send the data to the observability stack. If not, add basic Prometheus endpoints and configure Prometheus to scrape them.

    b For logs, ensure that the application writes to the console and consider using FluentBit to ship these logs.

    c Run the application to generate the necessary traffic.

4 Check and make sure that the data is showing up on the observability dashboard.

    a Open your dashboard, say Grafana, and verify Metrics, Logs, and Traces.

    b Create a basic panel in Grafana to visualize traffic or request rates.

    c Try introducing a simple error, like a database timeout or even a 404, and validate if this appears in the telemetry data.

5.3 *Observability platform as a separate internal product*

We started this discussion focusing on the observability features of our engineering platform. Most organizations will launch a simple internal observability tooling team during their early years, as the operational requirements increase as the company transitions from startup to successful growth. Companies tend to stall there, and it will be after a successful launch of an internal engineering platform that the value from a platform experience demonstrates that perhaps doing something similar with the broad category of observability can deliver significant value to all the other parts of the organization, outside developers, who rely on data for decision-making.

    Figure 5.7 shows how the approach to observability often changes over time and why investing in a centralized observability platform becomes increasingly important as the organization grows.

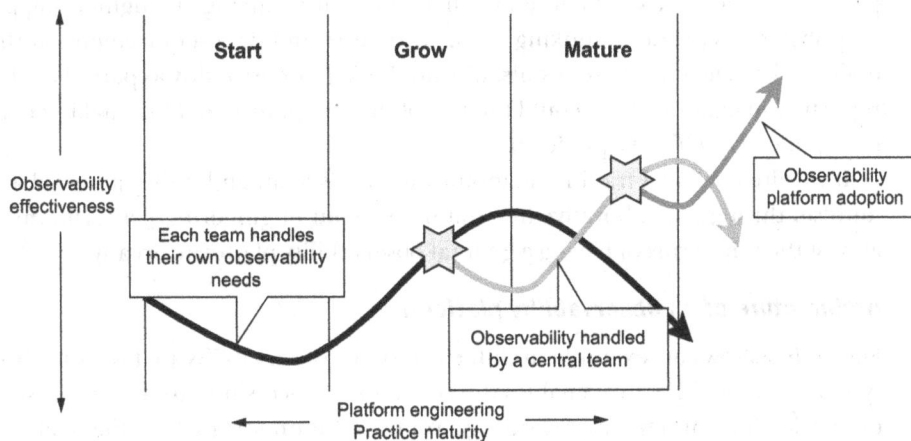

Figure 5.7 When the adoption of platform engineering services starts, there may not be a need for a fully functional observability platform distinct from the engineering platform. Over time, however, the needs of a growing number of stakeholders, teams, and systems will make investing in this a more feasible option.

In the start phase, observability is usually handled by individual teams. Each team might set up its tools and processes to monitor their specific applications or services. This approach works when the organization is small, with few teams operating independently. At this stage, you can quickly get some level of observability without much overhead. However, because each team uses different tools and methods, the overall effectiveness of observability across the entire organization may be limited. There will be gaps in visibility, and it's likely impossible to get a unified view of many systems. This fragmented approach leads to difficulties in diagnosing problems across multiple services.

As a company moves into the growth phase, these inconsistencies and difficulties lead to frequent outages. A dedicated monitoring team is created to set up Enterprise-style tooling, which all other teams are required to use, and there is a massive Project-style initiative to fix the problem. It is still the responsibility of each software or commercial off-the-shelf (COTS) team to manage integration with the new tooling.

At this point, the limitations of each team handling observability separately become apparent. The lack of a unified observability approach can lead to a longer mean time to recover during incidents because it's hard to trace problems that involve multiple services. Not all developer teams are as effective in setting up standard patterns, resulting in varying degrees of quality.

About this time, the overall pace of software development significantly declines from the early startup days, which, combined with the operational problems, leads to a DevOps initiative. The consistency this provides is fantastic, and this starts to have a real positive effect on the outage problems. But development speed, though initially there was a noticeable bump, has not taken off as expected, and engineering friction is still the most significant culprit.

At this point, the strategy changes to make self-serve and preconfigured architecture patterns the norm. Expectations are changed by introducing an engineering platform. If applying this product thinking to infrastructure and data requirements at the developer level can lead to these results, why not look at observability as part of analytics and reporting in general? How could the rest of the company benefit by making observability in general a self-serve platform?

If we already had a traditional monitoring tools team and if they adopted a product mindset through collaborative integration into our engineering platform, then we are almost there in terms of having a general observability platform already.

5.3.1   Architecture of an observability platform

Figure 5.8 shows an example architecture of an observability platform in distributed systems. This architecture enables the collection, processing, storage, and visualization of metrics, logs, and traces, providing a robust solution for tracking the health and performance of applications and infrastructure.

At the forefront of the data flow is the external data collection agent, the primary entry point for gathering metrics, logs, and traces from any external sources. Once collected, this data is forwarded to the message bus for further processing.

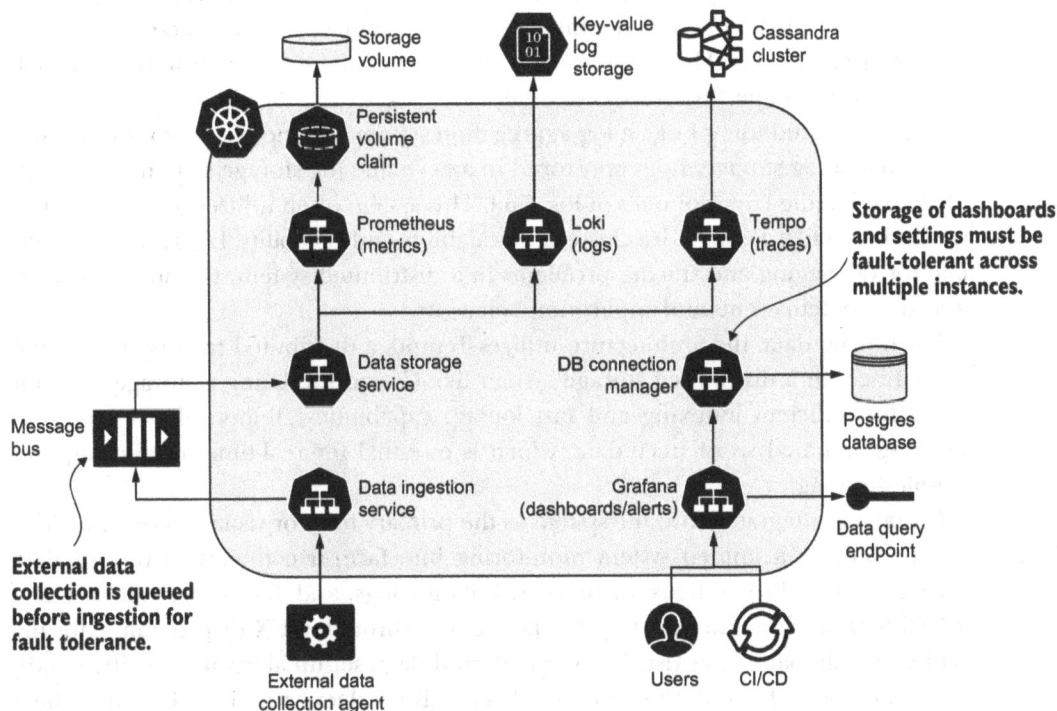

Figure 5.8 Most observability platforms, whether open source software or commercial, will use a similar high-level architecture. Specific technology components will be different depending on scale, but understanding this footprint will be important when considering build versus buy options.

The message bus acts as a buffering layer in this architecture, ensuring fault tolerance. It queues incoming data, temporarily storing it until the system is ready to process it. Effective architectures will have a specific strategy, like buffering, for preventing data loss, especially during peak times or when the downstream systems are temporarily unavailable or overwhelmed. A message bus is one way of smoothing out the data flow by decoupling the data collection from the processing components, ensuring the ingestion process is resilient and scalable.

Once data is in the message bus, the data ingestion service takes over. Its primary responsibility is to consume the queued data and format it to fit our storage and data analytics systems before storing. By separating the ingestion process from data collection, the architecture allows for greater flexibility and scalability in processing and storing data.

The next critical component is the data storage service, the conduit for routing the processed data to the appropriate storage backend. Depending on the data type—metrics, logs, or traces—the storage service directs it to the corresponding storage solution. For example, metrics data is routed to Prometheus, a time-series database for storing high-resolution metrics data. Prometheus is often paired with block storage managed via Persistent Volume Claims to ensure data persistence even across container restarts or migrations. This persistence is vital for maintaining a continuous and reliable view of system performance over time.

Logs are stored using Loki, a log aggregation system designed for high throughput and efficient log storage. Logs are stored in a key-value log storage system, which can efficiently handle large volumes of log data. This system often utilizes distributed storage backends like a Cassandra cluster for scalability and reliability. Logs are indispensable for debugging and tracing problems in a distributed system, providing detailed records of system events and application behaviors.

For tracing data, the architecture utilizes Tempo, a distributed tracing system that stores traces in a distributed storage system like Cassandra. Using a storage solution that offers efficient indexing and fast lookup capabilities, Tempo allows for rapid querying and analysis of trace data, which is essential for real-time monitoring and troubleshooting.

Grafana is integrated into the system as the primary tool for visualization and alerting. To provide a unified system monitoring interface, it connects to various data sources, such as Prometheus for metrics, Loki for logs, and Tempo for traces. Users and CI/CD pipelines interact with Grafana either through a UX or programmatically to create dashboards that visualize the collected data, set up alerts for specific conditions, and query the underlying storage backends for deeper analysis. Grafana's flexibility and extensibility make it a critical operational monitoring and decision-making component.

To support Grafana's operation, the architecture includes a DB connection manager that interfaces with a Postgres database. This database stores the configurations, dashboard settings, and alert rules Grafana uses. By using a relational database like Postgres, the architecture ensures that these configurations are stored fault-tolerantly, capable of surviving failures and scaling across multiple instances if necessary.

Finally, the architecture provides a data query endpoint. This endpoint is the access point for users and CI/CD systems to query stored data. Whether for real-time analysis, historical data review, or automated responses to certain conditions, this endpoint facilitates flexible and efficient access to the telemetry data.

Many different technologies could be substituted within this architecture. This example hopefully highlights the basic capabilities of any effective observability platform's underlying architecture.

5.3.2   *Should you build or buy?*

Buying versus building for observability technologies is no different from that of any software system. The following chapter will provide a sound methodology for foundational review. An observability platform is a platform that allows us to apply platform engineering practices in its delivery. Things like evolutionary architecture, software-defined delivery, and domain design all still apply. It will be more effective over time to select a handful of smaller technologies that each excel at meeting specific needs and interoperate well over bloated, do-it-all-for-you stacks that do a vast number of things poorly and can be architected more for vendor lock-in than flexibility (see figure 5.9).

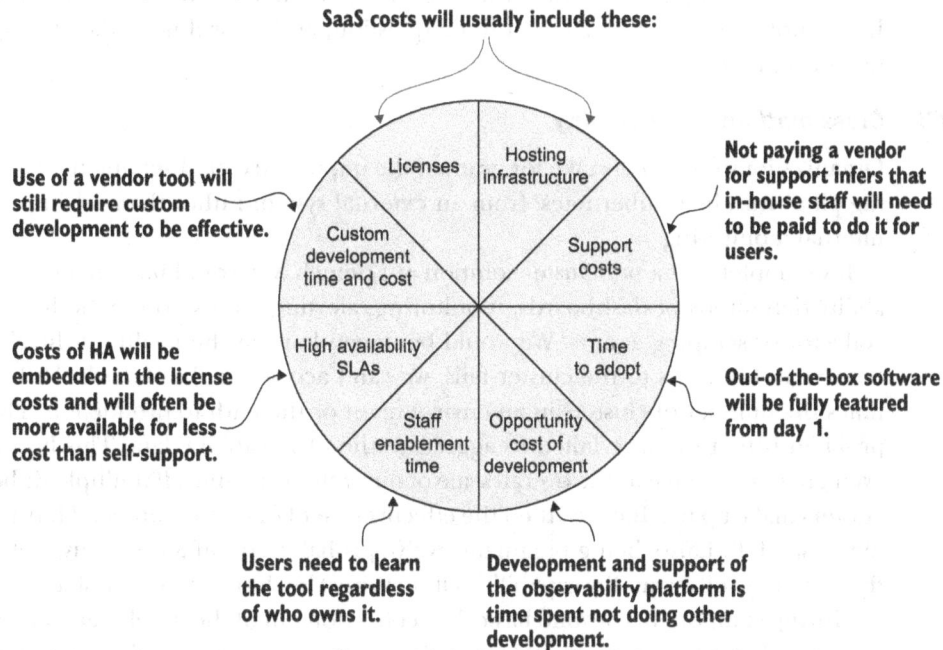

SaaS costs will usually include these:

Use of a vendor tool will still require custom development to be effective.

Licenses

Hosting infrastructure

Not paying a vendor for support infers that in-house staff will need to be paid to do it for users.

Custom development time and cost

Support costs

Costs of HA will be embedded in the license costs and will often be more available for less cost than self-support.

High availability SLAs

Time to adopt

Out-of-the-box software will be fully featured from day 1.

Staff enablement time

Opportunity cost of development

Users need to learn the tool regardless of who owns it.

Development and support of the observability platform is time spent not doing other development.

Figure 5.9 Finding the total cost of ownership of buying or building an observability platform, or any commercial software, is much more than just license costs and infrastructure hosting.

Time to value, support team sizes, and opportunity costs of what your team members are doing are all equally important when calculating the actual cost of an implementation to the organization. Don't forget that while we need an effective solution in this category, this is not going to be a strategic differentiator for practically any company. Whenever we pay our engineers to operate observability tooling, they are not spending their time on strategic work. Seriously investigate any of the assumptions or acceptance criteria put forward by both users and stakeholders alike. If someone says, "Security requires that all our logging and monitoring systems be in-house," find a courageous senior leader to ask why. If many of the largest and most rule-bound kinds of organizations, from finance to national defense, can successfully use partially or fully hosted solutions, then maybe you can too.

The decision boils down to a trade-off between cost, time, and control. Subscribing to a flexible SaaS observability platform can get Epetech up and running quickly, with support, high availability guarantees, and a wealth of prebuilt features. However, it comes with recurring costs such as subscriptions, support, and data storage fees. Building an in-house solution can lower subscription costs and provide more flexibility for data costs, but it will require a significant short-term and long-term investment in labor costs.

Adopt an evolutionary architectural approach, avoid being locked into either direction early, and experiment with real systems to get real data to drive decision-making. It may not need to be an all-or-nothing question, and we will need data to support a hybrid approach as well.

5.3.3   *Cross-platform observability*

Organizations sometimes take for granted the importance of observing their engineering platforms, like Kubernetes, from an external system rather than relying solely on internal monitoring.

If we implement a per-cluster solution at Epetech, we would have all of the observability definitions of dashboards, monitoring, alerting, and so on, in addition to the collector or scraping agents. We would be dependent on the health of the cluster to observe it. If ingress to the cluster fails, we can't access the dashboards. Multiply this times the number of clusters in an environment or the path to production. The main problem is that we have failed to aggregate the observability data. This becomes an even greater problem as the overall scale of our system expands. If multiple Kubernetes clusters make up production, then the effectiveness of on-cluster observability is greatly diminished. But also, being pragmatic, we've probably cut off any serious evolution of the rest of the observability capabilities if they must be duplicated to be shared.

Moving components beyond basic data collection out of the developer control plane and onto dedicated infrastructure provides a more sustainable and evolutionary strategy (see figure 5.10). For example, let's say Epetech sets up an external monitoring

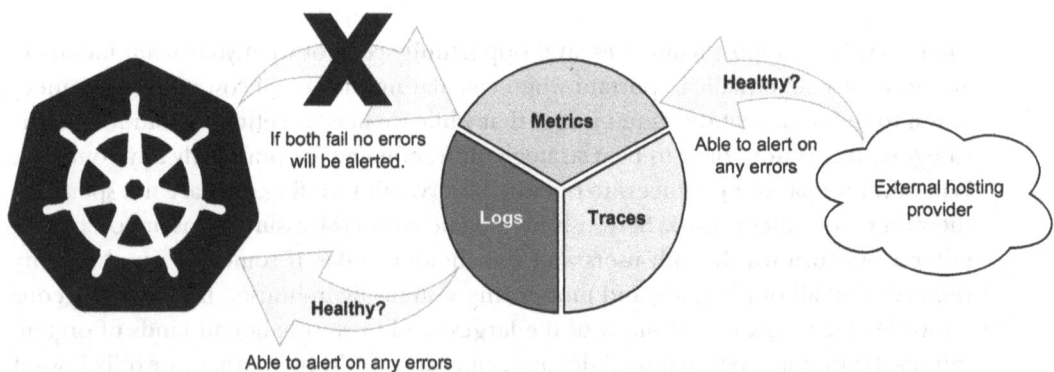

Figure 5.10   Observing your engineering platform should be done external to the platform itself. Otherwise, you risk not being alerted properly about a total outage because the observability system would also be down. Similarly, your observability platform is an equally critical system component and should also be observed externally.

service like Datadog or PagerDuty that checks the health of the Kubernetes cluster and the observability platform itself. If Kubernetes or the internal observability tools (collecting metrics, logs, and traces) go down, the external service can detect the problem and send an alert. This external monitoring is a safeguard, ensuring that we are always aware of critical system outages, even when the internal tools are not functioning. Of course, any system can fail, including the monitoring service on our external system. But being separate creates less coupling and better long-term results.

5.3.4 Strategies to drive adoption

Some organizations struggle with the adoption of observability platform capabilities. There is more than one reason this can happen. Driving the adoption of observability in both development teams and the overall business requires an intentional approach that balances the benefits of enhanced monitoring with the potential friction that may arise from introducing new tools and practices. Here are several strategies to encourage adoption:

- *Start with education and awareness.* One of the biggest challenges in adopting observability is helping teams understand what is possible and why it's valuable. You can begin by educating developers, operations teams, and other stakeholders about the benefits of observability. Hold workshops, lunch-and-learn sessions, and training to explain how metrics, logs, and traces can help detect and resolve problems faster, improve system performance, and enhance user experience. When people see observability as a tool that makes their jobs easier rather than as just another requirement, they are more likely to embrace it.

- *Provide easy-to-use tools and automation.* To reduce friction, provide teams with easy-to-use observability tools. For example, set up automated metrics collection and log aggregation so developers don't have to configure these for each service manually. Offer prebuilt dashboards and templates that teams can use out of the box. If the tools are intuitive and save time, developers will be more inclined to adopt them voluntarily.

- *Highlight quick wins and success stories.* Showcase how observability has led to quick wins within the organization. For example, share stories where a team quickly identified and resolved a production problem thanks to detailed metrics or where a performance bottleneck was uncovered using traces. These are the kind of quick wins that can be achieved with observability. Publicize these successes. When teams see real-world examples of how observability can make them more successful in their job, they'll be more motivated to incorporate it into their processes.

- *Offer support and make it a collaborative effort.* Adopting observability can be a significant change for some teams, so it's essential to provide support throughout the transition. One way to do this is by creating a central group of observability champions. These groups can assist other teams in setting up and using the observability platform, providing guidance, troubleshooting problems, and sharing best practices. Encourage a culture of collaboration where teams can share best practices, dashboards, and alerts. This makes adoption smoother and aligns with the shared responsibility model we provided earlier.

- *Balance enforced versus voluntary usage.* Decide where observability should be mandatory and where it can be optional. For example, a baseline level of observability with metrics, logs, and alerts should exist for every system. This can be done through platform-level integrations that automatically apply observability settings to these services. For tracing, teams should be required to install the basic language-level instrumentation, which is a package integration. Beyond this, teams can have the option to add tracing in spans at more detailed levels within their code. For certain services, simple tracing is sufficient. Naturally, for many teams managing COTS software, there may be no way to add even simple tracing.

- *Integrate observability into the development workflow.* Make observability a natural part of the development and deployment workflow. Integrate it with CI/CD pipelines so that new services automatically include observability instrumentation when deployed. Include observability requirements in the definition of "done" for every story or feature, ensuring that monitoring, logging, and alerting are considered from the start. When observability is baked into the development process rather than being an afterthought, teams are more likely to adopt it effectively.

- *Incentivize adoption.* Offer incentives to teams that actively use the observability platform and contribute to its improvement. This can include recognition through awards, spotlighting teams that have demonstrated best practices, or even tying observability adoption to performance goals. When teams see tangible rewards for adopting observability, they are more likely to participate enthusiastically.

- *Demonstrate business value and trust.* Tie observability to business outcomes to get buy-in from leadership and business stakeholders. Show how improved observability has reduced downtime and led to faster recovery times, better performance, and a smoother customer experience. Use metrics to demonstrate how these improvements translate into financial benefits, such as higher customer satisfaction, reduced operational costs, and increased revenue. When the business understands the value of observability, securing resources and support for its adoption becomes easier. Trust is an important factor here as it is easy for the stakeholders to lose trust in incomplete or incorrect data, even if that was injected inadvertently.

- *Iterate and adapt.* Adoption is not a one-time effort; it requires continuous improvement. Gather team feedback about what works and what doesn't, and use this input to refine the observability platform and practices. Adjust the strategies as the organization evolves, scaling the observability platform to accommodate new services, tools, and requirements.

- *Encourage a culture of observability.* Foster a culture where observability is essential to delivering high-quality software. Promote the idea that observability is a mindset more than a tool, emphasizing proactive monitoring, learning, and continuous improvement. Encourage teams to view observability as a shared goal rather than a task that is the responsibility of a specific team.

- *Generate comprehensive reports with suggestions for enhancements and remediation of systems based on observability data.* This is a powerful application of generative AI (GenAI). By combining templated reports with AI-generated suggestions, proactive measures can be taken when critical functions start behaving outside expected baselines.

While it is outside the scope of this book to look at the effect of GenAI and agentic AI on observability, we highly recommend that you do further research to study how observability can be improved across these five aspects:

- Anomaly detection and root cause analysis
- Predictive analytics and proactive remediation
- Automated incident response and resolution
- Security observability and threat detection
- Automated log analysis and insights

All major observability tool vendors are incorporating GenAI features across all these axes. However, your success in using a tool or a combination of tools depends on your understanding, as a platform engineer, of how these work and how to apply that knowledge to your environment.

Exercise 5.3   Evaluate the total cost of ownership of an observability strategy

In this exercise, we will imagine two options for Epetech. The goal of this exercise is for you to make appropriate decisions concerning build versus buy decisions. Your task is to discuss how you would choose the best initial option. Write a short analysis.

- Option 1: In this option, the platform engineering team at Epetech decides to build a custom observability platform as a subdomain of the overall platform, as they conclude that there are a lot of custom requirements that they cannnot find in a COTS solution. It will likely be based on using open-source tools such as Grafana LGTM, and Prometheus, among others. Based on the starting scope, they recommend four platform engineers and a technical product manager to work on the observability platform domain team.
- Option 2: In the second option, the platform engineering team at Epetech decides to buy a third-party SaaS observability platform from Chronosphere with Fluentd. This platform comes with built-in scalability, cloud-native application integration, and comprehensive features except for tracing. While tracing data could be aggregated, there is minimal visualization support, as this is still in

(continued)

the early stages of development at the vendor. They will have to deploy and self-manage something like Jaeger as a general interface for platform users. The team plans to incorporate the integration and operating tasks into their existing backlog of work. It will take two sprints of work across two platform engineers to rollout and a single full-time equivalent of two sprints per year to maintain going forward.

What are the requirements and ground realities you need to know to pick an option? Why?

5.4   *Observability of published service-level indicators, service-level objectives, and service-level agreements*

We build trust with our end users (developers) by how successfully we meet the service level objectives (SLOs) and agreements (SLAs) that we offer for our platform. Where vendor-managed technologies or tools are involved, we will incorporate them into our calculations. Most people will focus on uptime in terms of 9s as a proxy for a good experience. It's not bad, but it doesn't tell the whole story. Which would you rather use? Service A has a response time of 40ns for 99.99% of the time every month and is down for the remaining 52 minutes in two outages of 25 minutes or more each. Service B has a response time of 40ns for only 99.9% of the time, but the remaining 0.1% of the time is made up of response times ranging from 200ns to 800ns. For human users, service B will be a better experience. For API integrations from other computers, it will depend on how those other services cope with the slowness. This is a typical example of why resilience is such an essential capability for platforms.

No matter how we decide which measures are most beneficial to our customers, using published service-level goals is an effective way to set customer expectations. This also means we can automate tracking these numbers and make them visible for the entire platform team. Not being able to track these through our observability system will be a critical shortcoming.

We need a shared understanding of the terms. Figure 5.11 explains the concept of service-level indicators (SLIs), SLOs, and SLAs and how they relate to one another. Let us now look at how Epetech would handle these three concepts.

SLIs are pivotal metrics that gauge a service's performance. For instance, if the response time of a custom platform API is consistently 200 milliseconds, that's an SLI. SLOs are targets based on SLIs. They set expectations for what the service should achieve. An SLO might state that an API should respond within 200 milliseconds 99.9% of the time. If the API takes longer to answer, it tells the team to investigate and fix potential problems.

While SLIs and SLOs can be automated measurements, SLAs are formal customer agreements. They outline what happens if the service doesn't meet customer expectations. For example, Epetech might have an SLA with its enterprise clients stating that if the platform response time exceeds 200 milliseconds for more than 0.1% of requests in a month, they will offer a discount or some other compensation. Internal products can't use money very well to soothe upset customers. As such, internal products generally don't have SLAs (see figure 5.11).

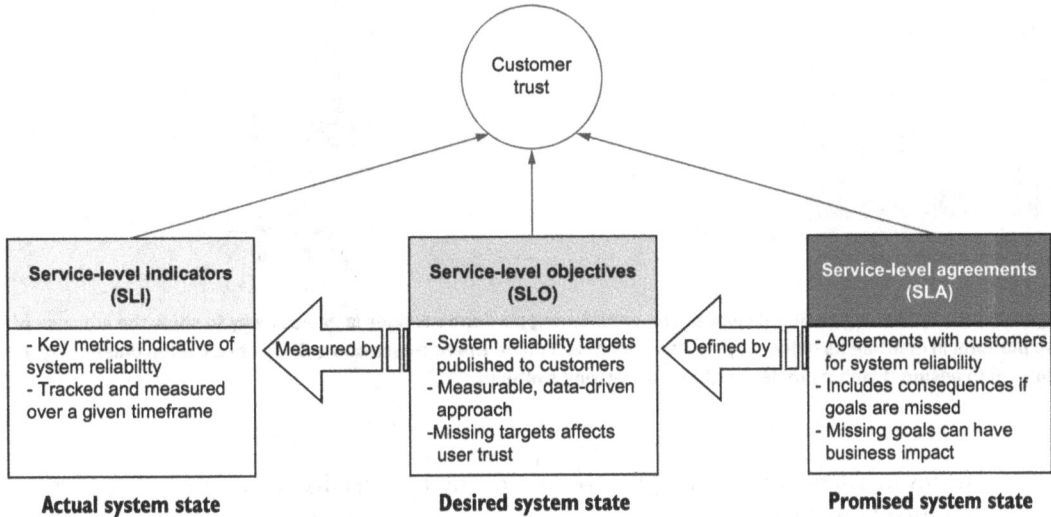

Figure 5.11 SLIs inform SLOs that can be used to notify and publish SLAs.

5.4.1 SLOs as code

Even though data collection, monitoring, and alerting for an SLO is fundamentally the same as for any type of health data for a system, it often doesn't naturally occur to developers to break out discrete dashboards. It monitors around SLOs to their end customers. The platform should set the example by creating these for the platform product and socializing the dashboards that show the state of SLOs.

Like everything else we do, these should be software-defined. Include examples of the platform's real SLO dashboard and the code backing them in the platform user documentation. Figure 5.12 shows an example SLO dashboard we might create for our engineering platform at Epetech.

The left side lists critical metrics such as the target SLO, the current error budget usage rate, and the remaining error budget for the month, providing a clear view of how much of the platform's tolerance for errors has been consumed. It also includes a 30-day overview of the error budget and status indicators for warning and critical alerts, helping teams quickly gauge the platform's health. To the right, various visual elements like line graphs and burn rate charts illustrate the platform's performance over time, highlighting trends or anomalies. This comprehensive dashboard enables platform

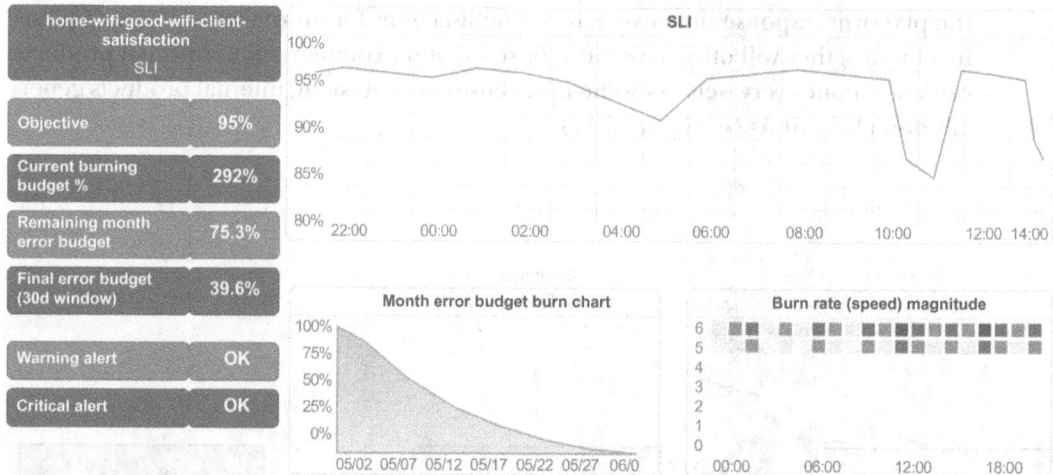

Figure 5.12 Publishing an SLO dashboard for engineering platform services is an easy way to show the success of the platform in meeting its objectives. It also becomes a place where teams can quickly check when diagnosing a problem to ensure it isn't a problem with the underlying systems.

teams to assess whether the platform is meeting its objectives at a glance and serves as a valuable tool for diagnosing problems efficiently, distinguishing whether problems stem from the platform itself or elsewhere in the system.

Optional Exercise 5.4   Use Prometheus data to create SLOs

In this exercise, decide on an SLO that you think should be set for our Epetech platform. What SLI will track this objective, and how do we collect the data needed?

Objectives:

1 Understand the importance of SLOs in a business context and how they are a crucial part of maintaining system reliability.
2 Align technical metrics to business needs by selecting appropriate metrics from Prometheus data that reflect business objectives.
3 Justify SLOs based on collected data by writing down the reasoning behind their chosen SLOs, aligning with business context and user expectations.
4 Use Prometheus monitoring data to formulate SLOs' conduct performance analysis and metric-based decision-making.

Deliverables:

1 Describe the SLO and how it relates to developer satisfaction in using our engineering platform.
2 Define the SLI to track this objective.
3 Describe how we will collect, visualize, and monitor the SLO.

Considerations:
For this exercise, we strongly urge you to consider some open source SLO generators like Sloth (https://github.com/slok/sloth). It helps you define, manage, and generate SLOs for Prometheus using a simple YAML-based configuration, abstracting away the complexity of writing long Prometheus recording rules and alerting rules manually.

Summary

- Observability is critical for engineering platforms themselves as well as the products these platforms are supporting.
- Observability is not monitoring or looking at metrics, logs, and traces. Instead, it goes beyond that by predicting a system's internal workings by examining its external behaviors.
- We should be monitoring and alerting on all known-knowns for any component or service.
- We should implement tracing and transaction IDs to accelerate resolving the unknowns that any complex system will exhibit.
- Flexible time-series data analysis visuals are table stakes for dealing with unknown and unanticipated problems. Analyzing all the observability data we collect and developing predictive models around these unknown unknowns is where we find greater value in evolving observability systems.
- Building an observability system includes five critical steps: (1) understanding your observability goals, (2) buying a tool or building one that provides the necessary framework to achieve these goals with a well-defined and predictable user experience framework, (3) instrumenting the code, (4) ensuring automated and verifiable data collection from all the sources, (5) establishing a transparent shared responsibility model.
- It's important to understand that building a world-class observability platform is an evolutionary process, not an immediate achievement.
- Building a platform is not enough. Getting the cultural aspects right to ensure your developers adopt the platform is challenging but crucial.
- Observability is critical to providing SLOs that will establish trust in the system for its customers.
- Workloads deployed on the platform should be observable by default with self-service.

Building a
software-defined
engineering platform

In this part of the book, we'll start building the initial Epetech engineering platform. Along the way, we'll put a lot of what we've talked about so far into practice and also take a deeper look at some of the architectural approaches that will help us succeed.

Earlier in the book, we talked about the challenges Epetech is facing. They're focusing on building their business services as APIs, using these capabilities themselves as well as selling them as a service to other companies. But without a clear strategy beyond a mix of tech silos and a DevOps team, developers at Epetech are now spending half their time on lead-time planning, coordinating with other teams to get DNS entries, firewall rules, storage, compute capacity, monitors, alerts, pipeline changes, and everything else needed to build, deploy, and operate their software, often under tight deadlines. Maintenance and operational problems are a constant headache and aren't seen as adding much value. Unsurprisingly, product incidents are rising, leading to frustrated customers and higher support costs.

We are a team within Epetech tasked with creating a better solution to these challenges (see figure 6.1).

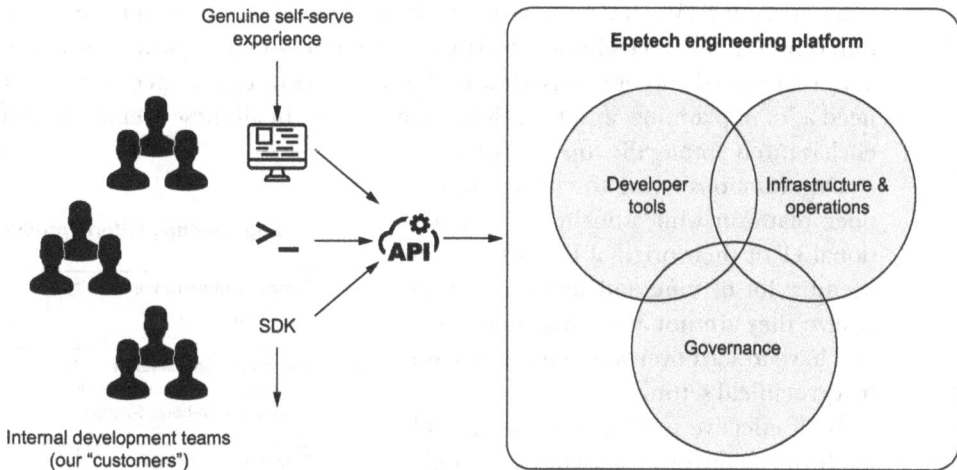

Figure 6.1 We want to create an internal product that provides a genuinely self-service experience where developers can imagine, design, build, release, and operate their applications with agility, high engineering quality, greater operational resiliency, and confidence in meeting compliance requirements, yet without all the engineering friction they usually experience. In other words, we are creating an engineering platform.

In the next couple of chapters, we will dive into applying platform engineering practices to create the foundational parts of an engineering platform for our imaginary company. These starting components are crucial for any effective platform. You'll see how platform domains relate to the pipelines we build, how we can extend the Kubernetes control plane for more value, and what a self-serve user experience can look like.

6.1 *Building our own example engineering platform*

Let's assume this will be a brand-new product. While this is a common approach for learning exercises, there are plenty of good reasons for an enterprise to take this viewpoint when building an engineering platform. The most pragmatic reason is described best by Gall's law:

A complex system that works is invariably found to have evolved from a simple sys-tem that worked. A complex system designed from scratch never works and cannot be patched up to make it work. You have to start over with a simple working system. [1]

By now, nearly every organization—at least those with modern development and deliv-ery practices—has been using many, if not all, of the various technologies that will go into an engineering platform. They have teams scattered everywhere using Kubernetes, creating infrastructure using Terraform, using Git, and "doing DevOps." These imple-mentations are often complex to adopt because they're either too focused on the needs and preferences of a small group of users or they were developed without user input and are instead optimized for the needs of the team providing the technology. In other cases, while the implementation is meant for general use, it is managed across many different traditional IT silos where API access and self-serve experiences were not origi-nally considered and by teams without the resources or experience to evolve. Changes need a lot of planning, and long delays are normal. In all these scenarios, user experi-ence is rarely among the top priorities.

Organizations trying to create a devel-oper platform while sticking to a tradi-tional IT or their original DevOps model spend a lot of time and money, only to realize they are not achieving their goals and have to start over with a unified team in a greenfield setting.

With effective product ownership and platform engineering practices, a single team can successfully manage the internal domain boundaries within the product during initial integration and MVP (min-imum viable platform) development. Then, as the product evolves and greater velocity in the platform features is needed, scale becomes a factor; subdomains can be handed off to other similarly organized teams effectively since the architecture has the right low-friction, loosely coupled boundary between the various parts of the platform product (see figure 6.2). But first let's talk about the prerequisites.

```
┌─── Engineering platform product ──────┐
│                                        │
│  ┌──────────────────────────────────┐ │
│  │ Cloud administrative identity    │ │
│  │ • aws-iam-profiles               │ │
│  └──────────────────────────────────┘ │
│  ┌──────────────────────────────────┐ │
│  │ Cloud account baseline           │ │
│  │ • aws-platform-observability-base│ │
│  │ • aws-platform-hosted-zones      │ │
│  └──────────────────────────────────┘ │
│  ┌──────────────────────────────────┐ │
│  │ Transit network layer            │ │
│  │ • aws-platform-vpc               │ │
│  └──────────────────────────────────┘ │
│  ┌──────────────────────────────────┐ │
│  │ Cloud identity provider          │ │
│  │ • platform-auth0-management       │ │
│  └──────────────────────────────────┘ │
│  ┌──────────────────────────────────┐ │
│  │ Cloud services control plane     │ │
│  │ • aws-control-plane-base         │ │
│  └──────────────────────────────────┘ │
│  ┌──────────────────────────────────┐ │
│  │ Managed control plane services   │ │
│  │ • aws-control-plane-services     │ │
│  └──────────────────────────────────┘ │
│  ┌──────────────────────────────────┐ │
│  │ Managed control-plane-extensions │ │
│  │ • aws-control-plane-extensions   │ │
│  └──────────────────────────────────┘ │
│  ┌──────────────────────────────────┐ │
│  │ Platform product services        │ │
│  │ • vsctl                          │ │
│  └──────────────────────────────────┘ │
└────────────────────────────────────────┘
```

Figure 6.2   The engineering platform product domains also show the basic dependencies and almost exactly the order in which we'll set up the initial product infrastructure pipelines. This diagram shows the pipelines we will build in each domain to create our Epetech starting engineering platform.

6.2   *Prerequisites to getting started*

What resources do we need to get started? See figure 6.3. Besides the cloud accounts where the platform infrastructure resides, you will notice that these tools are included

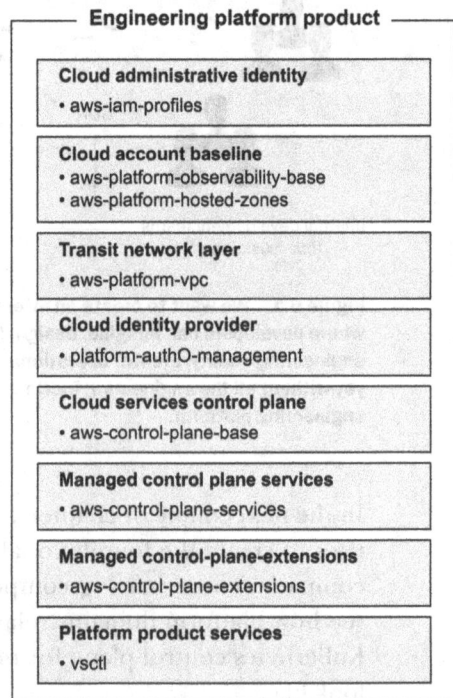

in the platform product for use by platform customers. As platform engineers, we will use these tools to deliver the platform.

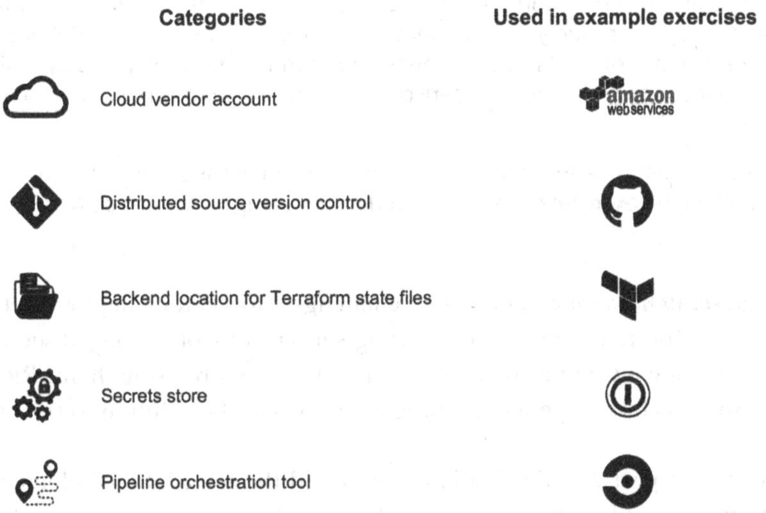

Categories		Used in example exercises
	Cloud vendor account	amazon webservices
	Distributed source version control	
	Backend location for Terraform state files	
	Secrets store	
	Pipeline orchestration tool	

Figure 6.3   Resources we will need to begin building our engineering platform product foundation

Not every potential developer tool is needed initially, so which tools are needed to bootstrap an engineering platform effectively? These are

- Source code version control
- Secrets store
- Infrastructure state store
- Pipeline orchestrator

Costs associated with using AWS

Our example platform will be built using AWS as the cloud infrastructure provider. Be conscious of the cost as you start these platform-building exercises. With careful management, such as de-provisioning resources, clearing data storage when not in active use, limiting the work to a single platform environment, and other similar strategies, you may be able to stay within the AWS free tier, but it can be challenging. A Kubernetes cluster supporting a service mesh and other platform technologies requires instances larger than micro. Presently, even at the small scale of a personal platform, fully sustaining the various resources of a two-environment platform 24/7 can run from $600 to $800 per month or higher.

Because these are learning exercises, you don't need 24/7 uptimes, and you can get these costs dramatically lower using the aforementioned careful management.

(continued)

Still, potentially significant costs may be involved, and consideration must be made at the start regarding access to the necessary resources. If you are applying these principles at your place of work in the actual delivery of an engineering platform, the cost has already been budgeted. Alternatively, many organizations fund limited use of cloud resources for skills improvement and learning, so that you may have the necessary access to cloud provider services through your employment or educational institution.

If you do not have access to cloud provider resources, many aspects of the engineering practices within the exercises can be explored locally using tools such as Minikube.

Starting from scratch, we have a bootstrap challenge. How can we deploy the first configuration in a software-defined manner using source control, managed secrets, state store, and a pipeline if we must first deploy these tools before using them? Right away, you can see the accelerating effect of using SaaS tools as the solution to the bootstrap challenge.

Over the rest of part 2 of this book, we will build the foundational elements of an effective starting point for an engineering platform. Naturally, to have an actual working example, we must use specific tools and technologies, even though there are multiple possible options. The reference code examples (https://mng.bz/pZG2) in the *Effective Platform Engineering* GitHub organization will demonstrate several highly effective tools and, for the initial requirements, will use

- GitHub
- 1Password
- Terraform Cloud
- CircleCI

Using these tools is not required to apply the principles in this book, and you are welcome to use equivalent tools if you wish. Using the listed ones, however, will allow you to get the most from the sample exercise solutions.

6.2.1   *Getting started with the example tools*

In an Enterprise setting, each tool would typically be integrated using a single sign-on solution. We introduced earlier how that fits into the product experience in section 4.3.3 on customer identity provider. But for now, let's go ahead and set up access to the initial tools as an individual user. The respective tool's product documentation provides detailed instructions for performing the following steps.

If you do not already have one, create a free personal account on github.com. Then, create a free-tier GitHub organization for our imaginary Epetech company, in which we and all the Epetech platform developers will be members. Create a GitHub team called `platform-team` to represent our product delivery team for the Epetech exercises.

Later, we will use GitHub Teams and team membership to manage access permissions. Add yourself to this team. Create a personal access token, and be sure to upload your personal SSH keys and enable support for signed commits (https://mng.bz/Owyo).

Create a free-tier Terraform Cloud organization. Go to the settings area (from the left-hand menu) within the organization, create a team, and add yourself to the team. From the team settings page, also generate a team API token.

Create a free-tier CircleCI organization and link it with our GitHub organization. Generate an access token.

Lastly, 1Password offers individual plans for less than $3 per month. Create a dedicated 1Password vault for these exercises, then go to the Developer options and generate a service account credential with read and write permissions (https://mng.bz/YZ0K). Or, if you are using some other secrets management tool, make sure you have the access credentials for pipeline usage available. Store all of these access tokens in this vault.

Most of the SaaS tools used in the example exercise solutions offer a free tier adequate to cover the exercises in this book or very affordable personal options, and alternative tools will often be discussed. Occasionally, we will use alternative tools to demonstrate the differences among effective choices within the example exercise solutions.

> **TIP** Alternative SaaS options for secrets management and Terraform state that have a free tier you could explore are doppler.com and tfstate.dev.

For any tool where you need an access token to use in automation, such as in our pipelines, if the tool doesn't allow you to create something like a team or an organizational-level token (where anyone on your team can manage it), then you must create a *personal* access token. This introduces a problem. What if you leave the company or take on a new role with a different team? Either of these events can cause your personal access token to be revoked, and any automation that depends on the token will break.

The two most effective ways of dealing with this situation are

- *Service accounts*—Sometimes called machine users, these are identities created within the appropriate system in the same way as are human users, except that no single person has control over the identity. It becomes a team resource with the username and password stored in the team secrets store for management. Often, systems provide an actual feature designed to support this type of user. We will use an example in AWS later in this chapter. Just for these exercises, creating and using a personal token when needed is fine.
- *OpenID Connect (OIDC) tokens*—Many tools and most cloud resources, such as AWS, also provide a means of establishing direct trust between other tools or cloud resources. This approach requires more behind-the-scenes automation to create a self-service experience for platform users, but it is certainly a viable option.

6.2.2   *Developer tools selection criteria*

The tools you choose aren't just neutral decisions—they can either support good platform engineering practices or get in the way.

NOTE   Platform engineering is not about the tool. Organizationally, this is true. Tools aren't magic. But that doesn't mean you can use just any tool without consequence. Some are well suited to platform engineering goals, and others simply aren't. When a consultant says, "The tool doesn't matter," they mean that no tool is going to overcome your organizational challenges.

The best place to start is by talking to your developers to understand their needs and preferences. But when it comes to making the final choice, it's important to include platform engineering considerations as part of your criteria to ensure you build and maintain a solid self-serve experience (see figure 6.4).

Choosing tools

👍	👎
Smaller, focused tool, exceptional in its implementation and interoperates easily	Large, monolithic product that tries to meet many different (or even all) developer needs
Strongly domain-bounded and can be implemented with replacement in mind	No or limited ability to test and experiment with tool before purchase
Qualified SaaS option that offers no or low cost access for testing and experimentation before purchase	Requires manual configuration by users
Has an API based on modern standards with good documentation that provides functional examples and does not require the use of a specific programming language	No or limited API access, or the API is based on out-of-date or otherwise unusual technology
The API provides access to all application functionality	Poor data security or API access to data maintained within the tool
Data stored in the product is secure at rest and in transit, and readable and writable through the API	No ability to support our platform's user authentication and authorization strategy
Can be integrated into our platform's user authentication and authorization strategy	Poor documentation, no visible community
Visible community	Must be deployed and maintained by the buyer, without support for a software-defined implementation
If self-managed, can be fully installed and maintained using software-defined practices	

Figure 6.4   Regardless of which tool we are examining, there are general criteria we should carefully consider in determining whether the tool will integrate effectively and help create the experience we want for our platform.

Where available, using high-quality, secure SaaS development tools is one of the most accelerating and long-term efficiency choices available, paying dividends not just at the start but continuously over the platform's life. Time spent deploying, operating, securing, or maintaining any of these tools is time taken away from doing strategically valuable work. Companies routinely underestimate the cost of self-managed or poorly administered tools.

ADDITIONAL CRITERIA FOR SPECIFIC KINDS OF TOOLS

In addition to these general criteria, each tool we implement has some additional attributes that will make it much easier to integrate and maintain a self-serve user experience (see figure 6.5).

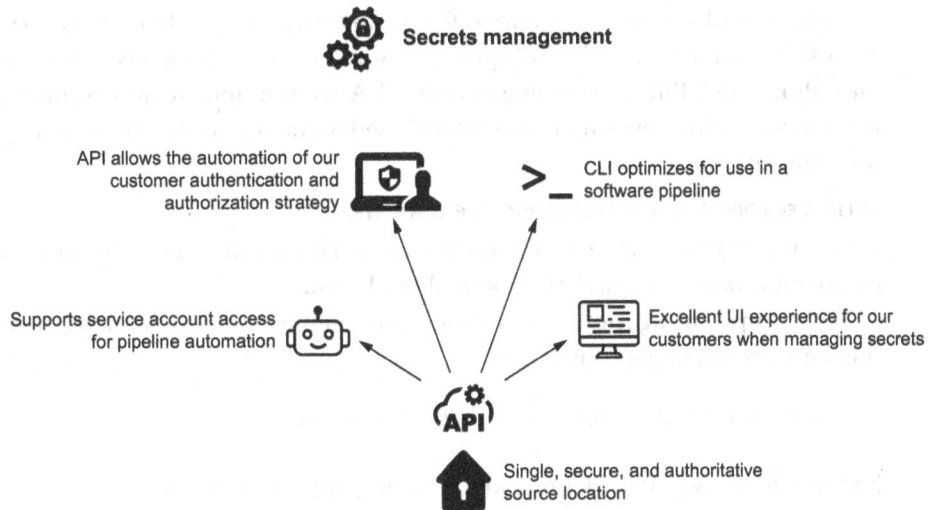

Secrets management

API allows the automation of our customer authentication and authorization strategy

CLI optimizes for use in a software pipeline

Supports service account access for pipeline automation

Excellent UI experience for our customers when managing secrets

API

Single, secure, and authoritative source location

Figure 6.5 We are using the same tools we will integrate with the platform for our customers' use. To create the truly self-service experience we want, beyond the general criteria, we need these from our secrets management tool.

First, the API should support our authentication and authorization strategy. While this may seem obvious, it can be challenging to achieve in practice. For instance, since we are building our platform on AWS, what about using AWS Secrets Manager? Recalling the discussion of customer identity from before, we want an independent customer identity model. Think of the complexities of using only AWS IAM to map individual secrets in Secrets Manager based on a user's team membership that is maintained in an external source. In practice, you must create a custom API to provide this experience. However, several tools are available that more closely align with our authentication and authorization goals.

Another aspect of access management relates to the onboarding experience for platform users to the secrets management tool supported by the platform. As with all external tools, we want to integrate the tool's configuration with the team onboarding.

In the case of secrets management, this typically means that a dedicated team space is set up for the onboarded team, with the associated team role-based access permissions. Any person on the team should automatically have the associated access to the team's secrets in the secrets management tool. The integration automation step can also automate the provision and rotation of any service account or OIDC trust used as part of the integrated deployment capability. That could mean a service account or trust for a team's pipelines, or it could be those credential sources used with something like an external-secrets-operator to enable all of a team's namespaces to retrieve secrets as part of an integrated Argo (https://argoproj.github.io/cd/) or Flux (https://fluxcd .io) deployment capability.

Also, the CLI should be optimized for use in a software pipeline. What do we mean by this? Pipelines are not the only places we will interact with secrets, nor will a CLI be the only method. But pipeline usage is critical. At a minimum, we need a command-line method for setting environment variables based on values in a file and injecting secrets into template files.

SETTING ENVIRONMENT VARIABLES FROM FILE CONTENTS

This is the most common pipeline use case. A clean, file-based method of sourcing secure information into a shell process should exist.

For example, using the 1Password CLI, you can inject secrets defined in a file into a shell process in a single command:

```
$ op run -env-file my_app.env -- bash_script.sh
```

Needed secrets would be defined in the file my_app.env as follows:

```
export SNYK_TOKEN=op://vault-name/snyk/api-token
export TFE_TOKEN=op://vault-name/terraform-cloud/team-api-token
export SLACK_BOT_TOKEN=op://vault-name/slack/post-bot-token
```

TEMPLATE INJECTION

There should be direct support for populating template files with secrets directly from the secrets manager. For example, a common method of providing credentials is through a credential file. Creating a template of the required file that can be populated and written to the correct location should be a single step. An example using Terraform Cloud would be

```
$ op inject -i terraformrc.tpl -o ~/.terraformrc
```

Where the contents of the –input file are

```
credentials "app.terraform.io" {
  token = "{{ op://vault-name/terraform-cloud/team-api-token }}"
}
```

Many widely used secrets management tools offer pretty poor support for these use cases. Unsurprisingly, this has inspired some open source projects to solve this problem (https://github.com/tellerops/teller).

As long as the secrets management tool meets the general software selection criteria listed at the start of this section, it is not difficult to create and maintain a simple CLI that provides the desired experience. It is worth the effort if the tool or an open source alternative does not provide the right experience.

When evaluating or extending a secrets management tool, ensure it delivers the following essential capabilities (see figure 6.6):

- *Supports service account access for pipeline automation*—Nearly all interactions with the secrets manager will be through automated integration, which will require some form of machine-to-machine credential. Usually, this means generating an API token or similar service account credential. There are other ways of supporting this automated integration, but however we implement this, we need to have experience to fully self-serve our customers.

- *Excellent UI experience*—Development teams will manage their own secrets. While this mainly involves using the secrets in integration and deployment pipelines or configurations, the interface for users to add or update secrets is also essential. Using a tool with a good interface means you won't need to build one from scratch.

- *Single, secure, and authoritative source of secrets*—There should be a single source of truth for secure values. Pipeline steps, deployment events, secret services deployed onto clusters, and all other automation should pull secrets from a single location. Not only does this reduce the opportunities for error, but it also dramatically simplifies sustaining secure configuration and good security practices such as automating the rotation of credentials.

- *Support for pipeline source code libraries*—Most modern pipeline tools have this feature. In CircleCI, these are called orbs. In GitHub Actions, they are shared actions and workflows. These shared code libraries are the key means of standardizing common activities or performing all the nonfunctional or cross-functional requirements. This must be a capability of the pipeline code itself rather than an extension to the pipeline server or runners. In other words, references to the shared pipeline code occur in the pipeline code itself, which lives in the repository with the infrastructure or application code. Modules or plugins that are instead loaded or installed on an orchestration server or runner are not the same thing and result in brittle, high-maintenance pipelines.

Most popular pipeline tools encourage community contributions to their growing library of version pipeline code (such as orbs or actions). Using these resources involves the same security practices needed for any shared library. With few exceptions, the most valuable orbs will be those created in-house to support your workflow needs directly. The internal development and management of customer pipeline libraries

Pipeline orchestration

SSH **>_**   Secure means of self-serve
access to runners for debugging

Support for external, versioned
pipeline action libraries,
incorporated at pipeline runtime

or   VM

pipeline.yaml   Event-based triggers

Pipelines are completely software
defined with the pipeline file(s)
expected to reside in the same
repo as the code being orchestrated

Dynamic, ephemeral runners with
both containerized and virtual
machine options, vendor-hosted
and self-hosted, and supporting
multiple parallel and serial jobs
within the same pipeline

Can support a secure
means of maintaining
artifacts and data between
independent jobs

No or limited manual mechanism for
building pipelines via a pipeline tool GUI

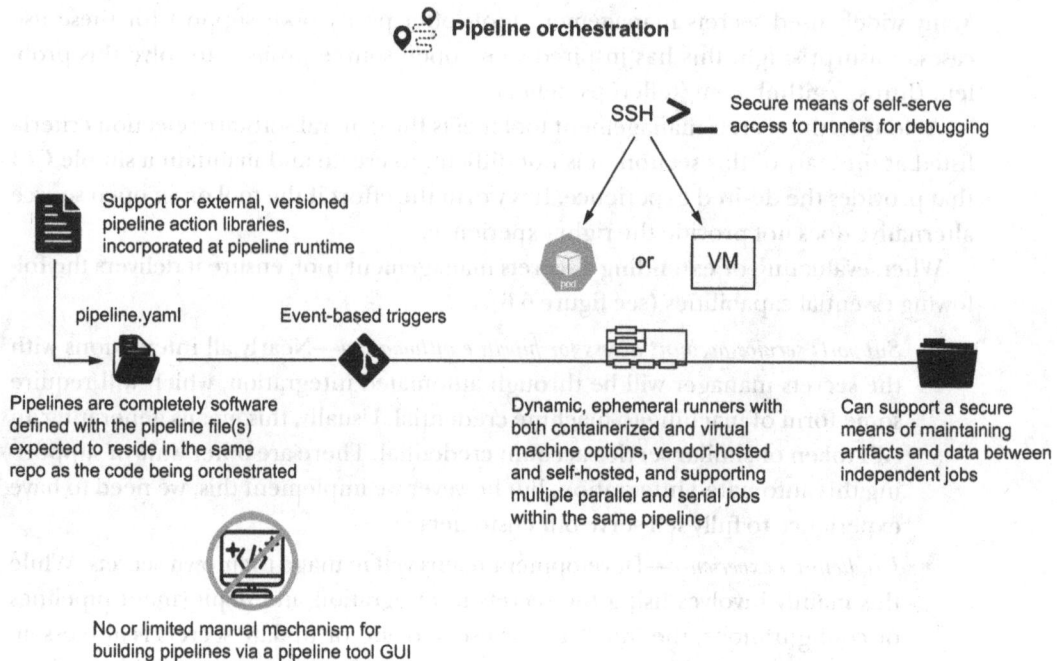

Figure 6.6   Our pipeline tool will determine the quality of the continuous integration and delivery experience and needs specific additional attributes beyond the general selection criteria.

must also follow traditional software development practices, such as integration tests and versioned releases.

- *Completely software-defined pipelines*—Teams must own their own pipeline code. Pipelines may be required to include remote orbs or actions to support cross-functional requirements, yet the CI pipelines triggered by source code changes must live in the same repository as the code being tested. When teams use the same language and architecture, they can easily use a common set of build or test steps and make those steps available through shared code referenced by the individual repository pipeline. Developer ownership is also a requirement for deployment pipelines. The essential outcome is that customers (developers) are never blocked, waiting for another team to make needed changes to their pipeline, nor should unexpected breaking changes get pushed into their pipelines. Changes in shared pipeline code must be introduced through version changes. Teams intentionally adopt the new version and will not be surprised even if the new version includes a breaking change. If a team needs a change in a shared pipeline resource and it's not happening fast enough, they can fork the shared code and make the changes themselves rather than remain blocked.

- *No GUI method for pipeline creation*—While not strictly necessary, this is an example of how the lack of a feature can effectively constrain complexity without compromising effectiveness. For the same reasons we don't want people going into the AWS console to make infrastructure changes, it is a poor practice to make manual pipeline changes. Where no manual option even exists, there is one less problem to manage.

- *Event-based triggers*—Optimally, triggering a pipeline via the pipeline tool should be limited to retries. This is not an absolute requirement, but triggering a pipeline within the pipeline tool itself should be treated as an anti-pattern. Confidence in continuous deployment automation is built upon the assumption that specific events will always occur in a specific order.

- *Dynamic, ephemeral, private, and hosted runners*—Slow pipelines mean wasted time. By installing packages and configuring runners as a stage in a pipeline, significant time may be recovered. Runners (or Executors as they are called in CircleCI) are where our pipeline jobs, steps, and commands occur. Having the environments already set up with the tools, testing frameworks, or any other packages the pipeline will need means the pipeline does not need to take the time to download and install those things. If you can shave 5 to 30 minutes off every pipeline, imagine how much time you could get back across a large organization with hundreds or thousands of developers, most of whom expect their pipelines to run multiple times daily. As a feature of your engineering platform, maintain a set of shared runners that includes a common base runner that has all the packages that need to be included with every kind of pipeline (such as the secrets manager CLI), along with language- or context-specific runners that have build, test, and reporting tools. Also, include Runner starter kits that customers can use to build upon the shared images to create fully customized runners that do not require any package installation or other configuration at pipeline runtime.

- *Access to runners*—A secure means of enabling developers to access pipeline runners for debugging is a significant time-saving feature. A pipeline step working locally but failing in the pipeline is a very common event. As long as the other pipeline tool requirements are true, you can build your own solution should the tool not already offer this capability, though it's easier if you don't need to.

- *Persist data and artifacts between jobs*—Though creating this feature is straightforward, it's still a missed opportunity since many reasonable solutions include this feature.

Exercise 6.1   Assess a platform developer tool according to the software selection criteria

Select a developer tool from one of the *prerequisite tool* categories. This can be a tool used in the example solutions or another tool you are interested in using. Use the general tool selection criteria and the additional requirements, if they apply, to assess whether the tool could be effectively integrated into a platform.

6.3   *Infrastructure pipeline orchestration practices*

Every component of our engineering platform will be software defined. Most of this software definition will be pipeline managed as it makes its way from initial testing to being used in production. The environments that make up the path to production depend on which part of our platform we are configuring.

6.3.1   *Account-level pipelines*

These are automated actions or infrastructure configurations that happen as a "once-per-account" kind of behavior (see figure 6.7). Each account is the *environment* in our account-level pipelines. There aren't many of these relative to the rest of our platform. In section 6.4, we introduce the first of these.

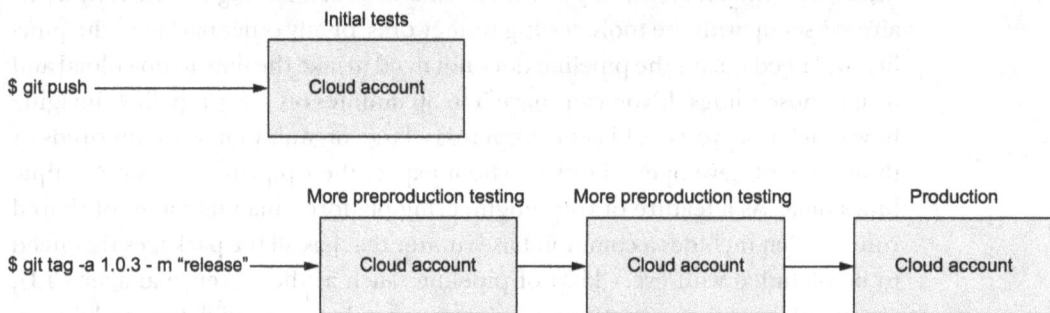

Figure 6.7   We will be using AWS in our Epetech example; some things we manage will be Account-level configurations. If we were using Google Cloud, these would be project-level configurations. Each cloud vendor will have some analogous structure.

6.3.2   *Control plane-level pipelines*

In addition to account-level pipelines, we will have control plane-level pipelines. In many ways, at the infrastructure level, an instance of the control plane amounts to an instance of the engineering platform. Along the path to production, our approach involves maintaining several instances of the platform, each representing a distinct stage in the promotion process and enabling the incremental validation of platform capabilities before reaching production (see figure 6.8).

Since we will be using Kubernetes as the technology to create our control plane, the environments in the path to production for cluster-level features are the clusters themselves. Production could be a single Kubernetes cluster to start. But as we grow, either in the number of developers, lines of business, or global regions needed for our software, *production* can grow to include more than one cluster. Where this is the case, the role of each of those clusters is still production. At that scale, the environment now becomes the set of clusters that share the same role.

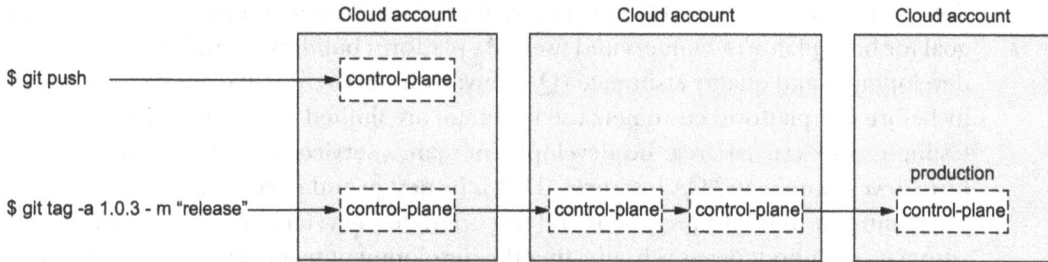

Figure 6.8 We want instances of our platform that we can use to develop and test new features or functionality before developers have access. We also want separate instances of our platform to provide developers with their preproduction environments.

The provisioning and configuration of the clusters would follow a *control plane* path to production. All the cluster-wide applications that platform engineers manage usually follow this same path since they are applications with a single instance per cluster.

6.3.3 Namespace-level pipelines

Anything else deployed on or through an engineering platform will have a namespace-level path to production. There are typically several applications managed by the platform team that will follow this pattern. However, most of this category will be made up of all the applications that the users of our platform (developers) deploy.

Nonproduction clusters hosting nonproduction namespaces and production clusters hosting production namespaces are ideas that are probably very familiar to most readers. But what is less familiar is the *preview* environment and cluster role shown in figure 6.9.

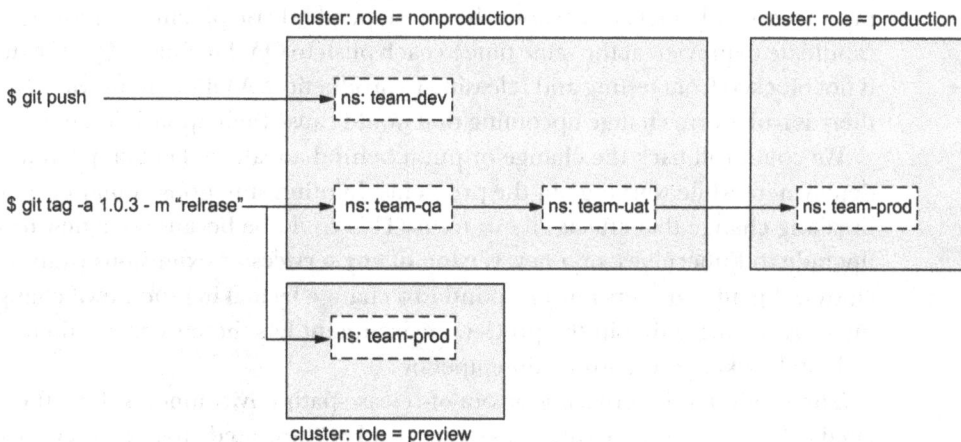

Figure 6.9 For users of the platform, an environment in the path-to-production is a Kubernetes namespace. There will be one or more namespaces in a preproduction cluster, or eventually multiple clusters, where development teams test their application before deploying to a production cluster. Something you may not have seen before is the *preview* environment in the similarly named *preview cluster*.

Catching bugs or breaking changes before they reach production is a key architectural goal for both platform builders and users. As platform builders, we will have dedicated development and quality assurance (QA) environments to test all platform functionality before our platform customers use it. Yet, we are limited in the effectiveness of our testing in one crucial area: no development team's services are running in the platform development and QA instances. That is by design and necessary.

We must be able to experiment and test upgrades, new technologies, or refactored automation without negatively affecting the development teams who use the platform. Doing this under the regular nonproduction environments our users depend on inevitably results in a much slower pace of operational maintenance and platform improvement. But at the same time, our testing will fall short if we cannot test with those same development team's services present. Hence, the preview role and cluster instance are invaluable. By providing the users of the platform with an environment (namespace) in our preview instance—an environment that is outside their usual path to production—we can see the effect of a change on our users without blocking their natural flow of development.

Imagine an internal team—let's call them the Payments team—handles various payment-supporting services and follows a path to production that includes development, QA, and stage environments before the final release. If we deploy a change to the control plane in the nonproduction cluster that causes their services to fail, they are blocked from development work until we fix the problem. Keeping nonproduction separate from production protected the production environments from this problem, which shields the end users of our software, but development work is still affected. This wastes time and is costly.

The preview role in our control plane path production gives us the ability to test platform changes against actual developer applications without disrupting their critical production path. Figure 6.9 shows the developers' release pipeline deploying a release candidate to preview at the same time as each push to QA. If it fails in QA, the developer is not blocked from testing and releasing to production. A failure in preview means that there is a platform change upcoming that would cause their application to fail.

We could roll back the change or put it behind a feature flag that prevents further deployment while working out the problems. In other situations, it may be a necessary breaking change that affects all our users. This could be because of a new feature, an upgrade to Kubernetes, or a new version of any services or extensions running on the cluster. If platform users must respond to a change by making their own changes, having those changes first in the preview environment lets them work out their response without blocking their production pipeline.

These nondeveloper-facing or out-of-release-path environments, how they are isolated and tested, and the software-defined and orchestrated change process from start to production release are central to how we build engineering quality into an engineering platform.

NOTE   *Engineering* in platform engineering is a verb.

What if a company doesn't want to maintain multiple platform testing environments? There will be additional costs associated with additional environments. But how much does a service outage in production cost? How much does it cost in developer productivity when developers' environments are down or upgrades and technology advancements in the platform are slow? For nearly all organizations, those costs are significantly higher than the costs of these environments.

Remember, we've simplified the scale and number of environments for these exercises. We'll keep using this simplified structure, but let's take a closer look at the recommended starting point if this were our actual Epetech enterprise platform build.

Before we get started on our first pipeline, we should define the platform engineering software development practices that make up a well-architected infrastructure pipeline (see figure 6.10).

The following seven principles form the foundation of a well-architected infrastructure pipeline:

- *Test-driven development*—In an infrastructure pipeline, the tests are less about confirming that the infrastructure SDK performs as expected and more about acting as a general smoke test after deployment and (more importantly) part of a nightly check to detect configuration drift caused by a manual change.

- *Trunk-based development*—Preferably, the platform team engages in pair programming and pushes directly to trunk. Short-lived story branches used to organize changes or to take advantage of the Pull Request process built into GitHub are fine, but you should still be merging changes frequently to main, at least daily and preferably more often.

- *Setting the path to production*—CI in this context refers to static code analysis, and deploying to DEV means the first infrastructure test environment. Naming the first environment *development* can create confusion, as this test environment is only for the builders of the engineering platform. A platform customer will never access this environment. *Sandbox* might be a better name for the first environment. It was recently brought to our attention that, for some organizations, the sandbox name is also used for a high-stakes nonproduction environment where they provide the first touchpoint to their B2B partners. These companies use a sandbox to give their partners a first glimpse of what it takes to connect to their APIs, and they are often referred to as sandboxes.

  Requiring a fixed, recurring release path to production is essential for maintaining the environmental stability needed for your customer to engage in continuous deployment successfully. Continuous deployment of application software depends upon the health and "sameness" of production and nonproduction environments, in addition to the rigor of the release process and automated testing. Successful continuous deployment of infrastructure has the exact requirements. Remember that every customer-facing environment is *production* from the platform delivery team's point of view, just as every customer's AWS account is a production environment from AWS's point of view.

Use test-driven development (TDD).

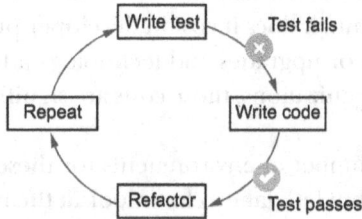

Write test → Test fails → Write code → Test passes → Refactor → Repeat

Use trunk-based development (TBD).

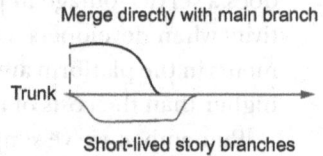

Merge directly with main branch

Trunk

Short-lived story branches

Test and release pipelines follow a set path to production.

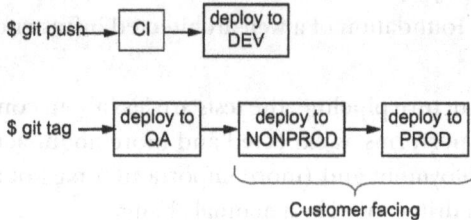

$ git push → CI → deploy to DEV

$ git tag → deploy to QA → deploy to NONPROD → deploy to PROD

Customer facing

Only one value is maintained in pipeline tool's ENV values.

Environment Variables

Environment variables are available to any job that request Environment Variables documentation.

Name	Value
OP_SERVICE_ACCOUNT_TOKEN	****YSJ9

Keep infrastructure code DRY.

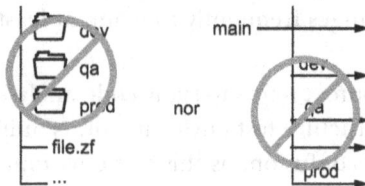

dev
qa
prod
file.zf
...

nor

main
dev
qa
prod

Build dumb pipelines and smart scripts.

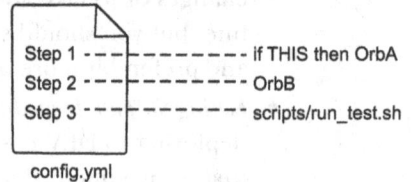

Step 1 -------- if THIS then OrbA
Step 2 -------- OrbB
Step 3 -------- scripts/run_test.sh

config.yml

Use local code protection and quality practices.

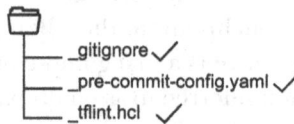

_gitignore ✓
_pre-commit-config.yaml ✓
_tflint.hcl ✓

Figure 6.10 Well-architected infrastructure-as-code pipelines are no different from well-architected regular software pipelines. This is why we prefer the term "software-defined infrastructure" to differentiate between simply using an infrastructure-as-code (IaC) framework like Terraform and the software engineering practices that are a part of sustainable, high-quality software developer lifecycle management of an engineering platform product.

- *Limited use of the pipeline tool ENVIRONMENT (ENV) variable solution*—Don't store all the secrets a pipeline needs in the pipeline tool's ENV value service. Pipelines pull in values from the secrets manager as needed. This practice will make us much more successful in the automated management and rotation of all forms of access credentials, reduce the security risks of human error through the repeated duplication of stored values, and significantly reduce the complexity of moving to either a different secrets manager or a different pipeline tool. The screenshot in the diagram is of a value entered into a CircleCI context that is associated with the GitHub Team *platform team*. Only the team's credential for accessing their secrets is retained in this secure location.

- *Keeping infrastructure code DRY ("Don't Repeat Yourself")*—None of our infrastructure code should be duplicated into folders or long-lived branches to account for environments. The minimal differences between environments are accounted for only through different configuration parameters (tfvars in our case). This is a standard practice in general software development, coming from years of painful learning (in many cases). Don't be tempted to reintroduce such strategies with infrastructure code as though it will be exempt from the consequences. It won't.

- *Dumb pipelines and smart scripts*—In other words, the pipeline or workflow triggered by the git event should contain only ordering logic. The individual steps of the pipeline will call external, versioned pipeline code (such as CircleCI orbs or shell script libraries) or local scripts for logic unique to the pipeline. This pipeline architecture has two important benefits. First, the *smart* shared code provides an effective, sustainable means of sharing standardized pipelines, keeping pipeline code DRY across teams and enabling developers to pass nonfunctional compliance checks successfully. Second, the relatively *dumb* pipeline code preserves a realistic ability to change out the pipeline tool should more effective or affordable options arise. (This is one example of *preserving domains of change* as described in chapter 2.)

- *Using local-code quality practices*—Use .gitignore, precommit hooks that run lint and style checks with each commit and all the usual repository-level code lifecycle practices.

If you have worked in software development, you will recognize that this list is standard for software pipelines. It may be because software-defined infrastructure is relatively recent. Still, it is common to find infrastructure engineers dismissing many of the hard-learned lessons of software development, not realizing that these apply to infrastructure code. The GitOps movement that began a few years ago has been a mixed bag of good and bad practices and has led many people to have to relearn all the lessons traditional software practitioners learned over the years of working with version control and pipeline orchestration. Managing code in a version control system and triggering automated build and deployment from changes in the source code is a well-understood practice. Labeling the practice as *GitOps* in an infrastructure context does not bring anything new to the domain.

There's one more thing about infrastructure code that's worth mentioning early on. When you're building an engineering platform product, the architecture, engineering choices, and implementation need to focus solely on optimizing for the platform itself.

Due to the history of DevOps and IaC initiatives in many companies, there's often a culture of continuously evolving Terraform code to support every possible use case. But many of those use cases will have nothing to do with the engineering platform. Some will need to stick around indefinitely but don't fit into self-serve patterns, or they're specific to just one team. Trying to create an architecture and code base that supports both an engineering platform and multiple unrelated use cases is not only impractical, but it will soon result in the delivery of capabilities and features for the platform being as slow and cumbersome as the traditional IT process it's meant to replace.

6.3.4   *Choosing an IaC framework*

In a cloud setting, infrastructure code should be declarative by design. Why? With very few exceptions, a cloud vendor's APIs are intentionally architected to be declarative. For example, we don't control how AWS sets up software-defined networks, deploys an RDS PostgreSQL database on an AWS-managed server (EC2 instance), or handles most tasks in any step-by-step way. When we interact with cloud vendor services, we just give them configuration values that get stored in some database we never see. Behind the scenes, an API does the actual setup and configuration based on the parameters we have provided. The frameworks provided by the cloud vendors themselves demonstrate this characteristic. Not surprisingly, many modern IaC frameworks are declarative by design.

Compare this to earlier IaC frameworks that had their start when the primary activity (often the only possible activity) was configuring virtual servers (e.g., Chef, Puppet, Ansible). Indeed, there was an end-state in mind, but the underlying purpose of the framework was to manage the steps required to arrive at a desired configuration. When this is still needed, then use tools well suited to those *imperative* configuration requirements.

But, particularly with the rise of cloud-native architectures, the vast majority of IaC tasks involved in using and managing cloud vendor infrastructure are highly declarative in nature. The optimal framework provides the most human-readable format for passing structured data to the cloud vendor's APIs while introducing the least processing overhead (wait time) beyond the vendor APIs' wait time.

We will use Terraform for our direct vendor infrastructure configuration as it meets our criteria. When we use Terraform to build and maintain an internal product, there's one key difference compared to how a typical DevOps or site reliability engineering team might use it. DevOps teams must focus on making their Terraform code flexible enough to handle a wide range of use cases. One week, they might need to provision a network (VPC) for one team with specific configurations, and the next week, it's a completely different setup for another team. Their priority is to support various requests efficiently, so they structure their Terraform code to simplify their workflow.

On the other hand, when we're building the internal components of an engineering platform, we're creating resources for a much more opinionated use case. The platform team is responsible for maintaining and evolving the platform over its entire lifetime. If we had to design our Terraform modules or resource definitions to support every possible use case across the company, every change would need extensive testing.

The structure of our Terraform code would shift to accommodate scenarios unrelated to our product, slowing down changes and making evolution within the code much more difficult and probably rare. The concern is there even when we choose to use a Terraform resource maintained by someone else. Most of the officially maintained modules related to cloud infrastructure are meant to be generic and provide access to all the configurations available for the resource. This makes it a low-risk choice. But when assessing outside modules, in addition to security considerations, try to determine whether there is some level of opinionation within the module that, should the goals of the maintainers change, would negatively affect our product.

6.3.5 *Test-driven development of infrastructure code*

In terms of the workflow pattern used by engineers, test-driven development (TDD) in infrastructure code is the same as in other software (see figure 6.11).

We said in the previous section that infrastructure is usually highly declarative. The action is happening inside the vendor APIs. But if this is the case, how much value is there in writing tests? You're not writing the code that technically performs the actions. You can write integration tests to confirm the infrastructure configuration, but isn't that just testing whether the AWS API works as advertised? True. If that were all testing inside of infrastructure pipelines could tell us, then it wouldn't be especially useful. However, integration tests for infrastructure code are still valuable.

First, exhaustive integration testing is very effective when building and maintaining a reusable module, as in a Terraform module. A traditional integration configuration test is the proper test to assess the module's internal workings. In this case, while the module also just accepts a set of configuration parameters, the specific resources provisioned are an opinionated decision of the module creator, not the cloud provider. As the developer of a reusable module, you will create a CI pipeline that applies the module in a dedicated cloud account or project with integration tests to confirm that your module correctly provisions the desired resources and configuration you intend.

Second, the TDD workflow provides an effective means of demonstrating story acceptance criteria. For example, the story might be that the subnet used for managed nodes in the control plane clusters supports the use of Karpenter, and an established naming convention will apply. In this case, while the AWS-provided VPC Terraform module can be counted on to successfully create and configure the VPC based on the parameters you provide, you will nonetheless want to confirm that tagging of the subnet uses the correct naming convention. The following snippet is an example of how the subnet parameters are provided to the VPC module:

```
...
private_subnets       = var.vpc_private_subnets
private_subnet_suffix = "private-subnet"
private_subnet_tags   = {
  "kubernetes.io/cluster/${var.cluster_name}" = "shared"
  "tier"                                       = "node"
  "karpenter.sh/discovery"                     = "${var.cluster_name}-vpc"
}
```

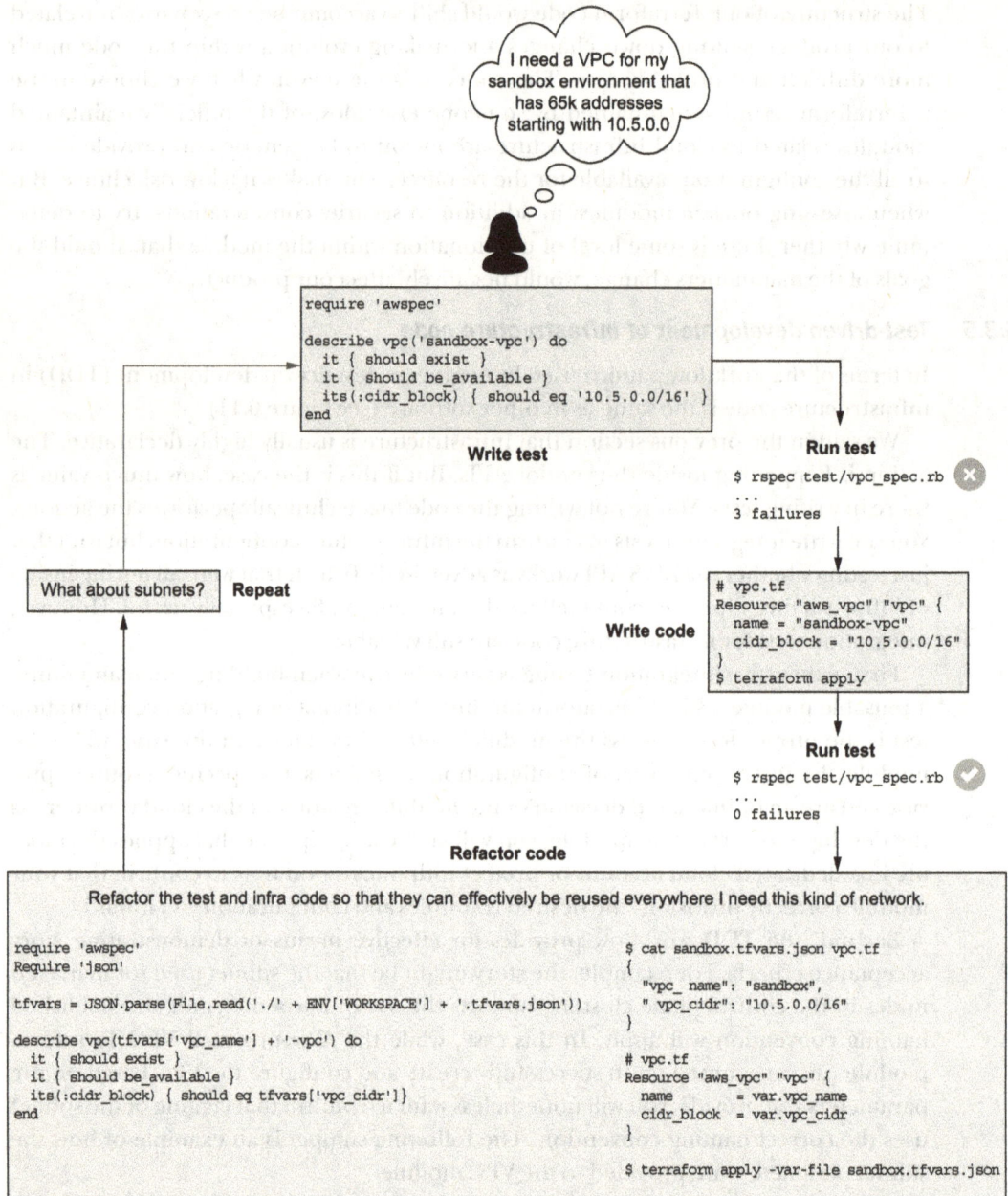

Figure 6.11 Write the tests. Run the tests. The tests are failing at this point. Then, start writing and applying the infrastructure code until the tests pass. Finally, refactor the code for dryness, readability, performance, etc.

An effective test is to confirm that the required tag values match the naming convention pattern, automating the proof that the acceptance criteria were met.

Third, integration tests can be practical as recurring tests aimed at early detection of configuration drift caused by actors outside the infrastructure pipeline. In a way, infrastructure code has the shortest potential shelf-life of any software because no matter what the code configures, there is always a manual way to change the infrastructure. An example is if someone makes a change through the console, and as a result, the actual state of the infrastructure does not match the desired state. There's very little chance of that with my Java app. Recurring configuration tests can be effective at detecting unexpected changes that can eventually become a breaking change.

Finally, don't overlook the long-term benefits of writing tests first. Writing the tests first forces you to work through your understanding of the intended outcome of the infrastructure code you are about to create. While creating the actual code (Terraform in our case), minor, unintended changes in direction, assumptions you didn't realize you were making, and even confirmation bias in favor of the implementation approach adopted can all creep into your thinking, with the result that tests written after primary development are statistically more likely to return false positives. In other words, the tests pass, yet the logic of the test is flawed and should have resulted in a fail based on the actual desired outcome.

Several tools exist for infrastructure configuration testing. Let's look at an open source example for AWS used in figure 6.11. Awspec (https://github.com/k1LoW/awspec) is an extension to the Ruby Rspec (https://rspec.info) framework that incorporates the AWS Ruby SDK to support comprehensive testing and has predefined assertions for the most commonly used resources.

One of the first things we will do in an upcoming section is create AWS IAM roles. The following is an example of testing for one of the built-in AWS roles, AdminUsersRole:

```
require 'awspec'
describe iam_role('AdminUsersRole') do
  it { should exist }
  it { should have_iam_policy('AdministratorAccess') }
end
```

iam_role is a predefined assertion in awspec. I only need to specify a role name.

This example tests for two things. First, does the named role exist?

Second, does it have an attached policy called AdministratorAccess?

InSpec (https://docs.chef.io/inspec/) is another tool originating from Rspec and now supports multiple clouds. The following example demonstrates a test for a Google Cloud project's existence and active state:

```
describe google_project(project: 'my-gc-project') do
  it { should exist }
  its('lifecycle_state') { should cmp 'ACTIVE' }
end
```

Notice the similar RSpec structure.

> **Exercise 6.2   Create and run a configuration test against a built-in AWS role**
>
> Use your personal, administrative-level AWS credentials and run the previous iam_
> role check against the AWS account you use for the exercises. Then, change the
> policy name to misspell it to test for a policy we know doesn't exist and see how
> Rspec reports the failure. (Exercise code samples are available in the companion
> code GitHub repository.)

6.3.6 *Static code analysis*

Like general programming languages, static code analysis of IaC code is an effective
means of maintaining general code quality and sustainability. However, as discussed
in section 6.3.5, IaC is highly declarative, so things like test coverage, cyclomatic
complexity, and other more traditional imperative code checks are not particularly
feasible or valuable. However, this still leaves some valuable analysis that can be
performed:

- Syntax
- Style and best practice conventions
- Static security analysis

There are dozens of paid and open source tools in this space. Whichever tool we use,
we want early feedback, locally and in our CI pipeline.

Let's look at a specific Terraform example for each category:

- Terraform (https://developer.hashicorp.com/terraform/install)
- Tflint (https://github.com/terraform-linters/tflint)
- Trivy (https://github.com/aquasecurity/trivy)

The Terraform CLI `validation` and `fmt` commands provide syntax validation and
canonical formatting checks.

Tflint is a linting framework for Terraform that warns about deprecations, validates
cloud vendor parameters such as instance types, and provides feedback around common best practices and naming conventions. The plugin architecture enables customization for the cloud provider we are using. Create a local file named `.tflint.hcl` with
the following contents and run `tflint --init` to configure for AWS:

```
plugin "terraform" {
  enabled = true
  preset  = "all"
}
plugin "aws" {
  enabled = true
  version = "0.30.0"
  source  = "github.com/terraform-linters/tflint-ruleset-aws"
}
```

Trivy is a multipurpose, open source security scanning tool created by Aquasec. It can scan various infrastructure technologies and frameworks, including Terraform files. The trivy `config` command can scan Terraform files for security problems.

Install these three tools and then complete the following exercise.

Exercise 6.3   Perform static analysis of Terraform code

Create a file called `main.tf` with the following contents:

```
resource "aws_vpc" "main" {
  cidr_block = "10.0.0.0"
  tags = {
    Name = "main"
    Pipeline = "https://github.com/my-org-name/my-repo-name"
  }
}
resource "aws_security_group_rule" "my_sg_rule" {
  type = "ingress"
  from_port = 0
  to_port = 65535
  protocol = "tcp"
  cidr_blocks = ["0.0.0.0/0"]
  security_group_id = "sg-123456"
}
```

1 Using the Terraform CLI, validate the syntax and canonical formatting of `main.tf`.
2 Correct the error and rerun the test.
3 Using the Terraform CLI, apply canonical formatting to `main.tf`.
4 Using Tflint, check the code style and formatting for best practices.
5 Make the recommended changes until Tflint no longer returns warnings.
6 Run a Trivy scan `main.tf`.
7 Finally, correct the security problems in `main.tf`. For the MEDIUM alert, rather than adding a VPC Flow Log configuration, research the Trivy documentation for instructions on how to add an inline comment to ignore that particular security check.

Before we leave the topic, let's implement the local git commit hooks recommendation from figure 6.7. The Python package pre-commit (https://pre-commit.com/) is an effective utility for managing local git commit hooks. Like the integration tests, the static analysis scans we examined earlier are steps that we want to include in our CI pipeline. Static tests can be applied locally against changed files with each commit for faster feedback rather than waiting for the pipeline to fail.

In the typical Terraform pipeline, an effective commit scan will include

- Static code analysis scans (same as will be applied in the pipeline) (https://mng .bz/Gw5R)

- Scan for secrets inadvertently committed (https://github.com/awslabs/git-secrets)
- Basic git syntax and configuration standards (https://github.com/pre-commit/pre-commit-hooks)
- Basic syntax scans for structured file types commonly found in Terraform repos

Exercise 6.4   Implement static analysis through commit hooks

Create a new git repository locally and add the uncorrected main.tf file from Exercise 6.3.

Using the Python package `pre-commit`, apply pre-commit hooks that perform each of the above four common scans for Terraform pipelines.

6.3.7 *Reusable pipeline code*

So far we've talked about seven essential infrastructure pipeline practices, discussed how to choose an IaC framework, and done a deeper dive into test-driven development of infrastructure code and performing static code analysis. Now, let's discuss reusable pipeline code (see figure 6.12).

An effective, sustainable pipeline architecture is built around a strategy described as "dumb pipelines and smart code." This is a play on words from the term "smart endpoints, dumb pipes" that has become well-known in the microservice development community. In figure 6.13, you can see specific triggering events and the steps. In the context of CircleCI, let us first define what triggers and steps are:

- *Triggers*—A change to the source code in our repository should be the only reason the vast majority of our pipelines are triggered. Running a build or integration test on a routine schedule (nightly) can be a helpful CI practice. Pipelines triggering other pipelines outside the same repository are nearly always a bad idea and indicate that code between those repositories is being coupled in unhealthy ways.
- *Steps*—In CircleCI, a command is a series of steps, and a job is a series of steps with a specified executor (the environment). In GitHub Actions, an action is a series of steps, and a workflow is a set of steps with the runner definition.

In CircleCI, the pipeline defined in the config.yml file is *triggered* any time there is a change to the repository, including when a tag is applied. Each job listed in the workflows can also have a filter added to limit the job to a more specific change. The following filter will limit a job to run only when a new tag is added:

```
filters:
  branches:
    ignore: /.*/
  tags:
    only: /.*/
```

Infrastructure pipeline orchestration practices

Use test-driven development (TDD).

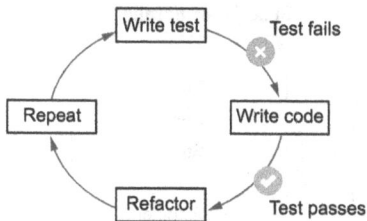

```
        Write test  ──→ Test fails
          ↑              ↓
       Repeat         Write code
          ↑              ↓
        Refactor ←── Test passes
```

Use trunk-based development (TBD).

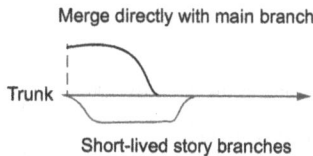

Merge directly with main branch

Trunk

Short-lived story branches

Test and release pipelines follow a set path to production.

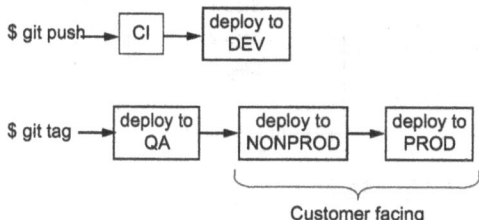

```
$ git push ──→ CI ──→ deploy to
                      DEV
```

```
$ git tag ──→ deploy to ──→ deploy to ──→ deploy to
              QA           NONPROD       PROD
```

Customer facing

Only one value is maintained in pipeline tool's ENV values.

Environment Variables

Environment variables are available to any job that request Environment Variables documentation.

Name	Value
OP_SERVICE_ACCOUNT_TOKEN	****YS_J9

Keep infrastructure code DRY.

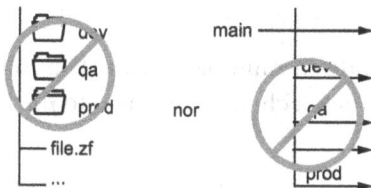

```
  dev
  qa
  prod
  file.zf
  ...
```

nor

```
main ──────────→
        dev ──────→
        qa ──────→
        prod ──────→
```

Build dumb pipelines and smart scripts. ◀━━━

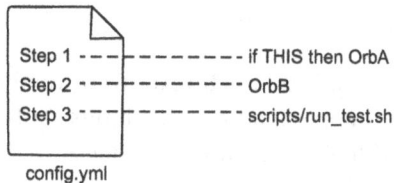

```
Step 1 ------------- if THIS then OrbA
Step 2 ------------- OrbB
Step 3 ------------- scripts/run_test.sh
```

config.yml

Use local code protection and quality practices.

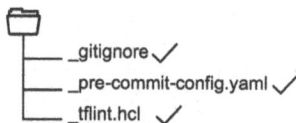

```
  _gitignore ✓
  _pre-commit-config.yaml ✓
  _tflint.hcl ✓
```

Figure 6.12 Essential practices for building reusable and sustainable infrastructure pipelines, including test-driven development, trunk-based development, path-to-production consistency, controlled environment variables, DRY principles, dumb pipelines with smart scripts, and local code protection

Jobs can also include a list of one or more other jobs that must be completed first. We can define a series of jobs that run in order upon a trigger or a list of jobs that will all run at the same time. Since many jobs in a pipeline can share the same trigger, we can

One or more automated
steps within a defined
environment

And there can be more
than one of these, either
in serial or parallel

Triggering event ⟹ Results in

• Git push or tag (most)
• Scheduled by time
• By another pipeline (rare)

Step 1
Step 2
Step 3

——— Environment ———

Step 1
Step 2
Step 3

——— Environment ———

...

Step 1
Step 2
Step 3

——— Environment ———

...

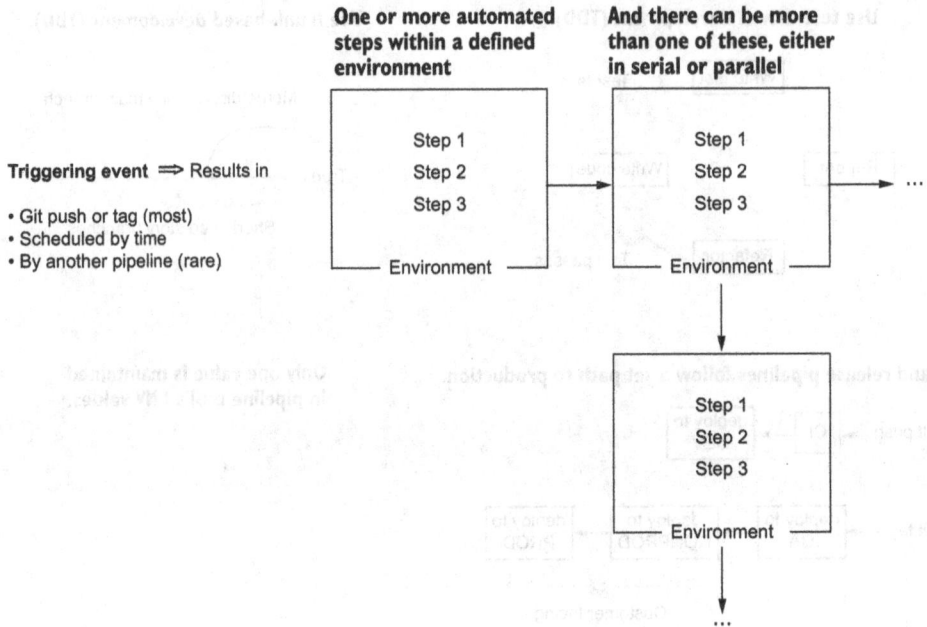

Figure 6.13   We intentionally want to constrain the complexity of our pipelines to these fundamental structures.

use a Yaml anchor to avoid duplicating this code in multiple places. The following example is a filter that limits a job to run only when a change is pushed to the branch called `main`, ignoring all tags:

```
on-push-main: &on-push-main
  branches:
    only: /main/
  tags:
    ignore: /.*/
...
workflows:
  jobs:

    my-job:
      filters: *on-push-main
```

We want to keep our local pipelines as dumb as possible. Here, "local" means the pipeline code that lives in the repository with the code it manages. This pipeline should focus only on when to run (triggers) and the order of events. Wherever possible, specifics about how to perform a step should be defined in shared, versioned libraries of pipeline code or similarly shared language libraries such as bash or Python. If the step details are unique to the pipeline, they should come from local scripts. Likewise, when the logic of a job or command is effectively unique to the pipeline, then local jobs and commands can be defined (see figure 6.14).

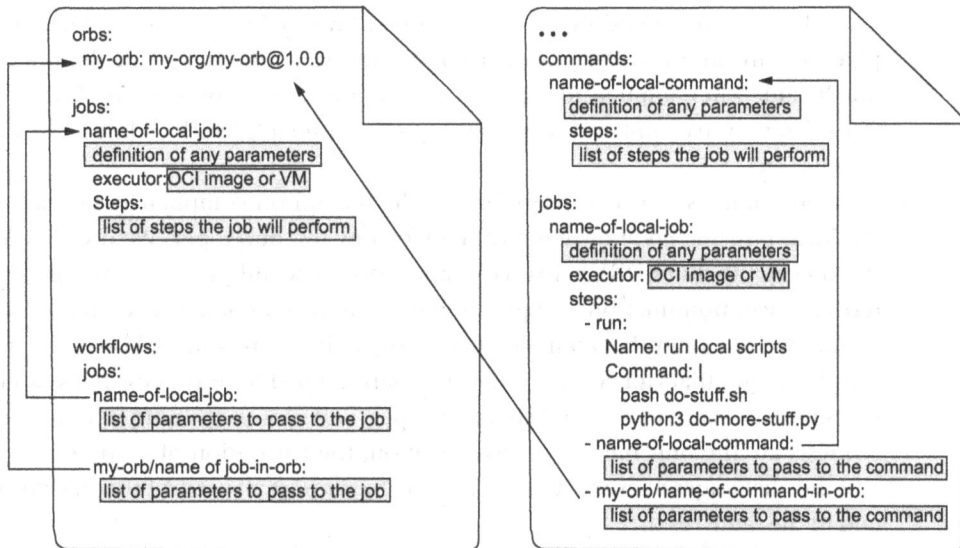

Figure 6.14 In CircleCI, you list all the jobs you want the pipeline to run beneath the workflows key. You can refer to a job that has been defined right in the same config.yml file, or you can refer to a job defined in an orb that will be pulled from the orb registry at pipeline runtime.

Jobs contain a list of steps to perform. The individual steps can run command-line instructions. But a step can also be the name of a command, defined in the same pipeline or an orb. Commands are also a list of steps. Jobs and commands can have required and optional parameters.

Any pipeline may have some steps that are unique to it. Still, most of what an infrastructure pipeline does depends on the IaC framework; the cloud vendor where the infrastructure is set up; and the tools used for testing, scanning, fetching secrets, compliance, and so on. This is no different than an application pipeline. If you decide to build an API with Python, most of what your pipeline will do is determined by that choice and by the specifics of the deployment environment for your API.

Because so much of what the local pipeline does will be common to the underlying type of code and environment, building and maintaining shared pipeline code libraries (orbs in CircleCI) will be a key part of what we do as the engineering platform product team. In practice, even with hundreds of teams using the platform, there will typically only be dozens of shared orbs or actions. These common libraries are also how we will manage the many nonfunctional (or cross-functional) requirements related to work normally done in the pipeline. Also, by sticking to this practice, we can prevent the implementation of a different pipeline tool from becoming so costly that it is impractical. This is an important feature of the product. And even though the first pipeline libraries we create in building the Epetech platform are for our own team's benefit, most will be equally useful to our eventual customers.

With so much depending on these shared libraries, how they are managed matters; pipelines are software. Assume that good software engineering practices will have as much value when applied to pipeline code as other types of software. When creating our orbs, we must apply software development principles such as linting, testing, versioning, etc.

In addition, as you read previously in the section on compliance, we want to keep the local pipeline code owned and managed by the developer. We use shared libraries to keep pipelines DRY across common workflows and provide developers with the tools to meet nonfunctional requirements, such as compliance. If we want developers to have the flexibility that comes from owning their own pipelines, how do we minimize the challenges that can come from using shared pipeline resources? If a shared job or command is too rigid or simplistic, developers will soon stop using it. Likewise, if pull requests are the only means of customization, the frustration of waiting on approvals and the challenges of every change needing to support all users of the shared code will end in the same result.

Versioning can address the problem of how changes from the orb owner can be released in a lower-friction manner. Users have time to understand any changes and can adapt to prevent being blocked. But this is not the only strategy. Additional strategies include

- Liberally include injection points throughout the job or command for custom steps.
- Provide overrides so the developer can customize the default parameters for tools or processes within the orb. Validate the parameters for needed guardrails.
- Allow tool or package version overrides wherever possible. Validate the parameters for needed guardrails.

The following sections show examples of each of these.

INJECTION POINTS FOR CUSTOM STEPS

A parameter to a CircleCI job or command can be defined as the type `steps`. Now, any valid list of steps can be passed as a parameter to the job.

Assume we are creating a shared job that performs the plan phase of a Terraform pipeline. The steps of the job could start out looking something like this:

```
Steps:
  - checkout
  - setup_remote_docker
  - run:
      name: terraform init
      working_directory: << parameters.working-directory >>
```

```
        command: |
          terraform version
          terraform init
    - run:
        name: terraform plan
        working_directory: << parameters.working-directory >>
        command: |
          terraform plan -var-file=<< parameters.terraform-var-file >> --out
tfplan.binary
          terraform show -json tfplan.binary | jq '.' > << parameters.
terraform-plan-outfile >>
    - when:
        name: run checkov scan of terraform source files
        condition: << parameters.checkov-scan >>
        Steps:
          - checkov:
              working-directory: << parameters.working-directory >>
              checkov-additional-args: << parameters.checkov-additional-args >>
              terraform-plan-outfile: << parameters.terraform-plan-outfile >>
```

Let's add the following parameters to the job definition:

```
after-checkout:
  description: Optional steps to run after checking out the repository code.
  type: steps
  default: []
after-init:
  description: Optional steps to run after running terraform init.
  type: steps
  default: []
after-plan:
  description: Optional steps to run after running terraform plan.
  type: steps
  default: []
after-complete:
  description: Optional steps to run after the entire plan job is complete.
  type: steps
  default: []
```

Within the orb job steps, add the following:

```
Steps:
  - checkout
  - setup_remote_docker
  - when:
      name: Run after-checkout custom steps
      condition: << parameters.after-checkout >>
      working_directory: << parameters.working-directory >>
      steps: << parameters.after-checkout >>
  - run:
      name: terraform init
      ...
```

Then do the same for each of the parameters at the respective location among the other job steps. Now, when using this shared job, a developer can include whatever additional steps they want, at any of the potentially useful locations within the job. Suppose they need to populate the contents of their varfile at runtime because some of the values are the result of computations the pipeline will perform. With the after-checkout parameter, they can create a local command that performs all the steps and pass it to the plan job to be performed right after checkout. No change is needed to the shared job, nor do they have to build into the shared job a feature that only they need and account for any negative effects on other users.

Keep this in mind when evaluating pipeline software. Generally, modern tools will have some means of passing or referencing custom pipeline steps from a shared job or command. For example, with GitHub Actions, when creating a shared workflow, you can have steps that reference specifically named workflows from the calling repository.

OVERRIDES TO TOOL PARAMETERS

Look back at the `terraform init` and `terraform plan` steps in the previous job. Let's change those steps:

```
- run:
      name: terraform init
      working_directory: << parameters.working-directory >>
      command: |
        terraform version
        terraform init << parameters.terraform-init-additional-args >>

- run:
      name: terraform plan
      working_directory: << parameters.working-directory >>
      command: |
        terraform plan \
          <<#parameters.terraform-var-file>>
  -var-file=<< parameters.terraform-var-file >>
  <</parameters.terraform-var-file>> \
          <<#parameters.terraform-plan-additional-args>>
  << parameters.terraform-plan-additional-args >>
  <</parameters.terraform-plan-additional-args>> \
          --out tfplan.binary
        terraform show -json tfplan.binary | jq '.' >
  << parameters.terraform-plan-outfile >>
```

In this version, the developer can pass additional parameters to the init step. There are many reasons they might need to do this. What if someone made a manual change to the AWS resource through the console and the result was the need to use the `--upgrade` or `--migrate-state` flag?

Also, note that the new version of the `terraform plan` step doesn't assume that a varfile is being passed. It is an option. This allows us to take advantage of a very effective varfile template strategy. There are several situations where the ability to populate the contents of a varfile while the pipeline is running is necessary. What if we needed a secret value? Or what if the parameter needed was a global value maintained in a remote location, such as a certificate? When we are preprocessing varfile contents, the version of the file maintained in the repository is now a kind of template. At pipeline runtime, we populate the dynamic values within the file and use the result as the varfile for the actual Terraform actions. And, in this situation, we also want some assurance that this resulting file never appears accidentally in the repository. We can prevent git from including these files by adding the `*.tfvars` extension to our `.gitignore` file. At runtime, we fetch the template varfile from a folder, populate it, and write it to the working directory as an `.auto.tfvars` file. Terraform will automatically include the file, and you do not need to manage the -varfile parameter, reducing the risk of typos.

The new plan step also has an additional-args parameter so users can self-manage their own unique circumstances if needed. If there are Terraform plan arguments that specifically must not be used, such as overriding the backend state location, add validation logic as a step.

OVERRIDES TO TOOL VERSIONS

Another common point of friction is where orb versions are either not providing minor and patch updates to tools promptly or a new orb is released that has updated tools or packages but is breaking for a small subset of users. In both situations, allowing developers to specify a different version, whether newer or older, is often the only adjustment needed for them to use the current version of the orb.

In tracking the problems and effects among teams in large organizations over several years from using shared pipeline libraries, we have found that these three practices significantly reduced the majority of the long-term management problems. It isn't possible to remove 100% of the challenges from shared pipeline code, any more than you can remove 100% of the challenges from using regular programming language libraries. But these practices will make the experience dramatically better.

Users of the platform should also be encouraged to submit pull requests against orbs as they find improved ways for the orb to function or to increase its flexibility. But users of shared orbs should not need to make pull requests to avoid being blocked. The orb maintainer may not always respond promptly or may reject the proposed change for legitimate reasons. Because the source code of the orb is visible to users, if at any point a platform user needs a change in the behavior of an orb for whatever reason, they will not be blocked waiting for the owner of the orb to make the change on their behalf as they can clone the orb or include the orb directly in-line within their pipeline and then modify as needed.

STANDARD PIPELINES FOR MAINTAINING SHARED PIPELINE CODE

Building and maintaining reusable pipeline code or runners is like any other kind of software development. CircleCI maintains an official orb designed to support the development lifecycle of shared orbs (see figure 6.15; https://mng.bz/z26X).

Shared orbs

Single tool or process	Collection of tools or processes (more efficient when packaged together)	Build or domain specific (complete language or resource specific workflows)

orb-lpassword:
    install: (install tool)
    env: (inject env variables into shell)
    tp.l: (inject secrets into template file)
 	
orb-slack:
    message: (send web-hook message to channel)
	orb-image-provenance: (cosign, syft, oras)
	    sign: (use cosign to sign QCI image)
	    sbom: (use syft to generate image sbom)
	    puhlish-sbom: (use oras to publish sbom to docker registry)
	
	orb-common-pipeline-events:
	    post-message: (slack)
	    publish-release: (github-release-notes)
	    scheduled-pipeline: (use API to define scheduled pipeline in tool)
		orb-tools (SDLC for shared pipeline code)
		executor-tools (SDLC for pipeline runners)
		
		orb-kube-ops (specific operational tasks)
		
		(specific language pipelines)
		orb-terraform
		orb-python-api
		orb-java
		
		(workflows for interacting with internal business product domains)
		Customer-profile

Shared executors

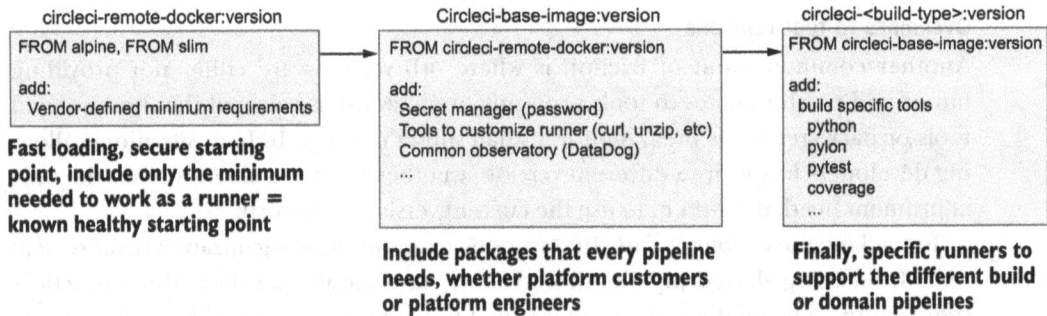

circleci-remote-docker:version	Circleci-base-image:version	circleci-<build-type>:version

FROM alpine, FROM slim
 	
add:
    Vendor-defined minimum requirements
	FROM circleci-remote-docker:version
	
	add:
	    Secret manager (password)
	    Tools to customize runner (curl, unzip, etc)
	    Common observatory (DataDog)
	    ...
		FROM circleci-base-image:version
		
		add:
		    build specific tools
		        python
		        pylon
		        pytest
		        coverage
		    ...

Fast loading, secure starting point, include only the minimum needed to work as a runner = known healthy starting point	**Include packages that every pipeline needs, whether platform customers or platform engineers**	**Finally, specific runners to support the different build or domain pipelines**

Figure 6.15   Specific tools or actions are the most basic type of shared pipeline code. But don't stop there.

The most accelerating shared pipeline libraries are those that are optimized to cover the entire lifecycle for specific resources and language builds, including all the internal cross-functional requirements along with the language CI needs. The smaller, single-tool, or domain collections are valuable in assembling into the larger workflows and also providing platform users with supported and standardized ways of using platform resources within custom portions of their pipelines. Along with the shared libraries, we want to maintain the underlying pipeline runners, which are preconfigured with expected packages.

The exercises in this book use open source orbs and executors. These are good representations of the kinds of pipeline resources you will typically need to build and use as part of getting started building an engineering platform. When you see later examples referencing these OSS resources, review the source code repositories to understand how to create an orb or executor build pipeline.

6.3.8 *Private executors (runners)*

Cloud vendors' API endpoints are exposed on the public internet. By following zero-trust networking engineering practices, every capability we include in our engineering platform, including how customers expose their APIs and UIs in each environment, can be effectively secured for similar public-facing access. This is the practice we recommend. But it is also true that most organizations require all services and infrastructure to be exposed only within internal, private networks unless and until they must be made available to customers. Despite the value that can be demonstrated by removing the network from the security equation, we should still take some time to talk about private runners when using SaaS-based pipeline tools, since this is the means of dealing with this challenge.

Private executors run on our cloud resources and are, therefore, a type of self-managed resource, unlike the executors hosted by CircleCI. We still want the same efficiency of use. This means we don't want executors that sit idle wasting resources, nor do we want pipelines waiting for executors to become available because they are a limited resource.

> **Exercise 6.5 Experiment with self-hosted runners**
>
> Let's do a simple experiment with private runners using our pipeline tool, CircleCI.
>
> Start a local instance of Kubernetes on your laptop and use the container-agent service provided by CircleCI to create a private runner resource that will watch for CircleCI projects configured to use it and run the pipelines on containers started within the local cluster (https://mng.bz/Ozol).
>
> For this exercise, we will need the following tools: CircleCI cli (https://circleci.com/docs/local-cli/), Kind (https://mng.bz/KwvZ), Kubectl (https://kubernetes.io/docs/tasks/tools/), and Helm (https://helm.sh/docs/intro/install/). These can be installed on macOS using the homebrew package manager as follows. See the tool documentation for installation on other operating systems:
>
> ```
> $ brew install kind kubectl helm circleci
> ```

6.4 *Cloud administrative identity*

With the preliminary stuff out of the way, let's start with the platform product domain, which is typically the first software-defined component in our platform. The cloud administrative identity domain encompasses the top-level cloud provider organization and account structure, along with the identities and permissions for the service accounts used in the foundational infrastructure automation (see figure 6.16).

The engineering platform should be assigned its own domain account, acting as a top-level account that can hold specific product-wide configurations, with subaccounts for platform test environments and nonproduction and production contexts. These are cloud vendor-specific. In AWS, these are "accounts." In Google Cloud, they are "projects," and in Azure, they are "subscriptions."

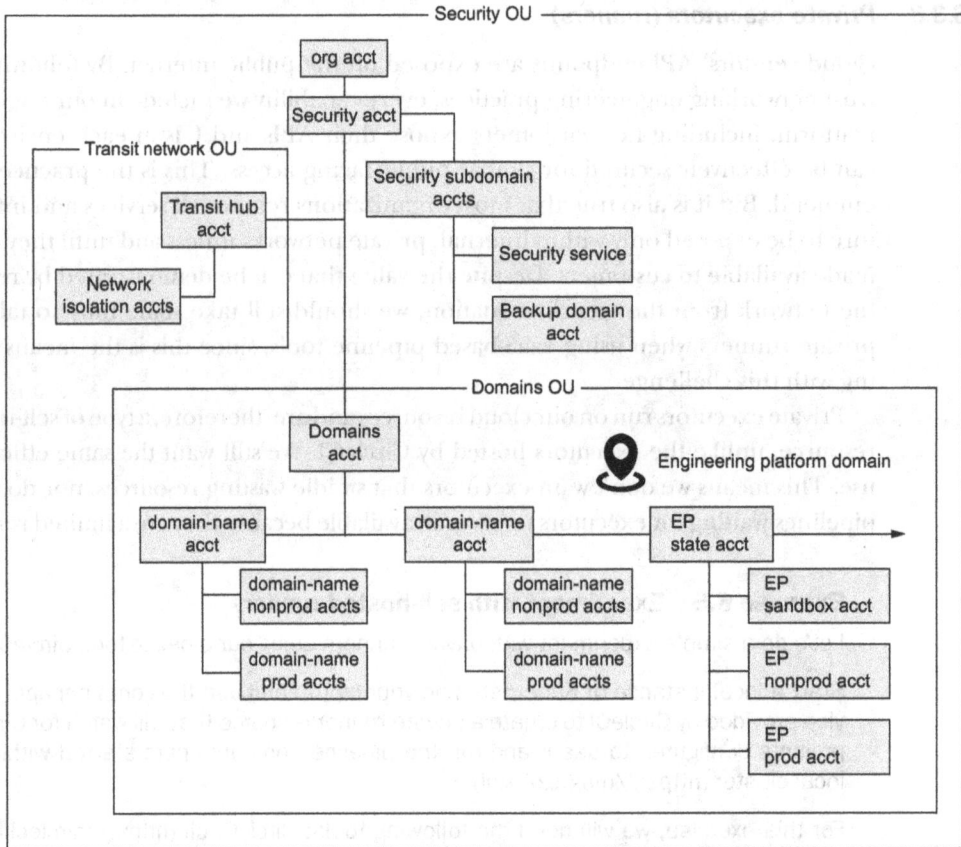

Figure 6.16 **An engineering platform exists within your organization's cloud structure, like any software product. This diagram shows a typical, well-formed AWS account structure with common organizational units (OUs) and clear product domain boundaries.**

A well-formed cloud vendor organizational structure will reflect the organization's business and technology domain capabilities. A platform engineering team has four distinct needs at the start of product development.

6.4.1 *Top-level Domain Account*

First, the product will have a certain amount of product-wide configuration. One example is where engineering platform-specific governance policies are applied at the cloud vendor level. If there is a top-level account, then such policies can be applied in a single location with confidence that if additional accounts or subaccounts are added in the future, the policies will consistently be applied. Another example is a configuration that is maintained on a product-wide basis. Service accounts, wide area network policies, or, in AWS, settings maintained in Parameter Store are examples of where there can be a value or an object that must have a single location or instance yet also have product-wide (or cross-account) implications. A dedicated top-level domain or *state* account is an effective means of addressing this problem. It is not uncommon for many of the top-level items mentioned here to be managed by other teams in your organization. So long as it is recognized that the delivery team for an engineering platform is an administrative-level team that must have administrator-level permissions to manage the cloud accounts in which their product will be created, this is manageable.

6.4.2 Platform product test environments

An engineering platform will create environments used by the platform engineers, delivering the product as development and test environments. The platform's internal customers never use these; they are solely for the development needs of the platform engineering team. It can be confusing to refer to this account as the *Dev* account since it is not where an internal platform customer has their *Dev* environments. We often refer to this account as the *sandbox* account.

There will also be many account-level settings incorporated into an engineering platform, and isolating platform test accounts from the internal customer-facing accounts is critical to enable the platform engineers to experiment, develop, and test without affecting platform users.

6.4.3 Internal customer nonproduction and production environments

An engineering platform separates nonproduction developer environments from production environments for governance and production stability risk management. From a product perspective, all internal customer-facing environments should be considered *Production* by a platform engineer. This is no different from our expectations when using AWS, Google Cloud, or any cloud infrastructure provider. While we may deploy cloud infrastructure that we consider *development* in a cloud account, we do not expect the cloud provider to maintain or support that infrastructure any differently. The only thing we expect from AWS is its *production* context.

Finally, the basic structure of accounts described here is the starting point for an engineering platform product. Increasing scale and complexity caused by regulatory or contractual problems can create the need for greater complexity than described here. Chapter 9 describes several architectural strategies for managing such complexity.

6.4.4 Service accounts and permissions

In AWS, roles are used to define a set of permissions. Each of our infrastructure pipelines will need a matching role that grants the permissions necessary to perform the pipeline's intended actions. Roles are assumed by the service account identity used in the pipeline. In other words, service accounts are defined only as having permission to assume roles (see figure 6.17).

The first pipeline we create will be responsible for managing the roles that service accounts assume when executing changes. These roles are kept consistent across all engineering platform product accounts to reduce complexity and maintain alignment. In the example shown in figure 6.17, we also manage IAM user service accounts, which are scoped to a single AWS account.

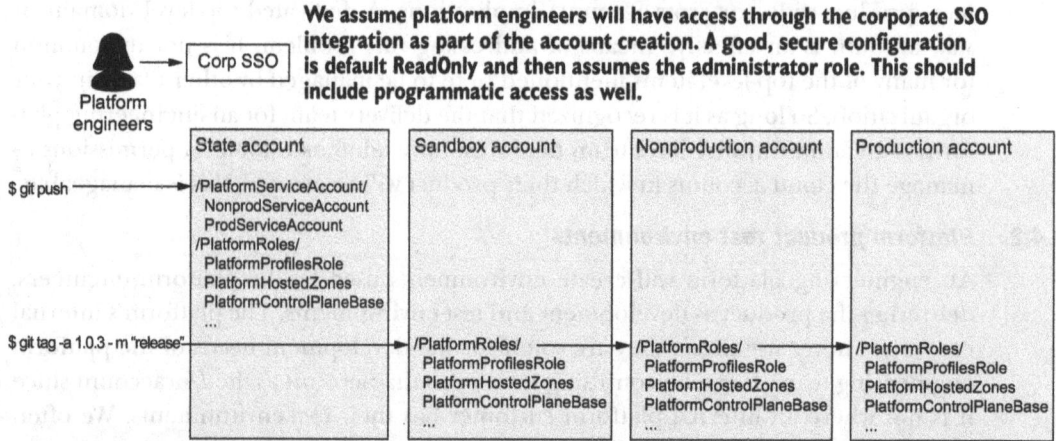

Figure 6.17 This diagram illustrates how service accounts and permissions are structured across multiple environments—state, sandbox, non-production, and production. Platform engineers interact with these accounts through a centralized SSO integration. Each environment contains a consistent set of roles that pipelines assume to execute changes, ensuring uniformity and security across the platform's lifecycle.

Since we will be using the Kubernetes API as the general control plane of the engineering platform, a relatively limited number of Terraform cloud infrastructure pipelines are needed. Many resources will be maintained via pipelines, but most will be services, controllers, and operators deployed to Kubernetes. We will use these operators and controllers to enable platform customers to create the infrastructure elements our platform supports, rather than additional Terraform workflows.

It is common to have fewer than a dozen pipelines using Terraform to configure cloud resources, even within a highly scaled engineering platform. No matter how few, these pipelines nonetheless need dedicated roles that enable the pipeline to manage just the resources for which they are responsible.

In these Epetech exercises, we will assume that we need to manage the creation and management of service accounts and credentials. The simplified exercise example solutions assume we are using only two accounts.

As we start creating service accounts, it is worth noting that many SaaS pipeline tools now offer OIDC integrations with the major cloud vendors. Defining an application identity for a pipeline tool still generates an associated ID and secret. From the integration owners' point of view, you are still creating an identifying credential in either case—and, frequently, one where the system doesn't offer an effective means of credential rotation. This also creates a completely new layer of automation complexity when applied broadly within the platform for developer use of the pipeline tool. Yet, the credential required to create this trust is used much less frequently. There are established, secure means of protecting automation service account credentials, and they are still the most broadly used industry standard. The option for system-to-system OIDC trust doesn't render the prior model insecure. Either one can be an appropriate choice.

An effective approach when launching an engineering platform with a single team is for the team to have just two service accounts used by their infrastructure pipelines: one for nonproduction use and one for production. The identities exist only in the State account. Use IAM Groups, one for nonproduction and one for production, to define in which accounts the service account may assume roles, and add the service account to the appropriate group.

We are ready to get started with the first infrastructure pipeline for our Epetech engineering platform. However, we can't start using git-push to trigger the first change since a pipeline will require an identity and a role that does not yet exist.

First, we will need to bootstrap, from our workstation, the minimum configuration necessary to enable our roles and service accounts pipeline to start managing these resources directly. Once those resources exist in the cloud account, we can add a pipeline to apply and manage the resources we just created and those that will be added to this pipeline as we go.

The minimum resources we need to put in place are

- An IAM role for the roles and service accounts pipeline that enables it to manage itself, plus all the other needed pipeline roles
- Two IAM users to be the nonproduction and production service account identities
- The initial credentials for our two service accounts

We will use the AWS-managed Terraform module for IAM resources (https://mng .bz/9ygo). As you create these resource definitions using modules, apply the following practices:

- Always pin modules, providers, and tools to a specific version to avoid unexpected breakage.
- Use a dedicated `role_path` for the roles created. It can greatly simplify ongoing management of pipeline roles when they are all kept in a single location.
- Place the IAM user on a dedicated path for the same reason.
- Name the backend state for each Terraform workspace with a combination of the pipeline repository name and workspace name. This makes it much easier to interact with the state store in a predictable way programmatically.
- Adopt a consistent tagging strategy. This is an organizational need as much as an engineering platform requirement. We will want to have a tagging strategy that lets us track and allocate costs. At a minimum, there should be a product identifier and a reference to the pipeline that orchestrates this code.
- Use Terraform variable validations wherever practical to help prevent errors in tfvar values.
- Keep Terraform DRY. Refrain from duplicating the code in folders or branches to deal with environmental differences. Having differences (apart from the

values passed in the tfvars file) between environments is a bad idea that we will surely regret.

Exercise 6.6   Bootstrap the nonproduction and production AWS accounts with the initial service accounts and pipeline role

Create a new repository called `aws-iam-profiles`. Create the following files and folder structure, and use the concepts we discussed previously to add the file contents that can be used to bootstrap our accounts. In these exercises, we will use only two AWS accounts:

```
aws-iam-profiles/
    environments/
        nonprod.auto.tfvars.json.tpl
        prod.auto.tfvars.json.tpl
    service-accounts.tf
    aws-iam-profiles-role.tf
    variables.tf
    versions.tf
```

Use your own credentials and administrator role permissions to apply the resources to the appropriate accounts with the matching tfvars.

Hint: Remember that we use Terraform Cloud for our backend state store. By default, a new workspace created in Terraform Cloud will be in *remote* execution mode; however, we will be operating in *local* execution mode. Local mode means we are not using the Terraform Cloud's additional paid features. Set our Terraform cloud organization default to local mode. The Terraform orb we are using can manage the settings on a per-workspace basis, or you can set it within the Terraform Cloud UI if you prefer.

Also, since you are using your credentials and permissions as part of this bootstrap, comment out the Terraform `assume_role` details in the AWS provider definition. We can uncomment those lines once the service accounts are set up and credentials are available.

BOOTSTRAPPING SERVICE ACCOUNT CREDENTIALS

After we have applied this configuration directly, the role that the pipeline in this repository needs exists in each account, and the service account identity the pipeline will use also exists in the correct account. Before implementing a pipeline for this repository that uses one of our new service account identities, we need to generate the associated access credentials and store these in our secrets management service. This pipeline will manage these credentials, rotating them in AWS and storing the current values in the secrets store. But the first time our pipeline runs, it will try to fetch the credentials from the secrets store. We will need to manually create and store those credentials for the pipeline to succeed and thereby take over the automated management of the service account credentials.

Use the AWS Console or CLI to generate credentials for each service account and store these in our secrets store. With that done, we can start on the first stage of our `platform_iam_roles` pipeline (see figure 6.18).

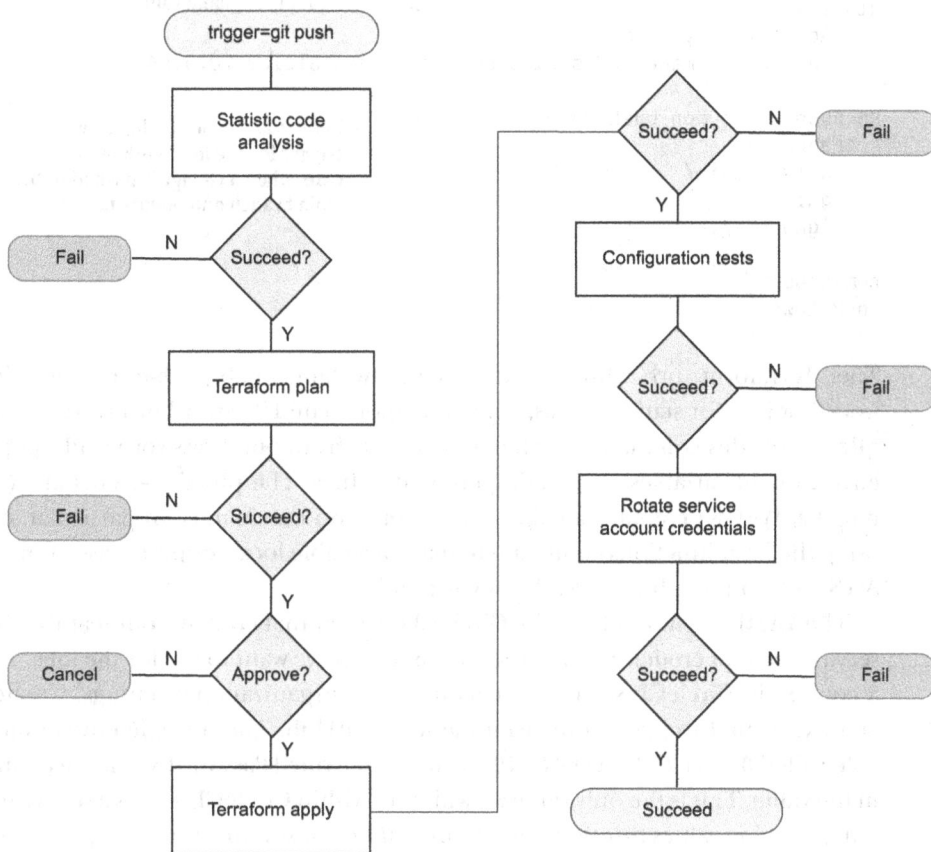

Figure 6.18 The logic of the first stage in our pipeline. We want to take these steps whenever a change is pushed to this repository.

This is a familiar Terraform flow. Terraform will generate a plan showing expected changes after the static code analysis, including a security scan. If it looks good, we want to apply the changes to our state account and compare the resulting actual configuration against our desired state. Finally, since we also store our service accounts in the state account, we will take this opportunity to perform a resilient credential rotation.

Create the file `config.yml` inside the `.circleci` folder and add the following snippet before starting the pipeline exercise:

```yaml
---
version: 2.1
orbs:
  terraform: twdps/terraform@3.1.1        ◄─┐  Uses these three orbs
  op: twdps/onepassword@3.0.0                 │  in creating our pipeline
  do: twdps/pipeline-events@5.1.0         ◄─┐  Uses a YAML anchor to define
globals:                                      │  a couple of global values
  - &context <my-team>
  - &executor-image twdps/circleci-infra-aws:alpine-2025.04

on-push-main: &on-push-main               ◄─┐  Defines an anchor to describe the
  branches:                                     trigger for the first workflows. In this
    only: /main/                                case, when a change is pushed to the
  tags:                                         main branch only, ignore tags.
    ignore: /.*/

commands:
workflows:
```

The Terraform orb (https://github.com/twplatformlabs/orb-terraform) includes workflow jobs for static analysis, plan, and apply. The 1Password orb (https://mng.bz/qRzE) provides commands for fetching secrets from our 1Password vault, populating environment variables, or creating credential files. The pipeline-events orb (https://mng.bz/WwGw) contains a collection of common commands. In particular, consider using the bash-functions command to make available local scripts for assuming roles in AWS and writing values into a 1Password vault.

The YAML anchor defines the CircleCI Context that contains our team's 1Password service account credentials and the runner image we want to use for the jobs. To create a context in CircleCI, select contexts from the organizational settings. Create a new context named to match our team name in GitHub. Add a single environment variable called OP_SERVICE_ACCOUNT_TOKEN and place our 1Password service account token in the value. This is the only value we will store within CircleCI. This is a secure location, but managing values through this feature is time-consuming and error-prone. All other values we need in the pipeline will be fetched at pipeline runtime. The OSS runner contains all the packages and dependencies for our Terraform pipeline (https://mng.bz/8XaB) and is part of a series of examples of maintaining preconfigured runners. The source code for these orbs and executors is open source, and you can review it to see exactly what the job or command does. CircleCI pipelines do not use the YAML key globals. Still, since it conforms to standard YAML, you can include additional data even though the pipeline processor itself will not do anything with it.

At this point, we are using some existing open source orbs to demonstrate versioned, shared pipeline code based on the tool we use for these examples. If you are using a different pipeline tool, of course, you can follow the pipeline code patterns of that tool. Just keep in mind the outcome. These bits of pipeline code need to be available from remote, versioned sources so that developer pipelines can self-manage the timing of pulling in upgrades. Most modern pipeline tools support this form of software-defined pipeline. What happens if you either choose a tool that does not support this or, even if it does, you don't implement it to enable developers to self-manage? Changes mean tickets and waiting.

> ### Exercise 6.7 Create the CI and development test pipeline for IAM service accounts and roles
>
> Now we are ready to complete the rest of the first stage of our pipeline according to figure 6.18 and test it against our nonproduction account. Complete the starting pipeline setup by adding the workflows and commands needed into the sections "commands" and "workflows." Wait until the following exercise to work on the credential rotation step. Don't forget to uncomment the lines from versions.tf that cause Terraform to attempt to assume the needed IAM role.

When using the static-code-analysis, plan, or apply jobs from the Terraform orb, remember that you can pass commands as a parameter, and they will be run at the specified location in the job. If we discover the need to set up some credentials or inject values into a tfvars template, we can easily do that without changing the orb directly.

When you are ready to start triggering the pipeline, go to our CircleCI organization, find the aws-iam-profiles repository among the projects, and start building. When you click set up project you will be asked whether you want to add a config.yml or use one already in the repository. Choose the option to use the pipeline you have created on the main branch. This step of setting up a project in CircleCI only happens when first connecting CircleCI to a repository.

You can see in this pipeline the effects of using versioned pipeline code steps or jobs. In this case, the Terraform orb we used provides most of the functionality we need for a typical Terraform pipeline, including hooks that let us provide custom commands at various points in the workflow. The orb provides preconfigured steps for calling the static analysis tools we have decided to use. In the future, should the technical details for interacting with the tool change or even a change in the tool itself, we can release a new version of the orb for users to adopt and afford a window of time for this before users deprecate the earlier pattern.

AUTOMATED ROTATION OF SERVICE ACCOUNT CREDENTIALS

The final step in the first stage of our pipeline is the automated rotation of service account credentials. Calling the AWS API to generate new credentials for an IAM user is straightforward. The complexity lies in safely updating those credentials in the secrets store. If new credentials are written while pipelines or workloads are still using the old ones, those jobs can fail. To avoid this race condition, we need a mechanism that ensures credentials remain valid and usable throughout the rotation process.

A common practice is to use a two-key pattern and perform a rotation at least twice within the desired frequency. What does this mean in practice? See figure 6.19.

IAM > Users > NonprodServiceAccount

SUMMARY		
ARN arn:aws:iam::123456789123:user/ PlatformServiceAccounts/ NonprodServiceAccount	Console access Disabled	Access key 1 AKIAR*****************-Active Used 6 days ago. 13 days old.
Created April 26, 2023, 21:40 (UTC-05:00)	Last console sign-in -	Access key 2 AKIAR*****************-Active Used 3 hours ago. 6 days old.

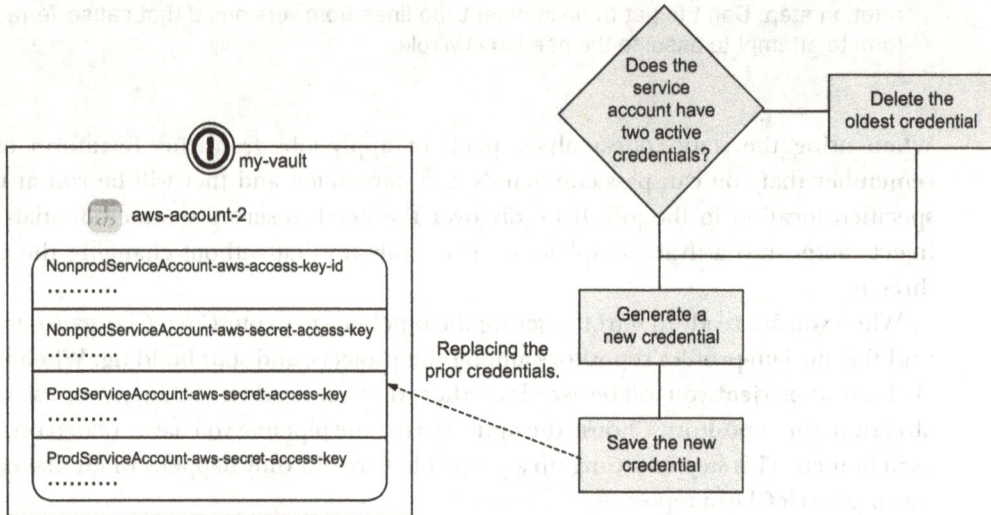

Figure 6.19 Our service account has two valid credentials at any given time. Only the latest credential is maintained in the secrets store, and the prior keys remain valid until the next rotation to prevent workloads and orchestration from failing due to the race condition of the key being changed while a job is already in process.

New jobs or pipelines launching constantly fetch the credentials from the secrets store and are therefore using the latest credentials. If you define an automated rotation to occur every 7 days, for example, the active key is never more than 7 days old, and both keys will be rotated every 14 days.

Support for this automated identity flow is one of the reasons IAM users can have two keys. This could be done using the AWS CLI. But there are a couple of steps, and if we use the AWS CLI, we will need to put these steps into a script. We only need to do this in this one pipeline, so that is not necessarily a problem. We could also create a shareable utility that can be used in any pipeline. Let's use the Python package `iam-credential-rotation` (https://pypi.org/project/iam-credential-rotation/).

The default method for the tool requires a single parameter: the IAM path where the service accounts are located. Recall we used the path `/PlatformServiceAccounts/` for the two service accounts we defined. Assuming you have appropriate credentials, the following command will apply the workflow from figure 6.18 for every IAM user found on the path specified as parameters. The resulting new credentials will be written to stdout:

```
$ iam-credential-rotation PlatformServiceAccounts
{
  "NonprodServiceAccount": {
    "AccessKeyId": "AKIARKL*************",
    "SecretAccessKey": "bCFqIBZUo**************************"
  },
  "ProdServiceAccount": {
    "AccessKeyId": "AKIARKLI*************",
    "SecretAccessKey": "cVSkOhunYxS**************************"
  }
}
```

Exercise 6.8   Add a credential rotation step to the first stage pipeline

Add a credential rotation step to the after-apply parameters of our Terraform apply pipeline step. This will come after the AWS integration tests:

```
After-apply:
  - aws-integration-tests:
      account: nonprod
  - rotate-service-account-credentials:
      account: nonprod
```

Now, define a local command that will use the iam-credential-rotation utility to rotate our service account credentials and store the resulting new credentials in our 1Password vault, overwriting the existing service account credentials.

RELEASING OUR CHANGES TO PRODUCTION

With every step in the first stage of our pipeline running successfully, we need a way to release this change to production. We trigger our release pipeline with a semantic tag to our latest commit.

Recall that our pipeline roles are deployed into each account. They are identical in each account. These roles are only assumed by our platform's dedicated infrastructure service accounts. And only the *ProdServiceAccount* can assume roles in the Production account. Our release workflow would look like figure 6.20, with three approval steps where an engineer can validate the Terraform plan results and decide to apply the changes to the following account. Any failure along the way will cause the entire release workflow to fail. That is the outcome we want. If we discover any environmental difference, the solution will be a code change, and all changes must go through this path to production to ensure that every instance of the product is built from the same code.

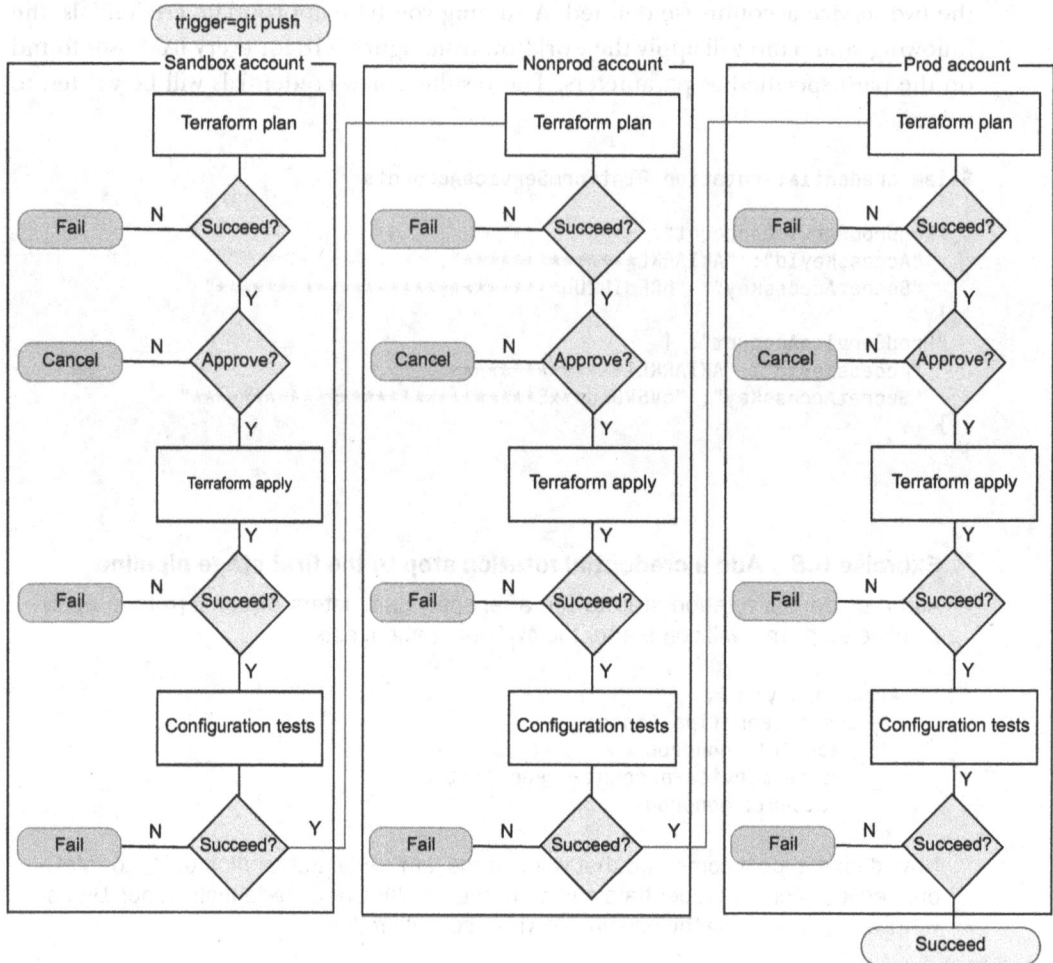

Figure 6.20 In the four-account strategy described at the start of this chapter, our service accounts are deployed to the State account only, and it is also in this account where we perform the initial configuration test of the roles.

The plan job will also write a plan file to the pipeline artifacts. You can download the plan through the CircleCI UI.

Working with Terraform

Terraform does a good job of listing the changes that will be made—something to think about when reviewing the plan output in the pipeline log. Over the years of using Terraform in an enterprise setting, we have made some observations that prove true nearly all the time:

- If you find the output of a Terraform plan so long that it is hard to follow the changes, this is the first sign that the amount of stuff being managed by the resources within the plan is simply too large. Entire production stacks of all related infrastructure managed by a single block of code are nearly always an anti-pattern. Good domain design within infrastructure code is essential for healthy change velocity.

- You can have Terraform Apply use the plan step output file rather than referencing the Terraform code directly when making the changes. This capability within Terraform arose during the early days when pipeline-orchestrated IaC was exceedingly rare, and the norm was for someone to generate a change plan that would not be applied for sometimes several days or even weeks. During that time, a human may have made manual changes to the same infrastructure.
- Including the "historical" state of the infrastructure within the plan logic when attempting the actual change was the best way of revealing those unintended changes before they created unexpected results. But recognize that the situation (e.g., an engineering team running Terraform from their laptops and requiring days to apply planned changes) is the symptom of a much greater problem.
- Plan feedback will always be valuable, and you could find yourself going back to the drawing board based on it. But confirming the expected results from Terraform Plan should always be quick, and there should never be delays between a successful plan and subsequent application.

Exercise 6.9 Create the release pipeline for IAM service accounts and roles

We need a trigger that will watch for new tags:

```
on-tag-main: &on-tag-main
  Branches:
    ignore: /.*/
  Tags:
    only: /.*/
```

Now add a workflow for the release job in the pipeline. We only need to deploy to a single account since we only use two accounts instead of four in our simplified example. This means we only need to add the first column from figure 6.20.

ADDITIONAL PIPELINE STEPS

What if we were to add some form of notification to our pipeline? We could add a command to send a message to a team chat channel. In practice, such messages can have value but have the same limitations as a monitoring alert. The message must be actionable, or it will be ignored. Sending a Fail message when a pipeline fails can be actionable. But then our pipeline tool will tell us when a pipeline fails. Most often, a pipeline is triggered because we made a change, and we will be watching for the pipeline results. And there are less complex ways of adding an additional pipeline status indicator than making this the general responsibility of the underlying pipeline code (https://ccmenu.org; https://github.com/build-canaries/nevergreen). Yet, there can be situations where a specific notification will be actionable and is worth adding to a pipeline.

The pipeline-events orb we are using includes a command for sending messages to Slack. We could notify our team of production changes just by adding these lines to the `after-apply` parameters:

```
- do/slack-bot:
      channel: engineering platform events
      message: New release of aws-iam-profiles
      include-link: true
      include-tag: true
```

How do we notify customers about new feature releases, incidents or outages, and events in general? A good experience will involve multiple channels, but subscribing to a chat channel is something most customers prefer.

A standard practice for a release pipeline is to generate release notes. Anyone affected by the changes can then read details about precisely what has changed. The pipeline-events orb includes a job that uses the github-release-notes utility to automatically generate a release and compile the completed problems and commit messages since the last release. Let's include this job as part of the release workflow:

```
- do/gh-release:
      name: generate release notes
      context: *context
      notes-from-file: release.md
      include-commit-msg: true
      before-release:
        - op/env:
            env-file: op.prod.env
      requires:
        - apply prod changes
      filters: *on-tag-main
- do/release:
      name: generate release notes
      context: *context
      on-tag: true
      additional-args: "--data-source=commits"
      Before-release:
        - op/env:
            env-file: op.prod.env
      Requires:
        - apply prod changes
      filters: *on-tag-main
```

Release notes will commit messages since the last release inserted into a customizable local file.

Add our GitHub token to the op.prod.env. export GH_TOKEN={{ op://my-vault/svc-github/access-token }}.

Don't post a message unless the release is successful.

When using git tokens, we would prefer to be able to create and use a GitHub service account to generate the token so that it is not tied to a specific user, at least in theory. However, this is not as straightforward as it used to be since GitHub requires all users to have two-factor authorization.

The final step we will add before leaving this section is a regularly scheduled run of our integration tests. Recall from section 6.3.5 that a recurring run of these tests can help catch unexpected changes made outside of our infrastructure code.

We should add a workflow that schedules a job each week to run our integration tests *and* rotate the service account credentials. The pipeline-events orb has a command that makes setting these schedules in CircleCI easy:

```
workflows:

. . .

  schedule weekly integration tests and sa credential rotation:
    jobs:
      - do/schedule-pipeline:
          name: weekly integration test and sa credential rotation
          context: *context
          scheduled-pipeline-name: weekly-iam-profiles-jobs
          scheduled-pipeline-description: |
            Weekly, automated run of integration tests
            and iam-credential-rotation
          hours-of-day: "[1]"
          days-of-week: "[\"SUN\"]"
          Before-schedule:
            - op/env:
                env-file: op.prod.env
          filters: *on-tag-main
```

Job runs every Sunday at 1:00 AM.

When the ProdServiceAccount can access both nonproduction and production resources, we need to schedule only a single recurring job. If we did not permit the prod sa to access nonprod resources, then we would have to schedule two jobs.

Now, define the scheduled job that runs the weekly IAM profile integration tests and credential rotation:

Pipeline name is UI label only.

Scheduled pipelines behave like git-push by default.

```
weekly iam profiles jobs:
  When:
    equal: [ scheduled_pipeline, << pipeline.trigger_source >> ]
  Jobs:
    - recurring-integration-tests:
        name: AWS integration test on Nonprod account
        context: *context
        account: nonprod
    - recurring-integration-tests:
        name: AWS integration test on Prod account
        context: *context
        account: prod
    - rotate-credentials:
        name: Rotate service account credentials
        context: *context
```

Runs integration tests on all configured accounts

Rotates service account credentials weekly

Let's take a closer look at this code:

- *Pipeline name label*—Although we are using the same name as the scheduled-pipeline name parameter we passed when scheduling a trigger, the pipeline name is just a label displayed in the UI when the trigger occurs.

- *Scheduled pipeline behavior*—A triggered pipeline is effectively the same as either a git push or a git tag in terms of how our filters will respond and, by default, is treated like git-push. In other words, when this pipeline is triggered because of a schedule, it will behave as though it were caused by git-push. Thus, when we start using the scheduled pipeline feature, individual workflows that should run only when scheduled or when caused by a code change need some additional configuration. The configuration you see here is saying, "Only run when the trigger source is actually because of a `scheduled_pipeline`."

- *Integration testing*—Runs the integration tests on all the accounts configured by the pipeline.

- *Credential rotation*—Rotates the service account credentials. Since the pipeline runs once a week, this means the credentials are fully rotated every two weeks.

We just defined two jobs that our workflow will trigger each week. But we haven't added these local jobs to our pipeline. In the jobs section, add these two jobs:

```
jobs:
  recurring-integration-tests:
    description: |
      Recurring job (weekly) to run pipeline integration tests to
  detect aws configuration drift
    docker:
      - image: *executor-image        ◀── Job requires executor
    parameters:                            definition, unlike orb jobs.
      account:
        description: nonprod or production account configuration
        type: string
    steps:
      - checkout
      - setup_remote_docker          ◀── Sets up credentials, the same
      - set-environment:                 as Terraform apply job
          account: << parameters.account >>
      - aws-integration-tests:       ◀── Uses same aws-integration-test
          account: << parameters.account >>   command as before

  rotate-credentials:
    description: Recurring job (weekly) to rotate PSK service  ◀──
  account credentials
    Docker:                          Similar to integration-test job
      - image: *executor-image          with added job configuration
    steps:
      - checkout
      - setup_remote_docker
      - set-environment:
          account: nonprod
      - rotate-service-account-credentials:
          account: nonprod
```

This code includes the following:

- *Job executor configuration*—This is a job, not just a command, so we need to define the executor to be used by the job. We can use the same executor as the Terraform job. The only jobs we have used so far have been defined in the Terraform orb. When you look at the source code for this orb, you will see that the job definition includes an executor configuration.
- *Credential setup*—Just like in our Terraform apply job, we need to set up our credentials.
- *Integration test*—Command We use the same aws-integration-test command, performing the same tests, as we did in the Terraform apply job.
- *Credential rotation job*—This job is similar to the integration-test job. We are calling the same `rotate-service-account-credentials` command that we did in the first stage of our pipeline. We just need to add the additional configuration that a job requires.

Finally, because our scheduled pipeline is treated like a git-push trigger, we need to add the configuration to our first stage so that it only runs on an actual change and not every time our scheduled pipeline runs:

```
deploy service accounts and roles to state account:
  When:
    Not:
      equal: [ scheduled_pipeline, << pipeline.trigger_source >> ]
  Jobs:
    . . .
```

Sending a Slack message and scheduling a CircleCI pipeline also require two more credentials to be added to our op.prod.env file:

```
export SLACK_BOT_TOKEN=op://my-vault/svc-slack/post-bot-token
export CIRCLE_TOKEN=op://my-vault/svc-circleci/api-token
```

With all the pieces in place, we have a fully software-defined lifecycle for our service accounts and needed pipeline roles.

With each new platform infrastructure pipeline we create, we will start by adding a new role in this aws-iam-profiles repository to provide the permissions the new pipeline needs.

Summary

- *Team and ownership*—
  - Start with a simple system that naturally evolves into complexity.
  - Traditional IT silos and DevOps alone fall short, favoring a unified platform team with clear domain boundaries.
  - Effective product ownership and platform engineering practices are essential for long-term success.

- *Tools and security—*
  - Tools must align with platform engineering practices, meet customer needs, and favor high-quality SaaS solutions for efficiency.
  - Tools should be easy to integrate, pipeline-friendly, and provide a single authoritative source of secrets.
  - Secrets management should support automation and rotation, minimizing manual intervention and human error.
- *Pipelines and testing—*
  - Developer ownership of pipeline code ensures agility while secure debugging access and performance optimization keep pipelines usable.
  - Define platform engineering practices for infrastructure pipelines, focusing on automation, secrets management, and eliminating duplicated code.
  - Adopt declarative Infrastructure-as-Code frameworks like Terraform, using best practices such as version pinning, role path organization, and consistent tagging.
  - Integration tests confirm reusable modules, enforce conventions, detect drift, and validate intended resources.
  - Tests should be written first to clarify outcomes, supported by tools like AWSpec and InSpec.
  - Recurring integration tests catch manual changes outside the pipeline and preserve stability.
- *Pipeline design and reuse—*
  - Pipelines should remain simple, focusing on triggers and orchestration, while logic is delegated to versioned shared libraries.
  - Flexibility is key: allow teams to inject custom steps, override parameters, and adapt tool versions as needed.
  - Shared pipeline code must be developed and maintained with proper software engineering principles to scale effectively.
  - Private runners (executors) should be used within secure internal networks to protect sensitive workloads.
- *Cloud organization and identity—*
  - A well-organized cloud structure should align with business and technology needs, anchored by a top-level domain account for governance.
  - Platform engineering teams need sandbox accounts separate from customer-facing environments, with clear nonproduction and production boundaries.
  - Service accounts and roles require precise permissions, assumed by pipelines with least privilege, including specialized roles for sensitive resources.
  - Initial service account setup begins with minimal configuration before pipelines take over autonomous management, while abstractions shield developers from unnecessary complexity.

Platform control plane foundations

This chapter covers

- Managing cloud account baseline settings
- Defining the transit network layer
- Separating customer identity
- Deploying the cloud service control plane

Previously, we started building the Epetech engineering platform by gathering the required resources. We also bootstrapped the initial pipeline, which manages the service accounts and roles that we will use in our infrastructure pipelines. We had to run the configuration from our laptops initially to create the service accounts and the role to manage permissions. But from this point on, both are now managed directly by the pipeline whenever we make changes to the repository. We began with the same developer tools we will provide our internal customers, like source control, secrets management, and pipeline orchestration. Remember that our goal in this section of the book will be to establish the foundation for the Epetech engineering platform. With the initial bootstrap of the IAM roles pipeline, we can proceed to the foundational components of the platform. The overall product goal for our engineering platform is to provide Epetech developers access to all the resources they need to build, release, and operate software independently, without the usual engineering friction. Every component of our platform needs to be resilient. This goes beyond merely including redundancy to minimize the effects of failure.

We want our services and the applications that our customers build and deploy to have a level of self-healing. If the actual state of something in our platform is not as we expect, or is not in the desired state, we want the platform to be able to correct this. Kubernetes provides us with this capability. Most people are familiar with Kubernetes' ability to redeploy a failing service, move services off of failing virtual machines, or scale up or down the number of instances of a service based on the amount of traffic. Yet, the Kubernetes API also allows us to tap into this orchestration logic and apply it in other ways to extend the API. This is why we refer to Kubernetes as the control plane. It is a key component among those that form the foundation of our engineering platform.

7.1   *Cloud account baseline*

While different cloud providers use different terminology, each provides a mechanism to sandbox organizational units, teams, software lifecycle environments, and workloads. This mechanism can be called accounts, subscriptions, projects, etc.; here, we refer to this capability as accounts since we will be using AWS in our later examples. Account baseline configuration implements requirements that are organization or account-wide in nature, applying in every setting and, in a sense, neither blocking nor enabling the account's purpose (see figure 7.1)

This domain might feel similar to the last one, as it also deals with cloud account-level settings. Just like with roles, these configurations are set up once per account. But, in reality, AWS account identity, authentication, and authorization have such a broad effect on the platform engineering team's ability to work effectively that it often becomes one of the first areas to need its own dedicated domain team. Because of this, administrative identity should be thought of as its domain. The rest of the account-level

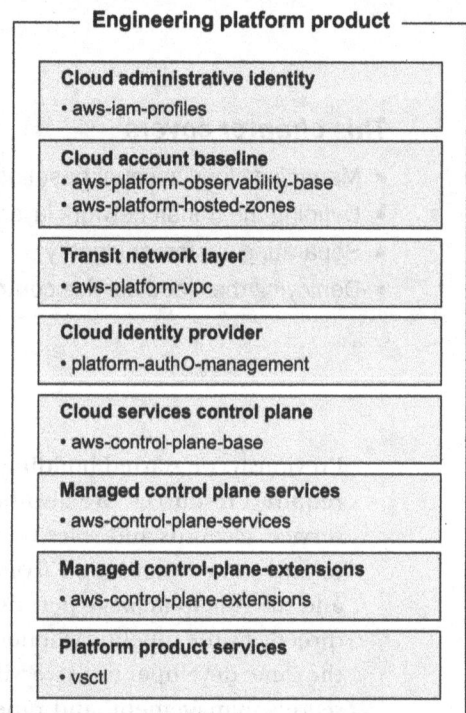

Figure 7.1   **The importance of domain-driven design and the platform product domains. The aws-iam-profiles pipeline we created was part of the cloud administrative identity product domain. We now continue to the cloud account baseline domain and create the account-level baseline resources.**

resources can be treated as a domain as well, and this is what we've named the cloud account baseline domain. Examples include

- Network flow and audit log aggregation
- Security information event management or security orchestration, automation, and response automation
- Account-level security scanning
- Domain name system (DNS) hosted zones and zone delegations
- Organization- or product-level networks or network-as-policy configuration

We will discuss three of the primary areas.

7.1.1 Account baseline security scanning

Account-level baseline security configuration can be effectively managed by a separate security team as long as the security leaders recognize the platform accounts as infrastructure-provider accounts and the platform engineers building the platform as the natural administrative owners of those cloud accounts. In this case, the baseline security configuration should be based on the configuration to which all cloud accounts within the enterprise must conform.

Examples include

- Permission that limits VPCs to connect only to the enterprise transit-gateway network
- Permission boundaries that require public networks only to contain load balancers integrated into a distributed configuration management architecture, such as AWS Firewall Manager.
- Permission boundaries that restrict access to cloud services that are not allowed based on enterprise technology standards
- Resources to automatically ingest all account-level logs into a centralized log aggregator
- Resources to automatically ingest specific logs that the security team is interested in to a centralized location

The recommended practice is that these kinds of baseline configurations be managed through a recurring, idempotent job that runs frequently (perhaps nightly) along with a similar, recurring scan designed to catch changes before they are automatically corrected.

It is also not uncommon for an enterprise to not adequately staff or fund its security teams to own this kind of configuration; instead, it requires that each infrastructure administrative team implement the security requirements as part of its responsibilities. If that is true in our organization, then as the owners of the engineering platform, we would include this configuration in our cloud account baseline domain and create the software-defined configuration with the same architectural goals we apply to everything we maintain.

We won't implement this configuration as part of our Epetech example. For an example of the configuration and scans commonly occurring in this domain, look at the CIS AWS Foundations Benchmark [1] and the Mitre example InSpec scan (https://mng.bz/NwX7) .

7.1.2   *Account baseline observability*

In chapter 5, we covered the key concepts. If Epetech were to adopt the same strategy as PETech in terms of technologies, at this point in our implementation of the Epetech engineering platform, we would be at the initial implementation stages for the Platform and Cloud Cost axes of observability. Within those, cloud account-level components are needed to begin aggregating system data generated by AWS account-level services (see figure 7.2).

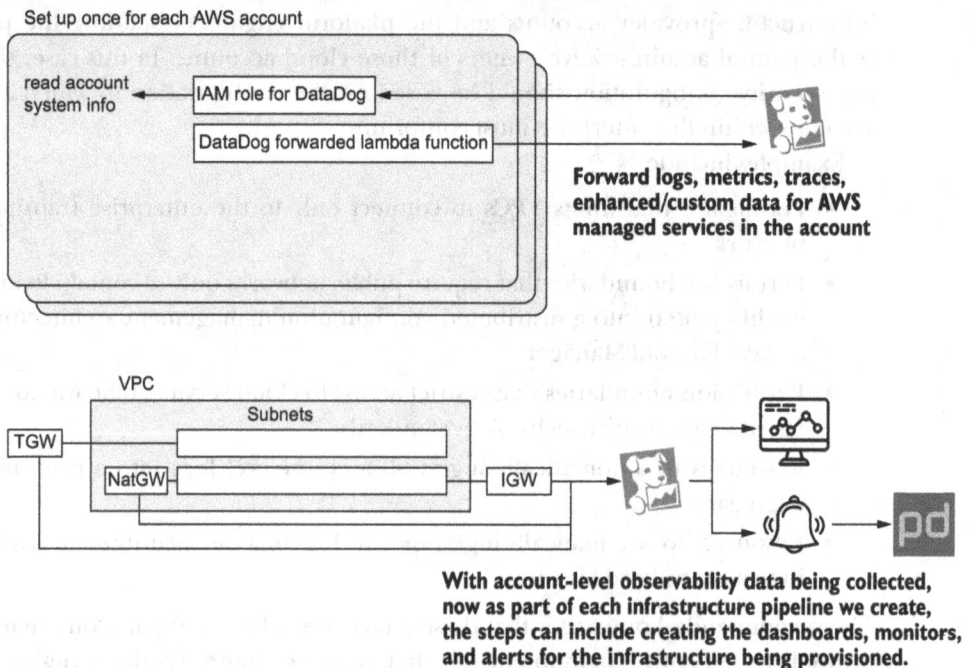

Figure 7.2   If Epetech were using DataDog, it is at this point that we would set up a repository and pipeline to manage the account-level integration provided by DataDog for AWS. With that integration in place, with each additional capability or feature we implement, such as the networks we will provision in section 7.2, observability would be a natural part of the definition of *done* for the implementation.

Creating and improving observability, both for operations and ongoing product development, is a part of everything we deploy. Due to cost and scope constraints, while we build out the Epetech platform, we won't include a complete implementation of observability as part of the exercises or solutions. Use the principles we learned earlier to think about what those solutions should look like. When we get to deploying applications onto the control plane, we will implement some basic cluster-level capabilities to demonstrate key aspects of the platform customer's (developer) experience.

WHAT ABOUT THE CLOUD INFRASTRUCTURE VENDORS' BUILT-IN SOLUTIONS?

Since we used DataDog in this example, what about using the built-in AWS solutions like CloudWatch or X-ray? Every infrastructure-as-a-service provider has some form of observability service. And of course, we should consider those services when deciding on the experience our engineering platform will provide.

The selection criteria are mostly like the criteria we covered while discussing the building of the software-defined platforms. The one critical factor frequently overlooked is how the observability tool will integrate with our customer identity architecture. Recall from earlier that we are creating a customer identity that is separate from the underlying cloud provider infrastructure IAM. We need the flexibility and security such an architecture provides for the same basic reasons as every SaaS provider. We will implement one example solution for customer identity later in this chapter, based on using GitHub and GitHub team membership for authentication and authorization. It's worth noting that cloud vendors like AWS do support federated identity integration. For instance, AWS IAM can work with third-party identity providers (IDPs) via federation, and services like Amazon Cognito Identity Pools allow for securely granting access to AWS services based on identities authenticated through external providers.

How will we integrate such a solution into the cloud vendor's observability dashboards, monitors, and alerting? We need to provide our customers with completely self-serve means of creating dashboards, setting monitors, triggering alerts, and accessing the resulting UI where available. There are certainly ways to deal with this, and they come with additional overhead, so cost is often a factor that will encourage the use of tools that already provide a separate identity integration point.

7.1.3   *Hosted zones and delegated domains*

When Epetech developers deploy their services, they need the services to be accessible. For example, the team that builds the customer profile service wants other services, including those from outside developers, to be able to access the profiles service at `https://api.epetech.io/v1/profiles`.

api.epetech.io is an internet domain name used by a DNS to translate human-readable words into an IP address that the network understands. We will use the AWS DNS service Route53 as our DNS. This is an account-level configuration. Our production services and customer production environments will be in one account, while non-production environments will be in another.

We will create a DNS zone for the epetech.io domain name in our production account. We will also delegate several subdomains, such as api.epetech.io, dev.api .epetech.io, etc. DNS architecture and management, in general, is beyond the scope of this book, but we will cover the setup necessary as a good starting point for our platform.

It is a business decision to create these services, and how internal and external users discover, understand, and use these services can be a good or a bad experience. In part, finding and accessing services starts with DNS. How are these services named, and how does naming affect the ability to understand and use the service?

This should be treated as a product decision first. For example, Google hosts APIs for most of its primary products on googleapis.com. You can programmatically interact with Google Chat on chat.googleapis.com, their docs applications on docs.googleapis .com, and so on. Yet there are dozens, even hundreds, of individual service resources for each of these products. These are referenced through the path that follows the domain in the API request URL. There is a specific product relationship tied to every subdomain of the Google API product domain named googleapis.com. Google has also worked hard to create consistency—both in terms of subdomain names, the products they support, and the naming conventions for the resources within the subdomain. In technical product language, there is an intentional taxonomy within the domain naming conventions and an equally intentional ontology in organizing the resources within each subdomain. While there can be a purely operational motivation to create such a convention, simplifying the process of identifying responsible teams and product owners, there is even greater product value. We want people to be able to successfully use our services, whether those people are other developers inside our company, the company's customers, or third-party developers who all use these services with different incentives but with the same outcome goal of providing value. A consistent and understandable naming strategy has a significant effect on discovery and ease of use (see figure 7.3).

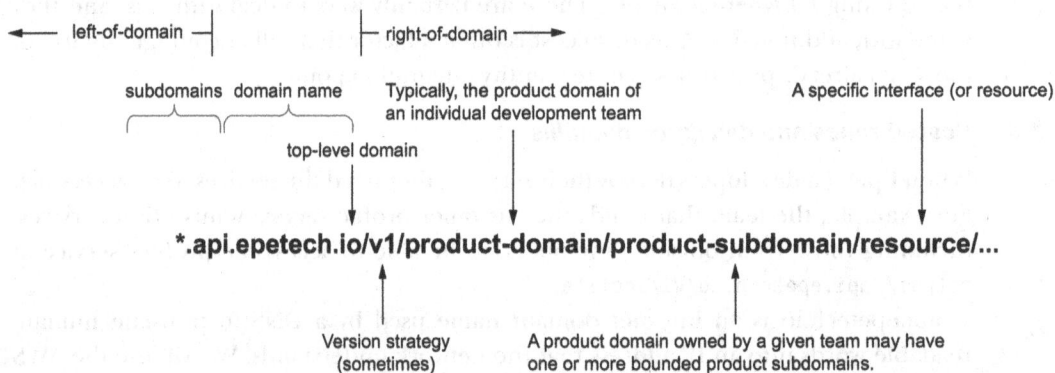

Figure 7.3   Our engineering platform must provide a self-serve experience for each internal customer (development team) to configure their service to receive traffic based on our company's "product" decision for how the DNS domain and subdomain names reflect our digital products.

There should be a left-of-domain strategy for how DNS subdomains organize separate products or subsets of capabilities within a single product. There should also be a right-of-domain strategy for organizing the capabilities and resources delivered by each development team deploying services accessed on a domain. Consider the following aspects:

- *Subdomain*—Google has many products marketed under the same *Google* brand. It makes sense for them to reserve subdomains for specific products. Developers familiar with their naming strategy will find it easy to search for documentation and resources even if they don't know the specific URL.

  But what if a company has just one main product? GitHub is a good example. Even though Microsoft now owns it, it still offers a single, focused product with lots of features. While not all of these features are strictly Git services, they're closely tied to Git workflows. And GitHub is a strong, recognizable brand. So, from a product perspective, it makes sense for it to use a single subdomain like `api.github.com` for all its APIs.

  Now imagine it went in a different direction and gave each central feature its subdomain. For example, what if the Orgs feature lived at `orgs.github.com` instead of `api.github.com/orgs`? That could get messy fast. GitHub is a multitenant product, and Orgs are just a way to manage permissions across the platform. Using paths like `api.github.com/orgs/ORG/teams` keeps everything consistent and easier to understand. In contrast, something like `orgs.github.com/teams?orgs=my-org` would be more challenging to maintain and less intuitive.

  This kind of decision matters even more when a company has multiple distinct products. Imagine Google launched Docs under a completely separate domain like `gdocs.com`. Docs is different from Search or Maps, but they all share the same customer identity. Would Docs still use `googleapis.com` for APIs, or would Google create something like `iam.gdocs.com`? Either way, it gets complicated.

  The bigger problem is when companies *don't* think these things through. Different teams end up doing their own thing, creating random subdomains, using confusing acronyms, or naming services in ways that don't match the product structure. Without a clear plan, it quickly becomes hard for developers to navigate and maintain.

- *Domain name*—If our company owns many distinct products, each with its own product brand, our engineering platform may need to support multiple primary domains. This commonly happens when a company grows through corporate acquisitions. Often, such acquisitions are meant to move into new product areas rather than consolidate the competition. These brands may stick around forever. In general, start with a solution for a single domain and then assume that as the product strategy matures, this will be expanded to enable teams to self-manage subdomains and eventually even domain names.

- *Version strategy*—There are many strategies for managing API version changes. While maintaining backward compatibility is tremendously valuable and the advised approach, there can be situations where the cost is simply not justified by the potential benefit. A straightforward method of dealing with these, hopefully rare, occurrences is to include the *Major* semantic version in the URL.

- *Product-domain*—The term "domain" here refers to our software architecture. Domain-driven design is an inherent part of a distributed service architecture. Regardless of our left-of-domain strategy, the product's architecture should result in multiple product domain teams. And frequently, a team will own more than one product domain, as these domains can sometimes be pretty small in terms of individual API functionality.

- *Product-subdomain*—It makes sense for a single product domain API to manage more than one resource. This is another way of saying that individual product domains can have valuable subdomain categorizations even when working on a single product-domain API.

- *Resource*—No matter the product domains or subdomains, there will always be the actual resources of an API.

An effective roadmap involves implementing the following capabilities in the following order. Regardless of where the general product organization goes in terms of adopting a better strategy, we can at least deal with most of the friction this absence causes.

PLATFORM-MANAGED DOMAINS

This is a left-of-domain strategy that reserves a specific domain as exclusively owned and managed by the engineering platform. For Epetech, we will make this epetech. io, and internal customers using the platform will have a standard set of DNS subdomains and ingress patterns they can use in a completely self-serve way. Users can't create new subdomains but are free to self-manage the right-of-domain pattern. This assumes (some would say, hopes) that the product side of the business is fully engaged and software development leadership is managing the decisions made.

CUSTOMER-MANAGED SUBDOMAINS FOR PLATFORM-MANAGED TOP-LEVEL DOMAINS

Eventually, we can add to this model and provide a self-serve means for developers to define and use custom subdomains within the epetech.io domain.

CUSTOMER-MANAGED DOMAINS

Finally, we create a means for developers to use custom domains. Many companies find that further customization isn't valuable once the first two experiences are available, and perhaps a couple more managed domains are added to the list. For our epetech example, we will implement only the first pattern. What will be our initial traffic patterns? See figure 7.4.

This will affect how DNS directs traffic based on our domain strategy. Since all our APIs will be on api.epetech.io, DNS would typically define that subdomain as pointing to an IP in our API gateway service. From there, it would redirect to the actual API with a different URL. A similar pattern would apply if our API offers a test or development instance, likewise, for UI traffic. While our platform will support deploying UI services directly, most modern approaches to the front end will involve some amount

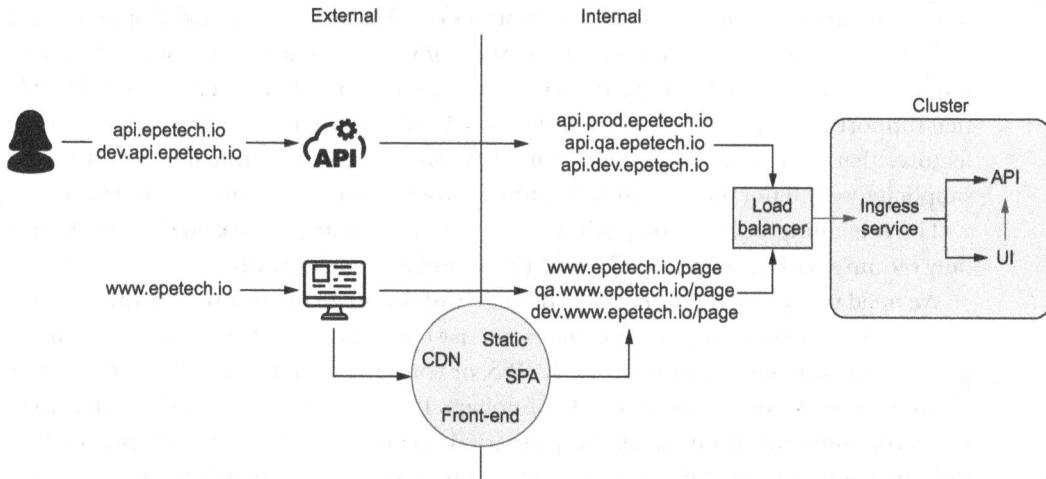

Figure 7.4 Traffic will come into services running on the platform in a couple of different ways.

of off-cluster processing, whether that is only graphical and static content, which our infrastructure cloud vendor may provide, or more extensive third-party solutions such as Next.js.

Since Epetech supports third-party developers using our API, we will need an API gateway for this external traffic. It is best not to think of API gateways as being a natural part of building APIs that will run on Kubernetes. In many cases, the core functionality that a gateway has historically provided is available through the Kubernetes API. Where a service mesh is included in the architecture, which we will do in our engineering platform, the mesh offers most of the rest. In fact, without the third-party developer aspect, incorporating an API gateway can simply increase traffic and configuration complexity (and cost) without adding technical or customer support value. If our organization's product APIs are only exposed for external access by the customers of our products, often the more straightforward approach is to add functionality to our products for customers to perform the authentication and authorization programmatically, so that the UI experience is incorporated. You've probably used third-party integration with popular products that use this integration. For example, Dropbox.com provides a means for third-party developers to incorporate into their products the process for their users, who are also Dropbox customers, to self-authorize. Dropbox could limit third-party functionality to this and not need to provide any mechanism for third-party developers to register and obtain developer keys to be successful.

However, not all third-party developers can use this approach. What if, as could be the case for Epetech, we want to monetize the part of our software that collects data from medical devices and reports it to the patient's doctor? Epetech may not want to build certain kinds of devices or may not want to operate in every country where there is demand for such a service. We could sell the software capabilities in a way that enables other companies to provide such an experience with much lower development and maintenance costs. Many vendors offer API gateway capabilities that make it easy to implement a means for third parties to register and obtain the sort of access credentials that support these other kinds of identity flows. In addition, such products often include features that provide documentation and developer resources at much lower costs. For simplicity, we will not include an API gateway in our Epetech platform architecture.

The remaining DNS configuration for our domain strategy is reasonably simple and only requires basic, account-level hosted zone and zone delegation.

We need to register our epetech.io domain with Route53 in our production account. Not everyone working on these exercises can use epetech.io. For the exercise, very inexpensive domains are available through AWS, or you can purchase one through another registrar, sometimes for just a couple of dollars. If you use a registrar other than AWS, you must configure Route53 as the primary domain name server before proceeding with the exercises. We will continue using epetech.io for the discussion and examples. Substitute your domain for this example domain.

Which subdomains should we delegate and to which account? In the more realistic four-account setup we discussed earlier, we split platform users' resources into separate nonproduction and production accounts—a recommended best practice. In our simplified example, `aws-account-1` represents the platform instance developers interact with, and `aws-account-2` is where we're building the platform itself. The main domain is registered in `aws-account-1`, so the hosted zone is already set up to route traffic.

For the Epetech platform, let's say our convention is to give each new team three environments by default: Dev, QA, and Prod. These environments start with Kubernetes namespaces, since most of our customers will be building APIs or user interfaces. We can decide that `epetech.io` (and `www.epetech.io`) is used for production UI traffic, while `dev.epetech.io` and `qa.epetech.io` handle preproduction testing.

Even though we'll support incoming traffic to the cluster on those domains for UI services, most of these UIs will likely use an S3/CDN setup, possibly with Lambda@ Edge, to serve content. To support that, we'll enforce a rule: any CDN route must explicitly manage a specific path under the primary domain. That way, all unmanaged traffic continues to flow into the cluster as expected.

For API traffic, our convention is to use `api.epetech.io` in production. This is a good example of using a single domain and defining clear subdomain conventions. We could have gone the route of separate domains, like `epetechdev.io`. Technically, either pattern works, and both can be automated by the platform with similar effort as long as the conventions are clearly defined and managed.

But the choice isn't just technical. From a product marketing and lifecycle perspective, `dev.epetech.io` and `epetechdev.io` may serve similar functions but signal different things. That's why decisions like these are best made with input from the product side of the business.

Normally, where your traffic is external and you plan to support customer and third-party developer use of your APIs, an API gateway solution that manages external developer access and provides the means of obtaining keys is the most effective way to implement it. If we were to implement such a gateway, traffic to api.epetech.io would instead be directed to our gateway. After it performed API gateway actions, it would pass the traffic on to us, and we would need a different subdomain to receive it—typically, something like api.prod.epetech.io. However, we will leave out the API gateway integration for the exercises in this book. We want the subdomain delegations shown in table 7.1.

Table 7.1 Zone delegations for the Epetech engineering platform

Subdomain hosted zone delegation	account-1	account-2
prod-i01-aws-us-east-2.epetech.io	X	
api.epetech.io	X	
qa.epetech.io	X	
dev.epetech.io	X	
sbx-i01-aws-us-east-1.epetech.io		x
preview.epetech.io		x

`prod-i01-aws-us-east-2` and `sbx-i01-aws-us-east-1` are our cluster names. In section 7.2, we will talk about cluster-naming conventions. Regardless of the naming convention we choose, we will want to have a dedicated subdomain for each cluster to support services that are both cluster-wide and cluster-specific. An example would be Kiali. When using a service mesh such as Istio, Kiali provides an excellent interface for viewing traffic between services and debugging mesh resources. It visualizes all activity within the mesh and is a per-cluster service.

Configuring Route53 using Terraform involves the following resource definitions. We first need a data resource to fetch information about the primary domains registered in our account-1 and a provider to define the role to assume when accessing:

```
$ cat domain_epetech_io.tf
locals {
  domain_epetech_io = "epetech.io"
}
provider "aws" {
  alias   = "domain_epetech_io"
  region = "us-east-1"
  assume_role {
    role_arn = "arn:aws:iam::${var.prod_account_id}:role/${var.assume_role}"
  }
}
# zone id for the top-level-zone
data "aws_route53_zone" "zone_id_epetech_io" {
  provider = aws.domain_epetech_io
  name     = local.domain_epetech_io
}
```

The primary domain has been registered in account-1, which we have been referring to as our production account.

Uses the access information defined in the provider

Finds the zone information for the primary domain registered there

Then, for each subdomain we want to delegate, create a dedicated file that defines a provider in the account where the delegation occurs, creates the hosted zone for the subdomain in that account, and makes a delegation of that hosted zone in the primary domain account we defined earlier. Here is an example of preview.epetech.io, which we will want in aws-account-2:

> **We want to delegate the preview subdomain to aws-account-2, which we have been calling our nonproduction account. Creates a provider that will configure resources in this specific account.**

```
$ cat zone_preview_epetech_io.tf
# define a provider in the account where this subdomain will be managed
provider "aws" {
  alias  = "subdomain_preview_epetech_io"
  region = "us-east-1"
  assume_role {
    role_arn = "arn:aws:iam::${var.nonprod_account_id}:role/${var.assume_role}"  ◀──
  }
}
# create a route53 hosted zone for the subdomain
module "subdomain_preview_epetech_io" {
  source  = "terraform-aws-modules/route53/aws//modules/zones"
  version = "3.1.0"
  create  = true                                          Uses the provider to create a
  providers = {                                   ◀────── zone resource in aws-account-2
    aws = aws.subdomain_preview_epetech_io
  }
  zones = {                                               The zone will be
    "preview.${local.domain_epetech_io}" = {      ◀────── preview.epetech.io.
      tags = {
        cluster = "sbx-i01-aws-us-east-1"          ◀────── We can add a tag that indicates
      }                                                    services in the sbx cluster manage
    }                                                      the rest of our DNS zone
  }                                                        management for this zone.
}


# Create a zone delegation (NS) from the primary domain
module "subdomain_zone_delegation_preview_epetech_io" {
  source  = "terraform-aws-modules/route53/aws//modules/records"
  version = "3.1.0"
  create  = true
  providers = {
    aws = aws.domain_epetech_io
  }                                               Finally, we create the zone delegation
  private_zone = false                            by defining a new nameserver within
  zone_name = local.domain_epetech_io             the primary hosted zone, pointing to
  records = [                              ◀───── the delegated zone.
    {
      name          = "preview"
      type          = "NS"
      ttl           = 172800
      zone_id       = data.aws_route53_zone.zone_id_epetech_io.id
      allow_overwrite = true
```

```
    records            = module.subdomain_preview_epetech_io.route53_zone_
name_servers["preview.${local.domain_epetech_io}"]
    }
  ]
  depends_on = [module.subdomain_preview_epetech_io]
}
```

Note how the hosted zone is created in the account where we want preview.epetech.io to be managed, and the delegation occurs in the account where the epetech.io domain is hosted. This is the same configuration even where the delegation occurs in the same account as the primary domain.

> **Exercise 7.1   Create a release pipeline for the hosted zone and zone delegation**
>
> Create the pipeline that will configure the hosted zones and delegations to support the subdomains from the platform-managed subdomain pattern described in table 7.1. Create a new repo called `aws-platform-hosted-zones`.
>
> Given the nature of DNS domains and hosting, testing a configuration before implementing is not possible. We can, however, use a different domain name to test a configuration strategy before implementing it in our product domain. You should plan on having a dedicated domain name for just this purpose in a real platform implementation. In this exercise, let's just deal with our example domain name. Though we are configuring information across two accounts, our pipeline can apply the configuration to both accounts simultaneously. In the pipeline, use stage 1 (git push) to perform linting, plan generation, and validation. Then, use the release stage to apply all changes. Because we apply the changes across both production and nonproduction accounts, we use the ProdServiceAccount since it can assume roles in both accounts.
>
> Since this is a new pipeline, we will need a new role for the service account to assume. Add this to the platform-iam-profiles pipeline.

7.2   Transit network layer

All deployed platform services and capabilities will require network connections for communication, the setup and management of which are handled in a dedicated domain. Networking can encompass many modes of communication, potentially including

- Access to and from the public internet
- Interservice (i.e., serverless functions to databases)
- Traffic across availability zones within a region
- Traffic across global regions
- Traffic between cloud providers
- Traffic between a cloud provider and a private cloud/data center

By handling this in a dedicated domain, we can ensure a strategy that covers all use cases optimally and minimizes conflicts that could surface between communication modes.

The word "transit" is a bit of an AWS term, but the concept is applicable across cloud providers. Architecturally, the goal is to have a network structure that enables low-friction expansion. Nonproduction and production transit gateways can be created in an account dedicated to forming the transit network. As new accounts are provisioned, they can include local transit gateways in supported regions and a configuration that allows any networks created within the account to be automatically accepted when configuring a connection to the TGW.

Alternatively, we could leave the approval step on the connection and create a lambda function that watches for such pending connections, queries our ticketing system for approval, and then accepts. This allows teams given AWS accounts to self-manage their networks, including connections to TGW, without needing to manage approval requests.

AWS CloudWAN services allow us to create broad network connections across multiple accounts and regions through a policy definition. AWS will manage all the required transit gateways and network connections. CloudWAN can simplify the management configuration needed to maintain large networks. But even with this network policy-based feature, VPCs are still required to host our Elastic Kubernetes Service (EKS) clusters and provide connectivity between services and other AWS services (see figure 7.5).

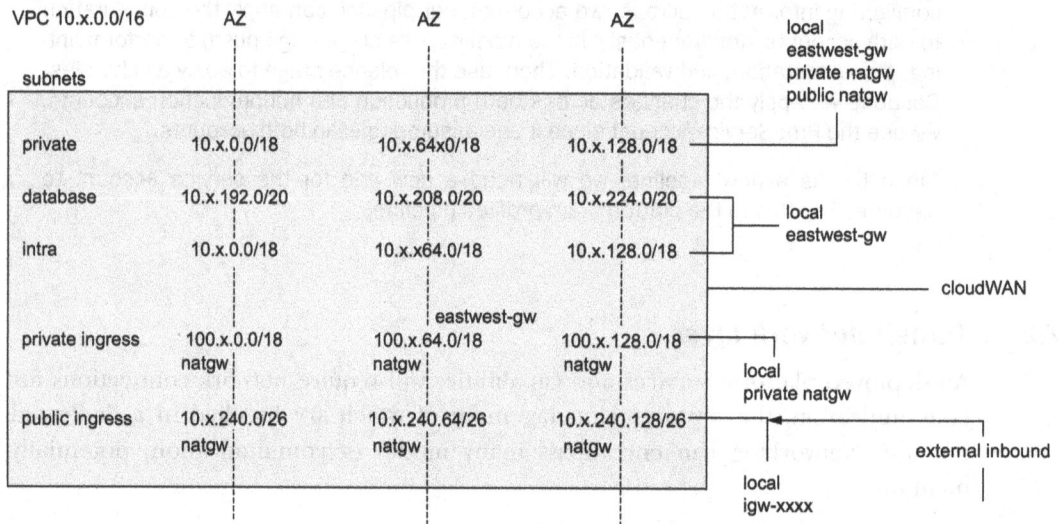

VPC 10.x.0.0/16	AZ	AZ	AZ	local eastwest-gw private natgw public natgw
subnets				
private	10.x.0.0/18	10.x.64x0/18	10.x.128.0/18	
database	10.x.192.0/20	10.x.208.0/20	10.x.224.0/20	local eastwest-gw
intra	10.x.0.0/18	10.x.x64.0/18	10.x.128.0/18	
				cloudWAN
private ingress	100.x.0.0/18 natgw	100.x.64.0/18 eastwest-gw natgw	100.x.128.0/18 natgw	local private natgw
public ingress	10.x.240.0/26 natgw	10.x.240.64/26 natgw	10.x.240.128/26 natgw	external inbound
				local igw-xxxx

Figure 7.5 This VPC structure creates a solid foundation for most starting EKS implementations.

This provides a large IP pool to support the AWS-CNI. There is a common database reservation and a large intra-pool to support a broader range of data sources and AWS resources that require IP claims, including network connects, lambda, and others.

There is a private ingress subnet based on an additional associated CIDR range that will come from the larger corporate, private IP range, and private NAT gateways that can receive internal load balancers, thereby isolating the VPC CIDR from the private corporate IP network, along with the public ingress subnet. This supports a wide variety of use cases but can be pared down to conform to less diverse strategies.

In our Epetech platform, let's simplify this general VPC architecture in the following ways:

- Remove the private ingress subnet. We fully expect to make all our APIs available externally, and all internal traffic will be on-cluster.
- Deploy only a single natgw in the public ingress network. We would not normally do this, as it introduces an outbound traffic vulnerability should there be problems with the gateway or the availability zone where it is deployed. The addition of a NAT gateway in each availability zone helps reduce this risk. But for our example exercises, we can reduce the cost by eliminating two-thirds of the gateways.
- The CloudWAN notation involves scaling the number of clusters in an environment. We will discuss this down the road on managing scale. We will not have CloudWAN integration for our VPCs at this point.

7.2.1 Role-based network structure

What we mean by role-based network structure is that each cluster provisioned will have a dedicated VPC. Initially, this is pretty ordinary, but as the scale of our platform grows, and we need to expand Prod (and therefore nonproduction, preview, etc.) to include multiple regions, Prod becomes more than just one cluster, and the role "Prod" applies to multiple clusters and networks. Initially, the primary consideration is to ensure that you reserve IP space sufficient to cover the Prod network, even if it includes multiple VPCs.

Since the VPCs we provision will match one to one with a Kubernetes cluster being deployed to the VPC, we should name our VPCs to match our cluster naming convention. There are many possible conventions for naming. We want to easily support future scale in the number of clusters per role, which includes even things like replacing clusters. For the example exercise, let's use the following identifiers for our two clusters:

```
sbx-i01-aws-us-east-1
prod-i01-aws-us-east-2
```

The first word indicates the role, the second could be the line of business and count of this instance, the third is the cloud provider, and finally, we have the region.

Based on these, we want to provision VPCs that include the cluster name so that we can later use a Terraform data resource to look up the VPCs. What would this look like if we used the complete four-account structure and the number of instances that implies? See figure 7.6.

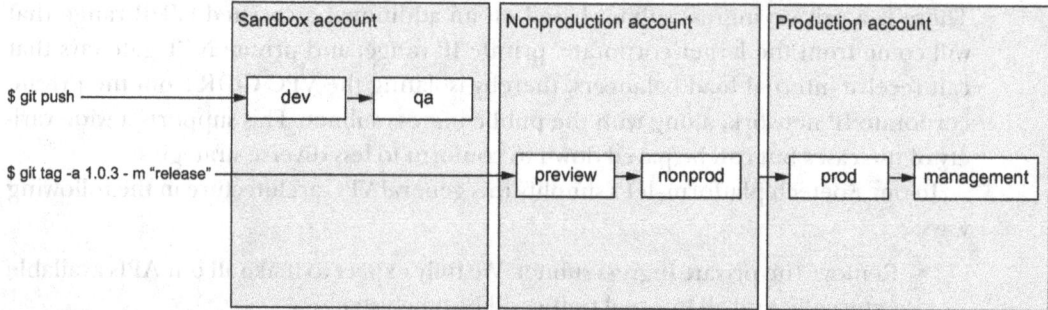

Figure 7.6   In an actual starting pipeline for our VPCs, we would also have the same number of VPCs as we have EKS clusters. But we typically have several more instances than we will create in our Epetech example.

This would include a development and quality assurance instance where the engineering platform team could thoroughly develop and test changes to the platform definition before putting these changes in front of platform users. Then, we would have a preview environment. Platform users would include this environment in their test environments, though failures would not be treated as breaking for their release. The preview environment is where their services can encounter changes to the platform definition before they appear in either nonproduction or production environments. Lastly, we would also have a product management cluster. Production instances of platform product services run here to prevent problems affecting platform customer environments and vice versa.

Exercise 7.2   Create a release pipeline for a role-based network

Let's create our Epetech engineering platform VPCs based on the previous recommendations. Create a new repository called `aws-platform-vpc` and use the terraform-aws-modules vpc module (https://mng.bz/DwWa) in a test and release pipeline to provision the two VPCs in our Epetech example using the details in the following table.

VPC configuration for our Epetech platform exercises

vpc/ subnets	region	az	az	az	Total IPs
account-2	us-east-1	us-east-1a	us-east-1b	us-east-1c	
sbx-i01- aws-us- east-1	10.80.0.0/16				
private (nodes)		10.80.0.0/18	10.80.64.0/18	10.80.128.0/18	49,146
intra		10.80.192.0/20	10.80.208.0/20	10.80.224.0/20	12,282

VPC configuration for our Epetech platform exercises (*continued*)

vpc/ subnets	region	az	az	az	Total IPs
account-2	us-east-1	us-east-1a	us-east-1b	us-east-1c	
database		10.80.240.0/23	10.80.242.0/23	10.80.244.0/23	1,530
public (ingress)		10.80.246.0/23	10.80.248.0/23	10.80.250.0/23	1,530
				unallocated	1047
account-1					
prod-i01- aws-us- east-2	10.90.0.0/16				
private (nodes)		10.90.0.0/18	10.90.64.0/18	10.90.128.0/18	49,146
intra		10.90.192.0/20	10.90.208.0/20	10.90.224.0/20	12,282
database		10.90.240.0/23	10.90.242.0/23	10.90.244.0/23	1,530
public (ingress)		10.90.246.0/23	10.90.248.0/23	10.90.250.0/23	1,530
				unallocated	1047

When using the AWS CNI, it is a good idea to have a large number of IPs in the node network since both the node and pod networks will draw IPs from the same range.

Include the following tag on the private network to support Karpenter in the upcoming aws-control-plane-base pipeline:

```
"karpenter.sh/discovery"                   = "${var.cluster_name}-vpc"
```

Usually, we would configure an S3 bucket for capturing VPC flow logs when provisioning a VPC. For our simplified example, skip this step. Additional VPC-level observability configuration that would take place alongside the VPC configuration includes provisioned components such as NAT and internet gateways. Because networks are central to all cloud provider-managed infrastructure, the providers will have additional health-monitoring services that enable users to track network health. (See the AWS Internet Monitoring services as an example.)

DEDICATED PLATFORM PRODUCT CODE

Though we've mentioned this before, it's worth calling out again here in this section on networking, as networking is a part of all infrastructure. The software we create to provision and manage any aspect of our engineering platform should be dedicated to this purpose alone. As an engineering practice, this means we should be continuously optimizing, at the software level, the structure and orchestration of this software for the product experience and delivery service-level objectives of our engineering platform and not the broader application of infrastructure-as-code within the rest of the enterprise.

What does this mean in practice? It means that the code that provisions and manages any part of the engineering platform should not also be designed to support any or all non-platform use cases within the enterprise. This platform VPC pipeline manages pipelines used by the engineering platform only.

If we were to wrap our implementation into an official, internal VPC definition module used across the organization for purposes beyond the engineering platform, we would then couple our platform code to all these other use cases. When we change our VPC implementation, we must test it against all these different use cases unrelated to our engineering platform product. The time it takes to make changes is now significantly longer and will only continue to grow. We may now be unable to make the desired changes within the platform due to external factors. Preserving the internal architectural independence of the infrastructure code of a product is a critical strategy in the practice of evolutionary architecture.

7.3   *Customer Identity*

In chapter 6, we discussed the importance of creating a platform customer identity independent of the underlying cloud vendor IAM.

This domain covers the identity and authorization framework implemented for the customers of the engineering platform. This domain is kept separate from the administrative identity defined earlier to enable us to create a cohesive experience across all platform capabilities, regardless of the underlying provider. This strategy should feel familiar since it follows the same pattern as many other products you likely use. For instance, Netflix hosts its service on AWS. When you stream a movie or TV show on Netflix, the file that contains the movie exists on a physical device where it is assigned access permissions based on AWS IAM roles and permissions. However, as a user of Netflix, you are not assigned an AWS IAM identity, nor is there a direct connection between you and the role used to access the file. When you subscribe to Netflix, you are assigned an identity within the Netflix customer identity system. When you stream a show, the service validates your permission to watch the show and then accesses and streams it on your behalf. This allows Netflix to design and deliver all of its services without directly coupling its customers to its infrastructure solutions. We will need this same flexibility to provide the same quality experience for engineering platform customers.

> **NOTE**   You may wonder about cases where a development team requires access to the underlying provider services to debug workloads or validate configurations. Part of addressing these concerns falls under the platform team principle of observability. Another way to manage this is by teams providing their backend services and *connecting* them to the platform. Both of these practices will be discussed later.

An important implementation detail for this customer identity service is that it will still have an authentication step tied to our organization's authoritative source. We still want single sign-on (SSO) across all the developer tools and other resources. However, we want our authorization step to enable permissions or access based on an individual developer's membership in a team.

7.3.1 *Authentication and authorization*

The product challenge is: how do we manage authorization to arrive at a team-oriented user experience? It is more effective to think about it like this: we want to onboard teams to our engineering platform more so than customers individually. The individual user experience is being added to a team. Once added to the team, a user should automatically have access to all team resources. This means that teams using the platform must be able to self-manage members (see figure 7.7).

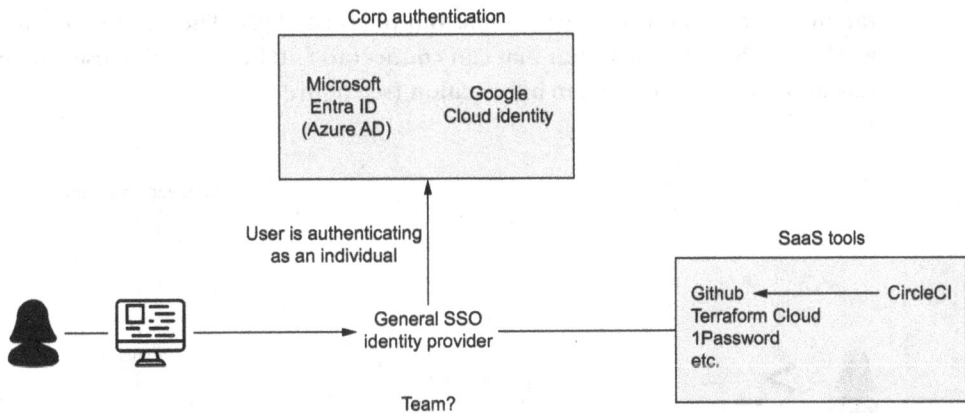

Figure 7.7 **For the SaaS tools that will be a part of our platform, the common enterprise SSO integration for authentication is a good starting point. Some tools, like CircleCI, can integrate directly with GitHub authentication and do not necessarily need an independent integration.**

The corporate identity source can define groups. We could use that source for groups to determine a team and manage the users who belong to a team. But how will we provide a self-service experience for a team on the engineering platform to self-manage their membership? We are creating a platform product and want a product experience.

Some IDP systems can be directly configured to provide this experience. We could also create custom automation around the corporate source of identity. A complete discussion of the options and implementation examples is beyond the scope of this book. We will take advantage of the team membership capabilities provided by our development tool, GitHub.

Assume that our SSO integration between GitHub and corporate identity is authentication only. Teams and team membership are maintained within GitHub's role-based access control (RBAC) capabilities. GitHub provides a good experience for users to self-manage teams and members. How will other parts of our platform use this team's information to provide access?

In the case of CircleCI, this feature is built in. Once connected to a GitHub org, CircleCI automatically does passthrough authentication, and you can connect context permissions to GitHub teams. For the other tools, we may need to create a custom API that will sync team membership information from GitHub to other SaaS tools that lack native support for this feature.

This only addresses the problem of access to tools. What about the platform infrastructure capabilities? We will need an authentication and authorization process based on the same internet-secure OAuth2 framework [2]. If we can implement this, the effectiveness of using Kubernetes as our product's general control plane will start to become apparent. We will enable access to Kubernetes resources based on team membership. From there, we can extend the Kubernetes API to allow teams to provision other platform infrastructure resources. We can also use the same authentication and authorization system to control access to custom platform APIs. The most efficient solution would be a SaaS IDP solution that can connect to GitHub to enable users to authenticate and return the user team information (see figure 7.8).

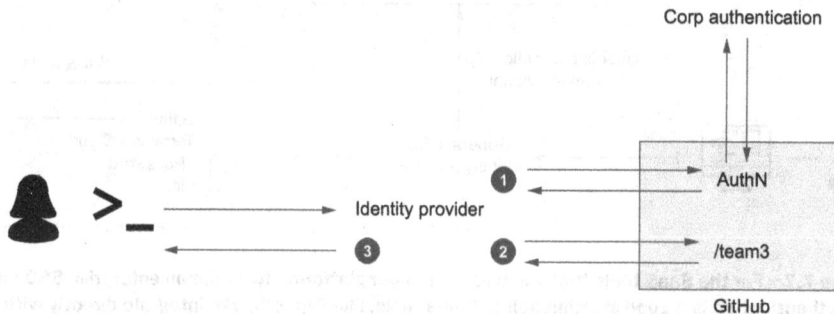

Figure 7.8   For Epetech, we would like our IDP service to have built-in or easily configurable means of integrating with GitHub, requiring authentication through whatever means we have set up in GitHub. As a result of (1) successful authentication, we want the IDP to (2) get the list of all teams the user is a member of in our GitHub organization. Finally, we want to (3) return to the user a secure means of accessing the platform infrastructure or custom API resources.

Most widely used IDP solutions (OneLogin, Okta, Entra AD SSO) provide at least part of the solution. Still, we will need to deploy and manage some form of authorization server if our GitHub organization is to be the authoritative source of authZ information. Because of this, engineering teams often decide to use solutions like Keycloak or Dex instead.

For our Epetech example, we will use a SaaS solution. Auth0, now an Okta product, offers a free tier for its product-oriented IDP capabilities that is sufficient for these exercises. This is exactly the functionality we need to create a product experience for our platform.

7.3.2 OpenID Connect device-auth-flow and team membership claims

Like any *connected* product experience, our internal platform customers (development teams) interact with platform infrastructure and custom services through a device. They use their laptop. However, they need to interact with these platform services programmatically and not merely utilize a dedicated browser or application interface. The programmatic context is typically a terminal window. Terminals have a limited ability to control user input or independently receive data from a browser or other application. The OAuth 2.0 device-authorization-grant [3] standard provides a secure means of dealing with this situation (see figure 7.9).

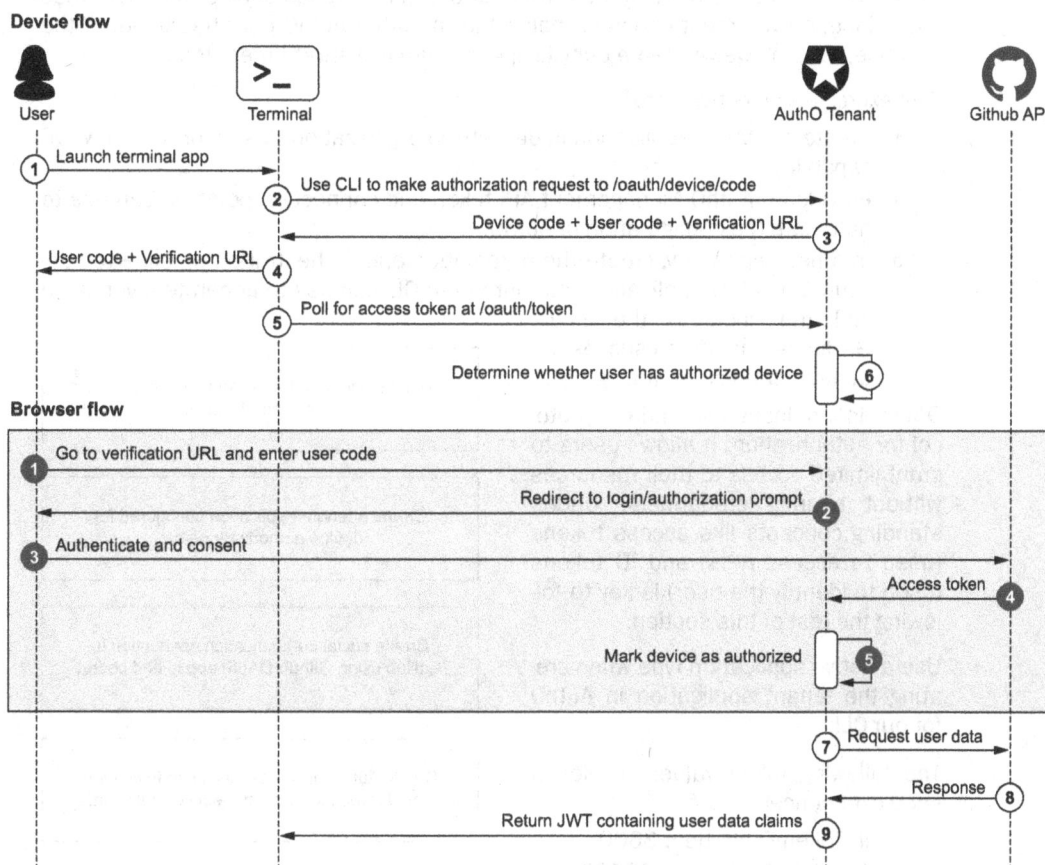

Figure 7.9 In this authentication and authorization flow, the IDP acts just as a secure go-between. The user must authenticate through GitHub and grant their device authorization to receive a JSON Web Token.

If the user successfully authenticates on GitHub, the IDP will use the resulting access token to request the list of teams within the organization where the user is a member. The IDP will then create a verifiable JSON Web Token (JWT) that includes the user's ID token containing the list of teams as a claim and can include a refresh token.

We will create a CLI that enables users of our platform to gain access to their team's resources within the platform. In the previous flow, this means our CLI will be responsible for steps 2, 4, and 5. GitHub provides the browser-step 4 capability. However, we need a service that offers the OAuth2 flow in steps 3, 6, 7, and 9. Auth0.com provides a free tier that supports exactly our use case.

Exercise 7.3   Configure SaaS IDP for device-auth-flow

Create a free-tier account on auth0.com and define a tenant (you can use your GitHub identity). The Auth0 application we create will primarily be visible to users through the CLI we will provide, so naming the tenant for the CLI is a good choice. Tenant names are unique, so you must choose a name that no other Auth0 user has used. In the exercise, assume we will name our CLI `epectl`, with `epe` short for epetech.

This exercise's objectives are

1 Create an OAuth application in our GitHub organization to support our new IDP capability.
2 Provide an Auth0 Management API token and connection point we can use to automate the configuration of Auth0.
3 In a new repository, create the automation and orchestration pipeline to configure an Auth0 application that our future CLI can use to generate a verifiable JWT that includes the user's GitHub teams after a successful authentication (see the figure).

OAuth is an industry-standard protocol for authorization. It allows users to grant limited access to their resources without sharing credentials. Understanding concepts like access tokens (used to access APIs) and ID tokens (used to identify the user) is key to following the rest of this section.

Use a native application type when creating the tenant application in Auth0 for our CLI.

The following token values provide a good experience:

- ID Token Expiration: 3600
- Absolute Expiration: 604800
- Inactivity Expiration: 172800

Include the Device and Refresh token grant types.

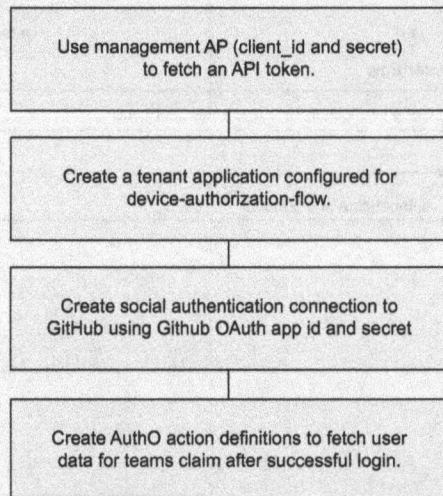

Use management AP (client_id and secret) to fetch an API token.

Create a tenant application configured for device-authorization-flow.

Create social authentication connection to GitHub using Github OAuth app id and secret

Create Auth0 action definitions to fetch user data for teams claim after successful login.

This configuration can be done through the Auth0 UI or programmatically. In a production environment, you should always manage configuration in code.

The tenant application should be created before the GitHub connection so that the connection can be assigned to the application.

The GitHub connection should support read:user, read:org, and read:public_key permissions. Include the user's email in the attributes and disable user profile syncing. We don't want Auth0 to maintain any user information.

The Auth0 tenant Actions settings are where you configure steps to take after a successful authentication. In our case, those steps are to use the token received from a successful social authentication with GitHub to fetch the user's GitHub teams and then return a JWT that includes those teams as an additional claim.

Auth0 provides excellent documentation, but obviously, this effort assumes you have a basic working knowledge of OAuth2 and web tokens. There is a complete solution in the GitHub repository associated with the book under chapter 7, which allows you to implement the solution by following a step-by-step guide.

7.4 *Cloud service control plane base*

This domain defines the platform's core control plane that enables and orchestrates all infrastructure components of the platform. Today, most enterprise engineering platforms rely on distributed service architectures, and therefore, Kubernetes can effectively be used as the platform's control plane. We've specifically labeled the domain with *Cloud* and *Base* to indicate that the scope should be limited to only those elements that are fully cloud vendor-managed operationally.

However, Kubernetes isn't the only way to build a control plane. If your organization isn't using Kubernetes, you'll need to set up a control plane through other means. The cloud vendors' API is a good starting point. But unlike Kubernetes, those APIs don't come with built-in extensibility, which means you'll need to create the service interface yourself.

Cloud vendors are continually enhancing their control plane-oriented services (an example is AWS Control Tower), making it easier to create a control plane when extended with serverless functions. Alternatively, you can explore solutions like HashiCorp's Terraform Cloud. When combined with Sentinel and well-defined account permission boundaries, these tools can help you achieve similar results.

With our VPCs provisioned and our customer OpenID Connect (OIDC) provider ready, we can deploy the EKS control plane base. The base pipeline is limited to EKS and just those Kubernetes services that AWS will fully manage.

The practical consequence of this from a platform engineering perspective is that the most effective way to minimize the long-term operational overhead and change management effort is to isolate the provisioning of these services into a single pipeline, along with reducing the amount of variance from officially supported resources, given our infrastructure-as-code framework.

Currently, the number of vendor-managed internals is relatively low. As the number of options grows or as vendors change the way that these services are managed, this domain boundary will change as well.

Figure 7.10 shows the elements we will manage in our aws-control-plane-base pipeline:

- EKS itself, naturally
- An AWS-managed node group to host the administrator-managed services and extensions for the cluster
- The default EKS Kubernetes required services
  - kube-proxy
  - coredns
- Two basic types of storage classes (which amount to the AWS defaults)
  - ebs-csi
  - efs-csi
- The current standard for OIDC assumable roles
  - eks-pod-identity-agent
- A node pool manager to support elastic compute for our platform customer needs
  - Karpenter

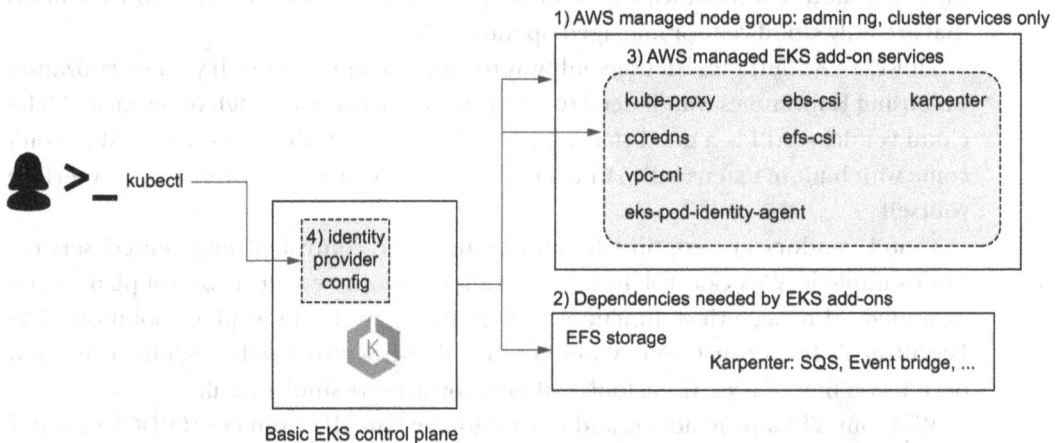

Figure 7.10   With vendor-managed services, we effectively decide which version of the service we want to be deployed and perhaps a handful of specific settings. Nearly all of what goes into deploying and managing the service is the cloud vendor's responsibility.

To provision the base vendor-managed components for Epetech, we will use the following Terraform modules:

- terraform-aws-modules/eks/aws
- aws-ia/eks-blueprints-addons/aws
- terraform-aws-modules/iam/aws
- cloudposse/efs/aws

AWS provides the first three. AWS also has an Elastic File System (EFS) module, but the CloudPosse module has more sensible defaults for our use case. Using modules from any source, including AWS, carries the same risks as using code libraries in any software, such as Springboot or Next.js. Always review such modules for implementation details and scan the source with tools like Trivy.

In addition to the AWS configuration tests we have been running in our earlier pipelines, we need to start testing for the general deployment health of these managed services running on the cluster. For basic validation of the provisioned AWS resources, we can continue to use AwSpec:

```
$ cat test/control_plane_base.rb
require 'awspec'
require 'json'

tfvars = JSON.parse(File.read('./' + ENV['CLUSTER'] + '.auto.tfvars.json'))

describe eks(tfvars["cluster_name"]) do
  it { should exist }
  it { should be_active }
  its(:version) { should eq tfvars['eks_version'] }
end

describe iam_role(tfvars["cluster_name"] + '-vpc-cni') do
  it { should exist }
end

describe iam_role(tfvars["cluster_name"] + '-ebs-csi-controller-sa') do
  it { should exist }
end

describe iam_role(tfvars["cluster_name"] + '-efs-csi-controller-sa') do
  it { should exist }
end

describe efs(tfvars["cluster_name"] + "-efs-csi-storage") do
  it { should exist }
end

describe sqs("Karpenter-" + tfvars["cluster_name"]) do
  it { should exist }
end
```

However, to test the EKS add-ons, we need to introduce some new approaches.

We will use Bats (https://github.com/bats-core/bats-core) for querying the Kubernetes API for the basic deployment health of these managed services. We can organize a series of command-line queries of the Kubernetes API using kubectl. This means we will need to have the necessary kubeconfig file available and be using the correct identity. We will need to include this in the setup commands of our pipeline:

> The following two tests will use kubectl to query for the number and status of nodes. We expect the number of nodes to be greater than zero, and none should be in Not Ready status.

> Our test namespace should exist. We will cover adding these system namespaces later.

> The clusterrolebinding for our platform team should exist. We will need to test the health of the configuration manually, as it is designed for human users.

> The remaining tests are looking for the Running status from all the EKS add-ons we selected.

```
$ bats test/baseline/baseline_resources.bats
#!/usr/bin/env bats

@test "validate nodes reporting" {
  run bash -c "kubectl get nodes | tail -n +2 | wc -l"
  [[ "${output}" != "0" ]]
}
@test "validate nodes Ready" {
  run bash -c "kubectl get nodes | grep 'Not Ready"
  [[ "${output}" != "Not Ready" ]]
}
@test "validate test system namespace" {
  run bash -c "kubectl get ns"
  [[ "${output}" =~ "test-system" ]]
}
@test "validate platform-adkmin clusterrolebinding" {
  run bash -c "kubectl get clusterrolebindings"
  [[ "${output}" =~ "platform-admin-clusterrolebinding" ]]
}

$ bats test/baseline/cluster_addons.bats
@test "evaluate kubeproxy" {
  run bash -c "kubectl get po -n kube-system -o wide | grep 'kube-proxy'"
  [[ "${output}" =~ "Running" ]]
}
@test "evaluate ebs csi node deployment" {
  run bash -c "kubectl get po -n kube-system -o wide | grep 'ebs-csi-node'"
  [[ "${output}" =~ "Running" ]]
}
@test "evaluate ebs csi controller deployment" {
run bash -c \ "kubectl get po -n kube-system -o wide | grep 'ebs-csi-controller'"
  [[ "${output}" =~ "Running" ]]
}
@test "evaluate efs csi node deployment" {
  run bash -c "kubectl get po -n kube-system -o wide | grep 'efs-csi-node'"
  [[ "${output}" =~ "Running" ]]
}
@test "evaluate efs csi controller deployment" {
  run bash -c
"kubectl get po -n kube-system -o wide | grep 'efs-csi-controller'"
  [[ "${output}" =~ "Running" ]]
}
@test "evaluate aws-node" {
  run bash -c "kubectl get po -n kube-system -o wide | grep 'aws-node'"
  [[ "${output}" =~ "Running" ]]
}
@test "evaluate core-dns" {
```

```
  run bash -c "kubectl get po -n kube-system -o wide | grep 'coredns'"
  [[ "${output}" =~ "Running" ]]
}
@test "evaluate eks-pod-identity-agent" {
  run bash -c
   "kubectl get po -n kube-system -o wide | grep 'eks-pod-identity-agent'"
  [[ "${output}" =~ "Running" ]]
}
@test "evaluate karpenter" {
  run bash -c "kubectl get po -n kube-system -o wide | grep 'karpenter'"
  [[ "${output}" =~ "Running" ]]
}
```

We can create and run these tests now, of course, expecting them to fail at this point. But beyond these general tests of the services reporting a ready status, we need tests that require the services to perform their expected function to test the actual operational health. We will come back to this type of testing later in this section.

> **NOTE** Recall that we use the aws-iam-profiles pipeline we created previously to manage the unique roles used by this base platform pipeline. For our aws-control-plane-base pipeline, we will need a platform-control-plane-base-role with the necessary permissions. You will need to add this role to the aws-iam-roles pipeline before our control plane base pipeline will work.

Let's now start provisioning the basic control plane. We need to define a few Terraform data resources to look up information that our cluster definition will require:

```
$ cat data.tf

data "aws_vpc" "vpc" {
  tags = {
    Name = "${var.cluster_name}-vpc"
  }
}
data "aws_subnets" "cluster_private_subnets" {
  filter {
    name   = "vpc-id"
    values = [data.aws_vpc.vpc.id]
  }
  tags = {
    Tier = var.node_subnet_identifier
  }
}
data "aws_subnet" "cluster_private_subnets" {
  for_each = toset(data.aws_subnets.cluster_private_subnets.ids)
  id       = each.value
}
data "aws_subnets" "cluster_intra_subnets" {
  filter {
    name   = "vpc-id"
    values = [data.aws_vpc.vpc.id]
  }
```

```
   tags = {
     Tier = var.intra_subnet_identifier
   }
}
```

The resources use the cluster name, VPC, and subnet naming convention to find the resources in our AWS account. With those available, we can use the standard EKS module to provision our control plane:

Our Kubernetes API endpoint will be accessible. The native API authorization and the additional OIDC provider we will attach are based on the same internet-standard security protocols. We can be safely managed over the public network.

```
$ cat main.tf
module "eks" {
  source  = "terraform-aws-modules/eks/aws"
  version = "20.36.0"
  cluster_name    = var.cluster_name
  cluster_version = var.eks_version
  cluster_endpoint_public_access = true
  authentication_mode            = "API"
  access_entries = {
    clusterAdmin = {
      principal_arn = "arn:aws:iam::${var.aws_account_id}:role/${var.aws_
assume_role}"
      policy_associations = {
        clusterAdmin = {
        policy_arn = "arn:aws:eks::aws:cluster-access-policy/AmazonEKS
ClusterAdminPolicy"
          access_scope = {
            type = "cluster"
          }
        }
      }
    }
  }
  vpc_id                  = data.aws_vpc.vpc.id
  subnet_ids              = data.aws_subnets.cluster_private_subnets.ids
  control_plane_subnet_ids = data.aws_subnets.cluster_intra_subnets.ids
  cluster_enabled_log_types = var.enable_log_types
  create_kms_key          = true
  # For longer cluster names using the prefix goes over 38 char limit
  iam_role_use_name_prefix = false
}
```

The current, recommended access mode for EKS is API. Other historical modes are still supported, but let's use the current standard.

Based on the API access mode, adds the role we will create for the pipeline to use as administrative access for cluster management

Uses an AWS-managed key management service key for cluster secrets encryption

We want all the available log types: ["api", "audit", "authenticator", "controllerManager", "scheduler"].

7.4.1 AWS managed node groups

Before we can use the EKS-managed services for our cluster, we need nodes to which the services can be deployed, and AWS provides an AWS-managed node group option. We can add a managed node group definition within the EKS module to host cluster services:

```
module "eks" {
  ...
  eks_managed_node_group_defaults = {
    version             = var.eks_version
    force_update_version = true
    enable_monitoring    = true
  }
  eks_managed_node_groups = {
    # dedicated mgmt node group, other node groups managed by karpenter
    (var.management_node_group_name) = {
      ami_type        = var.management_node_group_ami_type
      instance_types = var.management_node_group_instance_types
      capacity_type  = var.management_node_group_capacity_type
      min_size        = var.management_node_group_min_size
      max_size        = var.management_node_group_max_size
      desired_size    = var.management_node_group_desired_size
      disk_size       = var.management_node_group_disk_size
      labels = {
        "nodegroup"              = var.management_node_group_name
        "node.kubernetes.io/role" = var.management_node_group_role
        "karpenter.sh/controller" = "true"
      }
      taints = {
        dedicated = {
          key    = "dedicated"
          value = var.management_node_group_role
          effect = "NO_SCHEDULE"
        }
      }
    }
  }
  node_security_group_additional_rules = {
    allow_data_plane_tcp = {
      description                  = "Allow TCP Protocol Port"
      protocol                     = "TCP"
      from_port                    = 1024
      to_port                      = 65535
      type                         = "ingress"
      source_cluster_security_group = true
    }
  }
  tags = {
    "karpenter.sh/discovery" = var.cluster_name
  }
  ...
}
```

Include a Karpenter controller schedule label so Karpenter knows it should run on these nodes.

Taint the node group so that only services with specific tolerations will run on the management node group.

Add an additional security group rule to support TCP traffic within the control plane nodes.

Include a discovery tag for Karpenter.

7.4.2   Dependencies for AWS-managed EKS services

The EFS storage class provider requires EFS targets to create persistent volumes. There are several strategies for managing EFS targets for use as a storage class. Still, for most situations, we can provision a single target and configure the class to segregate volume claims into distinct folders and namespace permissions. We need to add this target for the storage class to work:

```
$ cat efs_csi_storage.tf
module "efs_csi_storage" {
  source  = "cloudposse/efs/aws"
  version = "1.1.0"
  name = "${var.cluster_name}-efs-csi-storage"
  region  = var.aws_region
  vpc_id  = data.aws_vpc.vpc.id
  subnets = data.aws_subnets.cluster_private_subnets.ids
  allowed_cidr_blocks          = [for s in data.aws_subnet.cluster_private_
subnets : s.cidr_block]
  associated_security_group_ids = [module.eks.cluster_security_group_id]
  transition_to_ia           = ["AFTER_7_DAYS"]
  efs_backup_policy_enabled = true
  encrypted                 = true
  tags = {
    "cluster"  = var.cluster_name
    "pipeline" = "control-plane-base"
  }
}
output "eks_efs_csi_storage_dns_name" {
  value = module.efs_csi_storage.dns_name
}
output "eks_efs_csi_storage_id" {
  value = module.efs_csi_storage.id
}
output "eks_efs_csi_storage_mount_target_dns_names" {
  value = module.efs_csi_storage.mount_target_dns_names
}
output "eks_efs_csi_storage_security_group_id" {
  value = module.efs_csi_storage.security_group_id
}
```

> **Access to the EFS instance is limited to the cluster for which it is provisioned.**

> **Choose a strategy that best fits your use case. This transition keeps costs low where performance is not critical (such as in these exercises).**

> **We must output the values needed for later storage provisioning. The pipeline should retrieve these and write them to our 1Password vault.**

Karpenter also has some AWS service dependencies. Karpenter can consume event information to manage Spot instance usage. The Karpenter submodule within the EKS module provisions the other AWS services and EKS node role configurations needed by the Karpenter services:

```
$ cat main.tf
...
module "karpenter" {
  source  = "terraform-aws-modules/eks/aws//modules/karpenter"
  version = "20.20.0"
  cluster_name = module.eks.cluster_name
  enable_pod_identity            = true
```

```
  create_pod_identity_association = true
  node_iam_role_additional_policies = {
    AmazonSSMManagedInstanceCore = "arn:aws:iam::aws:policy/
      AmazonSSMManagedInstanceCore"
  }
}
output "karpenter_iam_role_arn" {
  value = module.karpenter.iam_role_arn
}
output "karpenter_node_iam_role_name" {
  value = module.karpenter.node_iam_role_name
}
output "karpenter_sqs_queue_name" {
  value = module.karpenter.queue_name
}
```

◀— **We must access ARNs and Queues from this configuration during the Karpenter service deployment.**

7.4.3 *AWS managed EKS add-ons*

With a place for the services to run, we can add the AWS-managed EKS services:

- kube-proxy
- vpc-cni
- coredns
- aws-ebs-csi-driver
- aws-efs-csi-driver
- eks-pod-identity-agent
- karpenter

You may notice that Karpenter is on this list even though it is not yet a fully AWS-managed add-on. Karpenter is close to becoming fully managed. Several of its dependent components are already. Services like this can be included in the base pipeline without creating excess management friction. A historical example of this is the AWS efs-csi storage class. For a couple of years, the service itself, while developed and provided by AWS, was nonetheless self-managed in terms of performing the deployment and upgrades, as well as monitoring and responding to problems. However, the EFS storage location was a fully managed AWS service. In practical terms, AWS provided significant support as long as you used the service in the intended configurations. It made sense to include it in the control plane base implementation pipeline. Now, EFS is a fully managed EKS 27add-on.

AWS maintains a set of Terraform modules called Blueprints to support these add-ons. It is possible to do even more with these Blueprints, but this comes at the price of overcoupling and increased complexity. For AWS-managed add-ons alone, it is a good fit. You will also notice in this pipeline example for these fully AWS-managed add-ons, we are using most_recent=true, which is the equivalent of saying "use the latest version of this particular managed add-on associated with this version of Kubernetes." AWS maintains separate version trees for their managed add-ons versions by specific

Kubernetes version to improve its service-level objectives across the supported versions of EKS. This has significantly improved the stability of the add-ons. But you may ask: why would we use the latest as the desired version when this pipeline runs? This vendor-managed pipeline is the only place we are doing this. This pipeline is the mechanism that updates the nodes in the management node pool to the latest security patch version. We expect to be running this pipeline routinely, every week or two at most, if for no other reason than to pick up those patches in that pool (Karpenter is configured to perform this function in the customer-facing node pools). Overall, the stability and resiliency experience we have set for our customers depends on our ability to push frequent changes to the platform definition confidently. Success depends on the architecture of our build automation, incorporating effective testing, and (partly through these internally subdomain-bound pipelines) enabling us to consistently release these changes as frequent small changes rather than infrequent significant changes. What checks or processes do we put in place to provide overall feedback on the effectiveness of the platform team's internal engineering culture regarding this behavior? A list of nonproduction or production environment incidents is a very poor indicator. We can get high marks on that by simply never allowing any change at all. And our platform would quickly be of little value.

We have found this setting, in this particular pipeline, to be a good leading indicator. In real-world settings, at both small and large scales, running this pipeline to production frequently, constantly reviewing the change plan and noting when actual version changes are occurring, while having a platform development, quality assurance, and preview context for testing, has resulted in a very low-friction outcome. Occasionally, bugs will escape to one of these AWS-managed services, but they are routinely caught before leaving the preview environment.

Where this will break down is when the pipeline is not run frequently or there are no prereleases to customer testing environments—if you are waiting months to run this pipeline, are multiple versions behind on Kubernetes, or are unable to do meaningful testing until the changes are deployed under your users' actual nonproduction environments. You will find you have had to pin these add-on versions. Treat that as a symptom of the bigger problem of insufficient investment in platform engineering operational practices.

Not every service or technology release pipeline is a candidate for this practice. The reason it can be so effective here is primarily the result of the predictability of the environment in which AWS EKS add-ons run. While companies can and do use EKS in unpredictable ways, AWS does not have to craft release testing in isolation from an upstream Kubernetes deployment definition. These are meant only for EKS and will be coupled to AWS's operational practices with EKS. What this also means is that the more we depart from the reference EKS service architecture, the more likely it is we will need to coordinate testing and therefore need to pin the add-ons here.

One example is if we chose to self-manage the pod network. If we decide not to use the AWS CNI and instead deploy something like Cilium (https://cilium.io), which could include not using kube-proxy, then we will have to determine how to alter our pipeline domain boundaries to account for this. If we keep AWS-managed EKS elements in the same pipeline, such as our AWS-managed management node group, then we need to include the self-managed CNI in the pipeline with pinned version changes.

We don't generally recommend deviating from the cloud vendor-provided (supported) CNI or the other standard add-ons. When you do deviate from these defaults, ensure the business value is easily understood and measurable. The cost to implement and maintain will be significant and measurable, and the business value should exceed this additional cost:

```
$ cat eks_addons.tf
module "eks_addons" {
  source      = "aws-ia/eks-blueprints-addons/aws"
  version     = "1.21.0"
  depends_on  = [module.eks]
  cluster_name      = module.eks.cluster_name
  cluster_endpoint  = module.eks.cluster_endpoint
  cluster_version   = module.eks.cluster_version
  oidc_provider_arn = module.eks.oidc_provider_arn
  eks_addons = {
    kube-proxy = { most_recent = true }
    vpc-cni = {
      most_recent               = true
      service_account_role_arn  = module.vpc_cni_irsa_role.
  iam_role_arn
    }
    coredns = {
      most_recent = true
      configuration_values = jsonencode({
        autoScaling = {
          "enabled" = true
        }
        nodeSelector = {
          "node.kubernetes.io/role" = "management"
        }
        tolerations = [
          {
            key      = "dedicated"
            operator = "Equal"
            value    = "management"
            effect   = "NoSchedule"
          }
        ]
      })
    }
    aws-ebs-csi-driver = {
      amost_recent              = true
      service_account_role_arn  = module.ebs_csi_irsa_role.iam_role_arn
      configuration_values = jsonencode({
        controller = {
          nodeSelector = {
            "node.kubernetes.io/role" = "management"
```

Daemonset deployment that will automatically be added to every node, whether part of a managed node group or a Karpenter node pool

Some of these add-ons require that we provide a specific role. The AWS IAM module has specific submodules just for EKS add-ons.

In the past, scaling coredns required a separate service. This is now managed as a setting in the add-on.

For services other than Daemonset, we need to add the tolerances and node selector to direct the service to run on our management services node group.

```
            }
            tolerations = [
              {
                key      = "dedicated"
                operator = "Equal"
                value    = "management"
                effect   = "NoSchedule"
              }
            ]
          }
        })
      }
      aws-efs-csi-driver = {
        amost_recent            = true
        service_account_role_arn = module.efs_csi_irsa_role.iam_role_arn
        configuration_values = jsonencode({
          controller = {
            nodeSelector = {
              "node.kubernetes.io/role" = "management"
            }
            tolerations = [
              {
                key      = "dedicated"
                operator = "Equal"
                value    = "management"
                effect   = "NoSchedule"
              }
            ]
          }
        })
      }
      eks-pod-identity-agent = { most_recent = true }
    }
  }
  module "vpc_cni_irsa_role" {
    source  = "terraform-aws-modules/iam/aws//modules/
  iam-role-for-service-accounts-eks"
    version = "~> 5.40.0"
    role_path              = "/PlatformRoles/"
    role_name              = "${var.cluster_name}-vpc-cni"
    attach_vpc_cni_policy = true
    vpc_cni_enable_ipv4   = true
    oidc_providers = {
      main = {
        provider_arn              = module.eks.oidc_provider_arn
        namespace_service_accounts = ["kube-system:aws-node"]
      }
    }
  }
  module "ebs_csi_irsa_role" {
    source  = "terraform-aws-modules/iam/aws//modules/
  iam-role-for-service-accounts-eks"
    version = "~> 5.40.0"
    role_path              = "/PlatformRoles/"
    role_name              = "${var.cluster_name}-ebs-csi-controller-sa"
```

◄——— **Some of these add-ons require that we provide a specific role. The AWS IAM module has specific submodules just for EKS add-ons.**

```
    attach_ebs_csi_policy = true
    oidc_providers = {
      main = {
        provider_arn                = module.eks.oidc_provider_arn
        namespace_service_accounts = ["kube-system:ebs-csi-controller-sa"]
      }
    }
  }
}
module "efs_csi_irsa_role" {
  source  = "terraform-aws-modules/iam/aws//modules/
   iam-role-for-service-accounts-eks"
  version = "~> 5.40.0"
  role_path             = "/PlatformRoles/"
  role_name             = "${var.cluster_name}-efs-csi-controller-sa"
  attach_efs_csi_policy = true
  oidc_providers = {
    main = {
      provider_arn                = module.eks.oidc_provider_arn
      namespace_service_accounts = ["kube-system:efs-csi-controller-sa"]
    }
  }
}
```

You would be correct if you called out that the configuration for these AWS-managed services will request an upgrade to the most recently released version each time the terraform-apply is performed. Without our testing environments, this isn't something we would do. But that is one of the reasons for nondeveloper-facing testing environments. These aren't deployments we manage, not even slightly. These are completely AWS-managed deployments, which means we are equally interested in testing their deployment strategy.

We will always know before a new version gets deployed because it is visible in the change plan. And we expect to have (in a real setting) at least two complete nondeveloper-facing environments for early testing, plus the preview environment for testing with developer code, yet not in their path to production. In practice, in the case of these AWS managed services, we've found this strategy to result in better outcomes and team maintenance habits—something to consider. But you can, of course, pin these. A potential risk with automatic upgrades in nonproduction environments is that newer versions of AWS-managed services may be available in a lower environment but not yet rolled out to the production region. This can lead to situations where code tested successfully in lower environments fails or behaves differently in production due to version mismatches. To mitigate this, promotion to production should always use explicitly versioned resources, not automatically upgraded ones.

Finally, to deploy the Karpenter service itself, we will use the Helm resource. We don't think using Terraform to deploy Helm is a good idea. Deploying applications is not the equivalent of a declarative infrastructure definition. Recall our discussion on selecting infrastructure code frameworks. Helm is well-suited to interacting with the Kubernetes API to manage deployments. In virtually every case, adding another framework around Helm merely adds complexity. But in this "vendor-managed only" pipeline, we can get some maintenance value from deploying Karpenter in this manner, given the number of configuration values it pulls from the rest of the deployment, and that this is an AWS-provided chart:

```
$ cat karpenter_deploy.tf
resource "helm_release" "karpenter-crd" {
  namespace  = "kube-system"
  name       = "karpenter-crd"
  repository = "oci://public.ecr.aws/karpenter"
  chart      = "karpenter-crd"
  version    = var.karpenter_chart_version
  wait       = true
  values     = []
}
resource "helm_release" "karpenter" {
  depends_on = [helm_release.karpenter-crd, module.karpenter]
  namespace  = "kube-system"
  name       = "karpenter"
  repository = "oci://public.ecr.aws/karpenter"
  chart      = "karpenter"
  version    = var.karpenter_chart_version
  wait       = true
  skip_crds  = true
  values = [
    templatefile("tpl/karpenter_values.tpl", {
      iam_role_arn               = module.karpenter.iam_role_arn
      management_node_group_name = var.management_node_group_name
      management_node_group_role = var.management_node_group_role
      cluster_name               = var.cluster_name
      cluster_endpoint           = module.eks.cluster_endpoint
      queue_name                 = module.karpenter.queue_name
    }),
  ]
}

$ cat tpl/karpenter_values.tpl
serviceAccount:
  annotations:
    eks.amazonaws.com/role-arn: ${iam_role_arn}
imagePullPolicy: Always
podDisruptionBudget:
  maxUnavailable: 1
replicas: 1
nodeSelector:
  nodegroup: ${management_node_group_name}
tolerations:
  - key: "dedicated"
    operator: "Equal"
    value: "${management_node_group_role}"
    effect: "NoSchedule"
settings:
  clusterName: ${cluster_name}
  clusterEndpoint: ${cluster_endpoint}
```

Set low for the exercise. Would typically run at 3 for resiliency.

We must set the node selector and tolerations for the service to run in our management node group.

```
      interruptionQueue: ${queue_name}
      featureGates:
        drift: true
        spotToSpotConsolidation: true
```

7.4.4 *Integrating an OIDC provider with the control plane base*

In exercise 7.3, we set up an OAuth2/OIDC authentication and authorization end-point that will let us manage developer access through their team memberships in GitHub. By integrating the OIDC provider with the control plane, we can create (enforce) these user access controls and enable SSO across multiple clusters—even between different cloud providers. If you complete the exercise, you will have the necessary values to allow EKS to create an integration point between our IDP and the Kubernetes API:

Use the group claim name used in the JWT. "https://github.org/epetech/teams".

This value is the Auth0 application client ID from the IDP project setup in exercise 7.3.

```
$ cat main.tf
...
resource "aws_eks_identity_provider_config" "auth0_oidc_config" {
  cluster_name = var.cluster_name
  oidc {
    client_id                   = var.oidc_client_id
    groups_claim                = var.oidc_groups_claim
    identity_provider_config_name = var.
  oidc_identity_provider_config_name
    issuer_url                  = var.oidc_issuer_url
  }
  depends_on = [module.eks]
}
output "cluster_url" {
  description = "Endpoint for EKS control plane."
  value       = module.eks.cluster_endpoint
}
output "cluster_oidc_issuer_url" {
  value = module.eks.cluster_oidc_issuer_url
}
output "cluster_public_certificate_authority_data" {
  value = module.eks.cluster_certificate_authority_data
}
```

The IDP vendor name "Auth0"

The URL for the application we defined in Auth0. "https://dev-epectl.us.auth0.com/" (or just epectl for the production cluster)

We should now have the complete resource definition to provision our clusters. Since we have two clusters in our Epetech platform, we will have two environment value files. The following is an example of the resulting tfvars file for one of our two cluster environments:

```
$ cat environments/sbx-i01-aws-us-east-1.auto.tfvars.json.tpl
{
  "cluster_name": "sbx-i01-aws-us-east-1",
```

This example will use the ARM architecture
and provision with the Bottlerocket OS.

To identify this node group, the name includes a
description of what the node group will be used for
(e.g., management). It includes the architecture, the
OS reference, and -mng to identify the resource type.

```
"aws_account_id": "{{ op://vault-name/aws-account-2/aws-account-id }}",
"aws_assume_role": "PlatformRoles/PlatformControlPlaneBaseRole",
"aws_region": "us-east-1",
"eks_version": "1.32",
"enable_log_types":
    ["api","audit","authenticator","controllerManager","scheduler"],
"node_subnet_identifier": "node",
"intra_subnet_identifier": "intra",
"auto_refresh_management_node_group": "true",
"management_node_group_name": "management-arm-rkt-mng",
"management_node_group_role": "management",
"management_node_group_ami_type": "BOTTLEROCKET_ARM_64",
"management_node_group_disk_size": "50",
"management_node_group_capacity_type": "SPOT",
"management_node_group_desired_size": "1",
"management_node_group_max_size": "3",
"management_node_group_min_size": "1",
"management_node_group_instance_types": ["t4g.2xlarge","m6g.2xlarge","m7g.2
xlarge","c7g.4xlarge"],
"karpenter_chart_version": "1.4.0",
"oidc_client_id": "{{ op://vault-name/svc-auth0/
vsctl-cli-client-id }}",
"oidc_groups_claim": "https://github.org/epetech/teams",
"oidc_identity_provider_config_name": "Auth0",
"oidc_issuer_url": "https://dev-epectl.us.auth0.com/"
}
```

Uses Spot instances and defines our management pool with only a single node as the preferred scale

These are the same values we provided to our aws_eks_identity_provider_config resource.

We define the version of Karpenter in our environment variables and likewise perform the upgrade by changing this value.

Note that to keep costs low for this exercise, we use Spot instances and define our management pool with only a single node as the preferred scale. In a real setting, three to five is a better starting point for the management node group scale. If you find that you will have management services that you expect to run on the management node group and that do not support ARM, then you may wish to provision the node group as AMD.

The production cluster values can be nearly identical for exercise 7.4. Introduced in section 7.1.2 and used throughout this chapter, we set our production cluster name to prod-i01-aws-us-east-2, in its own account, which we have been referring to as aws-account-1, and in the us-east-2 region.

7.4.5   *Post-Terraform configuration*

After the terraform apply step in our pipeline, we need to gather and save certain cluster information. In addition, there are additional resources to deploy to the cluster via the Kubernetes API.

CLUSTER KUBECONFIG FILE

As part of provisioning the cluster, we set the cluster administrator to the role we used to create the cluster. For pipeline-orchestrated cluster administration, this is the role we will use in combination with our service account, including the current pipeline. Let's generate the needed Kubeconfig file:

```
$ cat scripts/generate_kubeconfig.sh
#!/usr/bin/env bash
source bash-functions.sh  # from orb-pipeline-events/bash-functions
set -eo pipefail
cluster_name=$1
export AWS_ACCOUNT_ID=$(jq -er .aws_account_id "$cluster_name".auto.tfvars.json)
export AWS_ASSUME_ROLE=$(jq -er .aws_assume_role "$cluster_name".auto.tfvars.json)
export AWS_REGION=$(jq -er .aws_region "$cluster_name".auto.tfvars.json)
awsAssumeRole "$AWS_ACCOUNT_ID" "$AWS_ASSUME_ROLE"
aws eks update-kubeconfig --name "$cluster_name" \
--region "$AWS_REGION" \
--role-arn "arn:aws:iam::$AWS_ACCOUNT_ID:role/$AWS_ASSUME_ROLE" \
--kubeconfig ~/.kube/config
```

We write the kubeconfig file to the default location. We could have alternatively written it locally and referenced it with $KUBECONFIG. We need to save a copy of this kubeconfig in our secrets store, and we will need some values from our Terraform outputs. Let's start the base_configuration.sh script, where we can take care of all the post-apply configuration:

```
$ cat scripts/base_configuration.sh

#!/usr/bin/env bash
source bash-functions.sh          ◄───┐  We will use a shared script
set -eo pipefail                       └  from the pipeline_events orb.

                                            Performs base64 encoding ┐
cluster_name=$1                                                      │
export AWS_REGION=$(jq -er .aws_region "$cluster_name".auto.tfvars.json)
kubeconfig=$(cat ~/.kube/config | base64)    ◄──────────────────────┘
# store cluster identifiers in 1password
vaultwrite1passwordField vault-name "${cluster_name}" kubeconfig-base64
  "$kubeconfig"
write1passwordField vault-name "${cluster_name}" cluster-url $(terraform
output -raw cluster_url)
write1passwordField vault-name "${cluster_name}"
  base64-certificate-authority-data $(terraform output -raw cluster_public_
certificate_authority_data)
write1passwordField vault-name "${cluster_name}" eks-efs-csi-storage-id
  $(terraform output -raw eks_efs_csi_storage_id)
```

```
write1passwordField vault-name "${cluster_name}" cluster-oidc-issuer-url
   $(terraform output -raw cluster_oidc_issuer_url)
eks_efs_csi_storage_id=$(terraform output -raw eks_efs_csi_storage_id)
karpenter_node_iam_role_name=$(terraform output -raw
   karpenter_node_iam_role_name)
```

Note that in the generate_kubeconfig.sh script, we wrote the kubeconfig to the standard location, allowing us to read it and store it with our secrets. Secrets management services do not always retain formatted data correctly. An easy way to deal with this problem is to first perform base64 encoding, so that basic string storage is all that is needed.

In this example, we store the values under a 1Password item with the same name as the cluster to which they are associated. The EFS storage ID is saved, and we will use it in creating the storage class. The EFS storage ID and the Karpenter node IAM role name will both be needed.

OIDC ADMINISTRATOR ACCESS

In exercise 7.3, we set up an authentication and authorization system based on GitHub team membership. If the IDP configuration is successful, a member of this GitHub team can use kubectl to access the cluster as an administrator. Create the administrative cluster role binding for our platform engineering team based on our GitHub team and include the deployment of this resource in the base_configuration script:

```
$ cat tpl/admin-clusterrolebinding.yaml
---
apiVersion: rbac.authorization.k8s.io/v1
kind: ClusterRoleBinding
metadata:
  name: platform-admin-clusterrolebinding
subjects:
  - apiGroup: rbac.authorization.k8s.io
    kind: Group
    name: epetech/platform-team          ◄——┐ Use your GitHub
roleRef:                                      │ organization name.
  apiGroup: rbac.authorization.k8s.io
  kind: ClusterRole
  name: cluster-admin
```

Add deployment to scripts/base_configuration.sh:

```
...
kubectl apply -f tpl/admin-clusterrolebinding.yaml
```

ADDITIONAL SYSTEM NAMESPACES

We will use a dedicated namespace for Karpenter resources, and we will deploy test applications to confirm the health of our services. Let's create those namespace definitions and add them to the configuration script:

```
$ cat tpl/system-namespaces.yaml
---
apiVersion: v1
kind: Namespace
metadata:
  name: karpenter
---
apiVersion: v1
kind: Namespace
metadata:
  name: test-system
```

Add deployment to scripts/base_configuration.sh:

```
...
kubectl apply -f tpl/psk-system-namespaces.yaml
```

STORAGE CLASSES FOR INITIALLY SUPPORTED PERSISTENT VOLUME CLAIM TYPES

We will preprovision the default Elastic Block Store (EBS) and EFS volume claim types. Initially, we will not provide a self-serve means for users of the platform to provision the underlying storage classes. If this type of storage is in high demand by our users, we can build an operator to allow for more extensive customization. By defining these initial standard defaults, however, we make the resources available for the most common use cases. These resource definitions have cluster-specific identifiers, but the complexity is low. Using a templating framework at this point adds complexity, so let's include this configuration directly within our base_configuration script:

```
...
cat <<EOF > tpl/ebs-csi-storage-class.yaml
---
kind: StorageClass
apiVersion: storage.k8s.io/v1
metadata:
  name: ${cluster_name}-ebs-csi-dynamic-storage
provisioner: ebs.csi.aws.com
volumeBindingMode: WaitForFirstConsumer
allowVolumeExpansion: true
Parameters:
  csi.storage.k8s.io/fstype: xfs
  type: io1
  iopsPerGB: "50"
  encrypted: "true"
EOF
cat <<EOF > tpl/efs-csi-storage-class.yaml
---
kind: StorageClass
apiVersion: storage.k8s.io/v1
metadata:
  name: ${cluster_name}-efs-csi-dynamic-storage
provisioner: efs.csi.aws.com
```

```
parameters:
  provisioningMode: efs-ap
  fileSystemId: $eks_efs_csi_storage_id
  directoryPerms: "700"
  basePath: "/dynamic_storage"
  subPathPattern: \${.PVC.namespace}/\${.PVC.name}
  ensureUniqueDirectory: "true"
  reuseAccessPoint: "false"
EOF

kubectl apply -f tpl/ebs-csi-storage-class.yaml
kubectl apply -f tpl/efs-csi-storage-class.yaml
```

> The EFS definition will automatically isolate volumes based on namespace and deployment when developers use it to create volume claims.

KARPENTER NODE CLASSES AND POOLS

We can begin by setting up the Karpenter EC2NodeClasses and node pools that will serve as the default node pool location for application developers to deploy to the platform. This approach is a good starting point. As the platform matures and developers' needs evolve, we can gradually introduce the capability for them to create additional node pools to address more specialized use cases. These include requirements for nodes with GPUs, specific processor architectures, or the need to isolate certain teams' services from others within the same environment.

We will instruct teams to build for the ARM architecture nodes by default since these are both cheaper and have better performance. Still, to ensure teams can deploy without any challenges, we should also have an Intel architecture pool. Our core strategy for managing customer compute resources will center around Karpenter. This decision is driven by Karpenter's advanced capabilities, including the ability to intelligently determine the optimal size and composition of nodes. Additionally, Karpenter's ability to regularly refresh nodes ensures that we can automatically incorporate newly patched, vendor-managed nodes, maintaining the highest levels of security and performance across the infrastructure.

Let's create the node pool resource definitions for both supported architectures. The following snippet shows the Intel definition. Also, create default-arm-node-pooo .yaml for the ARM pool by duplicating the resource definition and changing the necessary name and instance parameters:

```
$ cat tpl/default-amd-node-pool.yaml
---
apiVersion: karpenter.sh/v1beta1
kind: NodePool
metadata:
  name: default-amd-node-pool
  namespace: karpenter
spec:
  template:
    spec:
      requirements:
        - key: kubernetes.io/arch
          operator: In
```

Specifies the Intel AMD64 architecture; changes this to arm64 for the ARM pool

Uses SPOT instances

```
            values: ["amd64"]
          - key: karpenter.sh/capacity-type
            operator: In
            values: ["spot"]
          - key: "karpenter.k8s.aws/instance-category"
            operator: In
            values: ["t","m","c"]
          - key: "karpenter.k8s.aws/instance-family"
            operator: In
            values: ["t2","t3","m4","m5","m6i","m7i","c4","c5","c6i","c7i"]
          - key: "karpenter.k8s.aws/instance-size"
            operator: In
            values: ["xlarge","2xlarge","4xlarge"]
      nodeClassRef:
        apiVersion: karpenter.k8s.aws/v1beta1
        kind: EC2NodeClass
        name: default-node-class
Limits:
  cpu: 80
  ram: 320Gi
Disruption:
  consolidationPolicy: WhenUnderutilized
  expireAfter: 336h
```

It is helpful to provide a wide range of instance categories and families for Karpenter to optimize effectively. Change these to Graviton categories and families for the ARM pool.

Limits will control how large the number of nodes in the pools may grow. We've set these pretty small for this exercise.

This setting allows Karpenter to continuously examine the orchestration requirements and decide if underutilized nodes exist. It will shrink capacity to avoid waste.

Sets nodes to expire at a relatively short interval. Karpenter will schedule workloads off the node and then replace it with a fresh VM.

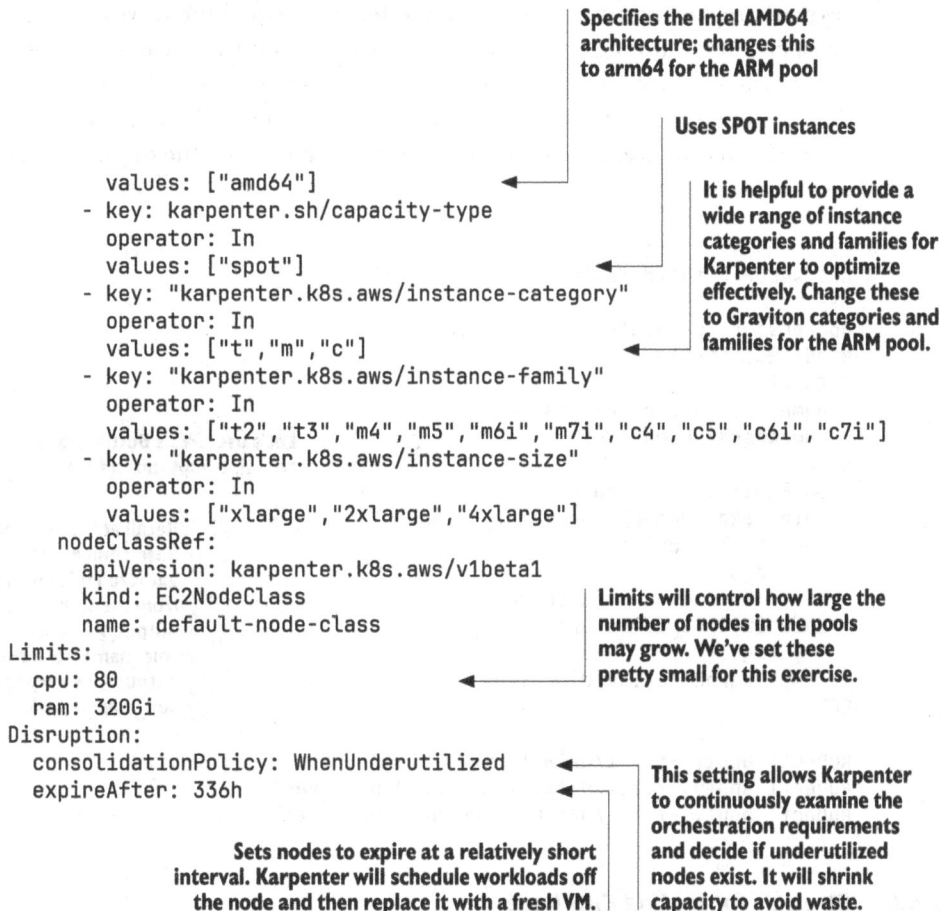

We use SPOT instances as they are the cheapest for our exercise. In a normal corporate setting, you will probably need to use a combination of pools that includes ON_DEMAND—based on your application's tolerance for Spot availability.

If we don't have good historical data about the applications running on a cluster to help choose instance types, a good exercise is to cover many possible instance types and then watch to see how Karpenter decides on optimization before tuning to a smaller list.

Set pool limits high enough that we don't hit them except in highly unexpected circumstances. We will want to be alerted if the limit is reached. But we also want to be alerted if we even get close. What if the unusual load is real traffic that we want to support? If we are alerted early, then we will have a chance to increase the limits before the node stops being provisioned.

When expired nodes are replaced, it will use the current, security-patched definition of the node for the Kubernetes version. This is an effective means of maintaining a strong security profile for nodes. There is no SSH access in this node definition, and by regularly replacing the nodes, we have effectively wiped the drives and picked up the latest patches. Allowing Karpenter to do this for us reduces the maintenance toil.

We will also need to create a node class resource. Like the storage class definition, we need to reference the cluster name, so let's include this as a heredoc template within our base_configuration script. Then include the deployment of all three resources:

```
...
cat <<EOF > tpl/default-node-class.yaml
---
apiVersion: karpenter.k8s.aws/v1beta1
kind: EC2NodeClass
Metadata:
  name: default-node-class
  namespace: karpenter
Spec:
  amiFamily: Bottlerocket
  role: $karpenter_node_iam_role_name
  subnetSelectorTerms:
    - tags:
        karpenter.sh/discovery: $cluster_name-vpc
  securityGroupSelectorTerms:
    - tags:
        karpenter.sh/discovery: $cluster_name
EOF

kubectl apply -f tpl/default-node-class.yaml
kubectl apply -f tpl/default-amd-node-pool.yaml
kubectl apply -f tpl/default-arm-node-pool.yaml
```

> Let's use AWS's Bottlerocket, container-optimized OS by default.

> Recall at the start of our base-configuration script, we gathered this information from the Terraform state output: karpenter_node_iam_role_name=$(terraform output -raw karpenter_node_iam_role_name).

7.4.6 *Strategy for testing EKS base*

Beyond simply testing that the Kubernetes orchestrator reports that the services indicate a Running status, we want to confirm that these services are all functioning as expected. To do that, we will need to deploy something to our cluster that will use the add-on services in a way that demonstrates healthy operation.

EBS STORAGE CLASS TEST

We created a default storage class for each cluster called `$cluster_name-ebs-csi-dynamic-storage`. To test whether the storage class is working, we need a script that will perform the following tasks:

1 Create a persistent volume claim.

2 Deploy an application that will write something to the volume.

3 Confirm that the write is successful.

4 Modify the volume claim size.

5 Confirm that the claim size has changed.

See the following EBS storage class test script:

```
$ cat scripts/ebs_storage_class_tests.sh
#!/usr/bin/env bash
set -eo pipefail

cluster_name=$1
export AWS_REGION=$(jq -er .aws_region "$cluster_name".auto.tfvars.json)

cat <<EOF > test/ebs/dynamic-volume/pvc.yaml
---
apiVersion: v1
kind: PersistentVolumeClaim
metadata:
  name: test-ebs-claim
  namespace: test-system
spec:
  accessModes:
    - ReadWriteOnce
  storageClassName: $cluster_name-ebs-csi-dynamic-storage
  resources:
    requests:
      storage: 4Gi
EOF
kubectl apply -f test/ebs/dynamic-volume/pvc.yaml

kubectl apply -f test/ebs/dynamic-volume/
  dynamic-volume-test-pod.yaml
sleep 30
bats test/ebs/dynamic-volume/initial-pvc-test.bats

cat <<EOF > test/ebs/dynamic-volume/pvc.yaml
---
apiVersion: v1
kind: PersistentVolumeClaim
metadata:
  name: test-ebs-claim
  namespace: test-system
spec:
  accessModes:
    - ReadWriteOnce
  storageClassName: $cluster_name-ebs-csi-dynamic-storage
  resources:
    requests:
      storage: 8Gi
EOF
kubectl apply -f test/ebs/dynamic-volume/pvc.yaml
sleep 90
bats test/ebs/dynamic-volume/expanded-pvc-test.bats

kubectl delete -f test/ebs/dynamic-volume/
  dynamic-volume-test-pod.yaml
kubectl delete -f test/ebs/dynamic-volume/pvc.yaml
```

◄— **Uses a heredoc template to generate the volume claim resource**

◄— **The test application deployment is in the following snippet.**

◄— **Let's wait a few seconds for the claim to be made and the application to launch and run.**

Now we can run a bats test to confirm the outcome. The test is shown below.

We can simply overwrite our initial volume claim resource with a new value and redeploy it.

◄— **Finally, test that the claim size increased as expected.**

◄— **Be sure to clean up our test fixtures.**

The following is a deployment that will use the EBS storage class test fixture. Remember, at this point, the only running nodes are those of the management node group.

We will support user workloads through Karpenter. Configure the test deployment to run in the management node group.

Node labels and tolerations represent two fundamental approaches for controlling where pods are scheduled in a Kubernetes cluster managed by Karpenter. The first method uses node affinity in the yaml file with label selectors to direct pods to specific nodes based on their labeled characteristics, such as targeting nodes with a particular role or hardware specification.

The second method, shown in the yaml file, employs tolerations to allow pods to be scheduled on nodes that have been "tainted" to restrict general workload placement, effectively creating dedicated node pools for specific workloads. While node labels pull pods toward desired nodes, tolerations enable pods to overcome barriers that would otherwise prevent their placement, and together these methods provide fine-grained control over workload distribution and resource allocation in your cluster:

```
$ cat test/ebs/dynamic-volume/dynamic-volume-test-pod.yaml
---
apiVersion: v1}
kind: Pod
metadata:
  name: claim-test-pod
  namespace: test-system
spec:                                   Configures this test deployment to
  affinity:                             run in the management node group
    nodeAffinity:
      requiredDuringSchedulingIgnoredDuringExecution:
        nodeSelectorTerms:
        - matchExpressions:
          - key: node.kubernetes.io/role
            operator: In
            values:                     The management node also
            - management               requires a certain tolerance
  tolerations:                          to accept a deployment.
    - key: "dedicated"
      operator: "Equal"
      value: "management"
      effect: "NoSchedule"              To test the volume claim, we launch a
  containers:                           simple OS container and provide a
    - name: claim-test-pod              shell command to write some text to
      image: centos:7                   the persistent volume claim.
      command: ["/bin/sh"]
      args: ["-c", "while true; do echo $(date -u) >> /data/out.txt; sleep 5;
  done"]
      volumeMounts:
      - name: persistent-storage
        mountPath: /data
      resources:
        requests:
          cpu: 10m
          memory: 50Mi
        limits:
          cpu: 100m
```

```
        memory: 200Mi
    securityContext:
      allowPrivilegeEscalation: false
      seccompProfile:
        type: RuntimeDefault
      capabilities:
        drop:
          - ALL
volumes:
  - name: persistent-storage
    persistentVolumeClaim:
      claimName: test-ebs-claim
```

The volume is created as a
persistentVolumeClaim and
references the claim we deployed.

After the pod has run, test the results using bats:

Confirms that our test pod is running. It can take a few seconds
for the volume claim to be created and for the pod to be up and
running. We should include some wait time in our test script.

Tests that the claim was created

```
#!/usr/bin/env bats
@test "validate dynamic ebs volume claim created" {
  run bash -c "kubectl describe pv | grep 'test-system/test-ebs-claim'"
  [[ "${output}" =~ "Claim" ]]
}
@test "validate claim-test-pod health" {
  run bash -c "kubectl get all -n test-system | grep 'pod/claim-test-pod'"
  [[ "${output}" =~ "Running" ]]
}
@test "validate dynamic ebs pvc write access" {
  run bash -c "kubectl exec -it -n test-system claim-test-pod
  -- cat /data/out.txt"
  [[ "${output}" =~ "UTC" ]]
}
```

Execs into the pods and check that the
contents of the file written to the claim
contain the expected information

If this is successful, we know the storage class is available and healthy. The default class
we initially created allowed for dynamically changing the size, and we should also confirm that it is working. To change the size, update the PersistentVolumeClaim (PVC) to
include more storage:

```
#!/usr/bin/env bats
@test "validate ebs volume expansion" {
  run bash -c "kubectl get pvc test-ebs-claim -n psk-system | grep '8Gi'"
  [[ "${output}" =~ "Bound" ]]
}
```

Be sure the test scripts delete all deployed items in testing.

EFS STORAGE CLASSTTEST

The EFS storage class is generally more useful and operationally resilient than the EBS
class. EFS storage is not tied to node groups as directly as EBS volumes and provides

automated backups. More importantly, EFS supports writes from multiple pods. As before, let's create a script that will provision a volume claim and use it to confirm the storage class health:

```
$ cat scripts/efs_storage_class_tests.sh
#!/usr/bin/env bash
set -eo pipefail

cluster_name=$1
export AWS_REGION=$(jq -er .aws_region "$cluster_name".auto.tfvars.json)

efs_eks_cis_storage_id=$(op read op://my-vault/
  $cluster_name/eks-efs-csi-storage-id)

cat <<EOF > test/efs/multi-write/pvc.yaml
apiVersion: v1
kind: PersistentVolumeClaim
metadata:
  name: efs-claim
  namespace: test-system
spec:
  accessModes:
    - ReadWriteMany
  storageClassName: $cluster_name-efs-csi-dynamic-storage
  resources:
    requests:
      storage: 5Gi

---
apiVersion: v1
kind: PersistentVolume
metadata:
  name: efs-pv
  namespace: test-system
spec:
  capacity:
    storage: 5Gi
  volumeMode: Filesystem
  accessModes:
    - ReadWriteMany
  persistentVolumeReclaimPolicy: Retain
  storageClassName: $cluster_name-efs-csi-dynamic-storage
  csi:
    driver: efs.csi.aws.com
    volumeHandle: $efs_eks_cis_storage_id
EOF

kubectl apply -f test/efs/multi-write/pvc.yaml
kubectl apply -f test/efs/multi-write/multi-write-test-pods.yaml
sleep 30
bats test/efs/multi-write/multi-write-test.bats

kubectl delete -f test/efs/multi-write/multi-write-test-pods.yaml
kubectl delete -f test/efs/multi-write/pvc.yaml
```

Recall that we created the default EFS storage location and stored the ID in our secrets store. We will make this value available to platform users.

Since these are simple test fixtures, let's again use a heredoc template to generate our resource template.

The test application deployment and associated bats tests are in the following snippet.

To test the write-many feature, we will need to deploy two pods that each use the same claim:

```
$ cat test/efs/multi-write/multi-write-test-pods.yaml
---
apiVersion: v1
kind: Pod
metadata:
  name: app1
  namespace: test-system
spec:
  affinity:
    nodeAffinity:
      requiredDuringSchedulingIgnoredDuringExecution:
        nodeSelectorTerms:
        - matchExpressions:
          - key: node.kubernetes.io/role
            operator: In
            values:
            - management
  tolerations:
    - key: "dedicated"
      operator: "Equal"
      value: "management"
      effect: "NoSchedule"
  containers:
  - name: app1
    image: busybox:1.36
    command: ["/bin/sh"]
    args: ["-c", "while true; do echo $(date -u) >> /data/out1.txt; sleep 5;
  [done"]
    volumeMounts:
    - name: persistent-storage
      mountPath: /data
    resources:
      requests:
        cpu: 10m
        memory: 50Mi
      limits:
        cpu: 100m
        memory: 200Mi
    securityContext:
      allowPrivilegeEscalation: false
      seccompProfile:
        type: RuntimeDefault
      capabilities:
        drop:
        - ALL
  volumes:
  - name: persistent-storage
    persistentVolumeClaim:
      claimName: efs-claim        ◀─────  Each pod's volume mount is
                                          connected to the same PVC.
---
```

```
apiVersion: v1
kind: Pod
metadata:
  name: app2
  namespace: test-system
spec:
  affinity:
    nodeAffinity:
      requiredDuringSchedulingIgnoredDuringExecution:
        nodeSelectorTerms:
        - matchExpressions:
          - key: node.kubernetes.io/role
            operator: In
            values:
            - management
  tolerations:
    - key: "dedicated"
      operator: "Equal"
      value: "management"
      effect: "NoSchedule"
  containers:
  - name: app2
    image: busybox:1.36
    command: ["/bin/sh"]
    args: ["-c", "while true; do echo $(date -u) >> /data/out2.txt; sleep 5;
  done"]
    volumeMounts:
    - name: persistent-storage
      mountPath: /data
    resources:
      requests:
        cpu: 10m
        memory: 50Mi
      limits:
        cpu: 100m
        memory: 200Mi
    securityContext:
      allowPrivilegeEscalation: false
      seccompProfile:
        type: RuntimeDefault
      capabilities:
        drop:
          - ALL
  volumes:
  - name: persistent-storage
    persistentVolumeClaim:
      claimName: efs-claim
```

Now we can test the results:

```
$ cat test/efs/multi-write/multi-write-test.bats
#!/usr/bin/env bats
@test "validate multi-write access on app1" {
  run bash -c "kubectl exec -it app1 -n test-system
```

Note that the test for pod App1 checks the contents of the file written by App2, and likewise pod App2 checks App1. Each pod is configured to write to the same PVC, and this test demonstrates that each pod can see the results of the others' actions.

```
  -- tail -n 5 /data/out2.txt"
  [[ "${output}" =~ "UTC" ]]
}
@test "validate multi-write access on app2" {
  run bash -c "kubectl exec -it app2 -n test-system
  -- tail -n 5 /data/out1.txt"
  [[ "${output}" =~ "UTC" ]]
}
```

It is also worth noting that deploying pods and communicating between various Kubernetes resources also effectively tests that components such as the CNI, kube-proxy, coredns, and so on are all working as expected.

KARPENTER NODE POOL TEST

The final resource to test is Karpenter. We have deployed a default node pool, and to test this resource, we need to deploy a container targeted to the node pool. If Karpenter is working as expected, a new node should be provisioned, and our test application should successfully run on the new node. So we need a script that deploys an application to each of our default node pools and confirms that Karpenter will provision the necessary node:

```
$ cat scripts/node_pool_test.sh
#!/usr/bin/env bash
set -eo pipefail

# deploy test pod to default NodePools
kubectl apply -f test/karpenter/amd-node-pool-deployment.yaml
kubectl apply -f test/karpenter/arm-node-pool-deployment.yaml
sleep 120
bats test/karpenter/test-dynamic-node-pools.bats

kubectl delete -f test/karpenter/amd-node-pool-deployment.yaml
kubectl delete -f test/karpenter/arm-node-pool-deployment.yaml
```

First, deploy a container to the default Karpenter node pool:

```
$ cat est/karpenter/amd-node-pool-deployment.yaml
---
apiVersion: apps/v1
kind: Deployment
metadata:
  name: test-amd-node-pool
  namespace: psk-system
spec:
  replicas: 2
  selector:
    matchLabels:
      app: test-amd-node-pool
  template:
    metadata:
      labels:
```

```
       app: test-amd-node-pool
spec:
  nodeSelector:
    kubernetes.io/arch: amd64
  containers:
    - name: test-amd-node-pool
      image: public.ecr.aws/eks-distro/kubernetes/pause:3.7
      resources:
        requests:
          cpu: 100m
          memory: 200Mi
        limits:
          cpu: 150m
          memory: 250Mi
      securityContext:
        allowPrivilegeEscalation: false
        seccompProfile:
          type: RuntimeDefault
        capabilities:
          drop:
            - ALL
```

> Here we add a nodeSelector that references our default AMD Karpenter node pool. This deployment will not be able to use our management node groups, as it is missing the necessary toleration.

Create an additional deployment for the ARM node pool:

```
$ cat test/karpenter/test-dynamic-node-pools.bat
#!/usr/bin/env bats
@test "validate amd node creation" {
  run bash -c "kubectl get po -n test-system | grep 'test-amd-node-pool'"
  [[ "${output}" =~ "Running" ]]
}

@test "validate arm node creation" {
  run bash -c "kubectl get po -n test-system | grep 'test-arm-node-pool'"
  [[ "${output}" =~ "Running" ]]
}
```

Can you identify a weakness in this test? It will work as expected at the start when there are no other deployments making use of the default node pools. But what about later? If Karpenter has been working successfully for a while but then stops, there could be room in the existing compute to run this test app, but no node provisioning would have taken place. How might you change the fixtures or the tests to deal with that eventuality?

Before starting our control plane base pipeline exercise, let's talk about upgrades.

We can trigger a Kubernetes version upgrade by changing the version defined in our environment tfvars, and AWS is responsible for performing the upgrade and maintaining the control plane health. AWS will automatically perform patch version upgrades, and we are only concerned with the 1.x upgrades. Be sure not to skip over versions in the upgrade process.

We configured the EKS add-ons to always use the latest release version of the add-on. The correct, latest version upgrade will be triggered whenever the pipeline runs. As official add-ons, AWS is responsible for performing upgrades and providing general service health support in the event of a failure. All we need to do is run our pipeline to ensure we are on the latest supported (and, more importantly, security-patched) version of the add-ons. The one exception is Karpenter. We still need to provide the specific chart version. Like an EKS upgrade, we just set the upgrade version in the tfvars files and run the pipeline.

We are using Karpenter to manage our customer node pools. We have defined a configuration that will cause Karpenter to use the latest, patched version of the AWS EKS-optimized Amazon Machine Images(AMIs) and automatically replace the nodes with the newest version approximately every two weeks.

But what about the nodes in our dedicated management node group? Since this is an AWS-managed node group, we need a way to trigger a refresh of those nodes through Terraform. Instead of using the now-deprecated `terraform taint`, we can achieve the same result using the -replace flag during `terraform apply`. The following command signals to the AWS API that the specified node group should be replaced, and because it's a managed node group, AWS handles this as a zero-downtime operation. The following example uses the node group name from our configuration:

```
terraform apply -replace="module.eks.module.eks_managed_node_group
  [\"management-arm-rkt-mng\"].aws_eks_node_group.this[0]"
```

AWS will provision the replacement nodes first, based on the node group size definition, and then move all workloads to the new nodes before deleting the old nodes. Any services deployed to the management node groups must include a Pod Disruption Budget if needed to prevent the service from failing due to rescheduling. The new nodes will be based on the latest patched AMI.

Finally we must consider the Terraform module versions. These are naturally pinned to specific versions to prevent unexpected breakage. However, we will still need to test and upgrade as the modules evolve routinely.

There are GitHub-integrated apps, such as Renovate (https://www.mend.io/mend-renovate/) or Dependabot (https://github.com/dependabot), that can help with this process. You can also create a custom solution. However you track such new releases, it is essential to set a monitoring system that will trigger an alert after a defined length of time, such as 30 days.

> **Exercise 7.4   Create a build and release pipeline for the control plane base**
>
> Create the pipeline to manage the cluster deployments for our example sbx and prod clusters. Use the four modules listed at the start of this section and the implementation goals detailed earlier. As before, incorporate all the platform engineering practices we have demonstrated in the prior pipelines. Be sure to think about how you are documenting your code. Documentation includes inline comments, README information, and commit messages. Detailed commit messages are among the most effective means of reporting changes and the evolution of an implementation. It is

(continued)

easier to be effective at frequent commits when you view the commit messages as a primary means of documenting your changes.

The previous implementation details for Karpenter included a default pool definition for AMD-based nodes. In addition to this, include in the exercise a pool resource definition for an additional default pool based on ARM architecture nodes and test the pool health as part of the integration testing.

Exercise 7.5   Create a platform CLI that uses the customer IDP to generate a customer identity token and a Kubeconfig file for accessing the Kubernetes clusters

In exercise 7.3, we configured our IDP to use GitHub authentication and generate our authorization claims based on the user's GitHub teams membership. We tested this using curl and our browser, which successfully interacted with an Auth0-based OIDC device-app flow for generating credentials for accessing the Kubernetes API.

Using curl to perform each step in the flow and then parsing the tokens from JSON isn't a very good developer experience—especially when, for example, they want to use Kubectl to query information about their application running on the platform.

This exercise aims to build a CLI and provide a much better experience. Your solution should provide the following features:

```
$ epectl list cluster
```

It should also provide the following information for each cluster:
- ClusterName
- ClusterEndpoint (URL to access the Kubernetes API)
- Base64CertificateAuthorityData (public certificate for transport layer security access to Kubernetes API)
- EfsCSIStorageID (storage ID needed to create PVC for EFS storage class)

We can keep things simple at this point and build this information into the CLI at build.

Next, we should be able to use the CLI to generate local credentials and a kubeconfig file for accessing the clusters:

```
$ epectl login
```

This should request a device code and auto-open a browser window to complete the authentication flow with the Auth0 CLI application. If the authentication is successful, the full jwt will be returned, and the following information should be present in the user's local ~/.epectl/config file:

```
accesstoken: *******
defaultcluster: prod-i01-aws-us-east-2
expiresin: 86400
idpissuerurl: https://vsctl.us.auth0.com/
idtoken: *****
loginaudience: https://vsctl.us.auth0.com/api/v2/
loginclientid: ******
loginscope: openid offline_access profile email
refreshtoken: *******
```

Remember, we are using the epectl name example from exercise 7.3. This should be the name you selected for your CLI application and configured in exercise 7.3. And finally:

```
$ epectl get kubeconfig
```

This should generate a kubeconfig file from the previous information in the following format:

```
apiVersion: v1
clusters:
- cluster:
    certificate-authority-data: ***S0tLS0K
    server: https://***B924.gr7.us-east-2.eks.amazonaws.com
  name: prod-i01-aws-us-east-2
contexts:
- context:
    cluster: prod-i01-aws-us-east-2
    user: oidc-user@prod-i01-aws-us-east-2
  name: prod-i01-aws-us-east-2
current-context: prod-i01-aws-us-east-2
kind: Config
preferences: {}
users:
- name: oidc-user@prod-i01-aws-us-east-2
  user:
    auth-provider:
      config:
        access-token: ***YOUTDA1w
        client-id: ***PCx6Q
        id-token: ***Ze1Vxn0w
        idp-issuer-url: https://vsctl.us.auth0.com/
        refresh-token: ***V4-h8E_h
      name: oidc
```

This should be the base64 version of the cluster Kubernetes API access certificate that was created and saved to our secrets store.

This should be the URL for accessing the cluster Kubernetes API, also saved to our secrets store after the Terraform apply step.

The access token returned by the device-auth-flow interaction with the Auth0 CLI application

The Auth0 CLI application client ID

The Auth0 CLI application endpoint

The refresh token returned by the device-auth-flow interaction with the Auth0 CLI application

As a member of the platform team in our GitHub organization, and with the valid Auth0 application configuration from exercise 7.3, you should be able to successfully

(continued)

log in and generate a kubeconfig file, which, when referenced in a kubectl command, enables you to interact with the prod cluster successfully.

Your CLI should allow you to specify overrides for the values needed to authenticate against the sbx cluster. Refer to the companion code in the GitHub repository for one possible solution based on Golang and the Cobra CLI framework.

Summary

- *Security and identity management*
  - Establish cloud account-level security configuration early and manage within the engineering platform if security stakeholders aren't equipped to provide product-bound capabilities.
  - Make platform customer identity a key capability within the engineering platform architecture for flexibility in creating user experiences and supporting evolutionary architecture.
  - Use a SaaS IDP like Auth0 to provide standards-based security protocols and act as the provider between authentication and authorization claims.
  - The OAuth2 OIDC device-auth-flow is an adequate standard for platform users to generate short-lived credentials for accessing infrastructure from their laptops.
  - The primary permission boundary (user claim) should be team membership, mapping well to domain-bound team topologies.
- *DNS and domain management*
  - A seamless and self-service experience for DNS and domain management is critical.
  - Decide on a platform-managed domain naming option and evolve to include custom subdomains and bring-your-own-domain capabilities.
  - The left-of and right-of domain naming patterns for APIs and services are primarily business-level product value decisions.
  - Set up release pipelines for DNS configurations and account-level resources to ensure consistent deployment across environments.
- *Networking and infrastructure*
  - Design a cloud-vendor-managed transit network that makes adding networks a low-complexity task.
  - Zero-trust networking can simplify business decisions to make internal resources available to customers or third-party partners.
  - Implement a role-based network structure where each Kubernetes cluster has a dedicated VPC, named according to the cluster.

- Provision VPCs and subnets in specific regions with designated IP spaces to support different roles.
- An API gateway may not be necessary unless supporting third-party developers; focus on zero-trust network patterns and internal API management.

- *Kubernetes and container orchestration*
  - Create a dedicated pipeline for orchestrating the cloud provider-managed aspects of the Kubernetes control plane.
  - Technologies like Karpenter provide more efficient means of maintaining short-lived nodes and node pools with optimal sizing.
  - Cloud-provided storage classes offer vendor-managed solutions for everyday attached storage needs.
  - Integrate Kubernetes directly with your IDP solution to provide users direct access to the Kubernetes API.
  - ARM nodes on most cloud providers offer more performant and cost-effective options.

- *Operations and monitoring*
  - Provision account-level observability dependencies early.
  - Include automated collection of Kubernetes configuration details in the control plane base pipeline.

- *Platform experience*
  - Integration testing of the EKS pipeline should include deploying test applications that utilize features in a customer-like manner.
  - A platform CLI provides an effective touchpoint for users to interact with platform APIs, with the service interface (API) always coming first.

Control plane services
and extensions

This chapter covers

- Reviewing the path to production
- Understanding the difference between control plane services and extensions
- Adding standard Kubernetes services
- Managing control plane extensions

After finishing the exercises so far, our Epetech engineering platform now has a sandbox and a production instance, each with its own network and Elastic Kubernetes Service (EKS) cluster. This way, we can test and debug each new platform capability before deploying it to our production instance. If we finish the two projects, we'll also have a CLI tool that platform team members can use to authenticate and generate individual credentials to access the Kubernetes API in both clusters. We now have the foundational components in six of our eight primary domains (see figure 8.1).

Our control plane is bare at this point. Apart from the few AWS-managed components, we do not yet have any of the services and extensions that enable our Kubernetes instance to serve as the control plane we need for our platform.

Now we get to two large domains—large in the sense that there are potentially lots of *services* and *extensions* deployed to a control plane, which continue to grow in number over time. Taken together, services and extensions make up all the cluster-wide services that will be deployed to our cluster. So why categorize these into either a service or an extension?

There are two reasons. The first applies to small platform engineering teams and platforms, and the second affects the management of cluster components as the platform grows and more teams are involved in the delivery of the platform.

8.1 Value of services and extension domains for smaller teams

There are some good reasons for an engineering platform to be delivered by no more than one or two teams. The most obvious is the size of your internal developer pool; if you only have a few dozen developers, there's rarely a need to go

Engineering platform product

Cloud administrative identity
- aws-iam-profiles

Cloud account baseline
- aws-platform-observability-base
- aws-platform-hosted-zones

Transit network layer
- aws-platform-vpc

Cloud identity provider
- platform-auth0-management

Cloud services control plane
- aws-control-plane-base

Managed control plane services
- aws-control-plane-services

Managed control-plane-extensions
- aws-control-plane-extensions

Platform product services
- vsctl

Figure 8.1   The six foundational components of our eight primary domains

beyond a single platform team. In addition, every platform team brings its own set of environments, infrastructure overhead, and coordination costs. When the organization is small, those added complexities can quickly outweigh the benefits of team specialization.

But it is also a highly effective strategy through the early stages of the creation and launch of a platform, even where we know the scale is expected to reach into the hundreds or thousands of developers using it. Large-scale platforms are an expensive investment. While the return on the investment is certainly a justification, there is also a significant risk that comes with that scale.

What if the platform fails to identify and deliver the capabilities that the developers need or gives the right capabilities but with such a poor user experience that developers don't use the platform and seek alternatives? Or what if, as the scale grows and the number of platform engineering teams needed to deliver and maintain the platform grows, the way we divide the ownership of the various platform components among those teams results in a return to the friction and delays that motivated us to create the platform in the first place?

Starting with a single team and only one or two development teams as *alpha* customers, scaling at later stages in the evolution of the platform allows us to mature the

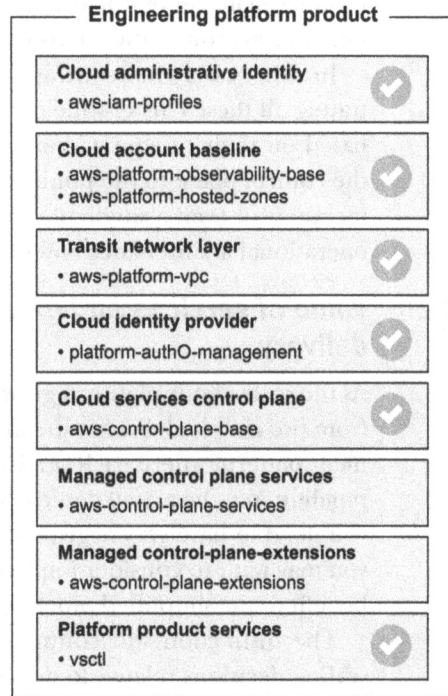

product management leadership and feedback skills while also allowing the domain boundaries around the components we want to scale to be tested and proven effective.

In either case, when starting with a single engineering platform team, initially orchestrating all these cluster-wide control plane applications through one of two pipelines, based on their categorization as either a service or an extension, accelerates getting the control plane to the point of being able to support alpha customers and helps the members of even a single platform team avoid overlapping work during both routine operational maintenance and new feature development.

8.2 *Value of services and extension domains for scaled platform delivery*

As the scale of our platform grows, one of the first changes we will make is to transition from two simple delivery pipelines for services and extensions to a distributed deployment pattern, where each service or extension will have its own release orchestration pipeline. Yet, the actual deploy event automation is happening locally on the cluster. If you need to have very aggressive adoption timelines for your platform, this is an area you may want to consider implementing from the start. But either way, the small-team benefit of the simplified pipelines is no longer present.

The distinction will continue to be valuable in informing future organizational scaling decisions related to delivering our platform. We use the term "organizational" because the kind of scale we mean is not configuring technology to handle more load but rather how the engineering platform product leadership can speed up the process of adding new features to the product. While a single team is the most effective way to launch an engineering platform, its delivery capacity will become strained once we start onboarding the first couple of development teams to use the early version of the platform. There will be pressure to divide the work among multiple teams, including teams not directly part of the unified platform product leadership. This distinction will help us navigate such a division of responsibilities more successfully.

When shifting responsibilities for cluster-wide applications to teams other than teams directly within the platform product delivery organization structure, first consider only the platform services. Extensions should only be considered after the platform product as a whole has progressed well beyond the early or minimal viable product (MVP) stage, and there has been meaningful scale in adoption. Even then, such an allocation should still be tested and proven first between two platform domain teams.

In our experience, technical product owners who apply this decision-making guideline when scaling delivery teams and allocating responsibilities are more likely to be successful than those who don't. By "successful," we mean the division of duties adequately increases the delivery velocity through the overall engineering platform product backlog without reintroducing manual processes and other engineering friction. The attributes that make something a service or an extension contribute to this effect. Let's look again at what makes something a service versus an extension (see figure 8.2).

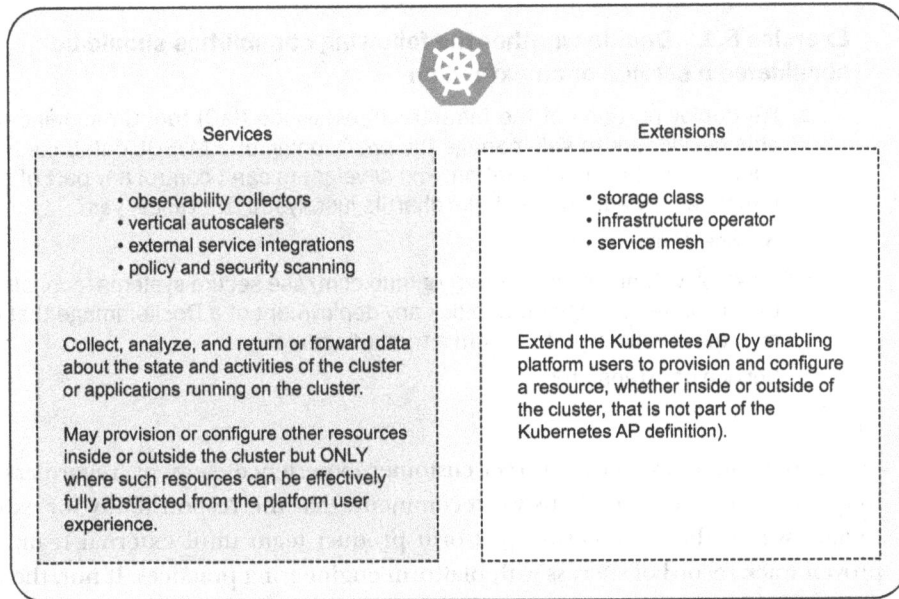

Figure 8.2 The easiest way to understand the difference is to focus on extensions. When deployed, an extension enables developers to provision a resource through the Kubernetes API that Kubernetes does not natively support.

Provisioning through the Kubernetes API means that a new resource type can be created using the same kind of Kubernetes YAML resource files used in deploying an application. An extension *extends* the Kubernetes API capabilities in terms of the user experience. Anything else the cluster maintainer deploys as part of the standard cluster configuration is a service.

A capability that sets up or configures another resource could still be considered a service when it's completely abstracted from the user. But what do we mean by "abstracted"? In this situation, *abstracted* means that nothing is being provisioned or configured uniquely to the developer's application or solely for their application's use. An example would be how we configured Karpenter in the previous chapter. As it is implemented, developers add node selection criteria to their application deployment to decide which node pool they want their application to use. Still, the pools don't exist for any individual team or application, and developers can't customize or alter the configuration of the pools available. If we changed the implementation to support development teams being able to deploy their own node pool resources, then it would be functioning as an *extension* in terms of the developer experience.

As you can start to see, not everything we deploy will be immediately apparent as one or the other just through examining the capability alone. How we implement also comes into play in terms of whether something is a service or an extension.

> ### Exercise 8.1   Decide whether the following capabilities should be considered a service or an extension
>
> 1 We deploy portions of the infrastructure-as-code (IaC) tool Crossplane to enable developers to self-manage the provisioning of a MySQL database. It only supports a single configuration, and developers can't control any part of it. The template they add to their helm chart is just `mysql_instance=yes`.
>
>   Service or extension?
>
> 2 We deploy Connaisseur (https://github.com/sse-secure-systems/connaisseur) to our cluster, configured to block any deployment of a Docker image that does not have a valid signature from a trusted source.
>
>   Service or extension?

Extensions will always have a direct customer experience element, regardless of how frequently they are used. Thus we recommend that the responsibility for extensions remain within the engineering platform product team until external teams have a proven track record of success with platform engineering practices. If not, the result is likely to be developers opening a ticket and waiting in a queue. (Pull requests are still tickets.)

8.2.1   Which services or extensions should be a part of every platform from the start?

The correct answer to the question of which services or extensions should be a part of every platform from the start in any organization will depend on several different factors. Which observability tools will we implement? What kind of secrets are required to support the chosen deployment strategy? Which security scanning tools have we selected? How will we manage ingress into the cluster? And how will we enable developers to provision additional infrastructure, such as databases?

A complete answer is simply beyond the scope of one book. However, specific capabilities will always be a part of any engineering platform. And, whether at the start or later, there are principles we can apply that will significantly increase our chances of success.

STAKEHOLDERS

There are often stakeholders outside the engineering platform team whose responsibilities overlap with or influence these decisions. Take the security team, for example—they naturally have a range of concerns they need to weigh in on, from security problems within the platform itself to broader organizational problems. For everyone to succeed in this situation, it's much more effective when stakeholders approach things in one of two ways:

- They focus on defining the outcomes that need to be achieved, while the teams affected by those standards determine the best way to meet them. For example, if the security team sets a standard like "all known vulnerabilities in our software must be fixed," the engineering platform team can choose the right technologies and build in automated scanning and alerting to make following this policy an automatic part of using the platform.

Or

- Stakeholders can apply platform engineering practices themselves by providing APIs that anyone in the organization can use to meet requirements. The engineering platform team can independently integrate the scanning and reporting tools from the security team to create the best possible platform experience for their users.

Problems arise where a stakeholder takes ownership of a solution that does not align with platform engineering practices. That's when you get manual handoffs, ticket queues, and unnecessary friction.

ALWAYS VALIDATE TECHNOLOGY CHOICES THROUGH EXPERIMENTATION AND ACTUAL RESULTS

There are a tremendous number of options available from a vast pool of vendors. There is also significant variation in how difficult these services can be to install, upgrade, and maintain in a Kubernetes context. In addition to evaluating any choice against the software selection criteria, regardless of who holds the final decision-making responsibility, no commitment should be made without performing an actual, as realistic as possible implementation on the actual engineering platform infrastructure: we must build the proof of concept.

OBSERVABILITY

No engineering platform would be usable without solid operational observability. That means centralizing logs, metrics, and events—not just for the apps running on the control plane but also for the control plane itself and for whatever node pool strategy we use. We also strongly recommend including tracing right from the start. Proper tracing instrumentation and developers skilled in using trace data are some of the most effective ways we've seen to manage the growing complexity of large distributed systems.

Metrics-server (https://kubernetes-sigs.github.io/metrics-server), kube-state-metrics (https://mng.bz/26m9), and some flavor of Kubernetes event exporter (https://mng.bz/15py) are always needed and even come bundled with some general observability agent installs.

The essential requirements for observability tooling selection are that it integrates with your platform's customer identity solution for authentication and team-level authorization and that it supports providing a completely self-serve experience for collecting custom metrics, building dashboards, setting monitors, and triggering alerts. Include a standard configuration for those things within the language starter kits you create for platform customers, but remember these are only starting points. Everything beyond that should be designed for developers to self-manage.

In just the past two years, the authors have implemented a wide range of observability technologies. A representative sample includes

- ELK stack variants
- PLG stack variants

- Cloud vendor native
- Open Telemetry (tracing) variants
- Proprietary variants (DataDog, Splunk, New Relic, Dynatrace, Sumo)
- FinOps variants (cloud vendor native, IBM Apptio/KubeCost, OpenCost)

CLUSTER AUTOSCALING

Node autoscaling should be considered a necessary component of Kubernetes resiliency. As this functionality becomes more of a built-in feature within cloud providers (as is nearly the case with the Karpenter on AWS, hence we included it in our control plane base pipeline), it is less likely that cluster-autoscaler will appear in the list of services platform operators need to manage. If we are not using a vendor-supported solution, then we would include the capability among the control plane services.

AUTOMATED DEPLOYMENT SUPPORT

Development teams need a means of deploying and testing their applications on the control plane. This can be as simple as a mechanism for teams to generate service account credentials for use in their deployment and release pipelines. In this configuration, consider creating a custom API to generate, store, and rotate such a credential in the secrets management service provided by the platform.

Alternatively, deployment services such as Flux (https://fluxcd.io) or Argo (https://argo-cd.readthedocs.io/en/stable/) are adopted to do the actual deployments. This can also be a means to avoid the need to provide service accounts that can directly interact with the Kubernetes API. Developers still orchestrate deployment timing, versions, and testing through the primary pipeline orchestration tool. However, the actual deployment, usually of Helm (https://helm.sh) or Kustomize (https://kustomize.io) generated deployment resources, is performed by the deployment service.

Whether the deployer needs to be part of the cluster definition depends on the implementation strategy. For example, assuming you are implementing the whole ArgoCD GUI experience for your platform customers: the experience that best fits a fully orchestrated software release pipeline will be a centralized Argo instance that manages deployments across all the clusters in the user's release pipeline. In this case, no Argo service is deployed to each cluster. However, at scale, performance will become a problem.

We will talk about some of the scaling strategies in part 3 of this book. Some methods will include running a deployer as part of the cluster definition, in which case this becomes part of the control plane services.

It is also typically the case when adopting a deployer-based solution like Argo or Flux that you must include some additional secrets management supporting service that doesn't depend on the release pipeline, since that pipeline is no longer performing the actual deployment. Hashi Vault (https://www.vaultproject.io) and the external-secrets-operator (https://external-secrets.io) are two examples of frequently used services that provide a means for developers to manage secrets needed by their applications from within the deployment definition. If a deployer is part of your required initial platform definition, on-cluster secrets management support for deployments is likely a requirement.

SECURITY STRATEGY

Over time, we want our security, compliance, and even governance requirements to be automated and integrated into the experience of using our engineering platform. Security, compliance, and governance should evolve into invisible, always-on elements of the platform experience—never an afterthought and never a barrier. To reach that state, we begin by establishing a baseline of essential security services that every cluster must provide from the outset. This foundation not only enables the first teams to adopt with confidence but also sets a standard the platform can consistently build on as adoption scales. Over time, these initial guardrails mature into fully automated, integrated governance, ensuring that security and compliance provide the assurance organizations need while enabling the speed and agility teams expect as the platform grows.

> NOTE In this section, we have been talking about initial services within a new engineering platform, which is what we are building with our Epetech example. Naturally, many organizations already use the underlying technologies of an engineering platform. The interest in platform engineering can be centered on maturing engineering and architecture practices. You may not be starting from scratch, which we call a brownfield, where you could be dealing with a mix of existing clusters, services, infrastructure, and automation scattered across different parts of the organization. These often come with a patchwork of overlapping or competing technology choices and a blend of legacy IT silos alongside DevOps practices at varying levels of maturity. Restructuring this into an internal product delivery organizational model with mature platform engineering patterns is still the path to success, even where many technologies that will make up the services and extensions of the new platform definition are already identified.

8.3 Control plane services

We want to start with a basic software-delivery lifecycle pipeline for managing services and extensions. Using a pipeline for deployment and keeping services together in one pipeline and extensions together in another is a great way to accelerate getting our alpha teams onto the platform while keeping the domain boundary between services and extensions clear during the early stages. Things can change quickly as the platform scales. We can start with simplicity at first by using basic release pipelines to manage all of these capabilities, while also keeping service and extension deployments in separate pipelines to make it easier to scale out the automation later.

If we don't test high-availability (HA) and resilience configurations outside of production, we shouldn't be surprised when production doesn't perform as expected.

For our Epetech platform services pipeline, we're limiting the initial services to metrics-server, kube-state-metrics, and event-exporter. You'll notice that the example configurations don't make full use of HA options; that's intentional for demo purposes only. In real production environments, of course, HA would be enabled. However, it's common to see organizations skip HA setups in nonproduction environments to reduce costs, under the assumption that failures in those environments won't directly affect customers. But this reasoning often falls short. The cost of developers being blocked, both in time and in delayed delivery of revenue-generating features, can be just as significant. More importantly, we need our nonproduction environments to reflect production-like behavior so we can trust what we're building and releasing. There are ways to scale nonproduction down, but skipping HA entirely undermines the reliability of our production confidence.

8.3.1   Services pipeline orchestration

The actions we want to perform for each cluster amount to an effortless flow. For each cluster, we want to use Helm to deploy a pinned version of each of our services. Then, we want to run integration tests to confirm the health of each service. Our extensions pipeline will follow the same pattern (see figure 8.3).

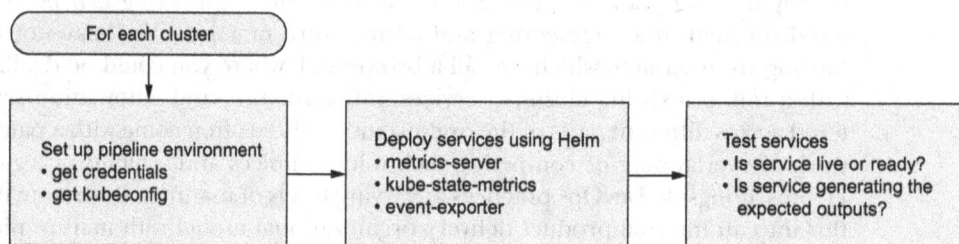

Figure 8.3   The pattern

The difference between the services and the extensions pipelines is less about *how* they release and more about *what* is being released.

With this pipeline, we are also switching to a context different from the prior pipelines. Rather than interacting with the AWS API to provision AWS-managed resources, we are interacting with the Kubernetes API to deploy and test services. Similar to how we used a general cloud vendor infrastructure pipeline image, we will want to have an administrative pipeline that is preconfigured to support all the general administrative pipelines we may need. We can use some of the same tools for scanning and testing, but we will need a variety of other packages based on the services and extensions we are managing. Pipelines primarily used for administrative automation of the control plane will have tools like the following:

- Kubectl (interacting with Kubernetes API)
- Helm (direct deployments)

- Kind (for continuous integration [CI] testing)
- Istio CLI (configuring or managing a service mesh)
- Trivy (best practice and security scanning)

Like our prior pipelines, we can make use of an open-source software CircleCI image and a Kubernetes-oriented orb to support our pipeline.

We will have two different kinds of environment-specific values. For each cluster, we will want to pin the version of the service to be deployed. But then, as we use Helm to deploy each service, we will want to be able to define cluster-specific values.yaml files to configure the service.

> **NOTE** We are intentionally not introducing a tool like ArgoCD or Flux as part of the cluster operators workflow at this scale. Those can certainly be part of the initial experience for developers using a platform. Still, at a smaller scale for cluster administrators, we consistently find that a dedicated deployer adds complexity. The inexperienced application of GitOps-style practices can create problems.

Let's start with the following basic pipeline outline, continuing the same foundational principles of our other pipelines. The outline has the headings for anchors, commands, jobs, and so on. Complete the outline and any underlying scripts:

```
---
version: 2.1
orbs:
  kube: twdps/kube-ops@1.1.2
  op: twdps/onepassword@3.0.0
  do: twdps/pipeline-events@5.0.1
globals:
  - &context <my-team>
  - &executor-image twdps/circleci-kube-ops:alpine-2025.04
on-push-main: &on-push-main
  branches:
    only: /main/
  tags:
    ignore: /.*/

on-tag-main: &on-tag-main
  branches:
    ignore: /.*/
  tags:
    only: /.*/
commands:
  set-environment:
  run-integration-tests:
jobs:
  deploy control plane services:
workflows:
  deploy sbx-i01-aws-us-east-1 control plane services:
    when:
      not:
```

The pipeline-events orb, which contains common actions that any pipeline could use, includes a bash function that can be sourced into a script to perform a basic Trivy scan of the Helm charts before using them.

For our pipeline environment setup, we will need most of the same *.env variables as we used in our control plane base pipeline, except we won't be using Terraform, so we won't need the Terraform cloud team API token.

What tests do we need to run after we install these services to confirm health?

Have a separate step in the deploy job for each service deployed. The step should just call a local script that contains the Helm deploy logic.

```
          equal: [ scheduled_pipeline, << pipeline.trigger_source >> ]
      jobs:
        - deploy control plane services:
            name: deploy sbx-i01-aws-us-east-1 control plane services
            context: *context
            cluster: sbx-i01-aws-us-east-1
            filters: *on-push-main

  release prod-i01-aws-us-east-2 control plane base:
      jobs:
        - deploy control plane services:
            name: deploy prod-i01-aws-us-east-2 control plane services
            context: *context
            cluster: prod-i01-aws-us-east-2
            filters: *on-tag-main
```

Let's take a closer look at three of the commands in the previous code:

- set-environment—We will need to use one of the bash functions available from
  the orb-pipeline-events. And we will also need the kubeconfig file for the pipeline service account. Recall that in the control plane base pipeline, we saved the
  kubeconfig to our secrets store. We encode the file as base64 before saving. The
  kube-ops orb includes a command to fetch the encoded string, decode it, and
  write it to the correct location for any of our tools that interact with the Kubernetes API. Add these steps to the set-environment command:

```
- kube/op-config:
    op-value: my-vault/<< parameters.cluster>>/kubeconfig-base64
- do/bash-functions
```

- run-integration-tests—The three services we are deploying provide information about the cluster. How should we test the services in the pipeline? In both
  the services pipeline and the extensions pipeline, an effective testing strategy will
  include both general smoke tests of container status, along with functional tests
  that confirm the operating results.

- deploy control plane services—In the solution code for the next exercise, you
  will see that when we deploy these services, we're pulling the community Helm
  chart directly from the source provided by the service's maintainer. A common
  best practice is to copy these charts from the official repository into your organization's Git store. Various reasons are offered for why this is important, yet in
  practical terms, these boil down to two. By mirroring the chart and then referencing from your local source, you can

  – Avoid a deployment failure during those times when the official source is
    unavailable for whatever reason.

  – Prevent deployments referencing external sources with the intention that all
    third-party charts have been subject to the appropriate review and security
    scan that should be applied when using any third-party code resource.

Those are solid principles not just for Helm charts but for all kinds of third-party resources such as code libraries, Docker images, and media content. But in practice, this approach has several weaknesses that often prevent it from delivering the intended benefits, especially in large corporate settings.

First, your organization's Git source is also at risk of outages, particularly if you're using a self-managed setup. Self-managed Git in many enterprises experiences more frequent problems than the major SaaS providers. Second, simply enforcing the use of the mirrored source doesn't guarantee that the proper reviews and scans are being done.

What often happens is that the responsibility gets centralized to a single team that has many other duties. Typically, a developer has to create some sort of ticketed request. When their request finally receives a response, the process is usually little more than a visual review. Every new version of the chart requires the same manual process.

The result is that adopting a third-party Helm chart—even updating to a new version—turns into a multiday, ticket-driven process with little to no meaningful security analysis. In the end, it just adds friction and delay without delivering any real value.

Just because this kind of organizational dysfunction is common doesn't mean we should throw out the practice entirely. Instead, let's be realistic about the challenges and focus on solutions that work.

Start by integrating security scanning directly into the pipelines that use the charts. Then, add admission controllers to verify the scan results for specific chart versions. When it comes to mirroring, make it fully automated and self-serve so any developer can easily add a chart into a system that continuously updates release versions and scans for vulnerabilities. And have an accelerated process for switching from the internal mirror to the official source, in case the internal is not available.

In our initial pipelines, let's include basic Helm chart scanning. In our deployment bash scripts, we can utilize a basic chart scanning function that can be pulled from our pipeline-events orb. Review the default values.yaml for each of these services and decide which values to provide. Don't forget: all our *management* applications will run on the management node group and will need node selector and tolerations:

```bash
#!/usr/bin/env bash
set -eo pipefail
source bash-functions.sh          ◄─── This shared function file is written to the
cluster_name=$1                        pipeline working directly when we call the
CHART_VERSION=$(jq -er .metrics_server_chart_version     do/bash-functions orb step in our set-
  environments/$cluster_name.json)     environment command shown previously.
echo "metrics-server chart version $CHART_VERSION"

helm repo add metrics-server
  https://kubernetes-sigs.github.io/metrics-server/
trivyScan "metrics-server/metrics-server
  " "metrics-server"  "$CHART_VERSION"
  "metrics-server-values/$cluster_name-values.yaml" ◄─── Use the trivyScan bash
                                                          function from the pipeline
                                                          events orb to perform a
                                                          security and best practice
                                                          scan of the chart we just
                                                          downloaded.
```

```
helm upgrade --install metrics-server metrics-server/metrics-server \
             --version $CHART_VERSION \
             --namespace kube-system \
             --values metrics-server/$cluster_name-values.yaml
```

The install script lets us reference a cluster-specific values file so we can manage any parameter differences between clusters (for example, the number of replicas, the amount of RAM or CPU, or similar scale-related settings). Normally, each cluster will have its own values.yaml. Charts have default settings for all the values, and often the default setting is tailored to suit the most common use cases. It is common to have only a handful of these settings that require a custom setting. Because of this, people often include only the values that are being changed from the default in a values.yaml of a Helm deployment.

We've noticed a couple of side effects from this practice. For third-party apps, if the chart isn't being mirrored into the lifecycle pipeline repository, administrators will need to switch back and forth between the repository containing the default values and the repository containing the cluster-specific override values. It is also not uncommon for this practice, in minor and occasionally even patch upgrades, to cause problems because the default value of a setting not being altered has changed unexpectedly.

A strategy that can reduce the effect of those situations is for each cluster's specific values file to include all the possible values, even if most remain set to the default settings. As upgrades come along, a single comparison of the new default values to any cluster values file will show every change. In our example cluster, apart from the node-selector and tolerations needed for the management node group, most of the changes will be in response to our security scan of the chart.

Exercise 8.2   Run Trivy scan on metrics-server chart and create a values.yaml to correct the findings

Use Helm to pull locally a copy of the version of the metrics-server helm chart you expect to deploy in our control plane services pipeline.

Use the Trivy `config` command to scan the chart for security problems. Review the results and identify the changes we can provide through values.yaml to address the scan concerns.

An effective practice for testing a deployed service or extension is to have both state and functional testing. State testing often assesses the same things that operational monitoring will be watching, such as whether the service is running and otherwise reporting a healthy state. Functional testing should use the service in a real-world way to confirm that it is usable.

Some common state checks include whether the Kubernetes API reports the service as running or inspecting the service logs to see whether healthy startup information has been generated. Here is an example using bats for the kube-state-metrics service:

```
@test "kube-state-metrics status is Running" {
  run bash -c "kubectl get po -n kube-system -o wide | grep 'kube-state-metrics'"
  [[ "${output}" =~ "Running" ]]
}
@test "kube-state-metrics logs show service has started successfully" {
  run bash -c "kubectl logs deployment/kube-state-metrics
 -n kube-system -c kube-state-metrics"
  [[ "${output}" =~ "Started kube-state-metrics self metrics server" ]]
}
```

What to functionally test depends on the service, naturally. In the case of metrics-server, since the horizontalpodautoscaler (https://mng.bz/Pwrg) uses this service, we want to deploy a test application that will use it. What simple image could we deploy with a Horizontal Pod Autoscaler definition and then generate load to see if the number of pods scales up in response? The Kubernetes documentation contains an example (https://mng.bz/JwRP) we can implement in our pipeline test automation. When we get to the testing exercise, consider adding this load test. There is an example solution in the companion code.

The other two services we are deploying don't have that sort of direct usage. But we can confirm that they are reporting metrics that we expect them to based on actions we have taken:

```
@test "is kube-state-metrics reporting metrics from running services" {
  run bash -c "kubectl get --raw
 /api/v1/namespaces/kube-system/services/
 kube-state-metrics:http/proxy/metrics
  [[ "${output}" =~ "kube_replicaset_spec_replicas" ]]
  [[ "${output}" =~ "karpenter" ]]
  [[ "${output}" =~ "event-exporter" ]]
}
@test "is event-exporter reporting events from our testing" {
un bash -c "kubectl logs deployment/event-exporter \
 -n kube-system -c event-exporter"
  [[ "${output}" =~ "Started container php-apache" ]]
}
```

> **Exercise 8.3 Create the set-environment command for our control-plane-services pipeline.**
>
> Let's start to fill out the pipeline from the previous snippet.
>
> In our set-environment steps, we need to
>
> 1 Load our secrets store env file for the environment parameter passed.
> 2 Set up the kubeconfig credentials for the associated cluster.
> 3 Load our shared bash functions from the pipeline_events orb.
>
> We aren't using any Terraform in this pipeline, which will simplify the deployment. The first stage of our pipeline will configure the services for the sandbox cluster and is triggered by any change pushed to the main branch.

(continued)

```
workflows:

  deploy sbx-i01-aws-us-east-1 control plane services:
    When:
      not:
        equal: [ scheduled_pipeline, << pipeline.trigger_source >> ]
      jobs:
        - deploy control plane services:
            name: deploy sbx-i01-aws-us-east-1 control plane services
            context: *context
            cluster: sbx-i01-aws-us-east-1
            filters: *on-push-main
```

> Like our previous pipelines, we will schedule a nightly run of our functional tests.

> We will create a local pipeline job to manage the deployment of services.

This will be a locally defined job rather than a job we reference from a shared orb. Remember that we will need to include an executor definition for the job to run on. Like the nightly test job, we will define this in the jobs section of our pipeline.

```
jobs:

  deploy control plane services:
    docker:
      - image: *executor-image
    parameters:
      cluster:
        description: cluster name
        type: string
  ...
```

Exercise 8.4   Add the necessary steps to the control plane services deployment job for our pipeline

The deploy job should do at least the following:

1 Check out the repository code.
2 Run the set-environment command for the sbx environment.
3 Install the metrics-server using the script from the previous code (remember, this service needs to run in our management node pool, not the Karpenter-managed pools, so be sure to add helm values for nodeselector and tolerations to target the correct pool).
4 Install kube-state-metrics (https://github.com/kubernetes/kube-state-metrics) following the same strategy.
5 Install kubernetes-event-export (https://github.com/resmoio/kubernetes-event-exporter) following the same strategy.
6 Assuming the pipeline succeeds to this point, run the tests described in the previous code to confirm the functional health of each of these services.

Since we know that we will want to schedule a nightly job to run these same tests, we can keep our pipeline DRY by putting the tests into a pipeline command that is called from the deployment job. The nightly job can then reuse the same command. At this point, we should be able to push these changes and work on getting the git-push-triggered portion of the pipeline running successfully. This pipeline will depend on basically the same env file values as our previous pipeline, except we won't need the team Terraform token.

NOTE Normally, the services pipeline is also where we would initially deploy our cluster observability services and then include the dashboard, monitors, alerts, and so on within this and all future pipelines as just another definition of done. We don't include actual observability tooling in our example solution for cost reasons. Refer to chapter 5 on observability for guidance on implementing this.

Exercise 8.5   Add the release stage to our control-plane-base pipeline

The final step in our pipeline is adding a workflow that triggers the production deployment when a Git tag is pushed and another workflow that runs tests on a nightly schedule.

8.4   Control plane extensions

Figure 8.4 lists a few of the most commonly used categories of extensions. There are many more out there, and that number will only increase as time passes. We will implement two of these three in our Epetech example and discuss the potential importance of operator extensions in terms of scaling the platform and the user experience.

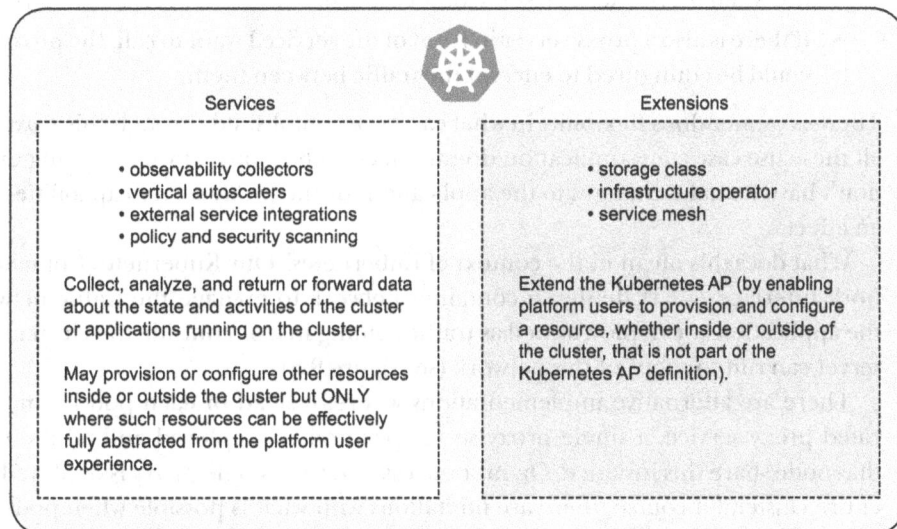

Services	Extensions
• observability collectors • vertical autoscalers • external service integrations • policy and security scanning	• storage class • infrastructure operator • service mesh
Collect, analyze, and return or forward data about the state and activities of the cluster or applications running on the cluster. May provision or configure other resources inside or outside the cluster but ONLY where such resources can be effectively fully abstracted from the platform user experience.	Extend the Kubernetes AP (by enabling platform users to provision and configure a resource, whether inside or outside of the cluster, that is not part of the Kubernetes AP definition).

Figure 8.4   Commonly used categories of extensions

8.4.1   Kubernetes storage classes

As cloud vendors have provided fully managed storage classes for the most common uses, there is no routine need to manage this capability as part of our other extensions. In the control-plane-base exercise, we specified both Elastic Block Store and Elastic File System storage classes among the fully AWS-managed features and included automated testing. The integration tests followed the same use pattern that customers would follow when using those resources. We will not add any additional storage classes to our Epetech platform.

If we need to extend those features or add other storage class technologies to our platform, they should be treated as control plane extensions since they extend the Kubernetes API and enable users to provision resources outside the cluster.

8.4.2   Service mesh

Implementing a service mesh provides a whole host of capabilities that we will need in our engineering platform. What is a service mesh? A service mesh is an infrastructure layer that manages secure, reliable, and observable communication between microservices. Let us dig a bit deeper into the concept of a service mesh.

At a high level, the power of a service mesh lies in what can be achieved through the use of sidecar proxy servers without changing application code:

- A proxy server acts as an intermediary, utilizing the TCP/IP networking protocol to manage the connection between applications, forwarding traffic, and even modifying or filtering the traffic based on its configuration.
- I could configure the proxy server to validate a web token in a request to my API.
- I could configure the proxy server to retry a connection before returning a failure when my API talks to some other service.
- If there is also a proxy server in front of the service I want to call, the proxy servers could be configured to encrypt the traffic between them.

There is tremendous flexibility in what can be accomplished through this *proxy*. And in all these use cases, my application doesn't need to be aware of what is going on, and I don't have to make changes to the application for the proxy server capabilities to have an effect.

What does this mean in the context of Kubernetes? Our Kubernetes Container Network Interface (CNI) defines a container network to manage the traffic between all the applications we deploy, as well as traffic coming in from outside the cluster. A proxy server can run "on top" of this network (see figure 8.5).

There are alternative implementations where, instead of each pod having a dedicated proxy service, a single proxy server per node is deployed and all the pods on that node share this instance. Or, in some cases, even a single proxy is deployed for the entire cluster. Of course, there are limitations with what is possible when pods share a proxy server, most notably around fine-grained traffic control, isolation, and observability. When multiple pods share a proxy, it becomes harder to enforce service-specific

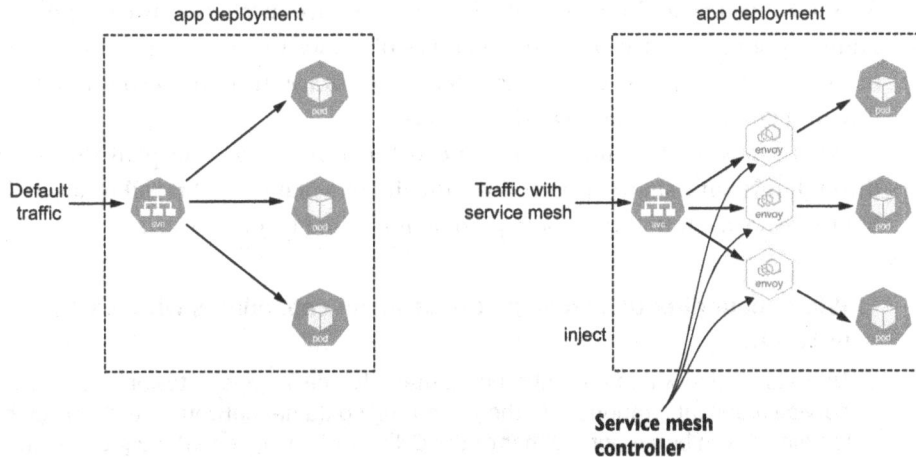

Figure 8.5 A service mesh acts as a control plane for proxy servers, deploying and configuring them based on our instructions, creating a standardized way of utilizing this integration point.

policies, capture metrics at the right granularity, or debug problems that are specific to a single workload. That said, depending on your needs, such tradeoffs may be acceptable, especially in environments where resource constraints or operational simplicity take precedence over strict isolation and detailed telemetry.

When a centralized control plane is managing these proxies, then you also have the option to enable the control plane to manage other capabilities that are dependencies for things you would like to do through the proxy. For example, because of this relationship between traffic routing and the applications deployed to the cluster, a service mesh is a practical approach to create the capabilities of the Kubernetes Gateway API (https://gateway-api.sigs.k8s.io). Early mesh architectures included similar capabilities, and much of the feedback that went into the Gateway API definition has come from this service mesh history. The Gateway API is quickly becoming an expected standard for Kubernetes because of the built-in design for enabling developers to have a self-managed experience for the ingress elements affecting their application.

While ingress is a capability we need from the start, there are several things we should expect to be part of our platform that a service mesh can provide:

- Kubernetes Gateway API
- Traffic control (dynamic routing: Canary, B/G, feature flags)
- Resiliency (retries, timeouts, failovers, circuit breakers, fault injection, rate limiting)
- Security and authorization (policy model, common authN/Z standards)
- Pluggable extension model (can direct traffic through any compatible service, e.g., open policy agent)
- Protocol adaptation (e.g., GraphQL resolution via filters or adapters)

Another effective architectural attribute of a service mesh, because of the proxy integration point, is that usually any features of a mesh can be toggled on or off. This makes it easier to preserve each as a *domain of change* (from our evolutionary architecture and domain-driven design discussions).

What kinds of capabilities do we need for our engineering platform to integrate through this same shared point? Over the life of a platform, this will be a very long list, but there are a few that we should plan on including from the start.

What about directly bundling service mesh capabilities with our container network?

There is a trend within the Kubernetes marketplace in general toward tightly coupling service mesh integrations with the underlying container network directly. Much of this is being driven by vendors, either of the CNIs or of services that integrate at the layer 7 level, all trying to expand their product capabilities to attract more customers and make their software stickier. But what does this mean from an architectural perspective? There are some principles that we should keep in mind:

- *Kubernetes API roadmap*—Like the Gateway API discussed earlier, there is growing maturity within the Kubernetes API around finding the right abstractions to enable the Kubernetes ecosystem to better integrate with the various privately managed or public cloud settings where it is being deployed. Be cautious with internal technologies, even a CNI, that start to diverge from the Kubernetes standards for common capabilities.
- *Preserving domains of change*—Where we can, we want to maintain the ability to change or evolve the technologies that make up our platform. The more things that are bundled together into a single offering, not intentionally designed to make individual features optional, the more challenging it becomes to change any of the bundled services.
- *Zero-trust networking*—One of the most valuable aspects of adopting a zero-trust networking strategy for application security is how greatly it can simplify the process of externalizing internal services and expanding the use of external services. But this comes from the consistent practice of applying security risk assessment that excludes the network. Many of the capabilities that take advantage of the service mesh integration points with the container network are security-oriented, such as automatic service-to-service mTLS. If the implementation of these capabilities within a cluster is fully coupled to our network, it becomes challenging to maintain a genuine separation for risk assessment purposes.

If we use a self-managed network (CNI) to provide service-mesh type features, and we lose these attributes, over time, our platform will become harder to evolve and upgrades will become larger and more complex.

For our Epetech platform, we will implement the Istio (https://istio.io) service mesh. Given its broad use among some of the largest Kubernetes implementations in existence over the last several years, we consider it the most mature mesh (see figure 8.6).

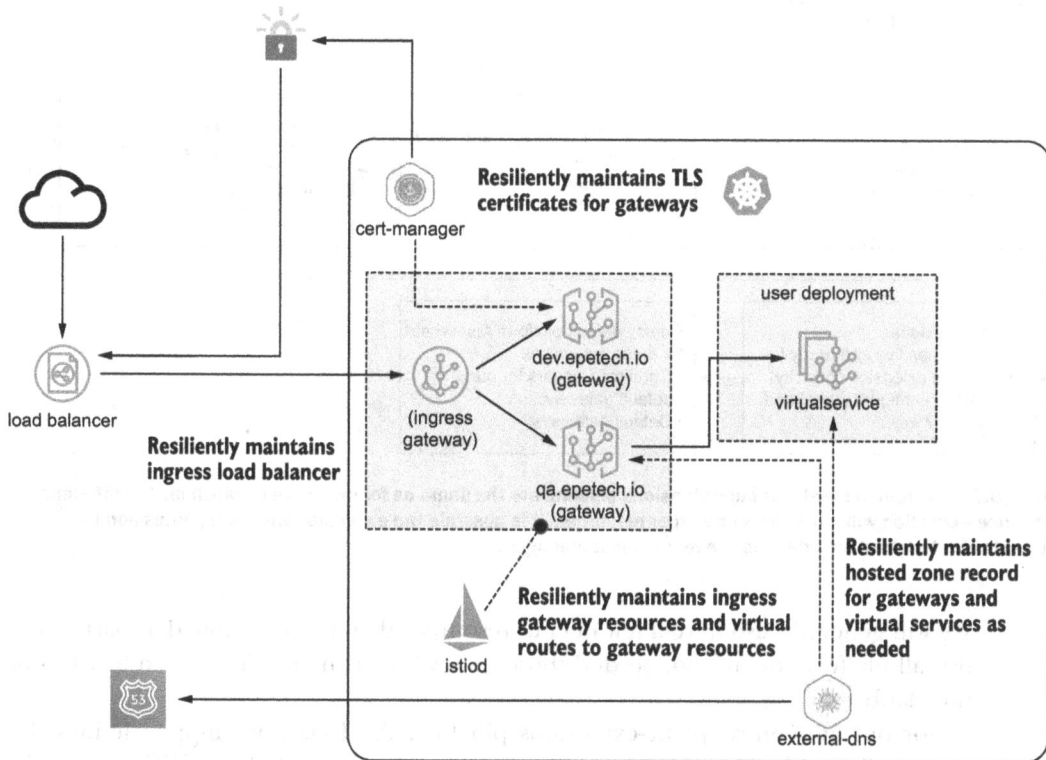

Figure 8.6 For our Epetech starting platform, we will deploy the Istio service mesh and configure it to support the platform-managed domain name system ingress pattern as a self-serve experience for our users.

By deploying an Istio ingressgateway, an external load balancer will be provisioned and managed by Istio for ingress traffic to the cluster. To support the domain name system (DNS) changes where needed for path routing of traffic to deployed services, we will deploy the external-dns extension to automate Route53 DNS changes. And, since we want to support HTTPS for secure inbound traffic, we will deploy the cert-manager extension and configure it to integrate with Let'sEncrypt to apply and rotate the needed TLS certificates.

We will use a basic in-place install and upgrade approach using the istioctl CLI. If you are new to Istio, this is a good starting point to become familiar with the initial capabilities and to get the early users of a platform running before the platform team begins practicing with the more full-featured revision install process. A service mesh, like Kubernetes itself, has a lot of capabilities and initially can feel complex to manage. But, also like Kubernetes, as you become more experienced and confident in using the capabilities, you will discover that a mesh has the long-term effect of constraining complexity, making it easier to maintain these capabilities.

Let's look at the basic installation flow for our extensions (see figure 8.7).

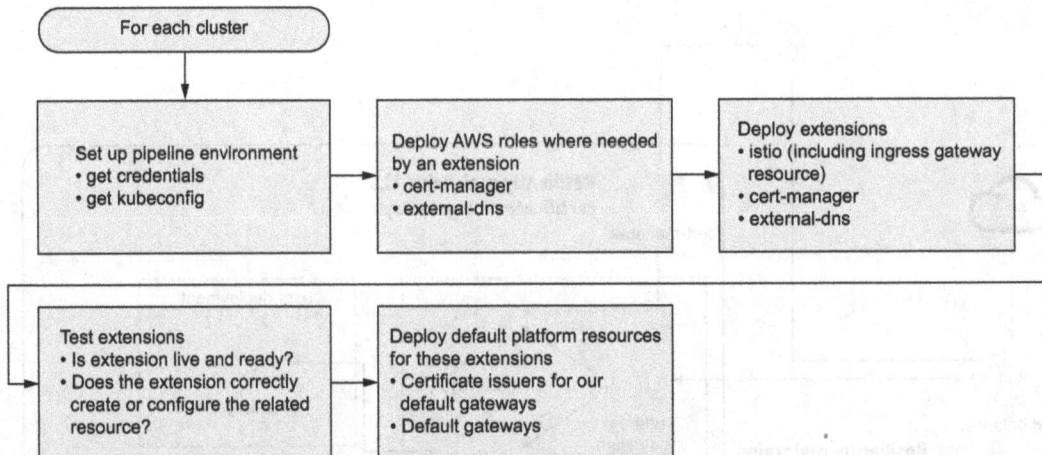

Figure 8.7 The requirements for our extensions pipeline are the same as for our services pipeline. The differences are, since extension will provision some other resources, it is possible the extension will need permission to interact with the cloud provider and the resources it manages.

We will generally also have a few default resources that are provisioned as part of the overall platform definition, beyond those that will be dynamically created by users of the platform.

For our aws-control-plane-extensions pipeline, the following snippet defines the basic outline of the pipeline contents, and a series of exercises follow to fill in the details of each command, job, or workflow:

In exercise 8.7, we will fill out the steps to set our environment values and credentials.

We will need to create AWS OpenID Connect assumable identity and access management roles for the cert-manager and external-dns services. A simple starting point is to use Terraform to make these roles. At scale, this approach will no longer be simple, as we discuss later.

```
---
version: 2.1
orbs:
  terraform: twdps/terraform@3.1.1
  kube: twdps/kube-ops@1.1.2
  op: twdps/onepassword@3.0.0
  do: twdps/pipeline-events@5.0.1
globals:
  - &context <my-team>
  - &executor-image twdps/circleci-kube-ops:alpine-3.2.1

on-push-main: &on-push-main
on-tag-main: &on-tag-main

commands:
  set-environment:
  validate-service-account-roles:
  run-integration-tests:
```

In exercise 8.6, we will complete the logic for these anchors.

We can use AwSpec to confirm our roles are provisioned. We will complete this in exercise 8.8.

The integration tests will need to use the extensions to confirm they are working as expected. We will complete these jobs in exercise 8.12.

```
Jobs:
  deploy control plane extensions:
  integration tests:

workflows:
  deploy sbx-i01-aws-us-east-1 control plane extensions:
  release prod-i01-aws-us-east-2 control plane extensions:
  run nightly integration tests:
```

Our pipeline will need two jobs: one to perform the extensions deployment and another to run the nightly integration tests. See exercises 8.9 and 10.

Finally, like our previous pipelines, we will have three workflows: one triggered by git-push for our sandbox testing environment, one triggered by git-tag to release changes to production, and a nightly workflow to continuously run our integration tests and confirm extension health. We will complete these in exercises 8.11 and 12.

Like before, you can see the proposed pipeline has a run-integration-tests command. We can use AWSpec to validate the role permissions. But since we are using AWS managed permission definitions, how much value is there in validating that each permission in the Terraform resource matches the resulting role permissions? We don't manage the contents of these permissions, so we can limit our test to whether the role has been created. Our later functional test will prove whether the role definition is successful.

Exercise 8.6 Complete the definition of our pipeline trigger filters in these anchors

We will use the same events as our other pipelines so far: one filter for git-push for our sandbox testing environment and one filter for git-tag to release changes to production.

Exercise 8.7 Complete the steps we will need for the set-environment command in our extensions pipeline

In our set-environment steps, we need to

1. Load our secrets store env file for the environment parameter passed.
2. Generate our environment auto.tfvars file from a values template.
3. Set up the kubeconfig credentials for the associated cluster.
4. Set up the Terraform API token to use cloud state.
5. Load our shared bash functions from the pipeline_events orb.

In the sandbox (CI) workflow, we will need the appropriate service account credentials along with our team's Terraform API token. In the release workflow, we will additionally need a GitHub token and a chatbot token to generate release notes or post a release announcement to chat.

Next, we can create the contents of the `validate-service-account-roles` command. Since we are going to use roles that AWS maintains through their Terraform module, as we discussed earlier, we can limit the test to confirming that the role was created.

What roles will we be creating and why? Let's look again at our service mesh figure (figure 8.8). Recall that we will be deploying three extensions: Istiod, cert-manager, and external-dns.

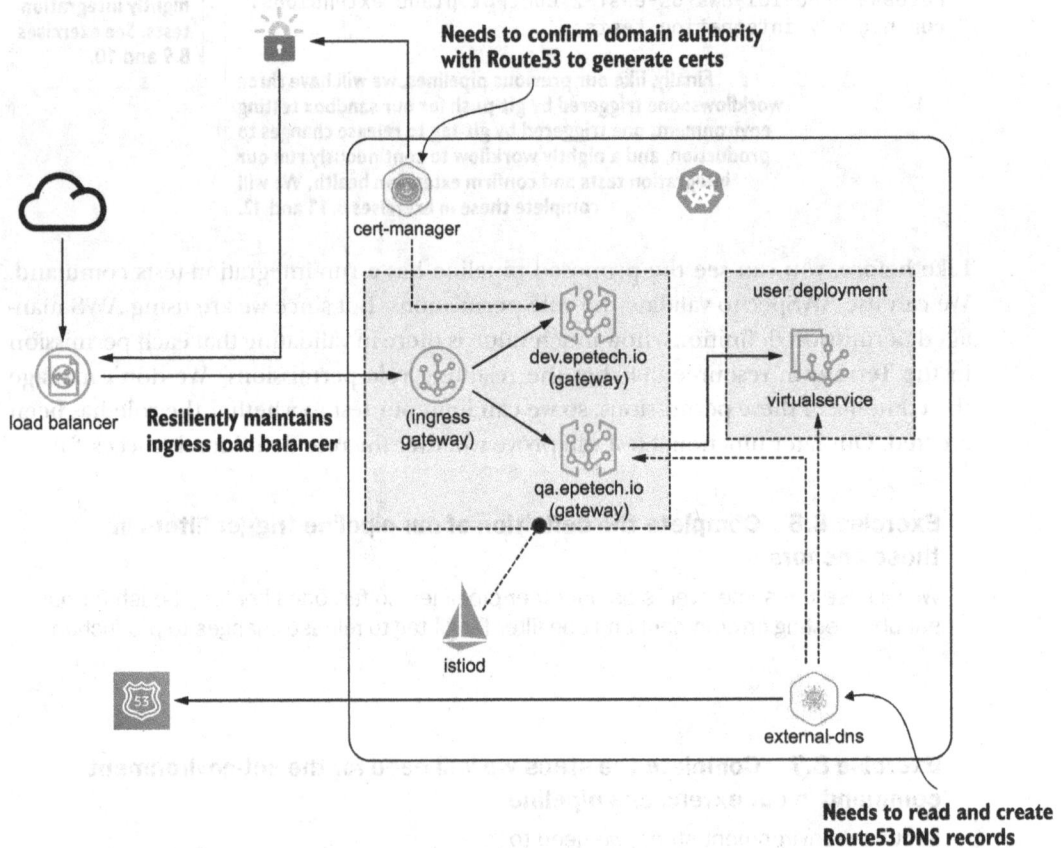

Figure 8.8   Istiod can use the Kubernetes API permissions to create a load balancer, but cert-manager and external-dns will need specific Route53 permissions.

We will need to create the oidc-assumable roles for two of our extensions before installing the extensions. The AWS Terraform module for IAM has roles for these services built in. We will then annotate the service account definition in the Helm charts with the associated role that can be assumed:

```
$ cat service-account-role-cert-manager.tf
module "cert_manager_irsa_role" {
  source = "terraform-aws-modules/iam/aws//modules/
  iam-role-for-service-accounts-eks"
  version = "~> 5.55.0"
```

```
  role_path                    = "/PlatformRoles/"
  role_name                    = "${var.cluster_name}-cert-manager-sa"
  attach_cert_manager_policy = true
  oidc_providers = {
    main = {
      provider_arn = data.aws_iam_openid_connect_provider.eks.arn
      namespace_service_accounts = ["cert-manager:cert-manager"]
    }
  }
}

$ cat service-account-role-external-dns.tf
module "external_dns_irsa_role" {
source = "terraform-aws-modules/iam/aws//modules/iam-role-\
for-service-accounts-eks"
  version = "~> 5.55.0"
  role_path                  = "/PlatformRoles/"
  role_name                  = "${var.cluster_name}-external-dns-sa"
  attach_external_dns_policy = true
  oidc_providers = {
    main = {
      provider_arn = data.aws_iam_openid_connect_provider.eks.arn
      namespace_service_accounts = ["istio-system:external-dns"]
    }
  }
}
```

Exercise 8.8   Create AwSpec test to confirm roles

Review the tests we created in the aws-iam-profiles pipeline and create AwSpec tests to confirm these two roles have been created.

DEPLOYING THE EXTENSIONS

When the git-push workflow is triggered, what steps do we need to take? We know that before we deploy cert-manager and external-dns, we will need to create the roles so the first part of our CI pipeline can perform our usual Terraform static analysis and deployment:

```
workflows:

  deploy sbx-i01-aws-us-east-1 control plane extensions:
    when:
      not:
        equal: [ scheduled_pipeline, << pipeline.trigger_source >> ]
    jobs:
      - terraform/static-analysis:
          name: static code analysis
          context: *context
          trivy-scan: true
```

```
    before-static-analysis:
      - set-environment:
          cluster: sbx-i01-aws-us-east-1
    filters: *on-push-main

  - terraform/apply:
      name: apply sbx-i01-aws-us-east-1 service account roles
      context: *context
      workspace: sbx-i01-aws-us-east-1
      before-apply:
        - set-environment:
            cluster: sbx-i01-aws-us-east-1
      after-apply:
        - validate-service-account-roles:
            cluster: sbx-i01-aws-us-east-1
      requires:
        - static code analysis
      filters: *on-push-main
```

Notice that we don't run a Terraform plan step. Of course, behind the scenes, Terraform is running a plan step, but unless we explicitly review the plan, we don't have the opportunity to review it before making the changes. That can be an essential step in an infrastructure pipeline. But as with any practice, the *standard* practice doesn't exist in a vacuum.

In the case of this pipeline, Terraform is only creating an OIDC assumable role with a permission definition that we don't maintain. And this is happening in a pipeline that will cease to exist with any meaningful scale of extensions and users. There is nothing to review that we are likely to successfully recognize as a problem from the results of the plan output. The functional tests we create are an effective means of finding bugs in these AWS-maintained roles, should they exist. Including a plan step in this situation can't provide the normally expected value of the step.

But what if you do want it anyway? One reasonable rationale could be that, even though the plan/approve step is not applicable in 100% of the situations where Terraform is used, the risk that some engineer might incorrectly assess a given situation should perhaps lead us to adopt the engineering standard that the plan step always occurs. We are willing to accept the increased cost overhead that will go along with that, as it is likely to be low.

The first two jobs will manage the roles. Let's look at our extension deployments.

DEPLOYING ISTIO

We are going to start with the *in-place* install and upgrade process for Istio using the istioctl CLI. This is a good starting point if you are new to Istio and the platform is being created as a greenfield build, where there will be a decent period of only alpha customer usage, as in our Epetech example. It is easier to manage and gives the platform engineering team some time to get familiar with all of the upgrade mechanics. The platform team can then refactor the Istio upgrade to follow a canary (or revision) upgrade process as the recommended practice, whether with the CLI or using the Helm chart. In-place upgrades will result in a momentary service interruption and should be done during a maintenance window.

When using the CLI to do the install, we will directly provision the istio-system namespace. In addition, we should create a dedicated namespace for functional testing service mesh capabilities. The namespace should be configured the same as the namespaces that will be provisioned for platform users:

```
$ cat tpl/istio-namespaces.yaml
---
apiVersion: v1
kind: Namespace
metadata:
  name: istio-system

---
apiVersion: v1
kind: Namespace
metadata:
  name: default-mtls
  labels:
    istio-injection: enabled
    pod-security.kubernetes.io/warn: restricted
    pod-security.kubernetes.io/audit: restricted
    pod-security.kubernetes.io/enforce: baseline

---
apiVersion: v1
kind: ResourceQuota
metadata:
  name: default-mtls-ns-quota
  namespace: default-mtls
spec:
  hard:
    requests.cpu: "2"
    requests.memory: 2Gi
    limits.cpu: "10"
    limits.memory: 20Gi
```

> We will configure Istio to only manage namespaces that have this label.

> We want Kubernetes to enforce the built-in baseline security requirements, and we will warn on deployment conflicts with the restricted requirements.

> All teams will start with a default amount of resources. These are pretty low just for this exercise.

We will include the deployment of these namespaces in the Istio deploy script. Beyond that, the install script should let us pass in the desired Istio version and perform either an install or an upgrade appropriately. When Istio is upgraded, applications running on the cluster that are included in the mesh using the sidecar proxy configuration will need to be restarted (or deployed) to upgrade the sidecar. In a Karpenter-managed node pool that is refreshing nodes every few days, we know that this will eventually happen, but we could also perform a restart after the upgrade:

```
# install_istio.sh
#!/usr/bin/env bash

set -eo pipefail
cluster_name=$1
```

```
istio_version=$(jq -er .istio_version $cluster_name.auto.tfvars.json)
echo "istio version $istio_version"

kubectl apply -f tpl/istio-namespaces.yaml

curl -L https://istio.io/downloadIstio | ISTIO_VERSION=$istio_version sh -
already_installed=$(kubectl get po --all-namespaces)

if [[ $already_installed == *"istiod"* ]]; then
  echo "inplace upgrade"
  istio-${istio_version}/bin/istioctl upgrade -y
  -f istio/values-$istio_version.yaml
  sleep 30
  kubectl get deployments --all-namespaces --field-selector=metadata.
    namespace!=kube-system,
  metadata.namespace!=cert-manager,
  metadata.namespace!=istio-system
  | tail +2 | awk '{ cmd=sprintf("kubectl rollout restart deployment
  -n %s %s", $1, $2) ; system(cmd) }'
else
  echo "new install"
  istio-${istio_version}/bin/istioctl install -y
  -f istio/values-$istio_version.yaml
fi
```

> Performs a simple check to see if Istio is already running to determine whether to perform a new install or an upgrade

Managing restarts safely

You will see in the previous code a simple method for doing a rolling restart of pods to pick up the upgrade. But is this a good approach? Rolling restarts are designed to be zero downtime, and an effective platform will include a requirement that everything developers deploy to the cluster has pod disruption budgets and horizontal scaling—configurations necessary to gain the advantage of the resilient orchestration of Kubernetes.

Yet, should we assume all the development teams are following this practice? Even if they are, it is also possible that their application could have a bug that makes it perform poorly during restarts or deployments—who knows? There is a debate to be had. But we can say that, in practice, being unable to manage Kubernetes based on the expectation that it is functionally healthy and that it is used correctly is a symptom of larger organizational problems.

Mature scaled cluster operations will include routine chaos automation, which is far more challenging than simple restarts. So if we are unable to safely include something like a rolling restart in system components like Istio because of disruptions to users' applications, recognize the situation for what it is. In many organizations, there simply isn't the will, and sometimes even the need, depending on the cost, to address a situation like this. If we find ourselves in that situation, then we can be realists and manage accordingly.

Similar to the values.yaml in a Helm install, we need to provide deployment setting values for the Istio CLI install. We will need version-specific values files for each upgrade, both to support easy rollback and also in anticipation of moving to a canary upgrade process very soon:

```
# istio-values/values-1.24.2.yaml
apiVersion: install.istio.io/v1alpha1
kind: IstioOperator
spec:
  profile: default
  hub: docker.io/istio
  tag: 1.24.2
  namespace: istio-system
  components:
    base:
      enabled: true
    pilot:
      enabled: true
      k8s:
        resources:
          requests:
            cpu: 10m
            memory: 128Mi
          limits:
            cpu: 2000m
            memory: 2024Mi
        nodeSelector:
          nodegroup: management-arm-rkt-mng
        tolerations:
          - key: "dedicated"
            operator: "Equal"
            value: "management"
            effect: "NoSchedule"
        podDisruptionBudget:
          maxUnavailable: 1
    cni:
      enabled: true
    ztunnel:
      enabled: false
    istiodRemote:
      enabled: false

    egressGateways:
      - enabled: false
        name: istio-egressgateway
    ingressGateways:
      - enabled: true
        name: istio-ingressgateway
        k8s:
          resources:
            requests:
              cpu: 10m
              memory: 128Mi
            limits:
              cpu: 2000m
              memory: 2024Mi
```

Like the rest of our management applications, we want the Istio control plane to run on the management node group.

We want to include a basic podDisruptionBudget so that Istio can reschedule effectively as nodes in the management node group are refreshed.

Run the CNI service so that elevated privileges aren't required for normal deployments.

We will have Istio use sidecar proxies. The ztunnel capabilities are for a per-node proxy server.

We do not want the installed Istio instance to be managed by a remote Istio instance.

An egress-gateway allows us to manage outbound traffic. We will not do that to start.

We do want an ingress-gateway. There are various ways this can be configured, depending on the type of load balancer we want to use. For Epetech, a classic load balancer will work fine, so we can start by using Istio's default method.

```
            nodeSelector:
              nodegroup: management-arm-rkt-mng
            tolerations:
              - key: "dedicated"
                operator: "Equal"
                value: "management"
                effect: "NoSchedule"
            podDisruptionBudget:
              maxUnavailable: 1
    values:
      base:
        enableCRDTemplates: false   ◄────
```

For an istioctl install, we will turn off the default Helm behavior for custom resource definitions

INSTALLING CERT-MANAGER AND EXTERNAL-DNS

We can manage these installs the same way we did in the services pipeline. The only difference is that we will need to provide the details for assigning the service account roles we created using Terraform:

```
helm upgrade --install cert-manager jetstack/cert-manager \
            --version v$chart_version \
            --namespace cert-manager --create-namespace \
            --set serviceAccount.annotations."eks\.amazonaws\.com/role-arn"=
  arn:aws:iam::${AWS_ACCOUNT_ID}:role/PlatformRoles/${cluster_name}-cert-
    manager-sa \
            --values cert-manager/$cluster_name-values.yaml

helm upgrade --install external-dns external-dns/external-dns \
            --version v$chart_version \
            --namespace istio-system \
            --set serviceAccount.annotations."eks\.amazonaws\.com/role-arn"=
  arn:aws:iam::${AWS_ACCOUNT_ID}:role/PlatformRoles/${cluster_name}-
    external-dns-sa \
            --set txtOwnerId=$cluster_name-epetech \
            --values cluster-domains-values.yaml \
            --values external-dns-values/$cluster_name-values.yaml
```

You will note that there is an additional values file being passed to external-dns: the cluster-domains-values.yaml file. External-dns needs to be configured with the domains it will be tracking and configuring. We will include these in our environment values file, and then, in our install script, we can fetch these and format them for Helm.

Here is an example of the values file for our environments:

```
$ cat environments/sbx-i01-aws-us-east-1.auto.tfvars.json.tpl
{
  "aws_account_id": "{{ op://my-vault/aws-account-2/aws-account-id }}",
  "aws_assume_role": "PlatformRoles/PlatformControlPlaneBaseRole",
  "aws_region": "us-east-1",
  "cluster_name": "sbx-i01-aws-us-east-1",
  "cert_manager_chart_version": "1.17.1",
  "external_dns_chart_version": "1.16.0",
  "istio_version": "1.25.1",
```

```
  "cluster_domains": [
    "sbx-i01-aws-us-east-1.epetech.io"
  ],
  "issuerEndpoint": "https://acme-v02.api.letsencrypt.org/directory",
  "issuerEmail": "owner@epetech.io"
}

$ cat environments/prod-i01-aws-us-east-2.auto.tfvars.json.tpl
{
  "aws_account_id": "{{ op://my-vault/aws-account-1/aws-account-id }}",
  "aws_assume_role": "PlatformRoles/PlatformControlPlaneBaseRole",
  "aws_region": "us-east-2",
  "cluster_name": "prod-i01-aws-us-east-2",
  "cert_manager_chart_version": "1.17.1",
  "external_dns_chart_version": "1.16.0",
  "istio_version": "1.25.1",

  "cluster_domains": [
    "epetech.io",
    "prod-i01-aws-us-east-2.epetech.io"
  ],
  "issuerEndpoint": "https://acme-v02.api.letsencrypt.org/directory",
  "issuerEmail": "owner@epetech.io"
}
```

Initially, we will only expect the sandbox cluster to be managing a cluster-specific ingress subdomain. Later in this chapter, we will talk about managed subdomains for developer environments.

Kubernetes service accounts on their own don't have AWS permissions. To bridge that gap, we can annotate the service account with an IAM role ARN. This way, external-dns will inherit the required AWS privileges at runtime, as shown in the following:

```
cluster_domains=$(jq -er .cluster_domains $cluster_name.auto.tfvars.json)
declare -a domains=($(echo $cluster_domains | jq -r '.[]'))
cat <<EOF > cluster-domains-values.yaml
domainFilters:
EOF

for domain in "${domains[@]}";
do
  echo "  - $domain" >> cluster-domains-values.yaml
done
```

> **Exercise 8.9   Create deployment scripts and values files for cert-manager and external-dns deployments**
>
> Using the deployment scripts and values.yaml files from our services pipeline as a guide, create the scripts we will use in our deployment job. For these exercises, we can use the same settings in both sbx and prod. Trivy will also remind you of some additional values to add.

Now that we have the deploy scripts and values for each of our deployments, we can fill in the deploy control plane extensions job:

```
Commands:
...

  run-integration-tests:
    parameters:
      cluster:
        description: cluster and tf workspace name
        type: string
    steps:
      - run:
          name: run control plane services state test
          command: bats test/services-state-test.bats
      - run:
          name: run control plane services functional test
          command: bash scripts/extensions_functional_test.sh
    << parameters.cluster >>

jobs:

  deploy control plane extensions:
    docker:
      - image: *executor-image
    parameters:
      cluster:
        description: cluster name
        type: string
    steps:
      - checkout
      - set-environment:
          cluster: << parameters.cluster >>
      - run:
          name: install istio
          command: bash scripts/install_istio.sh << parameters.cluster >>
      - run:
          name: install cert-manager
          command: bash scripts/install_cert_manager.sh \
    << parameters.cluster >>
      - run:
          name: install external-dns
          command: bash scripts/install_external_dns.sh
    << parameters.cluster >>
      - run:
          name: deploy cluster certificate issuer
          command: bash scripts/deploy_certificate_issuer.sh
    << parameters.cluster >>
      - run:
          name: deploy cluster default gateways
          command: bash scripts/deploy_gateways.sh << parameters.cluster >>
      - run-integration-tests:
          cluster: << parameters.cluster >>
```

Notice that after we install our three extensions, we also deploy a few resources that use these extensions before we run the integration tests. What are those resources?

DEFAULT RESOURCES USING OUR INITIAL EXTENSIONS

When we described the components to be deployed in our extensions pipeline, we said that we could also include any default resources. For Epetech, this means the resources that create our initial platform-managed subdomains. Each requires a gateway and a certificate.

With all three extensions deployed, we can deploy the standard gateways and then test that everything is functioning as expected. What are the resource requests we need to make?

- We need a cert-manager certificate issuer created that can communicate with the AWS Route53 hosted zones for our domain.
- We need to have the certificate issuer generate a certificate that we can provide to a gateway, so that the gateway will support secure TLS (HTTPS) communication.
- We need the gateway resource for the respective domain.

External-dns will automatically create the DNS records to direct traffic for the desired domain to the Istio-managed load balancer.

With those items in place, if we deploy an application to the cluster, we can include an Istio VirtualService resource that contains the path for our application. If everything is configured correctly, traffic on the defined path will hit the defined application service.

To use cert-manager, we deploy a certificate-issuer resource, and then we deploy certificate resources that will use the issuer to generate certificates for our ingress URLs. We can use the free Let'sEncrypt certificate authority. This is what that additional configuration is in our environments file:

```
"issuerEndpoint": "https://acme-v02.api.letsencrypt.org/directory",
"issuerEmail": "owner@epetech.io"
```

With that, we can generate a ClusterIssuer resource file to deploy to our cluster:

```
$ cat scripts/deploy_certificate_issuer.yaml
#!/usr/bin/env bash
source bash-functions.sh
set -eo pipefail

cluster_name=$1
export aws_account_id=$(jq -er .aws_account_id
  "$cluster_name".auto.tfvars.json)
export aws_assume_role=$(jq -er .aws_assume_role
  "$cluster_name".auto.tfvars.json)
export AWS_DEFAULT_REGION=$(jq -er .aws_region "$cluster_name".auto.tfvars.
    json)

export cluster_domains=$(jq -er .cluster_domains
  "$cluster_name".auto.tfvars.json)
```

```
export issuer_email=$(jq -er .issuerEmail "$cluster_name".auto.tfvars.json)
export issuer_endpoint=$(jq -er .issuerEndpoint
 ⇒ "$cluster_name".auto.tfvars.json)

awsAssumeRole "${aws_account_id}" "${aws_assume_role}"          ◄─────────

# generate cluster issuer resource template
cat <<EOF > "${cluster_name}-cluster-issuer.yaml"
apiVersion: cert-manager.io/v1
kind: ClusterIssuer
metadata:
  name: letsencrypt-$cluster_name-issuer
spec:
  acme:
    server: $issuer_endpoint
    email: $issuer_email
    privateKeySecretRef:
      name: letsencrypt-$cluster_name
    solvers:
EOF

# add cluster managed domains to issuer
declare -a domains=($(echo $cluster_domains | jq -r '.[]'))
for domain in "${domains[@]}";
do
  export zone_id=$(aws route53 list-hosted-zones-by-name |
 ⇒ jq --arg name "$domain." -r '.HostedZones | .[] |
 ⇒ select(.Name=="\($name)") | .Id')
  cat <<EOF >> ${cluster_name}-cluster-issuer.yaml
    - selector:
        dnsZones:
          - "$domain"
      dns01:
        route53:
          region: ${AWS_DEFAULT_REGION}
          hostedZoneID: ${zone_id}
EOF
done

kubectl apply -f "$cluster_name-cluster-issuer.yaml"
```

We will need to assume the **PlatformControlPlaneBaseRole** role to call the AWS API.

The script uses the AWS CLI to get the certificate challenge information from Route53 for each domain or subdomain for which we generate a certificate.

Once we have a cluster issue, we can deploy the Istio gateways that will manage traffic on the domains or subdomains that we want to set up in this pipeline.

At this point, that will mean the epetech.io wildcard domain in the production cluster and then a cluster-name-specific subdomain in each. Those are the values we included in the environment values file. We need to deploy a certificate resource in each cluster for the domains that we expect to receive traffic. Then we will deploy a matching Istio gateway to which the ingress-gateway (load balancer) will send the traffic:

```
# deploy_gateways.sh
#!/usr/bin/env bash
set -eo pipefail
export cluster_name=$1
```

```
export cluster_domains=$(jq -er .cluster_domains
  "$cluster_name".auto.tfvars.json)
echo $cluster_name
echo $cluster_domains
declare -a domains=($(echo $cluster_domains | jq -r '.[]'))
for domain in "${domains[@]}";
do
  echo "create certificate for $domain"
  cat <<EOF > tpl/$domain-certificate.yaml
---
apiVersion: cert-manager.io/v1
kind: Certificate
metadata:
  name: $domain-certificate
  namespace: istio-system
spec:
  secretName: $domain-certificate
  issuerRef:
    name: "letsencrypt-${cluster_name}-issuer"
    kind: ClusterIssuer
  commonName: "*.$domain"
  dnsNames:
    - "$domain"
    - "*.$domain"
EOF
  cat tpl/$domain-certificate.yaml
  kubectl apply -f tpl/$domain-certificate.yaml
  echo "define gateway for $domain"
  export gateway=$( echo $domain | tr . - )
  cat <<EOF > tpl/$domain-gateway.yaml
---
apiVersion: networking.istio.io/v1beta1
kind: Gateway
metadata:
  name: $gateway-gateway
  namespace: istio-system
  labels:
    istio: istio-ingressgateway
spec:
  selector:
    app: istio-ingressgateway
  servers:
    - port:
        number: 80
        name: http-$domain
        protocol: HTTP
      hosts:
      - "$domain"
      - "*.$domain"
      tls:
        httpsRedirect: true
    - port:
        number: 443
        name: https-$domain
        protocol: HTTPS
```

Loop through our list of default domains and create a certificate for each.

For each, we will provision certificates that support the subdomain and a wildcard subdomain. Of course, including a wildcard is optional and will depend on your security risk profile.

For each domain, we also create the gateway that uses the associated certificate.

We associate this gateway with the istio-ingress-gateway, which provisions and configures the external load balancer. External-dns, monitoring ingress and gateway deployments, will update Route53 so that traffic on these defined domain names is directed to this load balancer and then to the gateway-connected service.

This gateway will accept traffic only from HTML ports 80 and 443. If someone tries to access the HTTP port, we want to redirect to the HTTPS port automatically.

```
        hosts:
        - "$domain"
        - "*.$domain"
        tls:
          mode: SIMPLE
          credentialName: "$domain-certificate"
EOF
  cat tpl/$domain-gateway.yaml
  kubectl apply -f tpl/$domain-gateway.yaml
done
sleep 360
```

> **Once all of our defined gateways are deployed, we will start testing. Completing the provisioning steps can take a couple of minutes, particularly if this is the initial deployment of Istio.**

By waiting at the end of this script, we give the system time to be ready before we start testing. An improvement to this wait strategy would be to put logic at the start of the test to poll and wait for the resources to report a Ready, with a timeout period to report failure.

With each of these additional scripts created, our deploy job just needs the integration tests to be complete. As you implement these tests, think about the circumstances in which some form of end-to-end test could alleviate the need for specific configuration tests. As a general principle, prefer having broader, detailed testing at the component level and fewer, though comprehensive, end-to-end tests.

For the extensions themselves, we will continue to want state tests and functional tests. What test is needed to prove that the ingress load balancer, domain gateways, TLS certificates, and DNS updates have occurred so that I can receive and process traffic to an application running on the cluster? We need a small application that can be deployed to utilize these features, and then we can test to confirm overall deployment health. Let's start with the simple state tests.

Exercise 8.10   Create state tests using Bats to confirm the extensions report a healthy status

Look back at the state health check example in the previous code for the metrics-server. Create similar tests that will confirm that the following pods in the istio-system namespace report as running:

1 istiod
2 ingressgateway
3 istio-cni-node
4 cert-manager
5 cert-manager-cainjector
6 cert-manager-webhook
7 external-dns

The critical test, which is a functional use of these extensions, will be to deploy an application that uses a cluster default gateway and verify that it can be accessed over HTTPS. Httpbin (https://github.com/postmanlabs/httpbin) is an excellent application for this kind of testing. Recall that we defined the default-mtls namespace for testing Istio-managed applications. The application deployment will be the same regardless of the cluster being tested:

```
$ cat test/httpbin/deployment.yaml
---
apiVersion: v1
kind: Service
metadata:
  name: httpbin
  namespace: default-mtls
  labels:
    app: httpbin
spec:
  ports:
  - name: http
    port: 80
    targetPort: 8080
  selector:
    app: httpbin
---
apiVersion: v1
kind: ServiceAccount
metadata:
  name: httpbin
  namespace: default-mtls
---
apiVersion: apps/v1
kind: Deployment
metadata:
  name: httpbin
  namespace: default-mtls
spec:
  replicas: 1
  selector:
    matchLabels:
      app: httpbin
  template:
    Metadata:
      labels:
        app: httpbin
    spec:
      nodeSelector:
        kubernetes.io/arch: amd64
      containers:
      - image: docker.io/kennethreitz/httpbin
        imagePullPolicy: Always
        name: httpbin
        command:
          - gunicorn
          - -b
          - 0.0.0.0:8080
          - httpbin:app
          - -k
```

The internal service definition accepts traffic on the regular HTTP port. We will receive traffic on HTTPS at the gateway and then terminate that certificate. Once inside the service mesh, the mesh will generate the MTLS certificates that encrypt the traffic from there.

Recall that we don't have a standing node group, but instead Karpenter manages our default node space. We must target the desired existing node pool and, in this case, select the AMD architecture nodes.

httpbin doesn't have version tags. Trivy will alert us to this, and we will either need to mirror the image to our registry and version-tag there or add a .trivyignore instruction to allow its use as is.

```
            - gevent
        ports:
          - containerPort: 8080
        securityContext:
          allowPrivilegeEscalation: false
          readOnlyRootFilesystem: false
          runAsNonRoot: true
          runAsUser: 65532
          runAsGroup: 65532
          seccompProfile:
            type: RuntimeDefault
          capabilities:
            drop: ["ALL"]
        resources:
          limits:
            cpu: 150m
            memory: 256Mi
          requests:
            cpu: 100m
            memory: 128Mi
```

Now, to connect this to our gateway, we need to include an Istio VirtualService. This will need to include cluster-specific info since we will use the cluster-specific gateway:

```
---
apiVersion: networking.istio.io/v1beta1
kind: VirtualService
metadata:
  name: httpbin
  namespace: default-mtls
spec:
  hosts:
    - "httpbin.$cluster_name.epetech.io"          ◄──┐  Here we define the domain name
  gateways:                                            and path we want traffic to our
    - istio-system/$cluster_name-epetech-io-gateway  ◄── httpbin service to use. We are
  http:                                                making use of the wildcard
    - route:                                           certificate to receive traffic on a
      - destination:                                   specific subdomain of the gateway.
          host: httpbin.default-mtls.svc.cluster.local
          port:                                        We provide the path
            number: 80                                 to the gateway that
                                                       has been configured
                                                       to receive this
                                                       subdomain name.
```

If cert-manager is correctly provisioning certificates for our gateways, external-dns is correctly making DNS entries to direct traffic to these gateways, and Istio is correctly deploying a load balancer and connecting VirtualServices to the defined gateways, then once we have deployed httpbin, we can run this command to confirm the end-to-end health of all of the extensions:

```
jsonResponse=$(curl -X GET
  "https://httpbin.$cluster_name.epetech.io/json"
  -H "accept: application/json")
```

A healthy response will be

```
response {
  "slideshow": {
    "author": "Yours Truly",
    "date": "date of publication",
    "slides": [
      {
        "title": "Wake up to WonderWidgets!",
        "type": "all"
      },
      {
        "items": [
          "Why <em>WonderWidgets</em> are great",
          "Who <em>buys</em> WonderWidgets"
        ],
        "title": "Overview",
        "type": "all"
      }
    ],
    "title": "Sample Slide Show"
  }
}
```

Think about how you could orchestrate this test in a bash script.

Exercise 8.11 Create a script that uses the HTTPbin deployment to test our extensions

Later, our integration job will call a script called `extensions_functional_test.sh`, so let's create that script. It will need to take the following actions:

1 Deploy Httpbin to our default-mtls namespace targeting the default AMD node pool.
2 Curl the JSON endpoint on the publicly accessible HTTPS endpoint. For the sandbox cluster, this would be httpbin.sbx-i01-aws-us-east-1.epetech.io/json (but, of course, using the domain name you provisioned for the exercise).
3 If we receive the expected response, then the script can exit with a success state. We know that our service mesh has deployed a load balancer, that external-dns has correctly been modified to direct traffic on our default cluster managed domain to our ingressgateway, and that cert-manager can successfully generate Let'sEncrypt certs for our gateway definition so that traffic to our httpbin service is encrypted.
4 If the `curl` fails, then the script should fail, and we will know we need to do some debugging.
5 Success or failure, we need to clean up our test app.
6 For an extra challenge:
   a Our mesh is configured to use only the current TLS standard. Test the endpoint to confirm this is working as expected.

(continued)

    b You will notice that the solution script uses some simplistic logic to uninstall the testing app, resulting in duplicate script code. How could this be made DRY?

With the script dependencies for our deploy and test jobs complete, we can add the deployment to our git-push–triggered workflow:

```
- deploy control plane extensions:
    name: deploy sbx-i01-aws-us-east-1 extensions
    context: *context
    cluster: sbx-i01-aws-us-east-1
    requires:
      - apply sbx-i01-aws-us-east-1 service account roles
    filters: *on-push-main
```

At this point, with all these changes pushed to the aws-control-plane-extensions repository, we should be able to deploy our extensions to our example sandbox cluster successfully. The last thing to do is add the release workflow to the pipeline so that we can tag the repository to release changes to production.

Exercise 8.12   Add the release workflow to the aws-control-plane-extensions pipeline.

Like the CI deployment, we need to run both the Terraform apply job to provision the assumable roles and our deploy job to deploy them and test the extensions. Since this is the production release, like our other pipelines, let's generate release notes and send a Slack notification. Also, don't forget to schedule a nightly test workflow.

8.4.3   *Using operators for persistent data platform capabilities*

Over the last couple of years, the maturity of operator SDKs and cloud vendor infrastructure component operators means we can effectively extend the Kubernetes API to provide a platform experience for using many of the most commonly needed persistent data resources for platform users. Remember that an engineering platform is not a wrapper for all infrastructure that a development team may need. In terms of cloud infrastructure, an engineering platform provides the common resources required for development teams building distributed service architecture applications. And while there are many capabilities within that definition, it is far short of *everything*.

The things that API teams tend to need are databases, message queues, file shares, and high-performance caches. These all tend to be about holding data, hence we refer to them as *persistent data* resources.

We can put the provisioning and use of these kinds of resources behind an API; then we can create the right experience for both the users and the team delivering the capabilities. This is where infrastructure operators come in. There are various options in this category. For more direct management, there are tools like Crossplane (https://www.crossplane.io), AWS ACK (https://github.com/aws-controllers-k8s/community), and the operator SDK (https://sdk.operatorframework.io). The Kubernetes API now becomes the interface for developer provisioning these resources, but, like the platform control plane itself, the platform engineers are responsible for the operational lifecycle. Maintaining infrastructure through operators differs from the traditional IaC lifecycle, and it has its own learning curve. Yet many large organizations have had great success in using operators to extend the acceleration of a platform experience to many more categories of infrastructure.

If you don't have the staff or the resources to build the new operational skills of fully operator-managed infrastructure, Terraform also has an offering in this category with the Terraform Operator (https://mng.bz/wZgW). This will wrap the entire Terraform workflow and operational process within the operator pattern, so it brings its own sort of complexity and performance implications.

Using the operator pattern, users of your platform can provision and manage common, needed persistent data infrastructure from within their Helm chart. A database becomes just another Kubernetes resource within the application deployment definition. Where credentials or roles are required for interaction with the infrastructure, the operator automates managing these on the developer's behalf while providing debugging access through their regular platform identity and thereby maintaining the separation.

An implementation example is beyond the scope of this book. But in our experience, where the number of developers using an engineering platform starts to go beyond 50 to 100, the other IaC approaches to managing these particular resources will create a noticeable drag on the overall platform experience.

NOTE The operational differences between the operator pattern and traditional IaC should not be underestimated. We don't recommend employing operators as an alternative to conventional IaC languages in any general sense until you have had substantial experience with the pattern on a smaller scale. Even in large-scale engineering platforms, we would expect to see no more than a dozen or so standard components made available using this method.

INFRASTRUCTURE STARTER KITS

You are probably familiar with the pattern of providing infrastructure resources to developers in the form of Terraform starter kits, or sample repositories that can be duplicated and then used to provision some piece of infrastructure. Developers are provided with a fully configured bundle of code that includes the needed Terraform files with sensible defaults, hopefully a pipeline, and even the observability configuration—all the things that a typical DevOps team might include in an infrastructure pipeline.

This can be a helpful strategy. It can increase the efficiency of a DevOps *team* strategy as they try to support a greater number of developers. However, this isn't a platform engineering strategy. It feels a lot like self-serve. Developers can independently get a copy of the code and, in short order, have the infrastructure up and running. This is precisely what we want from language starter kits. A Python API starter kit can contain the API framework; logging, tracing, and any other language libraries; the complete development-to-production pipeline; initial operational observability; and generally everything needed for the developer to almost immediately begin coding business logic that can flow to production equally rapidly. So, what's the difference?

In the case of the Python starter kit, the developer assumes full responsibility. It is rare within a company for the user of a database starter kit to take much responsibility at all. All of the real responsibility is still with the DevOps team that created the starter kit. If there are any operational issues at all, they are called back to own both the response and the follow-through. And most of the time, when there are changes within the definition of the starter kit, anything that needs to be pushed out to users of the kit will also end up being the responsibility of the DevOps team.

Recall that an essential part of the product architecture of a platform is that the features of a platform are delivered as a service interface first–an API. A platform engineer team is responsible for providing the user with access to the user behind an API.

This doesn't mean that there is no place for infrastructure starter kits. There absolutely is. There are also a couple of essential characteristics to keep in mind as you use them and as you think about their relationship to engineering platforms.

KNOW THE VALUE AND THE COST

Infrastructure starter kits will not enable the development acceleration or economies of scale possible through an engineering platform. This isn't a criticism.

At almost any scale, starter kits save DevOps teams time when creating new resources and resolving everyday problems. But as versions multiply and the kits themselves evolve, the overhead of maintaining them creates friction of its own. As more infrastructure instances are created with these kits, the number of DevOps engineers required to support them also grows. While there are moments in an organization's journey where the accelerating effect of starter kits is measurable, over the long term and with broad adoption, their true value lies in improving and sustaining quality, not simply in acceleration or cost savings, and that contribution should not be overlooked.

KEEP SEPARATE FROM THE PRINCIPAL ENGINEERING PLATFORM DELIVERY TEAMS

We also strongly recommend that, if Terraform starter kit-style resources are curated as part of your internal developer resources, the engineering platform product teams should never be the team maintaining them. At the very least, if such resources are to be part of the overall platform product roadmap, then a separate subdomain product team should have ownership within the overall platform. And this team's only responsibility should be the curating and supporting of these particular accelerators. The reason for this is that, fundamentally, these are not self-serve resources. Inevitably, the maintenance team will be required to provide a material level of traditional DevOps-style support. They are a service team that will prevent them from delivering against a product backlog effectively.

8.5   *Platform management APIs*

We have the foundations of our engineering platform at this point. But as it is, only the platform administrators have access. How do we enable access to platform features for our internal platform customers?

We want the development team to be the primary authorization mechanism for our platform, and we want the users of our platform to be able to self-manage team onboarding and membership. This means that developers should not need to request access to all the various systems that make up the engineering platform capabilities. And there will be dozens of such systems. It is pretty standard, within organizations of all sizes, for a developer to have to request access to every developer resource individually. In large companies, developers are constantly being hired or quitting, moving between teams, or joining multiple teams, spending weeks to get access to the systems they need to do their job. Part of the function of an engineering platform is to own this experience. When a team is onboarded, every member of the team should automatically have access to all the features of the platform within the bounds of their team.

In our Epetech platform, we have used Auth0 to create an identity integration between GitHub and the control plane. We could expand the use of Auth0 to include all the access points. Every organization has some central source of authentication, whether that's Active Directory, Google Identity, or something else. We could connect Auth0 to our corporate authentication system and then integrate all of our SaaS tools with Auth0. Auth0 is an Okta product, and many companies use the flagship Okta product for this purpose. But authentication is the easy part. The challenge is managing authorization. What will be the source of truth for teams and team membership within our platform product? No matter how we solve this, not all the systems we use may have a built-in integration ideally suited to our solution.

We have started by using GitHub teams to track team membership. Using our OIDC integration, a user would authenticate through GitHub, and their authorization comes from the team to which they belong.

If you completed the OIDC integration and CLI projects, then you can already authenticate and access the control plane using your personal GitHub credentials. Recall that in the control plane base pipeline, we also applied a ClusterRoleBinding for the GitHub team in which we, as the platform building team, are members. We could have integrated GitHub with the Epetech corporate identity system. If that were Active Directory (AD), for example, we could configure the integration such that AD groups are synced as GitHub groups, and then AD would be the place where teams needed to be formed and people added and removed from teams. How would we provide a self-serve experience there for teams to self-manage?

Whether we use GitHub as the authoritative source for team membership or something else, we still need a means of knowing which "teams" are teams that are engineering platform customers. If we had such a list, we could then automate the process of

- Creating the standard team namespaces in the appropriate clusters. For example, when the payments team is onboarded, these teams are created:
  - payments-dev, payments-qa in the nonproduction cluster
  - payments-preview in the preview cluster
  - payments-prod in the production cluster
- Creating the RoleBindings in each cluster that authorize members of a team to
  access their namespace.
- Creating the matching gateways for the standard namespaces.
- Syncing teams and team membership information, as needed, with any other
  system that we integrate with our platform that doesn't have a built-in integration
  with our authorization source.

This is just the basic set of things we could do. Many of the systems we will want to
use will have easily integrated access controls—but never all of them. And we need a
mechanism that gives us confidence that the platform experience can be maintained
regardless of platform feature evolution. Far too frequently, organizations just decide
they can't be bothered to solve this problem, and the waste amounts to thousands of
hours a year.

A practical and sustainable strategy is to build a handful of lightweight custom platform management APIs to manage any integration needs that the tools or technologies
we use don't already support. Our experience is that these APIs primarily focus on control plane configuration. Still, they also play a critical role in enabling an organization
to broaden its ability to have multiple technical teams outside the primary engineering
platform team easily integrate with the platform roadmap requirements (see figure 8.9).

In this way, a namespace API could maintain the standard namespaces across all
the clusters for a team and also be the interface to provide support for teams creating
and managing custom namespaces. An integrations API can subscribe and be used to
maintain any configurations related to team authorization within a tool or system that
doesn't easily provide the same experience through our regular identity provider. The
teams API can also generate these sync events on a frequent, recurring basis so that the
configuration settings become resilient and able to self-heal from unintended external
changes. You can see how the introduction of the event architecture provides an easy
integration point for teams outside the primary platform team. For example, if there
were a separate team that managed an Enterprise secret store (like Hashi Vault), they
could support the platform roadmap directly by creating a service that subscribed to
the Teams events and then performed any necessary configuration within the store to
provide that part of the comprehensive platform user experience.

It does require an investment to create and maintain these services. Still, the time
saved over the life of an engineering platform through being able to resiliently support a unified platform user access experience more than makes up for the cost. The
larger the scale of the organization, the greater the return there is on this kind of
investment.

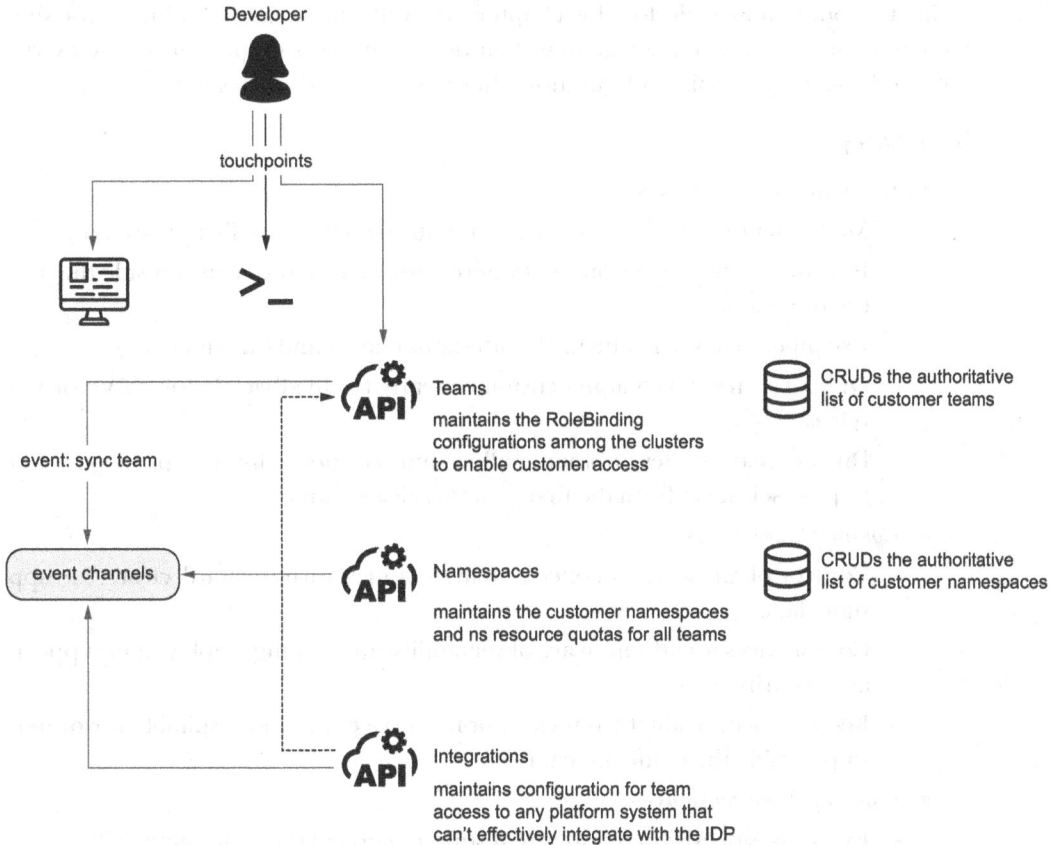

Figure 8.9 A "teams" API can be the interface to onboard a team and maintain the authoritative database for customer teams. This API will maintain the correct RoleBindings on the respective clusters. It can also populate the "sync team" events stream to which other services can subscribe.

8.5.1 Managing teams and namespaces for early adopters

How do we deal with these factors in the early stages of engineering platform development before we deploy our management API? If we added the necessary configuration to the clusters, we could have a couple of early-adopter teams already in our Epetech control plane getting started deploying their applications and providing feedback While the management APIs are not especially complicated, it will still take some time before they can automate this step.

A straightforward approach would be to create a dedicated pipeline that uses something as basic as a JSON file containing our initial teams and standard namespaces. This simple customer management pipeline would follow the same release pattern as our other cluster configuration pipelines. We will not be supporting more than a couple of teams and standard namespaces in this alpha stage, so we should rarely need to make changes to this configuration until the management API is ready.

In the companion code for this chapter, you will find a sample solution for simple team and namespace management that demonstrates a simple and not self-serve method for managing this configuration while working on the API solution.

Summary

- *Environments and testing—*
  - Maintain multiple dev/test environments to enable nondisruptive change.
  - Provide a preview environment where customers deploy code outside the production path.
  - Use pipeline tests that include both status checks and functional tests.
  - Onboard one to two alpha customers early for feedback before MVP or GA release.
  - During feature development, allow limited non-self-serve processes, but require self-serve from the first general release onward.
- *Control plane services—*
  - Control plane services collect, analyze, and return/forward cluster or app state data.
  - Core services for adoption are observability, autoscaling, deployment support, and security.
  - Keep services distinct from extensions; services are more suitable for ownership outside the platform team.
- *Control plane extensions—*
  - Extensions provision/configure resources beyond the Kubernetes API.
  - Core extensions for adoption are storage classes, ingress/gateway API, resiliency, and authN/authZ.
  - Moving extensions to external teams risks friction and waste.
  - A service mesh is the most effective way to deliver gateway API, routing, traffic policies, and zero-trust networking.
- *Platform management APIs—*
  - Provide lightweight, custom platform management APIs to maintain product experience.
  - These APIs enable teams outside platform ownership to participate effectively in the roadmap.
- *Platform roadmap considerations—*
  - Include self-serve provisioning of external infrastructure (databases, queues, API gateways) in roadmap but not necessarily at MVP.
  - Starter kits (e.g., Terraform templates) are useful accelerators but should remain outside the core platform roadmap.

## Part 3

Scaling engineering platforms

Imagine your platform team has built a rock-solid internal developer platform that works beautifully for five teams. It's reliable and fast, and everyone's happy. Then the company doubles in size overnight through an acquisition. Suddenly, your once-sleek platform is straining under the weight. Disparate tools start popping up, support queues swell, carefully designed golden paths are ignored, and developers quietly spin up shadow systems just to keep shipping code. The problem isn't that the platform was bad; it's that it didn't scale with the organization. What once felt elegant now feels brittle, with friction at every turn.

Or take another, subtler scenario. Your platform is technically sound with solid architecture and acceptable uptime and feature-compliant, but developers avoid it. They say it's too rigid, doesn't fit their real-world workflows, or feels like more overhead than help. Leadership begins to see it as a cost center rather than a value driver. Here, the missing ingredient is evolution: treating the platform as a living product. That means engaging in user research, building roadmaps, and gathering constant feedback so the platform grows alongside its users' needs rather than drifting away from them.

This part of the book is about meeting those two challenges head-on: scaling and evolving your engineering platform. In chapter 9, we'll explore how to scale platform architecture and operations across teams, clusters, and pipelines. You'll learn practical patterns like event-driven automation, federated control planes, and distributed orchestration that keep things reliable and cost-effective at scale. In chapter 10, the focus shifts to product evolution: how to measure success in ways that resonate with both engineering and the business, how to embed feedback loops, and how to create long-term vision and roadmaps. We'll also look at cultural shifts, site reliability engineering practices, and developer-centric experiences such as internal developer platforms, portals, and intelligent assistants.

By the end of part 3, you'll have a toolkit for building platforms that not only handle growth but also keep getting better over time, scaling like a product, evolving like a service, and learning like a living system. The goal isn't just to keep up with your organization's needs but to anticipate and enable them.

Architecture changes
to support scale

This chapter covers

- Scaling the control plane roles
- Scaling the pipeline orchestration for many clusters
- Scaling the orchestration of control plane services and extensions
- Using events to increase the scale of automation

Scaling an engineering platform isn't just about adding more servers or improving performance numbers—it's about smart, intentional architectural changes that keep teams moving quickly without causing chaos. When the business needs to support more developers or deliver engineering platform capabilities faster, scaling the engineering platform product team is just as important as scaling the technology. We need the right people, roles, and processes in place to effectively expand the platform control plane as well as the services and extensions. And scaling isn't just about speed; it's about cost too. What was efficient for a handful of teams can become brittle or expensive as the number of teams using the platform, or the number of services running on the platform, scales.

We may have started with a single engineering platform product team to establish a good architectural foundation. Still, we won't remain there, at least not at a medium or large business scale, if there are dozens or hundreds of development teams. Multiple domain teams within a product mean domain boundaries. To be effective, these teams need to be sufficiently autonomous. In other words, the independent and self-serve experience we create for the users of our platform is the same experience we need between the teams within the platform as they create, deliver, and operate the platform. How will these teams work together, and how do we decide which boundaries to create?

When you're scaling, event-driven platform releases and contract tests between platform teams and their consumers are game-changers for keeping things reliable and maintaining trust between teams. At the same time, managing a software-defined delivery architecture across a growing number of control planes, each with increasing capabilities, is all about finding that balance between our initial centralized strategy and the distributed patterns that perform better at scale rather than creating a one-size-fits-all solution. It's about creating an architecture that can adapt, making innovation and experimentation possible and affordable. In this chapter, we'll dig into a few key things to keep in mind to keep scaling both sustainable and meaningful.

As shown in figure 9.1, each domain within our platform product can have its own strategies for scaling. When to scale and which areas to scale should be driven by

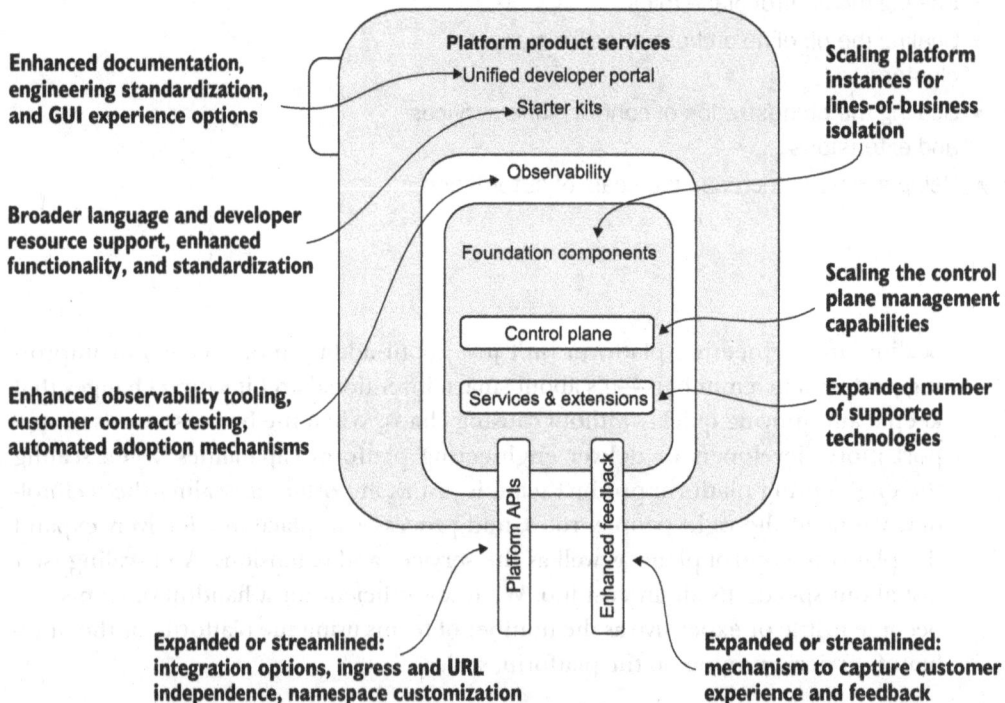

Figure 9.1   Practical examples of evolutionary scaling strategies for engineering platform components

business priorities. For example, suppose your organization is in the financial services industry and needs to improve in both banking and investing software development equally. In that case, we may need to provide isolated replication of the engineering platform to support the strict regulations about separation sooner than we need support for a greater scale of developers in general.

On the other hand, if a top business priority were the ability to expose internal APIs to external, third-party developers, then we would probably prioritize the control plane extensions to enable developers to self-manage integration with our public API gateway before giving developers a way to create custom namespaces.

In this chapter, we cover some effective scaling strategies that commonly arise in the foundational components, which we started in the previous chapters.

9.1 Scaling the control plane roles

We've started with a single cluster instance for each control plane role. This structure can meet the needs of a large segment of business categories and sizes.

However, as organizations scale, the regulatory, contractual, or capacity and locality performance demands will mean we need to scale our engineering platform capabilities. Figure 9.2 visualizes the control plane scaling that happens across two dimensions.

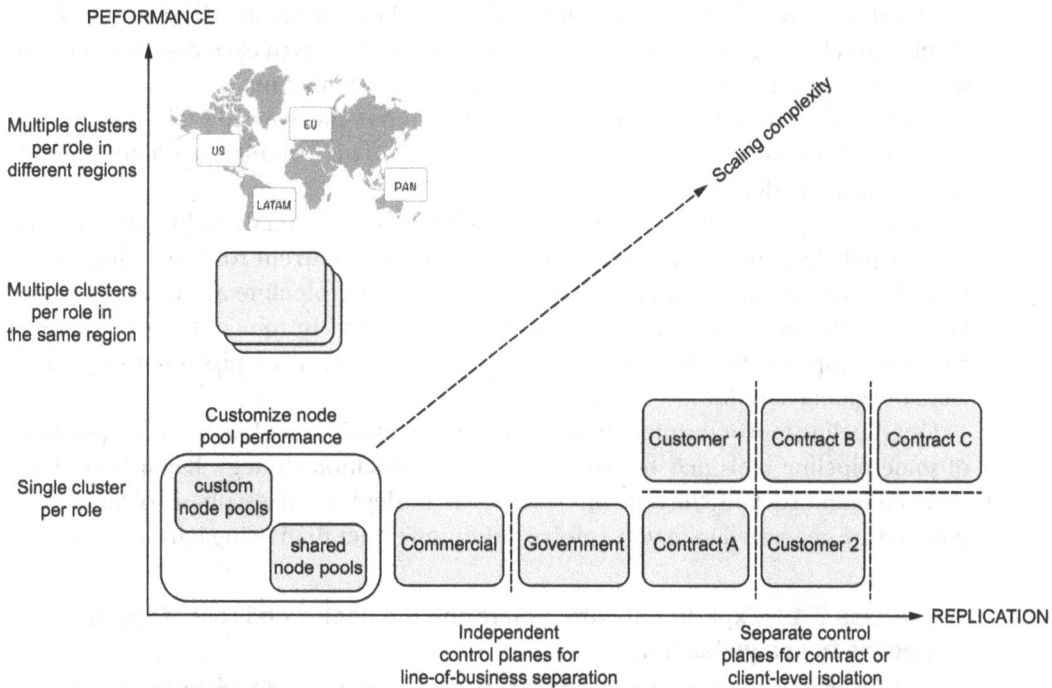

Figure 9.2   Control plane scaling happens along two general axes. Performance requirements for specific control plane roles will grow, requiring node pool customization capabilities or multiple clusters within a single role. Alternatively, legal requirements or contractual decisions mean that we need multiple isolated instances of the same role.

Having multiple clusters within a single role, whether within the same region or across different regions, will require changes to our ingress architecture. This affects the control plane architecture in two ways. First, we will need another layer of load balancing before the normal cluster ingress point. This could be followed by rebalancing services among the clusters or a round-robin or lease-requests traffic routing for all clusters in the same region. For regionally distributed clusters, this usually means georouting capabilities. Second, the self-serve ingress capability we provide to developers now needs to support the ability to simultaneously deploy the same version of a service in multiple clusters, along with customizing traffic flows between clusters or among external technologies provided by the extensions. The dynamic routing capabilities of a service mesh are well-suited to provide this experience.

When we need isolation between lines of business within the organization or at even higher granularity based on market demands of the customers the business serves, this will mean even greater scale in the number of clusters, regardless of the individual load. This could mean complete duplication of the entire platform product definition. Even in this situation, we still recommend maintaining a single product roadmap rather than each line of business creating its platform product definition.

9.1.1 *Dynamic release pipeline*

Where a single, static orchestration pipeline is responsible for more than 20 to 30 clusters (and growing), the release pipeline will start to become brittle. Hardcoding, at the pipeline level, a large and effectively dynamic pool of clusters in each role doesn't scale well. An effective first step is to move to dynamic release pipelines.

At run time, a dynamic release pipeline will generate the workflow that matches the details for all clusters currently defined within a role. This is similar to a "matrix build" in an application development pipeline.

Rather than a fixed list of clusters per role maintained directly within our pipeline code, a globally available data set is created that lists the current roles and clusters per role. The deploy and test steps for any part of a release pipeline are then generated before execution. For example, if there are four clusters in four different regions in a role, our pipeline automation will create the matching release pipeline using values from the global definition.

Our pipeline tool determines how we implement this. The built-in matrix capabilities of some pipeline tools may be part of the implementation strategy. Regardless of the implementation details, the outcome will be that the deploy and test phases of our release pipeline are generated to match a global definition rather than being hard-coded.

> #### Exercise 9.1   Experiment with generating the deploy and test steps of a pipeline from a global list
>
> Imagine that in the Epetech foundation pipelines, we wanted the deploy and test stages of the pipelines to be dynamically created at pipeline runtime. The VPC pipeline is the first pipeline to have a one-to-one relationship with our control plane roles.

We are just using a single sandbox and production cluster for exercise purposes, but let's assume we have a complete set of roles that include development and quality assurance in our testing environments. This exercise is an experiment; you could work out a complete solution or just list the capabilities needed in a solution. While pipelines and team-specific ownership can help decentralize certain aspects, an increased number of pipelines can also introduce side effects, such as more time spent by engineers maintaining CI/CD definitions, dealing with merge conflicts, or resolving transient test failures that block progress.

If we created a globally available definition of our test roles, what information would we need to generate that part of our pipeline successfully?

```
test:
  filter: "*on-push-main"          ◄——  We will likely need a filter value that indicates how
  deploy:                    ◄——         the deploy and test steps are triggered. A git push
    - platform-dev                         triggers CI and test environment deployments,
    - platform-qa                          whereas the release pipeline is based on a git tag.
  roles:
    platform-dev:                          We might include a list of all the
      deploy:                              roles we will want to deploy through
        - platform-dev-i01-aws-us-west-2   the push-triggered pipeline.
        - platform-dev-i01-aws-eu-west-1
      instances:                   ◄——     For each role, we will need
        platform-dev-i01-aws-us-west-2: ◄——  to provide some values.
          aws_region: us-west-2
          aws_account_id: '10100000000'    We will need some way
        platform-dev-i01-aws-eu-west-1:    to specify the clusters
          aws_region: eu-west-1    ◄——     that are part of the role.
          aws_account_id: '10100000000'
    platform-qa:                           It's likely we will need to be able
      deploy:                              to provide cluster-specific
        - platform-qa-i01-aws-us-west-2    values for each cluster in a role.
        - platform-qa-i01-aws-eu-west-1
      instances:
        platform-qa-i01-aws-us-west-2:
          aws_region: us-west-2
          aws_account_id: '10100000000'
        platform-qa-i01-aws-eu-west-1:
          aws_region: eu-west-1
          aws_account_id: '10100000000'
```

Looking at our existing VPC pipeline, everything up to the sbx deployment would be the same, no matter how many clusters we were managing. Ignore the nightly testing for the moment. How could we use the CircleCI-generated pipeline capability (https://circleci.com/docs/dynamic-config/) to generate a deploy and test pipeline for our testing environments after the static analysis portion is complete?

Generating a pipeline will require code, but depending on the amount of flexibility needed and how broadly we want to use the automation, a solution could be as simple as a bash script that populates a template or a more feature-rich CLI. You can look at one CircleCI solution example here: https://github.com/ThoughtWorks-DPS/circlepipe.

> **NOTE** If the pipeline tool we are using does not support dynamic pipelines, this limitation should be addressed before scaling our clusters beyond the limits of a static pipeline. That means using a different tool or stepping up to even more scalable cluster provisioning strategies. Imagine a cluster-engine made up of a dedicated Elastic Kubernetes Service (EKS) instance that had elements of a crossplane running sufficiently to support provisioning the equivalent of our control-plane-base configuration. Now our pipeline could have a step that dynamically generates the set of custom resource requests that match each cluster within a role, rather than individual pipeline steps.

Even this strategy has limitations. While it works well for ongoing scale in the number of supported regions within a role, it is not necessarily suited to other scale needs. Looking back at figure 9.2, if our primary scaling need for cluster roles is *customer* or *contract* isolation, this means that it will be the production role that scales far more than the other roles. And in that situation, the demand for those additional clusters originates within the development teams using the platform. Therefore, we will need to provide a self-service experience for those teams to trigger new control plane instances that are nonetheless still managed through our general cluster health processes.

We are not saying that a low-scale technique will simply be unable to create a higher scale. It is just that there will be consequences. If you stick with a static pipeline while your regional footprint keeps growing, eventually, operational and evolutionary changes to your control plane and pipeline will take longer and become more error-prone, even if you catch problems early. A simpler, low-complexity approach might be much cheaper to set up, but if it's at scale, it makes routine operations five times slower—then you've lost whatever gain you hoped to achieve.

9.2   *Scaling the orchestration of control plane services and extensions*

At Epetech, we started out using straightforward deploy and test pipelines to manage services and extensions, as shown in figure 9.3. While this worked well when there were just a handful of clusters, this approach is showing cracks as the number of clusters grows. Longer deployment times, pipeline bottlenecks, and challenges with performing routine upgrades on multiple services or extensions at once make it clear we need a better strategy. We can solve the challenges as shown in figure 9.4, with multiple simultaneous changes by breaking out each service into its lifecycle pipeline.

When each pipeline has to reach out to each cluster to manage the service, as the number of clusters grows, managing these pipelines becomes increasingly challenging. As discussed in section 9.1, dynamically generating the release portion of the pipeline could improve the pipeline management challenges. However, at the individual service

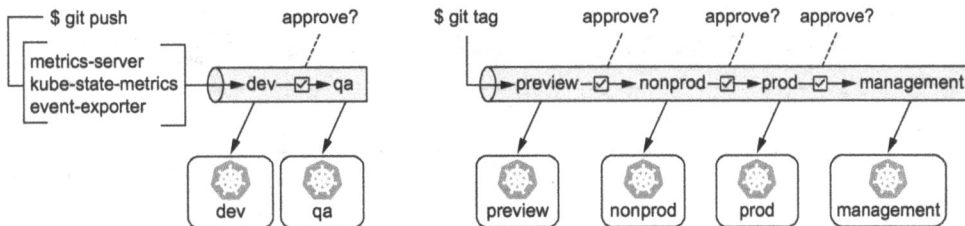

Figure 9.3   At first, we deploy and test all our services through a single pipeline. We do the same with extensions.

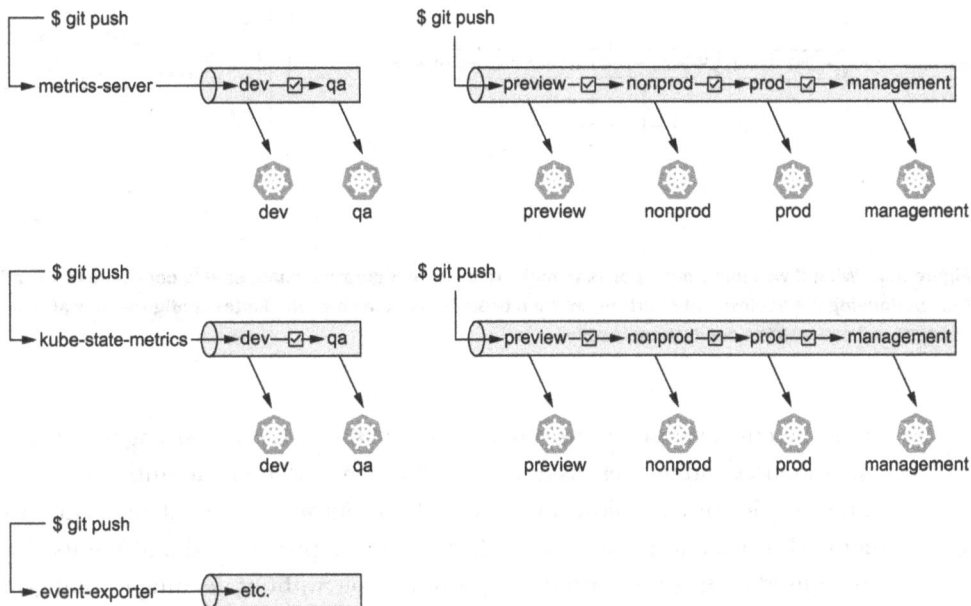

Figure 9.4   Dedicated software lifecycle pipelines for each service and extension is one of the first modifications we can make to improve the health of our routine operational activities as the scale grows. While necessary, this will aggravate the problems that the scale has created.

or extension level, the scale of the problem is growing faster than just the number of clusters. For our control-plane-base pipeline, adding a region would mean adding three more clusters (one each for preview, nonproduction, and production). But with three services, as we have at the moment, that means nine additional service deployments to manage. There will be more than just three services in a real-world setting. What we need is a way to limit the scope within an individual service pipeline to just the number of roles we define in our platform, without needing to modify these software lifecycle pipelines, as shown in figure 9.5, every time clusters are added or removed.

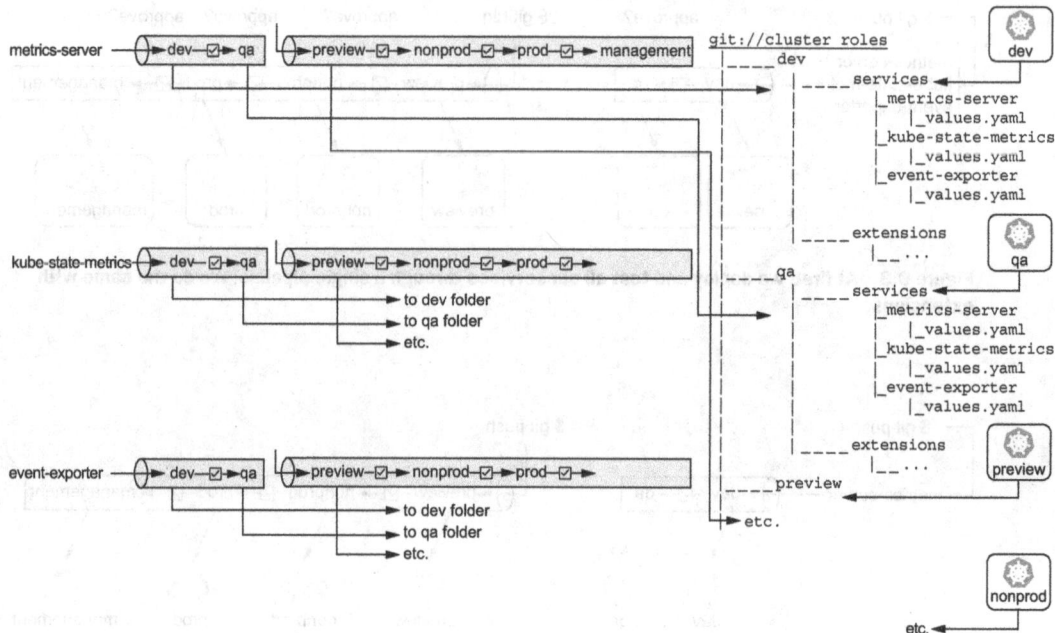

Figure 9.5   What if we modify our pipeline to make release configuration changes to a code repository rather than performing the deployment? Further, we then deploy a service on each cluster configured to watch for those changes and execute the deployment locally.

With the effective use of our observability tooling, we can easily aggregate all deployment metrics and test results into a single view and a single definition for monitoring. A new service or extension can be added without needing to change cluster configuration directly, and likewise, new clusters can be provisioned and the local deployer configured to integrate with the appropriate role without needing to change any individual service or extension pipeline.

A centralized datastore for observability data is a requirement for this distributed management architecture. But that is already a core requirement for an engineering platform in general.

We recommend making all three of these changes so

- There are individual lifecycle pipelines for each service or extension that make updates to a central configuration definition for each cluster role.
- Clusters individually pull their configuration from the central definition and perform the deployment and health tests locally.
- There is central visibility for the status, monitoring, and alerting of this distributed architecture built on top of our observability tools, deployed by the service, extension, or distributed deployer lifecycle pipelines.

We can now effectively scale both the number of services and extensions being managed and the number of clusters where these are deployed without a proportionate increase in operational time. By moving the deployment activity out of a centralized location and distributing the workload to the cluster where the deployment is occurring, the cumulative deployment event is much quicker, the cross-cluster effect from individual deployment problems is reduced, and we can create a loose boundary between the lifecycle of a cluster and the administrative services that run on it.

You will no doubt recognize the pattern of the deployment engine running independent of the CI/CD pipeline, though triggered by the same events. Within IT or DevOps circles, GitOps is the popular term now associated with what is a long-established software delivery approach. ArgoCD (https://argoproj.github.io/cd/) and Flux (https://fluxcd.io) are the most popular deployers for Kubernetes resources. As part of a scaled cluster-level configuration, we recommend running this service without all the GUI and other overhead. Flux has consistently been a very small and fast agent and has the added benefit of having built-in support for defining cluster-specific values to enable a shared role deployment configuration, and it can also easily incorporate cluster-specific values from the cluster at deploy time. But with some added setup, you can do the same with Argo, and Argo has recently introduced a core version that is just the deploy engine.

9.2.1 Scaling the creation of OpenID Connect Assumable Roles

In the earlier discussions, we used a simple Terraform resource as part of our extensions pipeline to create the OpenID Connect assumable roles needed by our extensions. This is fine as a simple starting point, but it too will not scale well. Although we aren't going to cover an example or exercise in this book, the use of an operator-based provisioner is a practical next step for scaling these roles. With an administrative operator deployed, we could include a role resource request in our external-dns deployment (for example) to define and provision the role without the need for a dedicated Terraform workflow. Having a running API manage these resources also provides a much less complex upgrade path at scale.

9.3 Scaling through platform event streaming

In section 9.2, the distributed cluster configuration process we describe makes use of an important scaling architecture pattern. We deploy a service to each cluster that is configured to watch for changes in a specific git repository and perform a Helm upgrade in response. This is a simple example of an event-driven architecture. GitHub provides an event-stream publisher in the form of a webhook. You can configure a subscriber application to listen for any of the events published by the webhook. Tools like Flux and ArgoCD have a subscriber capability for watching git repositories. They can be configured to respond to a variety of common git events, such as pushing a change or applying a tag.

Event-driven architectures play a critical role in scaling our engineering platform in much the same way they do for distributed services software in general and can afford the same type of benefits:

- *Decoupling services*—A service only needs to know about the events it is interested in, allowing for independent development and deployment.
- *Asynchronous scalability*—By processing events asynchronously, a system can more easily scale to handle high volumes of data by distributing processing across multiple services.
- *Resilience*—If one service fails, other services can still operate as long as the event stream remains functional. It is easier to configure a graceful response to a dependent service failure among loosely coupled services.
- *Agility*—New capabilities can be added or modified without significantly affecting existing ones by simply publishing or subscribing to relevant events.
- *Real-time updates*—Near-real-time data updates are enabled across a distributed system by allowing services to respond to events as they occur.
- *Simplified integration*—Seamless integration with external systems is possible by publishing and consuming events from any source.

As the scale of developers on an engineering platform grows, more of the scaling and coordinating strategies used in general software architecture become valuable and essential considerations in our platform architecture.

The strategies we discussed in section 9.2 are effective for scaling the performance of the cluster configuration. But as the number and features of services and extensions grow, there will be a growing need for varying degrees of coordination between the platform team and users of the platform during upgrades and technology replacement. As a platform engineering team, when we have hundreds or thousands of teams deploying to our platform, how can we better scale coordination activities related to upgrades and changes to foundational components of our platform?

While the majority of changes amount to patches or minor revisions, where the combination of CI and preview environment testing can be counted on to expose most problems that the platform team can deal with alone, throughout each year, there will still be releases that require a change on the part of platform users.

Kubernetes itself is a good example. Kubernetes has an evolutionary cycle of three minor revisions per year. The project follows a process of deprecation with its APIs, where each release will deprecate or promote APIs using a standard schema. Similar principles apply to other container services such as AWS Fargate, which also evolve with new features, configuration changes, and occasional deprecations. Understanding this lifecycle is important so that platform teams can anticipate changes and plan upgrades or migrations accordingly.

Coming back to Kubernetes, the API schema looks like this:

```
apiVersion: admissionregistration.k8s.io/v1alpha1
Kind: MutatingWebHook

apiVersion: apps/v1
Kind: Deployment
```

When an API is promoted, say in the previous example, the "admission registration" API goes from v1alpha1 to v1beta1—the v1alpha1 will be marked as deprecated in the next release. Two cycles later, it will be removed entirely. During the two cycles before the v1alpha1 API is removed, it will still be usable to provide a period of backward compatibility. But anything deployed to the cluster using the v1alph1 version will have to be updated to the newer v1beta1 by the removal time.

Suppose at any time there is a Kubernetes upgrade. In that case, an event is published, we could set up a service to catch that event, check the Kubernetes API for any changed apiVersions, and scan everything running in the cluster to see which services are using outdated versions. That would give us a clear list of deployments that need updating, within the next eight months, to avoid breaking when the next Kubernetes release rolls out.

Now, if we also required every deployment to include team information in its metadata, our *upgrade watcher* service could take things a step further. It could automatically create Jira issues for each team, detailing exactly what's changing in the apiVersion, including links to recommended upgrade strategies. That way, teams would get a heads-up with clear next steps, making the upgrade process much smoother.

Let's look at how to design and implement an event-driven release process that can be consumed and used by both the platform team and the platform users.

9.3.1 release-api

Our goal should be to reduce friction between the platform and application teams by providing a mechanism to iterate and evolve without constantly interfering with each other. In figure 9.6, we have a sample of events as we roll out a new version of Service Mesh.

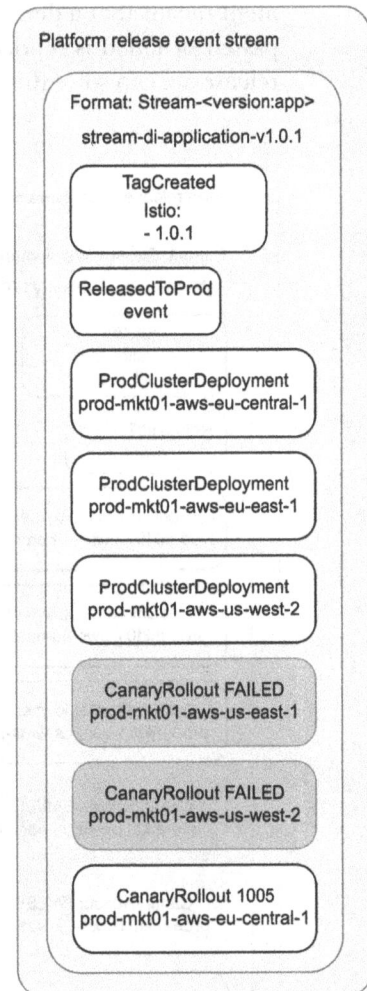

Platform release event stream

Format: Stream-<version:app>

stream-di-application-v1.0.1

TagCreated
Istio:
- 1.0.1

ReleasedToProd
event

ProdClusterDeployment
prod-mkt01-aws-eu-central-1

ProdClusterDeployment
prod-mkt01-aws-eu-east-1

ProdClusterDeployment
prod-mkt01-aws-us-west-2

CanaryRollout FAILED
prod-mkt01-aws-us-east-1

CanaryRollout FAILED
prod-mkt01-aws-us-west-2

CanaryRollout 1005
prod-mkt01-aws-eu-central-1

Figure 9.6   A sample of events that represent the rollout of a new version of Istio to our engineering platform

In this example, we assume that the platform comprises several Kubernetes clusters spanning three regions. When we release the update to production, each participating cluster will attempt its rollout of the Istio upgrade. The progress of these events could be represented as events. Events should be kept simple and lightweight by asking a few simple questions like

1 Where did it happen?
2 What happened?
3 Optional: pass/fail

Pass/fail is optional because some events exist for "something" that happened, but there is no state other than "It happened." For example, the triggering of a deployment means that a deployment was attempted. The state of whether that deployment passed or failed is reported back in a unique event later on. Figure 9.7 shows how a release-api can solve this.

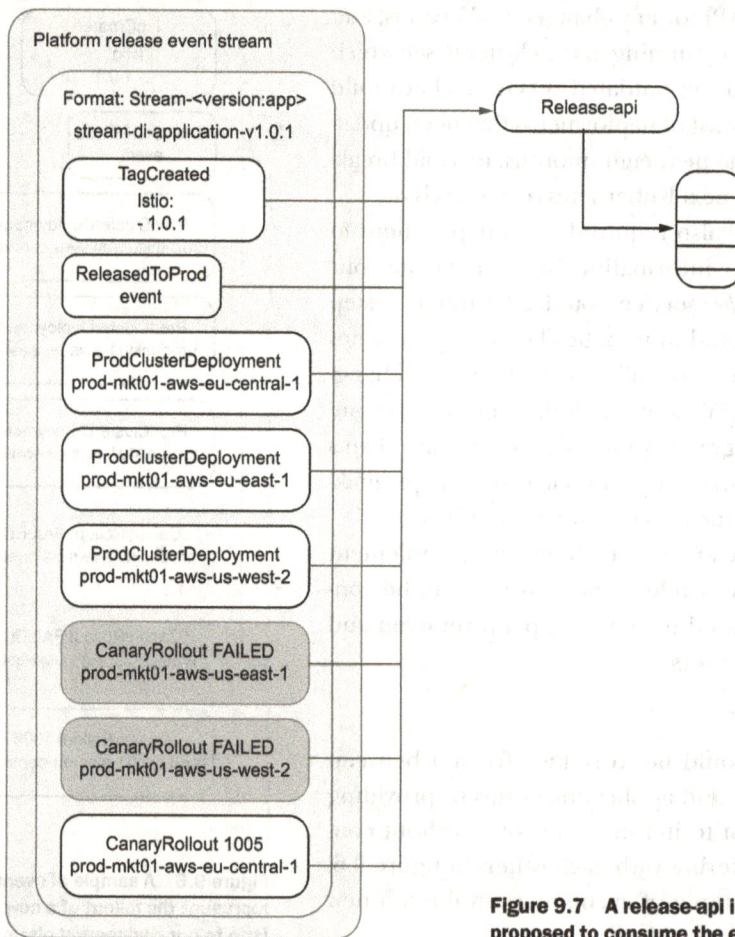

Figure 9.7   A release-api is proposed to consume the events.

When we look at these example events, they could be thought of as an immutable event stream. A release api could be configured to watch these events and take action based on the events that occur. However, the most complex aspect is that the events come from many different places.

9.3.2 Adapter pattern

In figure 9.7, the *TagCreated* event is coming from GitHub. The *ReleasedToProd* event may come from a CircleCI workflow. The *ProdClusterDeployment* event could come from a workflow's CircleCI step or the deployments API (via an admission controller) in the Kubernetes cluster. The *CanaryRollout* event would come from our canary controller (i.e., ArgoCD or Flagger).

Our events come from many places in many different formats. Figure 9.8 shows the release-API expanded to show the specific resources you might want to consider.

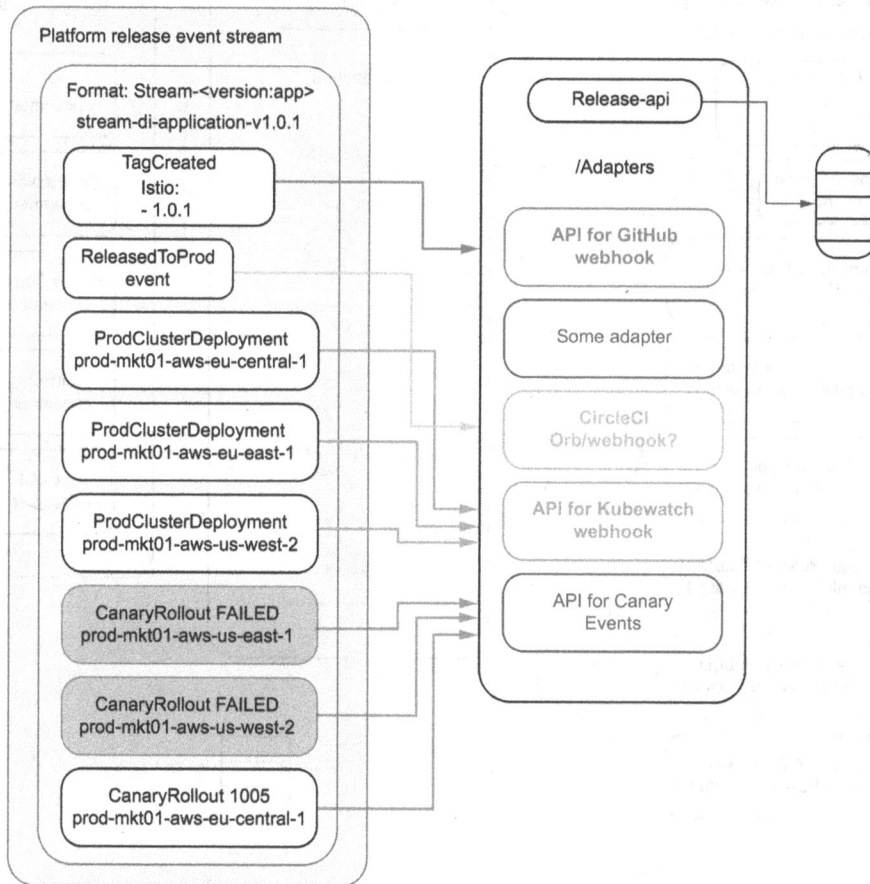

Figure 9.8 To consume the events in our release-api, we'll need a pattern from the many systems that produce them.

Each type of event will require an adapter to consume the events and convert them into our standardized event model. While this may sound complex initially, keep in mind that monitoring our enterprise systems requires many different types of instrumentation and agents. This pattern is something we already do to aggregate data. We are just focusing on event data and getting events into a stream to which any API could subscribe. By separating the publishing of the events from the consuming, we greatly simplify creating a successful event collection process. This dual benefit has a massive time-saving effect, creating a flexible and repeatable pattern for adding new systems into the service event stream. Figure 9.9 shows the relationship between this event stream and consumer plugins for standard services like JIRA, ServiceNow, and CircleCI.

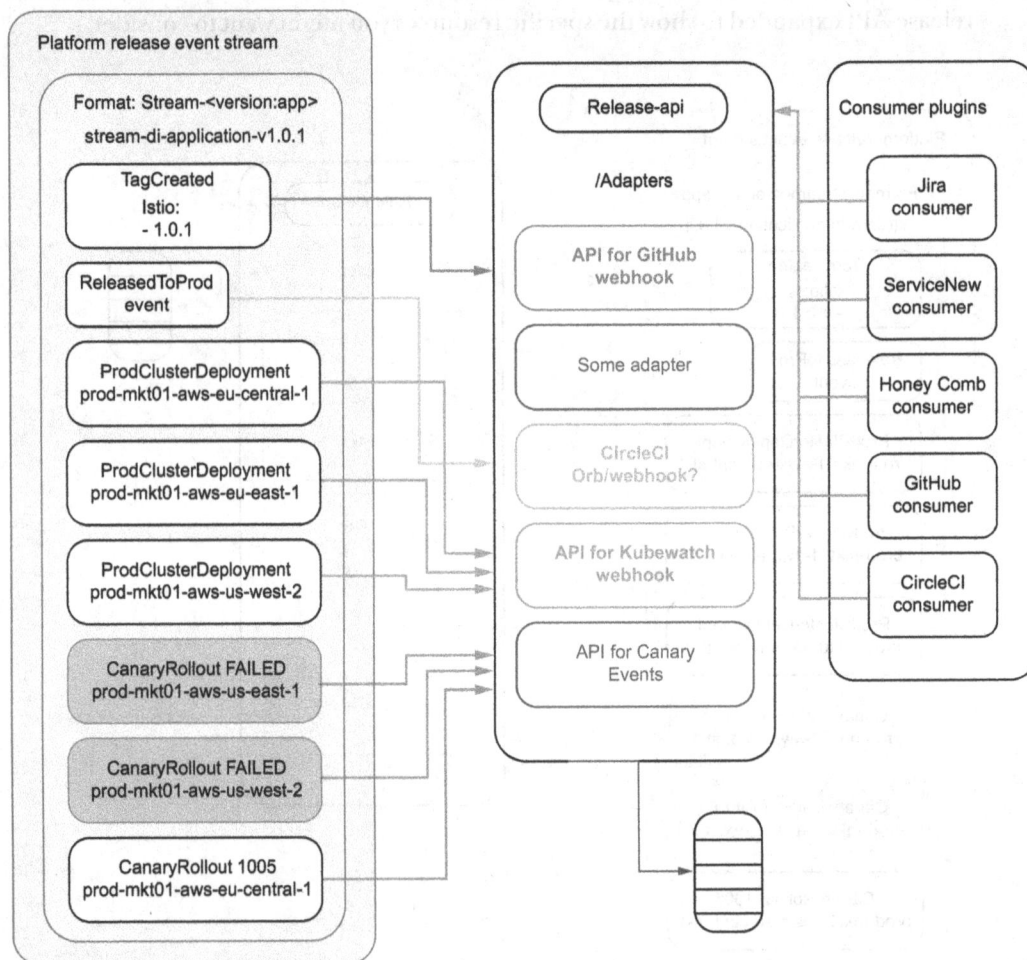

Figure 9.9   With a consolidated consumption model, consumers can now be developed to talk to the release API and do something with the data. Examples of consumer plugins will be services used for issue tracking, configuration management database, source control, and CI/CD.

These are custom consumers used to enhance the capabilities of our platform and create more effective and scalable platform lifecycle patterns, and they are not meant to replace the normal integrations for these tools or services.

With a standard model for event formats, regardless of the source, enabling consumers to provide enhanced capabilities is now very easy. This opportunity is not limited to just the platform product teams. The platform team can provide starter kits for building a consumer service that pulls an event stream from the release API. Application teams can use the kits to create communities around the events that matter most to them.

Let's look at some of the more common event types that can be used to create an improved experience for both platform maintainers and users.

9.3.3 *Adapter pattern: Issue tracking*

Our first example is issue management (see figure 9.10). Imagine the platform team has published an event that signals a new release of Kubernetes that will be going out soon. This could be done by publishing an event that says the preview environment has received a new version of Kubernetes, and the standard policy is that the preview environment is updated 1 month before production environments are, giving teams time to review their application health on the new version.

Now that we have the release-API, instead of publishing a company-wide Slack announcement that nobody will read, we can have a Jira consumer that creates a new issue on our application team's work board with an urgency level of medium. Figure 9.11 shows the platform team publishing the events.

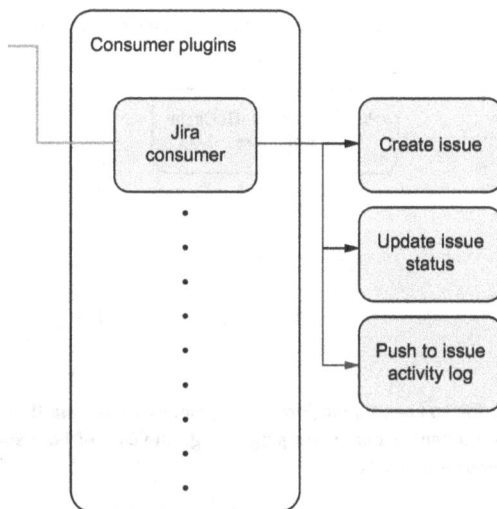

Figure 9.10 An issue-tracking consumer might create and manage problems in response to specific events.

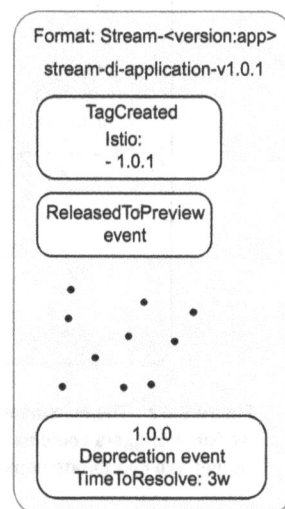

Figure 9.11 The platform team will continue to publish events regarding the state of the upgrade, including deprecation notices.

As the time to production release grows closer, if the task isn't completed, the consumer can update the task urgency to ensure our application team prioritizes verifying their service on the new version simply by consuming the deprecation events and updating the upstream task statuses.

9.3.4   *Adapter pattern: CI hooks*

Let's continue with our platform upgrade example. A consumer could also be created to respond to all of these routine upgrade announcements, most of which will not require developers to make any changes but will need to be verified.

Figure 9.12 illustrates how application teams can enhance collaboration with platform consumers by exposing inbound webhooks from their CI systems of choice and opting into a consumer-driven model for deployment events.

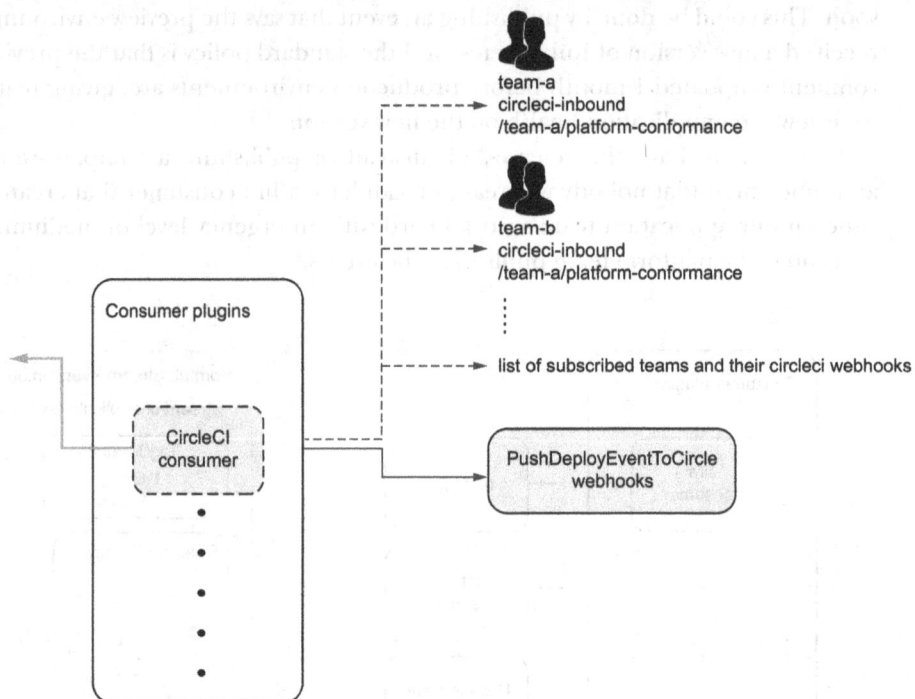

team-a
circleci-inbound
/team-a/platform-conformance

team-b
circleci-inbound
/team-a/platform-conformance

list of subscribed teams and their circleci webhooks

Consumer plugins

CircleCI
consumer

PushDeployEventToCircle
webhooks

Figure 9.12 The consumer API can subscribe to specific platform deployment events, and then inbound workflow triggers could be created, allowing a central consumer plugin (e.g., the CircleCI consumer) to trigger and coordinate deployment workflows seamlessly.

Any time a cluster component upgrade occurs in the preview environment, users' conformance test pipelines could trigger to deploy and test the current version to reveal any conflicts created by the change. If all tests are passed, nobody needs to do anything! The consumer API could even find and close the Jira ticket we talked about earlier. If there are errors, it could add relevant logs and pipeline links to the Jira ticket to make responding and fixing faster.

This is often the case with the upgrade of platform services. Because technologies like Istio and Kubernetes make considerable efforts to provide backward compatibility and are highly selective with the graduation and deprecation of APIs, more often than not, upgrading our core services is a nonevent. But because of the massive uncertainty in the absence of a system like this, our organization, before our release-API, had to manually check with every single team before moving forward with the changes. This also meant that changes had to be scheduled way in advance, and the schedule would be pushed back if any interruptions or new priorities emerged.

Where this sort of event-driven conformance testing is made an engineering practice requirement, then the platform product could extend the automation a step further. Figure 9.13 illustrates how a platform team can use automation to monitor Jira upgrade-notice problems and track their resolution status.

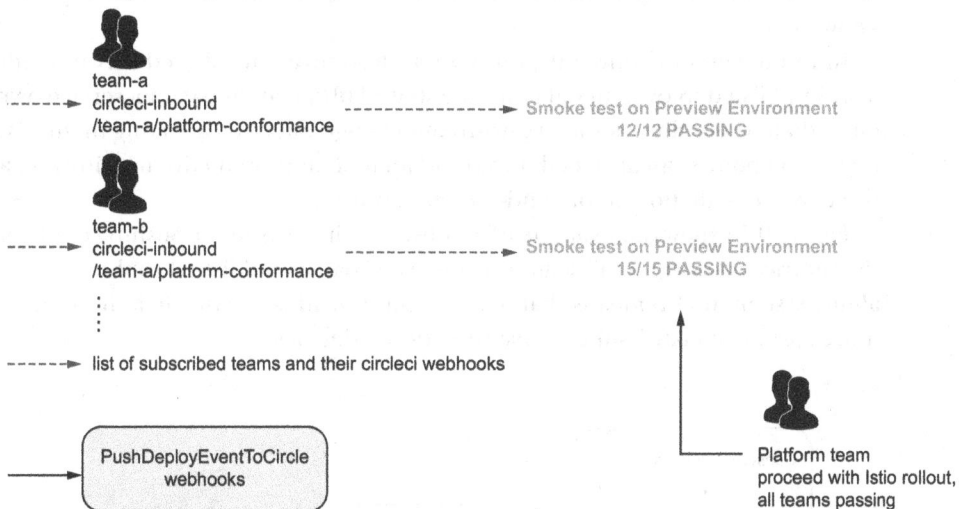

team-a
circleci-inbound
/team-a/platform-conformance
Smoke test on Preview Environment
12/12 PASSING

team-b
circleci-inbound
/team-a/platform-conformance
Smoke test on Preview Environment
15/15 PASSING

list of subscribed teams and their circleci webhooks

PushDeployEventToCircle webhooks

Platform team
proceed with Istio rollout,
all teams passing

Figure 9.13 The platform team could create a consumer API that watched for the creation of all the Jira upgrade-notice problems and whether they were all auto-closed after successful conformance tests. They could proceed with greater confidence in releasing the changes to production or have a detailed list of the affected services and the problems found.

This is a very effective replication of human behavior. Even when people do respond to the global chat messages about checking their service in preview against a new cluster component upgrade, almost universally, they will only look at the monitors to see if anything is red or run automated tests if they have them. Automating that response guarantees fast and universal coverage. This doesn't mean that every team will have bulletproof testing or that automated testing is ever 100% accurate, but it does mean that what can be done will be done rapidly. That covers most of the changes, and the overall effect is to maintain a higher operational maintenance velocity.

9.3.5   *Adapter pattern: Observability hooks*

An observability consumer could process and publish all of these new kinds of events into the observability tool (data logs), including application deployment events (`PublishAppDeployed`), rollout statuses (`PublishRolloutStatus`), and dependency updates (`PublishDependencyUpdates`). All of these events can then be added to the normal observability indicators, providing teams with better real-time visibility into the operational health and performance of their systems.

Beyond improving situational awareness, these hooks create a stronger link between delivery workflows and operational insights. By automatically publishing deployment-related events, platform teams ensure that any change, whether it's a major rollout or a minor dependency bump, becomes part of the observable history of the system. This traceability helps correlate performance changes, error spikes, or downstream failures to specific deployments without relying solely on manual incident reports or tribal knowledge.

In multiteam environments, this pattern also promotes shared accountability. If all teams publish deployment data into the shared observability system, service owners can immediately identify whether an upstream change might be affecting them. Over time, these data points can also feed into trend analysis and predictive monitoring, allowing proactive remediation before end-user effects occur.

Figure 9.14 shows an example of an observability consumer pushing deployments to the metrics platform. If all team release event data is published to the general observability system, it also means that teams' own individual service health monitoring can more easily correlate issues against their dependencies.

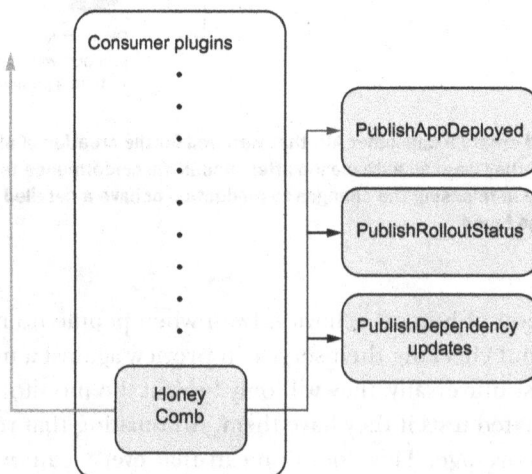

Figure 9.14   Example of an observability consumer that pushes deployment events to our metrics platform

Figure 9.15 demonstrates the value of this correlation. Here, Team A experiences a sudden increase in HTTP errors. Because the observability platform already has a deployment event recorded from Team B (version 1.2 release), the relationship between the upstream change and the downstream error spike becomes obvious. This not only speeds up root cause analysis but also reduces the number of unnecessary escalations and handoffs between teams.

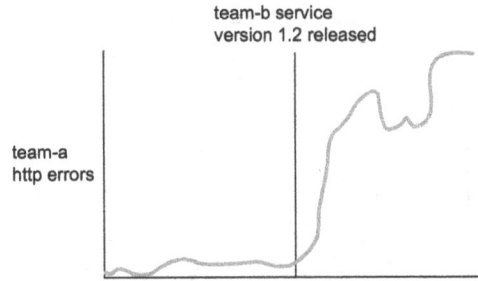

Figure 9.15 Team A's dashboards can show events from internal services on which they depend and make it easier to diagnose remote changes that affect their services.

From a practical standpoint, this adapter pattern can be implemented using standard tooling in modern engineering platforms. For example, OpenTelemetry can instrument services to emit deployment and dependency update events, while systems like Prometheus, Datadog, and New Relic ingest these events alongside performance metrics. In Kubernetes environments, tools like Argo CD or Flux can trigger event hooks on deployments, which are then pushed to these observability platforms for correlation and dashboarding. This ensures the connection between delivery pipelines and operational insights is automated, consistent, and visible across the organization.

9.3.6 *Adapter pattern: Configuration management database and audit gathering*

Consumer APIs can be created to automate audit-gathering requirements. For example, assume our organization uses ServiceNow to track change management data that includes the current list of all services running and versions, as shown in figure 9.16. From an audit perspective, as illustrated in figure 9.17, we can configure a ServiceNow consumer that pushes all new release events to ServiceNow.

We can then consume the events in our ServiceNow configuration management database (CMBD) API and portal. In most CMDB systems, the expectation is that we have a catalog of the deployed services and the information that explains what they are, who owns them, and what they are connected to. In our case, all of this information is already handy in the deployment event (because it was necessary to create the deployment anyway), so we can readily forward the deployment event information to our CMDB in ServiceNow, allowing ServiceNow to update its application map.

In section 9.3, we have covered several situations in which deployment event data can be used to automate necessary but laborious processes. But this is just one kind of event. There are all manner of events being generated or that can be captured. Becoming confident in building solid event-driven capabilities is a necessary skill for platform engineers.

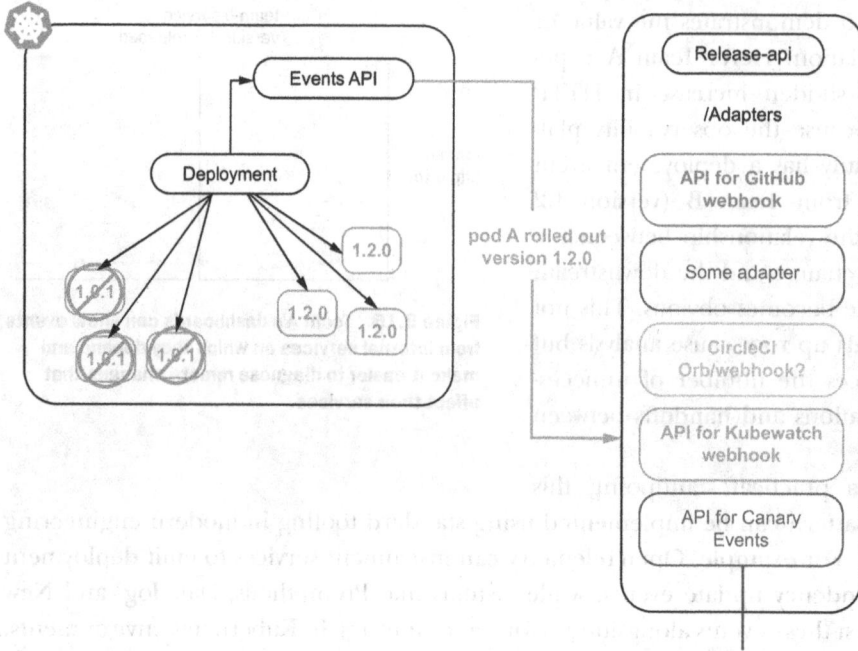

Figure 9.16   If events are being propagated from our Kubernetes cluster to the release API, then all deployments will generate events. Every single pod event is published. So, when one of the 1.0.1 pods is terminated, that is a unique event. And when one of the 1.2.0 pods successfully deploys and starts taking traffic, that is also an event.

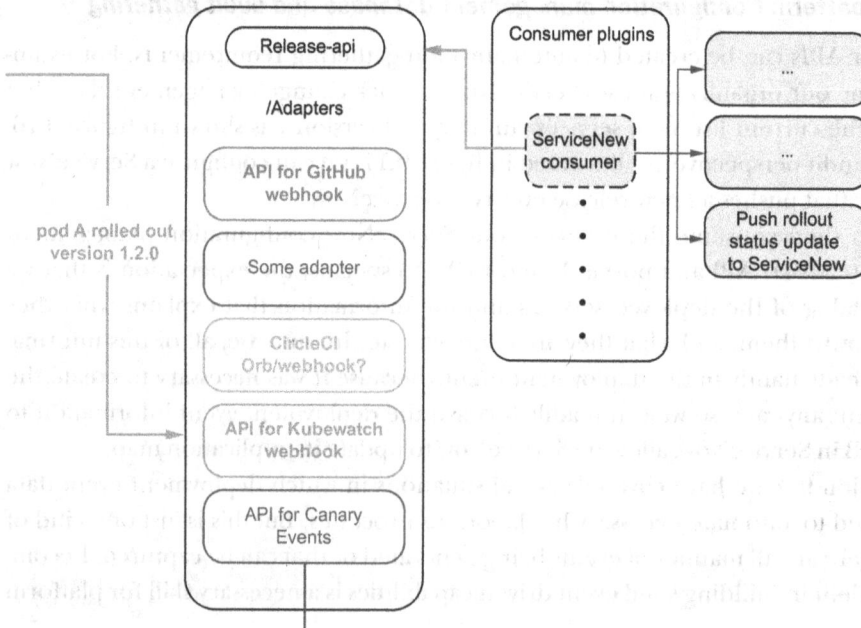

Figure 9.17
The event for Pod A is sent to the release-api, where our ServiceNow consumer consumes it. Our consumer pushes the update to ServiceNow's configuration management database.

Summary

- Scaling an engineering platform requires intentional architectural changes, not just adding servers.
- Cost assessments, including the cost of delay, are critical to justifying investments in scaling platform capabilities.
- Effective scaling includes aligning platform team structures, roles, and processes to match evolving business needs.
- Establishing domain boundaries and autonomy between teams enables efficient collaboration and scalability.
- Event-driven release architectures enhance reliability and trust by reducing friction between platform and consumer teams.
- Dynamic pipelines that adapt to the number and configuration of clusters improve deployment efficiency at scale.
- Lifecycle pipelines for individual services and extensions improve release quality and remove bottlenecks.
- Distributed deployers at the cluster level reduce centralized orchestration overhead and enable quicker rollouts while reducing blast radius from many kinds of common errors.
- Platform APIs should be the foundation for all capabilities, ensuring seamless integration and extensibility.
- Scaling strategies should prioritize the platform user/consumer experience, reducing wasted time and friction.
- Developer portals like Backstage improve discoverability but must align with API-first principles to avoid creating support burdens.
- Event-driven architectures are a key skill in scaling engineering platforms.
- Adapter patterns standardize data flow across diverse systems, simplifying integration and reducing complexity.
- Observability integrations allow real-time tracking of deployment events, enhancing system visibility and troubleshooting.
- Event-driven notifications ensure platform consumers stay informed about upgrades and deprecations, reducing coordination overhead.
- Integrating release events into CMDBs and audit systems supports compliance while maintaining lightweight, scalable architectures.

Platform product evolution

This chapter covers

- Measuring the success of your platform organization
- How platforms as products are a differentiation in your platform evolution
- Intelligent assistants
- Internal developer platforms and products

In the dynamic world of software development, organizations are continually seeking ways to accelerate delivery, improve reliability, and enhance the developer experience. As companies grow and their software ecosystems become more complex, an effective platform strategy becomes critical. This chapter explores the evolution of platform products, focusing on how treating platforms as products can be a differentiator and how measuring success, embracing cultural shifts, and using modern tools and methodologies can drive organizational success.

We'll revisit our favorite company, Epetech, which we've discussed throughout the book, to illustrate these concepts in practice. Epetech's journey from monolithic applications to a microservices architecture highlights the challenges and opportunities in evolving platform products, providing practical insights into how organizations can navigate similar transitions.

10.1 Measuring the success of your platform organization

Now that you have embarked on a platform journey and have started seeing some improvements, it is essential to measure your progress. As we have discussed, evolving your platform to the next level almost always requires knowing your progress.

10.1.1 The platform value model

For any platform initiative to be successful, it's essential to establish metrics that align with organizational goals. Measuring the success of your platform implementation provides insights into its effectiveness, adoption, and areas for improvement. It ensures that the platform delivers value to its users, primarily the developers and operators, and, ultimately, the business by facilitating better decision-making and strategic planning.

Key metrics to consider include waste and friction indicators (e.g., lead time for changes, deployment frequency, developer wait time), product adoption and engagement (e.g., percentage of teams using the platform's golden paths, active daily/weekly users), buy versus build efficiency gains (e.g., cost savings or time saved by using third-party services instead of custom builds), system reliability and observability coverage (e.g., mean time to detect/resolve incidents, percentage of services with full telemetry), and autonomy measures (e.g., number of self-service deployments without platform team intervention). These metrics, when tracked over time, provide a tangible view of platform value and highlight opportunities for optimization.

As discussed in part 1, the platform value model offers a framework for quantifying the value delivered by a platform. It focuses on several key areas. Figure 10.1 shows the

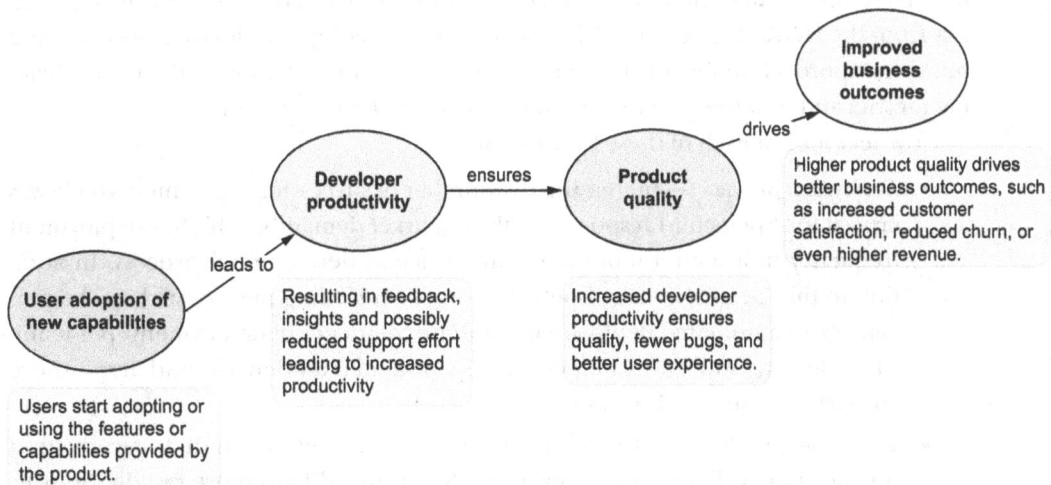

Figure 10.1 Quantifying the value across multiple levels, from building the capabilities to addressing the business outcomes

evolution of value quantification as we translate the engineering capabilities to business outcomes.

Now let us look at the relevant metrics for each of these steps in the value articulation process:

- *User adoption metrics*—Tracking the number of teams and developers using the platform helps gauge its relevance and usefulness. High adoption rates often correlate with increased efficiency and satisfaction among users.
- *Productivity metrics*—Measure improvements in four key DORA metrics, highlighting the platform's effect on operational efficiency. These metrics reflect how quickly and reliably the organization can deliver customer value.
- *Quality metrics*—Assessing the reduction in incidents, failures, and defects provides insights into the platform's role in enhancing system stability and reliability. Improved quality metrics can lead to better customer satisfaction and trust.
- *Business metrics*—Evaluating the effect on revenue, customer satisfaction, and market competitiveness directly connects the platform's performance to organizational success. These metrics demonstrate how the platform contributes to achieving strategic business objectives.

Organizations can make data-driven decisions to optimize platform strategies by integrating these metrics into regular reporting and analysis.

10.1.2 Epetech's approach to measurement

At Epetech, the platform team recognized the importance of measuring success early in their platform evolution journey. They established key performance indicators aligned with the platform value model to ensure their efforts were focused and effective. They also aligned their key performance indicators (KPIs) with the four key metrics from the DORA framework while incorporating leading metrics to provide a more proactive approach to performance improvement. Figure 10.2 shows the typical leading metrics and how they are related to the popular DORA four key metrics.

Now, let's look at each of these four metrics:

- *Deployment frequency*—Increasing the number of successful deployments daily was crucial for Epetech to respond swiftly to market demands. A higher deployment frequency indicated a more agile and efficient development process. In addition to this lagging metric, Epetech monitored leading metrics such as the percentage of automated deployments and the frequency of deployments per team. These leading indicators helped identify potential bottlenecks and areas where automation could be further enhanced.
- *Lead time for changes*—Reducing the time from code commit to production release allowed Epetech to deliver new features and fixes more rapidly. Shorter lead times improved competitiveness and customer satisfaction. As a leading metric, it tracked the time spent in different deployment pipeline stages, such as

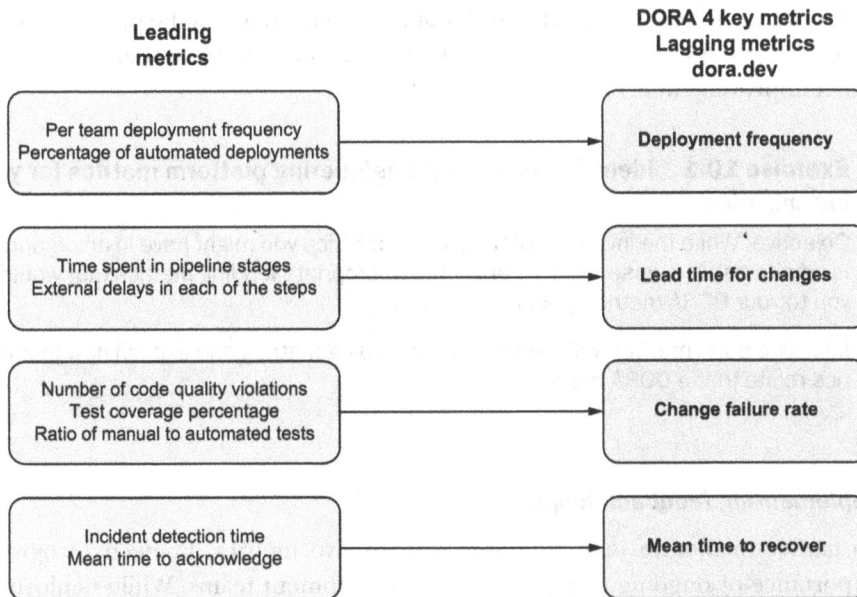

Figure 10.2   Key leading metrics used by Epetech to understand and use the DORA lagging metrics

build, test, and approval. Epetech could identify specific stages causing delays by analyzing these breakdowns and implementing targeted optimizations.

- *Change failure rate*—Lowering the percentage of deployments that failed in production was essential for maintaining system reliability. A lower change failure rate reduced downtime and enhanced user trust. To proactively address this, Epetech also tracked leading indicators like the number of code quality violations, test coverage percentage, and ratio of manual to automated tests. These metrics provided early warning signs of potential problems, allowing teams to address quality concerns before they affected production. In addition, the percentage of faulty deployments that were rolled back versus those that were not was measured to understand the effectiveness of remediation actions. Even when a deployment was not classified as erroneous, it could still result in a suboptimal customer experience. These cases were captured through mechanisms like Correction of Error documents, which many organizations use to document and analyze such incidents.

- *Mean time to recovery (MTTR)*—Decreasing the time it takes to restore service after an incident minimizes the effect of outages. A shorter MTTR improves overall service availability and customer experience. Epetech complemented this with leading metrics such as incident detection time and mean time to acknowledge. Focusing on these early stages of incident response could improve its monitoring and alerting processes, ensuring faster resolution times.

By focusing on these metrics, Epetech could objectively assess the platform's effects on developer productivity and operational efficiency, enabling it to identify successes and target improvement areas.

Exercise 10.1   Identify the leading engineering platform metrics for your organization

Objective: While the inventory of the leading metrics you might have in an organization is a finite set, it is essential to identify the appropriate leading metrics that would lead you to your DORA metrics (four key metrics).

Intended outcome: You will create a list of leading metrics and explain how those metrics relate to the DORA metrics.

10.1.3 *Implementing feedback loops*

To gather qualitative data alongside quantitative metrics, Epetech recognized the importance of ongoing dialogue with its development teams. While deployment frequency and lead time provide valuable insights into the platform's performance, they do not always capture the nuances of developer experience, usability problems, or the specific needs of different teams. To address this, Epetech implemented regular feedback loops, employing various methods to engage with developers and stakeholders, as shown in figure 10.3.

Now let's look at how Epetech built each of the core pieces (surveys, interviews, community forums, and advisory groups) of the feedback loop ecosystem.

SURVEYS AND INTERVIEWS

Epetech conducted periodic surveys (both quantitative and qualitative) to collect developer satisfaction scores and feedback on the platform's usability, performance, and features. By structuring surveys around different aspects of the platform—such as ease of use, documentation quality, and the effectiveness of automated workflows—Epetech could identify which elements were working well and which required attention.

In addition to surveys, the platform team held one-on-one and group interviews with developers, team leads, and operations personnel. This enabled the team to delve into the context behind survey responses, uncovering underlying problems that might not be evident from quantitative data alone. For instance, developers might express frustration over certain features during an interview, which could be traced back to a lack of documentation or unclear workflows. The interviews also fostered a sense of involvement, making developers feel their voices were heard and valued in the platform evolution process.

By combining surveys and interviews, Epetech gathered rich data that informed its decisions on platform enhancements. This process ensured that platform improvements were directly aligned with user needs, driving higher adoption and satisfaction.

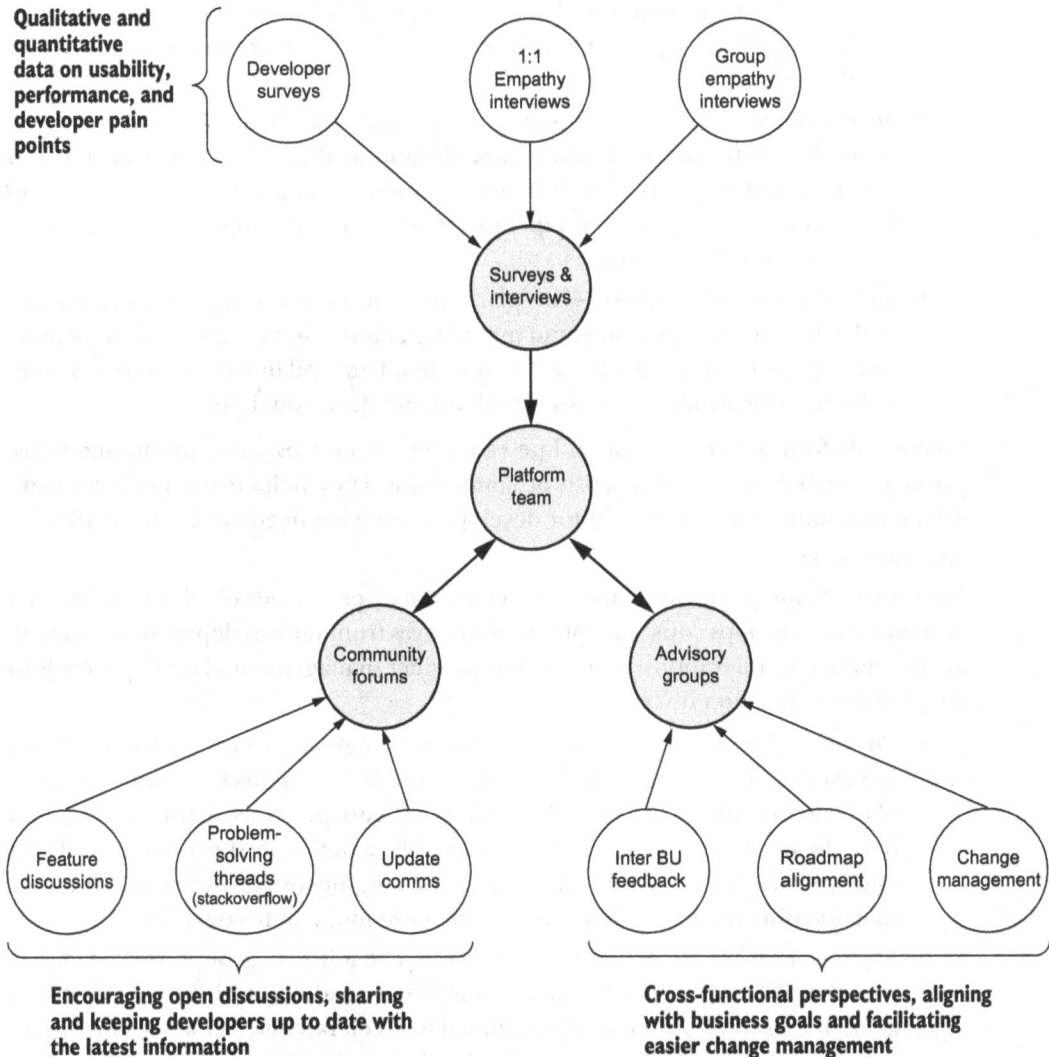

Figure 10.3 Feedback loop ecosystem for the platform engineering team, enabling comprehensive end-user-driven development

COMMUNITY FORUMS

Epetech established community forums as an open space for developers and platform users to discuss features, challenges, and best practices. These forums were designed to be more than just a feedback channel; they became a collaboration and knowledge-sharing hub. Developers used these forums to

- *Voice concerns and suggest improvements*—Developers could report problems, request new features, or suggest enhancements in a public setting, allowing the platform team to gauge the demand for specific changes. This open dialogue made prioritizing improvements based on real-world usage and developer sentiment easier.

- *Share experiences and solutions*—Developers often face similar challenges while using the platform. The forums allowed them to share tips, workarounds, and solutions, fostering a collaborative environment. For example, a developer who had optimized a deployment pipeline could share their approach, helping others achieve similar efficiencies.

- *Stay informed about updates*—The platform team used the forums to announce updates, share release notes, and provide guidance on new features. Proactively communicating changes helped teams adapt to updates more smoothly and reduced the learning curve associated with new functionalities.

Community forums became vital to Epetech's developer ecosystem, promoting transparency, collaboration, and a sense of community. They helped the platform team dynamically and interactively monitor developers' evolving needs and experiences.

ADVISORY GROUPS

To ensure that the platform roadmap reflected the diverse needs of all teams, Epetech formed advisory groups consisting of representatives from various departments, including development, operations, security, and product management. Their approach to the platform's evolution involved

- *Prioritizing features*—The advisory groups met regularly to review feedback and discuss upcoming features and improvements. With insights from different areas of the organization, they helped the platform team prioritize features that would have the most significant effects. This cross-functional perspective ensured that platform development was balanced, addressing needs across the board rather than focusing on the loudest voices or the most immediate concerns.

- *Aligning the roadmap with business objectives*—The advisory groups worked closely with the platform team to align the platform's roadmap with broader business goals. For example, if the company aimed to accelerate the rollout of a new product line, the advisory group might prioritize platform features that streamline deployment and testing processes. This alignment ensured platform investments delivered tangible business value and supported strategic initiatives.

- *Facilitating change management*—Platform changes often require updates to workflows, processes, or team responsibilities. Advisory group members acted as change champions within their respective teams, helping to communicate the benefits and implications of platform changes. They facilitated the adoption of new features and practices, reducing resistance and smoothing the transition process.

The advisory groups ensured platform development was inclusive and aligned with user needs and business goals. This collaborative approach led to a more targeted and effective platform roadmap, ultimately driving higher adoption and satisfaction.

COMPREHENSIVE APPROACH TO FEEDBACK

By implementing a multifaceted feedback loop that included surveys, interviews, community forums, and advisory groups, Epetech created a holistic feedback ecosystem. This approach ensured that the platform evolved in response to real user needs, capturing both the quantitative and qualitative aspects of developer experience. It allowed the platform team to

- *Identify pain points promptly*—Regular feedback cycles helped detect problems early, preventing the embers from becoming full-blown fires. For example, feedback about a cumbersome deployment process led to the development of a new automated pipeline, significantly improving efficiency.
- *Celebrate successes*—By engaging with developers and recognizing areas where the platform excelled, Epetech fostered a culture of continuous improvement and collaboration. Celebrating successes, such as the successful rollout of a new feature or the reduction of deployment time, reinforced positive behaviors and motivated further progress.
- *Adapt to changing needs*—As the organization grew and its needs evolved, the feedback mechanisms allowed the platform team to adapt quickly. For instance, as security requirements became more stringent, feedback from the advisory groups guided the integration of enhanced security features into the platform.

This comprehensive feedback approach not only improved the platform itself but also fostered a culture of continuous improvement. Developers felt a sense of ownership and investment in the platform, leading to higher engagement, more innovative ideas, and a platform that genuinely served users' needs.

Now we have looked at how Epetech is using the feedback mechanism. However, having some hands-on practice to implement in your organization is essential. To do so, let us see how Epetech does it.

Exercise 10.2 Create an approach for a feedback mechanism at Epetech

Objective: Implement a feedback mechanism to gather qualitative and quantitative insights from internal developers, third-party developers, and partners regarding the usability, performance, and challenges of using Epetech's API services.

Answer the following questions:

1. What are the steps for setting up a surveys and interviews process as shown in the Epetech case described previously?
2. How would you form a platform team responsible for feedback analysis?
3. Based on the example provided, how would you create community forums for discussions?
4. Should you be forming advisory groups for strategic feedback?

Intended outcome:By implementing this simple feedback mechanism, Epetech should be able to continuously improve its developer platform, ensuring both internal and external stakeholders are satisfied with the usability and performance of their APIs.

10.2   Platform-as-a-product as the differentiator

As introduced in part 1, treating the platform as a product involves applying product management principles to its development. This means prioritizing user-centric design, continuous improvement, and a clear value proposition. By adopting this mindset, organizations can create functional and delightful platforms, driving higher adoption and satisfaction rates.

At Epetech, the platform team adopted the platform-as-a-product mindset by taking deliberate steps to ensure that the platform was not just a set of tools but a product designed to solve specific problems and deliver value to its users. This approach involved strategic planning, continuous alignment with organizational goals, and adopting best practices to foster a culture of adaptability and innovation. The following describes how Epetech approached this transformation.

10.2.1   Defining the platform vision and mission

The first step in adopting the platform-as-a-product mindset was to establish a clear vision and mission for the platform. The platform team at Epetech recognized that without a well-defined purpose, the platform could quickly become a collection of ad hoc features and tools, lacking coherence and strategic direction. To avoid this, it focused on answering fundamental questions: What is the platform's primary purpose? Who are its users? What problems is it designed to solve?

The team articulated a vision that described the long-term effects it wanted the platform to have on the organization. For Epetech, the platform vision centered around creating a seamless developer experience that empowered teams to build, deploy, and operate their applications efficiently. The vision was about technology and fostering a culture of innovation, speed, and reliability across the organization. This overarching vision provided a guiding star for all development efforts, ensuring every feature, enhancement, or decision contributed toward a unified goal.

Building on this vision, the team crafted a mission statement outlining how the platform would achieve its vision. The mission focused on specific outcomes, such as reducing the time-to-market for new features, ensuring high system reliability, and providing robust tools that abstracted the complexities of infrastructure management. By defining a clear mission, the team established a concrete set of objectives that shaped the platform's development path.

This clarity in vision and mission had a profound effect. It gave the platform team the ability to prioritize their fundamental problems. It also helped align stakeholders across the organization, from developers to business leaders, around a shared understanding of the platform's objectives. This alignment ensured that every feature and improvement was evaluated based on its contribution to the platform's overarching goals.

10.2.2   Establishing a product roadmap

With the vision and mission in place, the next step was to develop a product roadmap that translated these high-level goals into actionable steps. The roadmap was a list of features and a strategic plan that prioritized work based on user needs, business objectives, and technical feasibility and included the following:

- *Planning features and enhancements*—The platform team conducted extensive user research, gathering feedback from developers, operations teams, and other stakeholders to identify pain points and opportunities for improvement. This research helped the team understand user groups' specific needs and challenges. For example, they discovered developers were spending significant time on manual deployment processes, leading to delays and errors. This insight led to prioritizing features like automated deployment pipelines and self-service infrastructure provisioning.

- *Strategic alignment*—The roadmap also considered the organization's strategic goals. For Epetech, this included objectives like accelerating the rollout of new digital services, improving system reliability, and reducing operational costs. The team ensured their work directly contributed to the company's success by aligning the platform roadmap with these goals. Features that had the potential to drive significant business value were prioritized, while items with lesser effect were scheduled for later iterations.

- *Communication tool*—The roadmap was a powerful communication tool, aligning stakeholders on expectations, timelines, and priorities. It provided transparency into the platform team's work and why they did it, helping manage stakeholder expectations. Regular roadmap reviews allowed the team to update stakeholders on progress, incorporate new feedback, and adjust plans as necessary. This open communication fostered trust and collaboration between the platform team and its users.

Establishing a product roadmap transformed the platform development process at Epetech. It provided a clear path forward, enabling the team to focus on delivering features that mattered most to their users and the organization. It also reduced ad hoc requests and scope creep, as stakeholders had a transparent view of the platform's direction and priorities.

Exercise 10.3   Create a platform product roadmap blueprint for Epetech

Objective: The objective of this exercise is to think about how Epetech would create a platform product roadmap. Remember: you are not creating the roadmap itself, as that would require an understanding of the domain-specific activities of Epetech.

To achieve this objective, answer the following questions:

1 What are the teams and types of requirements analysis you will be doing if you are creating a platform product roadmap (hint: conduct stakeholder management)?
2 What are the strategic goals for the overall business that will be addressed by the platform product capabilities being built?
3 What are the communication tools you will need to increase trust among your stakeholders on the progress of the platform capability buildout?

10.2.3 *Implementing agile practices*

To bring the platform vision and roadmap to life, Epetech adopted agile practices, focusing on delivering value incrementally and responding quickly to change. Traditional, long development cycles replaced iterative processes, allowing the platform team to adapt to feedback and evolving requirements. This involved the following concepts:

- *Iterative development cycles*—The team broke the roadmap into smaller, manageable increments, delivering new features and improvements in short sprints. This approach enabled them to release updates more frequently, providing users with immediate value and gathering feedback. For example, they started with a minimal viable product (MVP) that automated basic deployment tasks instead of building a full-fledged deployment automation tool over several months. This MVP was then iteratively enhanced based on user feedback, progressively adding more complex features like automated testing and rollback mechanisms.

- *Continuous feedback and adaptation*—Agile practices emphasize the importance of constant feedback loops. After each sprint, the platform team conducted reviews and retrospectives to assess what went well and what could be improved. This process allowed them to adapt their plans in real-time, incorporating user feedback, addressing new requirements, and improving workflows. If a newly released feature received feedback indicating usability problems, the team could quickly iterate on the design in the next sprint rather than waiting for a major release cycle.

- *Cross-functional collaboration*—Agile practices also promoted collaboration across different functions. The platform team included developers, operations engineers, security specialists, and user representatives. This cross-functional approach ensured the platform was built with a holistic view of user needs, operational requirements, and security considerations. Regular stand-ups, planning sessions, and collaborative tooling helped keep everyone aligned and moving toward common goals.

Implementing agile practices had a transformative effect on the platform's evolution. The platform team became more responsive to user needs and changing requirements and was able to pivot quickly when necessary. They moved away from the pitfalls of lengthy development cycles, where features could become outdated when released. Instead, they embraced a continuous delivery and improvement culture, where the platform evolved organically based on real-world usage and feedback.

10.2.4 *The role of the platform product manager*

To drive the approach of agile practices introduced in the last section, Epetech appointed a platform product manager, Alex, whose role was crucial in ensuring the platform's success. Alex had three key tasks:

- *User research*—Alex invested time in understanding developer workflows, pain points, and requirements. By conducting interviews, surveys, and observational studies, he gathered valuable insights that shaped the platform's features and user experience.

- *Stakeholder engagement*—Collaborating with leadership, development teams, and operations helped align the platform's priorities with business objectives. Alex facilitated group communication, ensuring the platform met technical and strategic needs.

- *Metric tracking*—Monitoring KPIs and adjusting strategies accordingly allowed Alex to make data-driven decisions. He regularly reviewed metrics to ensure the platform delivered tangible value and identified areas needing attention.

Alex's role was pivotal in bridging the gap between technical implementation and user expectations, ensuring the platform aligned with user needs and business objectives.

10.2.5 *Differentiating through user experience*

By focusing on the developer experience, Epetech's platform became a clear differentiator in several ways. The approach was grounded in a platform-as-a-product mindset, where every feature, process, and interaction was designed with the end-user—the developer or operator—in mind.

Key aspects of differentiation included

- *Simplifying complexity*—Abstracting infrastructure complexities allowed developers to concentrate on coding and innovation instead of wrestling with underlying technical details. This reduction in cognitive load not only accelerated development cycles but also improved the overall developer satisfaction index.

- *Providing self-service capabilities*—By enabling teams to provision resources and deploy applications without bottlenecks, the platform promoted autonomy and speed. Self-service tooling empowered developers to act decisively while fostering a stronger sense of ownership and responsibility.

- *Ensuring consistency and compliance*—Standardized configurations aligned with security and governance requirements minimized vulnerabilities and human error. This created a uniform operating model across teams, ensuring adherence to organizational policies while safeguarding system integrity.

By adopting a platform-as-a-product mindset, defining a clear vision and mission, establishing a strategic roadmap, and implementing agile practices, Epetech created a technically robust platform aligned with its users' needs and the organization's strategic objectives. The result was a measurable increase in productivity and innovation, accompanied by a positive cultural shift where developers felt supported, valued, and trusted. Figure 10.4 introduces the evolution of the platform-as-a-product mindset.

Let us look at each of the five steps in this evolution:

1 *Platform vision and mission*—
    a Define the platform's purpose, goals, and user-centric outcomes.
    b Align stakeholders early to establish a unified direction and clear expectations.
    c Anchor all future platform decisions to this vision to prevent scope drift.

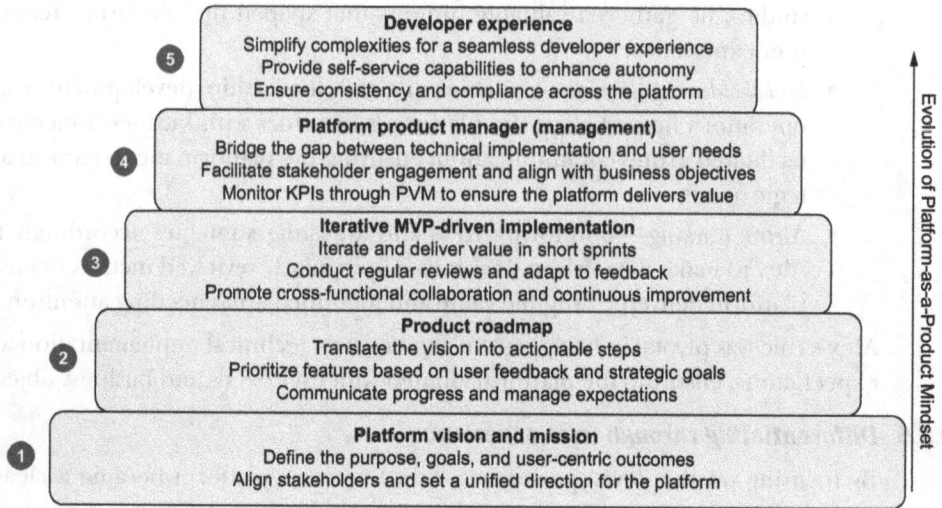

Figure 10.4 Visual representation of the lifecycle of the platform-as-a-product approach, highlighting how to transition from vision and mission to a fully operational, developer-centric platform

2 *Product roadmap—*

   a Translate the vision into actionable, prioritized steps based on user feedback and strategic goals.

   b Continuously communicate progress, upcoming changes, and tradeoffs to maintain stakeholder confidence.

   c Use the roadmap to balance short-term delivery with long-term scalability and maintainability.

3 *Iterative MVP-driven implementation—*

   a Deliver platform capabilities in short, iterative sprints to validate assumptions quickly.

   b Conduct regular reviews and adapt features based on real-world usage patterns and developer feedback.

   c Promote collaboration across functional teams to encourage innovation and reduce rework.

4 *Platform product manager (management)—*

   a Act as the bridge between technical implementation and business needs.

   b Facilitate stakeholder engagement, ensuring that priorities reflect both developer needs and organizational objectives.

   c Monitor KPIs such as adoption rate, time-to-onboard, and satisfaction scores to ensure the platform delivers tangible value.

5 *Developer experience (outcome)—*

  a Simplify complexities to create a seamless developer experience that minimizes friction.

  b Provide robust self-service capabilities to enable rapid, autonomous action.

  c Ensure consistency, compliance, and reliability across all platform-provided services.

Case study: Epetech's LaunchPad: An internal developer platform

To bring the platform-as-a-product vision to life, Epetech developed LaunchPad, its internal developer platform (IDP), which became a cornerstone of its development ecosystem.

Features of LaunchPad included

- *Standardized service templates*—Preconfigured setups for common microservices ensured best practices were followed across teams. These templates reduced setup time and provided a solid foundation for new services.
- *Integrated continuous integration/continuous deployment (CI/CD) pipelines*—Automated testing, security scans, and deployments streamlined the release process; integration with existing tools minimized disruptions and enhanced efficiency.
- *User-friendly interface*—An intuitive portal for managing services, environments, and deployments made it easy for developers to navigate and utilize the platform's capabilities. A focus on usability reduced the learning curve and encouraged adoption.
- *Extensive documentation*—Guides, tutorials, and FAQs supported developers at every step, providing resources for troubleshooting and learning. Comprehensive documentation fostered self-sufficiency and continuous learning.

By offering a seamless and empowering developer experience, LaunchPad increased adoption and accelerated feature delivery, becoming a critical asset in Epetech's technology stack.

Exercise 10.4   Adopt a platform-as-a-product mindset

Objective: Develop a product vision and roadmap for your internal platform, incorporating user-centric design principles.

The recommended steps for this exercise are as follows:

1 *Conduct user research—*
  a *Coding activity*—Build a survey application using a web framework (e.g., Flask, Django, Express.js). Collect responses and store them in a database like SQLite or MongoDB.
  b *Data analysis*—Write scripts in Python or R to analyze survey data and extract critical insights.

(continued)

    c Define the platform's vision and mission.

    d Summarize the findings from your analysis.

    e Craft clear and concise vision and mission statements.

6 *Develop a product roadmap—Modeling activity*: Use project management tools like Trello, Jira, or Azure DevOps to create a visual roadmap. Organize features into sprints or releases.

7 *Create user personas—Modeling activity*: Design personas using visual tools, including demographic information, goals, challenges, and preferred tools.

8 *Design a prototype or mockup—Coding activity*: Develop an interactive prototype of a critical platform feature. Use frontend technologies like HTML, CSS, or JavaScript or frameworks like React or Angular. Alternatively, use prototyping tools like Figma for noncoded mockups.

9 *Gather feedback*—Present the prototype to stakeholders and users.

Expected deliverables for this exercise are

- Platform vision and mission statements in a documented format
- Product roadmap visualized with project management tools
- User personas with detailed descriptions and visuals
- Interactive coded prototype of crucial platform features
- Feedback summary with action items and planned improvements

10.3 Cultural shift from a traditional operations world

Epetech's initial challenges stemmed not only from technical complexities but also from cultural and organizational silos. The traditional separation between development and operations hindered collaboration and slowed down processes. Recognizing that technology alone couldn't solve these problems, Epetech understood that a cultural transformation was necessary to achieve its goals.

10.3.1 Embracing DevOps cultural principles

To address the challenges of slow deployments, siloed teams, and inefficient workflows, Epetech embraced DevOps principles, fostering a culture of collaboration, automation, and shared responsibility. This shift aimed to break down barriers between teams, streamline processes, and create a more agile and responsive organization capable of rapidly delivering value to customers.

KEY DEVOPS PRACTICES ADOPTED

The key DevOps practices and concepts Epetech adopted are

- *Cross-functional teams*—Epetech reorganized its teams to be cross-functional, integrating developers, operations personnel, quality assurance (QA) engineers, and security professionals into unified teams working toward common goals. This integration allowed for diverse perspectives and expertise within each team, promoting a shared understanding of the project's objectives and challenges, and consisted of the following concepts:

- *Shared responsibility*—Team members collectively owned the development, deployment, and maintenance of their services, reducing handoffs and delays.

- *Improved communication*—Regular interactions among team members from different disciplines enhanced collaboration and reduced misunderstandings.

- *Faster problem resolution*—With all relevant expertise within the team, problems could be identified and resolved more rapidly without involving external departments.

For example, the Customer Account Team at Epetech included software developers, an operations specialist, a QA engineer, and a security analyst. This team was responsible for developing new features, ensuring code quality, deploying updates, and maintaining security compliance for the customer account services.

- *CI/CD*—Epetech implemented CI/CD pipelines to automate the build, test, and deployment processes. This automation reduced manual errors, accelerated release cycles, and ensured consistent team deployment practices and included the following practices:

  - *Continuous integration (CI)*—Developers frequently merge their code, build it, and test it early to detect integration problems.

  - *Continuous deployment (CD)*—Successful builds were automatically deployed to staging and, after passing necessary checks, to production environments, minimizing the time between code completion and deployment.

  - *Rapid feedback loop*—Automated testing and deployment provided fast feedback to developers.

For example, upon committing code changes to the repository, the CI/CD pipeline would automatically run unit tests, integration tests, and security scans before deploying to the staging environment.

- *Infrastructure-as-code (IaC)*—Epetech adopted IaC practices using code and automation tools to manage its infrastructure configurations. This approach ensured consistency, repeatability, and version control for infrastructure provisioning and changes and included the following:

  - *Consistency and repeatability*—Infrastructure could be provisioned and configured consistently across different environments (development, staging, production), reducing configuration drift.

  - *Version control*—Infrastructure code was stored in version control systems, allowing teams to track changes, roll back if necessary, and collaborate effectively.

  - *Scalability and disaster recovery*—Automated provisioning enabled rapid scaling of resources and efficient recovery in case of failures.

Epetech utilized tools like Terraform and Ansible to define and manage its infrastructure. For instance, it defined its cloud resources (servers, databases, networking) in code, which could be deployed consistently across multiple environments.

- *Monitoring and observability*—Implementing robust monitoring and observability practices allowed Epetech to gain real-time insights into system performance, availability, and health. Proactive monitoring helped detect problems early and improve system reliability. This included the following:
  - *Real-time visibility*—Dashboards and alerts provided immediate insights into key metrics such as CPU, memory, response times, and error rates.
  - *Proactive issue detection*—Automated alerts were configured to notify teams of anomalies or thresholds being exceeded, enabling swift response to potential problems.
  - *End-to-end tracing*—Observability tools enabled tracing requests throughout the system, facilitating root-cause analysis of performance problems or failures.

Epetech employed tools like Prometheus for metrics collection, Grafana for visualization, and the ELK Stack for log aggregation and analysis.

By embracing DevOps practices, Epetech experienced significant improvements across its operations. Automation reduced the time from code commit to deployment from weeks to hours, allowing the company to respond quickly to market demands with faster deployment cycles. Continuous testing and monitoring led to the early detection of problems, reducing defects in production by 60% and markedly improving quality. Cross-functional teams fostered a culture of shared responsibility and teamwork, increasing developer satisfaction by 40% and enhancing collaboration. The organization became more agile and responsive, adapting swiftly to changing customer needs and technological advancements.

Adopting DevOps principles at Epetech was not merely a procedural change but a fundamental transformation of the company's culture and operations. Breaking down silos between departments encouraged open communication and collaboration, empowering teams to make decisions and take ownership of their work—a significant cultural shift. Streamlined workflows eliminated bottlenecks and inefficiencies, while the integration of automation tools reduced manual intervention and errors, leading to process optimization. With the ability to deploy updates rapidly and reliably, Epetech enhanced customer satisfaction and competitive positioning by delivering new features and improvements more frequently. For example, after implementing these practices, Epetech successfully launched a new feature for its e-commerce platform ahead of schedule; the cross-functional team collaborated seamlessly, and the CI/CD pipeline ensured thorough testing and problem-free deployment. Real-time monitoring allowed for immediate observation of user interactions, and any minor problems were quickly addressed, resulting in positive customer feedback and increased sales.

Epetech adopted DevOps principles and practices to transform its software development and delivery processes. The focus on collaboration, automation, and shared responsibility led to

- *Operational excellence*—This allowed for enhanced efficiency and effectiveness in delivering high-quality software.
- *Innovation enablement*—Freed from the constraints of manual processes, teams could focus on innovation and strategic initiatives.
- *Sustainable growth*—The ability to adapt quickly to market changes positioned Epetech for continued success in a competitive industry.

This transformation serves as a model for other organizations seeking to overcome similar challenges and underscores the value of embracing DevOps principles to drive organizational success.

10.3.2 *Breaking down silos with team topologies*

Epetech realized that the organization of their teams significantly affected their ability to collaborate and deliver value. To improve collaboration and efficiency, it restructured its teams using concepts from the Team Topologies framework, which we first introduced at the beginning of the book. This approach helped it align its organizational structure with business goals and enhance team communication.

TEAM TYPES IMPLEMENTED

Epetech created stream-aligned teams that focused on delivering end-to-end value for specific business domains. These teams were aligned with key business areas and had the autonomy to make decisions and move quickly. Examples were

- *E-commerce team*—This team was responsible for the online shopping platform, including the user interface, shopping cart, and checkout process. They worked on features that directly affected customer experience and sales.
- *Mobile app team*—The mobile app team focused on developing and maintaining Epetech's mobile applications, ensuring a seamless experience across devices.
- *Inventory management team*—It handled the systems that tracked product stock levels, warehouse logistics, and supply chain integrations.

By aligning teams with specific business streams, Epetech ensured that each team's work directly contributed to organizational goals. These teams owned their services from development to production, enabling them to respond rapidly to customer needs and market changes.

Epetech also established a dedicated platform team tasked with developing and maintaining the internal platform that other teams used. The platform team reduced the cognitive load on the stream-aligned teams by handling common infrastructure and tooling needs. Their responsibilities included

- *Developing self-service tools*—Creating tools that allow other teams to provide resources like databases, servers, and networking components without manual intervention
- *Managing CI/CD pipelines*—Maintaining continuous integration and deployment pipelines that standardized the build and release processes
- *Providing shared services*—Offering services such as logging, monitoring, authentication, and authorization that could be reused across multiple teams. For example, when the stream-aligned teams needed to deploy their applications, they used the deployment pipelines provided by the platform team. This allowed them to focus on writing code and delivering features rather than dealing with the complexities of infrastructure management.

Finally, to support adopting new technologies and practices, Epetech formed enabling teams. These teams provided expertise and guidance to other teams, helping them overcome obstacles and improve their capabilities. Their functions included

- *Training and workshops*—Conducting sessions on DevOps practices, cloud migration strategies, and security best practices
- *Consultation and support*—Working closely with teams adopting new technologies, offering hands-on assistance and advice
- *Developing standards and guidelines*—Creating documentation and templates to help teams follow best practices and maintain consistency.

For instance, when Epetech decided to migrate some of its services to the cloud, the enabling team specializing in cloud technologies assisted the stream-aligned teams in understanding cloud architecture, selecting appropriate services, and implementing best practices for scalability and security.

INTERACTION MODES

Teams are fine, but the real win is realized when a clear interaction and communication pattern is established. Let us now look at how Epetech did this.

Epetech defined explicit interaction modes to ensure effective collaboration between teams. These modes clarified how teams should work together in different scenarios.

Collaboration occurred when teams needed to work closely on complex projects or transitions. This mode was characterized by

- *Joint planning and execution*—Teams coordinated their efforts, shared responsibilities, and worked toward common goals.
- *Knowledge sharing*—Teams exchanged expertise and insights, learning from each other's experiences.
- *Problem-solving together*—Collaborative efforts led to innovative solutions that might have yet to emerge in isolation.

For example, when Epetech undertook a significant overhaul of its customer loyalty program, the e-commerce, mobile app, and inventory management teams collaborated to ensure a seamless experience across all platforms. They held joint planning sessions, integrated their development efforts, and tested the new features collectively.

In the X-as-a-service mode, the platform team provided services that other teams could consume as needed. This approach streamlined interactions and clarified responsibilities:

- *Service provisioning*—Teams requested services through well-defined interfaces or APIs.
- *Clear contracts and service-level agreements*—The platform team established service-level agreements that specified performance expectations and support commitments.
- *Decoupling dependencies*—Teams could only use the services with an understanding of the underlying implementation details.

For example, if the mobile app team needed a new database instance, they could request it through the platform team's database-as-a-service offering. The platform team would handle provisioning, backups, and maintenance, allowing the mobile app team to focus on developing app features.

Lastly, the facilitation mode involved enabling teams to assist other teams in building their capabilities without doing the work for them and involved

- *Mentoring and coaching*—These provided guidance and support, helping teams develop new skills.
- *Temporary support*—They might be embedded with a team for a short period to help them become familiar with a new technology or practice.
- *Promoting best practices*—Teams were encouraged to adopt standards that improve efficiency and quality.

For example, when the e-commerce team wanted to implement automated testing for their applications, an enabling team specializing in test automation facilitated workshops and paired programming sessions. They helped the e-commerce team set up testing frameworks and write initial test cases, empowering them to continue independently afterward.

By restructuring its teams and defining explicit interaction modes, Epetech achieved several benefits:

- *Improved focus and efficiency*—Stream-aligned teams could concentrate on delivering features and value to customers without being burdened by infrastructure concerns or needing more expertise in certain areas.
- *Reduced cognitive load*—The platform and enabling teams took on specialized responsibilities, allowing other teams to work more efficiently and effectively.
- *Enhanced collaboration*—Clear interaction modes minimized confusion and conflict between teams. Teams knew when and how to engage with others, leading to smoother workflows and better relationships.

- *Accelerated innovation*—With empowered and supported teams, Epetech brought new features and improvements to the market more quickly, responding to customer needs and staying ahead of competitors.

Case study: Epetech needs to improve the inventory management system

To illustrate the application of the team topologies framework at Epetech, let's consider a real-world scenario that showcases how different team types and interaction modes lead to successful outcomes.

Challenge:

The *inventory management team* needed to implement real-time inventory level tracking to improve order fulfillment accuracy. This enhancement was critical to

- Reduce stock discrepancies.
- Minimize order errors.
- Enhance overall customer satisfaction.

Solution:

To address this challenge, Epetech used the strengths of various team types and defined interaction modes:

- *Collaboration*—
  - The inventory management team collaborated with the platform team to integrate a new messaging system capable of handling real-time data streams.
  - This close cooperation allowed them to combine the inventory management team's domain expertise with the platform team's technical proficiency in infrastructure and tooling.
- *Facilitation*—
  - An enabling team with expertise in real-time data processing facilitated training sessions.
  - They helped the inventory management team understand how to work with the new messaging system, transferring knowledge without taking over the project.
  - This empowerment enabled the inventory management team to develop new capabilities and become more self-sufficient.
- *X-as-a-service*—
  - The platform team provided the messaging system as a service, handling its maintenance and scalability.
  - By consuming this service, the inventory management team could focus on implementing business logic without worrying about underlying infrastructure complexities.
- *Clear boundaries and expectations*—Boundaries and expectations should be clear with streamlined interactions between the teams.

Outcome:

As a result of these coordinated efforts

- The inventory management team successfully implemented real-time inventory tracking.
- Order errors were reduced by 25%, leading to fewer customer complaints and returns.
- Customer satisfaction improved significantly, as accurate inventory levels ensured better product availability and timely order fulfillment.
- The company saw an increase in repeat purchases and positive customer reviews.

Exercise 10.5 Implement team topologies in your organization

Objective: Restructure team interactions based on team topologies to improve collaboration and flow efficiency.

The recommended steps for this exercise are as follows:

1 *Map current team structures—*
   a *Modeling activity*—Create organizational charts and team interaction diagrams using tools like draw.io, Visio, or Miro. Highlight communication channels and dependencies.
   b *Coding activity*—Use network analysis libraries in Python (e.g., NetworkX) to model and visualize team communication patterns based on data from communication tools (e.g., Slack API).
2 *Identify appropriate team types—*
   a Analyze the data to determine optimal team structures.
   b *Modeling activity*—Update diagrams to reflect proposed stream-aligned, platform, enabling, or complicated-subsystem teams.
3 *Define interaction modes—*
   a *Modeling activity*—Create sequence diagrams or flowcharts illustrating new interaction modes between teams.
   b *Coding activity*—Simulate interactions using scripts or tools to model workflows.
4 *Propose a restructured team topology—*
   a *Modeling activity*—Present the new organizational structure using visual aids.
   b *Coding activity*—Develop a simple application to showcase how teams interact with shared tools or platforms.
5 *Develop a transition plan*—Outline the steps and timelines.
6 *Pilot the changes—*
   a Implement the new structure in a pilot area.
   b *Coding activity*—Create collaborative coding projects on platforms like GitHub or GitLab to reflect new team interactions.
7 *Collect feedback and iterate—*
   a *Coding activity*—Use custom scripts to collect metrics on collaboration (e.g., pull requests and code reviews).
   b Analyze the effectiveness of the new topology and make adjustments.

(continued)

The expected deliverables are

- Organizational charts of current and proposed structures
- Communication patterns analysis using visualizations from coding activities
- Interaction diagrams showing new workflows
- Simulated interaction models or applications
- Transition plan with automated project management tasks
- Pilot implementation report with data-driven insights

10.3.3 *Effects on Epetech's culture*

This reorganization led to significant positive changes within Epetech. Enhanced communication through open channels and regular interactions reduced misunderstandings and delays, while transparent communication built trust and aligned efforts across the organization. Stream-aligned teams were empowered with autonomy and ownership over their services, increasing motivation and accountability. This empowerment led to higher engagement and job satisfaction among team members. Additionally, reduced handoffs and streamlined processes resulted in faster delivery, accelerating time-to-market and allowing Epetech to respond swiftly to customer needs and competitive pressures. The collaborative environment improved morale, increasing job satisfaction and retention as teams felt valued and connected to the organization's success.

By embracing a cultural shift alongside technical changes, Epetech created a more resilient and adaptable organization capable of sustaining long-term growth and innovation. This combination of cultural transformation and strategic reorganization positioned the company to meet future challenges effectively, fostering an environment where continuous improvement and collaboration drive ongoing success.

Exercise 10.6   Plan a cultural shift toward DevOps and collaboration

Objective: Develop a strategic plan to initiate a cultural shift from a traditional operations model to a DevOps-oriented, collaborative culture within your organization. This includes modeling current processes and coding automation scripts to support new practices. Follow these steps for this exercise:

1 *Assess the current culture—*
   a *Modeling activity—*Create process flow diagrams of your current software development lifecycle using tools like Visio, Lucidchart, or draw.io. Map out handoffs, bottlenecks, and feedback loops.
   b *Coding activity—*Develop scripts (e.g., using Python or Bash) to collect and analyze data on current deployment frequencies, lead times, and failure rates. Use APIs from tools like Jenkins, GitLab, or Jira to extract metrics.

2 *Define the desired culture—*
   a *Modeling activity*—Design future-state process models that incorporate DevOps practices. Highlight differences from the current state using annotations or overlays.
   b *Coding activity*—Prototype automation scripts for CI/CD pipelines using tools like Jenkinsfiles, GitLab CI/CD YAML configurations, or GitHub Actions workflows.
3 *Develop a change management plan—*
   a *Leadership engagement*—Present your models and findings to stakeholders using visual aids.
   b *Communication strategy*—Create infographics or presentations illustrating the benefits of the cultural shift.
   c *Coding activity*—Implement the new CI/CD pipelines in a controlled environment with selected teams. Build a simple web application or use a service like Google Forms to collect anonymous feedback. Write scripts to analyze feedback data.
4 *Implement and measure the plan—*
   a *Rollout*—Implement the initiatives according to the change management plan. Use the coded automation scripts in pilot teams to demonstrate the benefits.
   b *Coding activity*—Rerun your data collection scripts to gather post-implementation metrics. Data visualization libraries like Matplotlib or D3.js can be used to compare before and after results.

The expected deliverables are

- Process flow diagrams of current and future software development lifecycle processes
- Automation scripts for CI/CD pipelines and data collection, with documentation
- Training materials, including coded exercises or labs
- Data analysis reports with visualizations of before and after metrics
- Feedback data that is collected via coded tools or forms
- Implementation progress report summarizing outcomes and lessons learned

10.4 Site reliability engineering strategy, models, and aligning with organizational needs

At Epetech, ensuring system reliability became significantly more important as the engineering velocity accelerated with the advent of the engineering platform. Site reliability engineering (SRE) offered a disciplined, engineering-first approach to its traditional operational practices. In this section, we will look at the approach Epetech took to generate the outcomes of reduced incidents and faster delivery, which led to an overall improvement in delivery.

10.4.1 Understanding SRE

As Epetech increased deployment frequency, maintaining system reliability became critical to ensuring customer satisfaction and trust. SRE provided a framework for balancing innovation with stability by applying software engineering practices to operations. The three core considerations in SRE are

- *Service level objectives (SLOs)*—Targeted performance and availability levels define the expected quality of service. SLOs provided clear goals for reliability that aligned with user expectations.
- *Service level indicators (SLIs)*—Metrics that measure compliance with SLOs, such as latency, throughput, and error rates, offer quantifiable data to assess system performance.
- *Error budgets*—Acceptable levels of risk to manage change velocity versus reliability. Error budgets allowed teams to balance the need for new features with maintaining system stability.

10.4.2 Implementing SRE at Epetech

Epetech embedded SRE practices into its teams to enhance reliability without stifling innovation. It began by defining SLOs and SLIs for critical services like payment processing. These clear objectives were established based on user needs and business priorities, guiding engineering efforts and resource allocation to ensure that vital services met performance and availability targets.

Additionally, Epetech implemented advanced monitoring and alerting tools like Prometheus and Grafana to gain real-time insights and enable proactive issue detection. This allowed teams to identify and address problems before they affected users. It also built automated remediation mechanisms to handle common failures, reducing manual intervention and downtime. This automation increased system resilience and recovery speed, contributing to a more robust and reliable overall system.

10.4.3 Aligning SRE with organizational goals

By aligning SRE practices with business objectives, Epetech ensured several vital outcomes that benefitted the organization and its customers. First, reliability metrics directly support customer satisfaction. By maintaining high availability and optimal performance, Epetech enhanced the user experience, which led to increased customer loyalty and a positive brand reputation. Customers enjoyed uninterrupted access to services, which fostered trust and encouraged repeat business.

Second, error budgets became a vital tool for team decision-making. By balancing feature development with reliability improvements, teams could make strategic choices about when to prioritize system stability over the introduction of new functionalities. This approach ensured that innovation did not compromise reliability, allowing Epetech to deliver new features without adversely affecting the user experience.

Lastly, Epetech fostered a culture of continuous improvement. Regular reviews of performance against SLOs and SLIs led to process enhancements and system optimizations. This practice embedded a culture of learning and adaptation within the organization, where teams consistently sought ways to improve reliability and efficiency. By embracing this mindset, Epetech was able to evolve with changing business needs while maintaining high levels of service reliability.

10.4.4 Outcomes of Implementing SRE

Implementing SRE practices yielded significant benefits for Epetech:

- Epetech experienced substantially reduced incidents, with fewer outages and performance problems, improving overall service quality. By proactively monitoring systems and addressing potential problems before they escalated, Epetech minimized service disruptions. This reduction in incidents enhanced the customer experience and reduced maintenance costs associated with emergency fixes and downtime.

- Epetech achieved faster recovery times when incidents did occur. Quicker resolution minimized the effect on customers and internal operations, ensuring that service interruptions were brief and managed efficiently. Implementing efficient recovery processes, such as automated rollbacks and self-healing mechanisms, enhanced the system's confidence among users and stakeholders. Teams were better prepared to handle unexpected problems, strengthening the company's reputation for reliability.

- The adoption of SRE practices enabled data-driven decision-making within the organization. Using metrics and performance data to guide prioritization and resource allocation, Epetech ensured that efforts were focused where they mattered most. This data-driven approach improved transparency and accountability, as teams could see the effects of their work on KPIs. By integrating SRE into its operational strategy, Epetech successfully balanced rapid innovation with dependable service delivery, aligning technological advancements with business objectives.

10.5 Using intelligent assistants to help enhance engineering platforms

Intelligent assistants and AI-driven automation are reshaping how engineering organizations operate today. With the prevalence of autonomous agents and model context protocol servers, the ability for teams to accelerate with existing toolsets and processes is abundant. Epetech's own AI bot, EpetechBot, demonstrated many of these capabilities, specifically in the areas of platform flexibility and reducing the cognitive load of the developers. It also helped Epetech grow the platform organically as the business requirements evolved.

10.5.1 The role of intelligent assistants

Generative and agentic AI can significantly enhance engineering platforms by automating routine tasks. This reduces manual effort and errors, freeing time for more complex and creative work. Automation improves efficiency and ensures consistency across processes so that the teams can focus on innovation and problem-solving. For example, automated testing and deployment pipelines speed up delivery cycles.

AI also provides valuable insights by analyzing vast amounts of data to offer recommendations. This enables teams to reduce their development times. AI-driven insights can reveal patterns and opportunities that might go unnoticed, helping teams optimize performance and anticipate future needs. Additionally, intelligent assistants can enhance communication by serving as interfaces between teams and tools, facilitating smoother interactions and collaboration. They centralize information and streamline workflows, making it easier for teams to access the needed resources and work together more effectively. While how to apply AI in platform engineering is outside the scope of this book, we share a simple example of how developer productivity was improved at Epetech by implementing an AI bot.

10.5.2 *Epetech's EpetechBot*

To further support its developers, Epetech developed EpetechBot, an intelligent assistant integrated with its platform. This AI-driven bot was designed to enhance the developer experience by automating routine tasks, providing real-time support, and streamlining workflows. By integrating EpetechBot into their daily operations, developers gained a powerful tool that simplified their processes and empowered them to work more efficiently and effectively.

EpetechBot had several key capabilities that transformed how developers interacted with the platform. One of its primary functions was deployment assistance, allowing developers to initiate deployments through simple chat commands. This feature greatly simplified the deployment process, reducing barriers and accelerating deployment cycles while minimizing errors. Additionally, EpetechBot provided monitoring alerts by notifying teams of problems detected through log and metrics analysis. These proactive alerts ensured that teams could quickly address potential problems, minimizing their effects on production environments. EpetechBot also offered knowledge base access, answering questions about platform usage, best practices, and troubleshooting. Acting as an always-available support resource reduced dependency on specific individuals and democratized knowledge across the team. Another valuable feature was code analysis, where EpetechBot provided real-time feedback on code quality and potential security vulnerabilities. This immediate insight helped developers improve their code before it reached production, enhancing the applications' quality and security.

Implementing EpetechBot led to several significant advantages for development teams. Increased efficiency was one of the most notable benefits, as developers saved time on routine tasks, allowing them to focus on innovation and more complex problem-solving. This efficiency gain translated into higher overall productivity. Moreover, improved quality was achieved through the early detection of problems, which reduced defects and the need for rework. As a result, applications became more stable and reliable, strengthening customer trust. Lastly, EpetechBot was a valuable training tool for new team members, facilitating onboarding and continuous skill development. By providing easy access to information and best practices, EpetechBot supported a culture of learning and growth within Epetech, enabling developers to continuously improve their skills and knowledge.

10.5.3 *Exploring advanced tools*

Epetech also explored a range of advanced tools to enhance its platform further, ensuring it remained at the forefront of technology trends and could meet evolving business needs. By incorporating these tools, Epetech aimed to simplify complex processes, streamline resource management, and provide its developers with a more robust and flexible platform.

Crossplane was one of the critical tools Epetech adopted to orchestrate applications and infrastructure across different environments. It provided a declarative API that allowed Epetech to manage resources consistently, regardless of where they were hosted. With Crossplane, the team could define infrastructure requirements as code, enabling them to quickly replicate environments and apply changes uniformly across multiple clouds or on-premises systems. Its extensibility was particularly valuable, as it supported diverse environments and could scale with Epetech's growing infrastructure needs. For example, if Epetech needed to deploy a new service that required a combination of cloud services like databases, storage, and networking, Crossplane enabled them to do so with a unified configuration, ensuring consistency and reducing manual overhead.

In addition to Crossplane, Epetech explored a cloud native operating environment (CNOE) to provide a standardized environment for its cloud-native applications. CNOE offered a simplified deployment and management process across various cloud providers, enhancing portability and reducing vendor lock-in. By standardizing the environment, CNOE allowed Epetech to deploy applications seamlessly on different cloud platforms without worrying about underlying infrastructure differences. This flexibility meant that Epetech could choose the right CSP based on cost, performance, or specific service offerings without being tied to a single vendor. Moreover, CNOE's standardized environment helped streamline the development process, reducing additional cognitive load.

Humanitec was another tool Epetech considered for building a flexible internal developer platform. Humanitec offered features like dynamic configuration management and resource orchestration as a platform orchestrator, providing higher automation and customization. With Humanitec, Epetech could abstract away many of the complexities developers typically face when deploying and managing applications, such as configuring environments, managing dependencies, and scaling resources. This level of orchestration enabled Epetech to provide developers with a more seamless and self-service platform experience. Developers could deploy their applications with a few clicks or API calls, knowing that the platform would handle the intricate details of infrastructure provisioning, resource allocation, and compliance with organizational standards.

By integrating these tools, Epetech abstracted much of the complexity of modern cloud environments. These technologies provided developers with powerful capabilities without overwhelming them with the details of infrastructure management. As a result, Epetech's platform remained adaptable and future-proof, capable of evolving alongside technological advancements and business demands. This strategic approach ensured the platform could support Epetech's growth while maintaining high flexibility and resilience.

Exercise 10.7   Integrate an intelligent assistant into your platform

Objective: Enhance your platform by developing or integrating an intelligent assistant (e.g., chatbot) to automate tasks and support developers.

The recommended steps are

1 *Identify use cases*—List potential functions the assistant could perform (e.g., deployment assistance, answering FAQs, monitoring alerts). Prioritize features based on effect and complexity.

2 *Choose a technology platform*—Select tools or frameworks for building the assistant (e.g., Botkit, Microsoft Bot Framework, Slack API). Decide on using APIs like Slack API, Microsoft Bot Framework, or custom solutions.

3 *Develop an MVP*—Implement core functionalities such as responding to simple commands, providing deployment status, and fetching documentation links. You should scope it out to the most essential activities you need in your organization. Code the assistant to handle core functionalities. Implement command parsing, API integrations with CI/CD tools, and response handling.

4 *Integrate with communication channels*—Use OAuth and webhooks to connect the assistant with platforms like Slack or Microsoft Teams. Ensure secure authentication and authorization.

5 *Test and refine*—Write unit and integration tests. Consider using frameworks like PyTest or Mocha. Set up CI to automatically run tests on code changes.

6 *Plan for advanced features*—

   a Outline how AI capabilities (e.g., natural language processing, machine learning) could enhance the assistant. Integrate natural language processing using libraries like spaCy or TensorFlow.

   b Implement machine learning models for predictive analytics.

7 *Consider document security and compliance*—Implement input validation, error handling, and logging. Secure sensitive data to ensure compliance with data protection laws.

The expected deliverables for your exercise are

- A working, intelligent assistant integrated with your team's communication tool
- Documentation of use cases and implemented features
- User feedback and planned improvements
- Security and compliance assessment

10.6 *Comparing IDPs and developer portals*

If you have been exposed to platform engineering before, you have undoubtedly heard a lot about IDPs and developer portals. These are complementary but distinct components of a modern platform engineering ecosystem. A detailed take on the platform orchestration or the front-end for developers to access the platform capabilities is outside the scope of this book. However, we need to take a quick look at what these are and how they help an organization before we conclude. IDPs focus primarily on operational efficiency by making sure that the self-serve deployments, provisioning, and abstraction are accelerated.

On the other hand, developer portals place greater emphasis on discoverability, documentation, and overall collaboration while also providing a cleaner, more intuitive interface to the world of platform engineering. Think of IDPs as *doing* things behind the scenes while portals streamline the act of *finding* things. Most organizations we work with, like Epetech, integrate these two components to create a unified interface that reduces context switching and improves collaboration, thereby supporting developers. In this section, we examine their specific, nonexhaustive capabilities while contrasting their roles to avoid the confusion we see in the industry where these terms and the tools used are used interchangeably and, at times, to the detriment of the organization.

10.6.1 *Understanding IDPs*

IDPs, like Epetech's LaunchPad, provide a crucial layer between developers and the underlying infrastructure, offering self-service capabilities and abstractions that simplify development and deployment. These platforms are characterized by self-service interfaces that empower developers to manage applications and environments independently, eliminating the need to wait for other teams and increasing autonomy and speed.

For example, suppose a developer needs to deploy a new microservice. In that case, they can use LaunchPad's self-service portal to configure and deploy it with a few clicks without involving the operations team. IDPs enforce standardization using templates and policies that promote best practices and compliance, ensuring consistency, standardization, and accuracy. Additionally, they emphasize automation, streamlining workflows with CI/CD integration and automated provisioning to minimize manual effort and errors. Once the developer sets up their service, LaunchPad automatically handles the build, testing, and deployment processes, allowing developers to focus more on the product domain-related features rather than dealing with infrastructure complexities.

The IDP and an engineering platform share similarities in that they aim to improve developer efficiency and streamline the software development process. However, they differ in scope, purpose, and the specific problems they address within an organization.

IDPs primarily provide a layer of abstraction over the underlying infrastructure. They aim to empower developers with self-service capabilities to manage applications and environments quickly. IDPs are designed to streamline the development and deployment process by offering tools, interfaces, and automation that enable developers to provision resources, deploy code, and monitor applications without needing to understand the intricacies of the underlying infrastructure.

An engineering platform, on the other hand, has a broader scope, encompassing not just deployment and infrastructure management but also the entire software development lifecycle. It enhances developer productivity, collaboration, and overall engineering efficiency. Engineering platforms often include capabilities such as source code management, build and test automation, security and compliance tooling, observability, and developer collaboration tools. The goal is to provide a comprehensive environment that supports all aspects of software engineering, from writing and testing code to monitoring and maintaining applications in production (see table 10.1).

Table 10.1   Five key features of an IDP

Key features	Description
Application configuration management	Manage application configuration in a dynamic, scalable, and reliable way
Infrastructure orchestration	Orchestrate the infrastructure dynamically and intelligently
Environments	Ephemeral environments on demand
Deployment management	Implement a delivery pipeline for continuous delivery or even continuous deployment
Role-based access control	Manage who can do what in a scalable way

Reproduced with permission from InternalDeveloperPlatforms.Org.

10.6.2 *Understanding developer portals*

Developer portals like Spotify's Backstage are a centralized hub where developers can access documentation, APIs, services, and tooling. These portals are designed with discoverability, making it easy for developers to find and use internal services and resources, enhancing efficiency and fostering collaboration across teams. They also focus on documentation and knowledge sharing, centralizing information to support learning and promoting best practices in the organization. Moreover, developer portals often feature plugin ecosystems that allow for extended functionality through integrations with other tools. This enables organizations to customize the portal to fit their needs and scale its capabilities as they grow.

Portal frameworks like Backstage streamline workflows and improve the developer experience by providing a UX for developer resources. The benefits of developer portals are summarized in table 10.2.

Table 10.2   Key capabilities of developer portals and how they might be used

What?	How
Centralized access to APIs and services	Discover new APIs and integrate them with their applications
Unified documentation and knowledge sharing	A single source of truth that consolidates documentation and guidelines
Standardized project templates	Quick and easy onboarding of a new service

Table 10.2 Key capabilities of developer portals and how they might be used (*continued*)

What?	How
Automated service provisioning	Easier provisioning of cloud services in a controlled environment
Streamlining collaboration	More accessible code reviews, team communication by collaborating with a GitHub repository
Plugin ecosystem for customization	Custom plugins used by multiple users are changed without changing user experience

10.6.3 *Comparing and contrasting IDPs and developer portals*

The interchangeable usage of the two terms "internal developer platforms" and "developer portals" indicates notable confusion surrounding their applicability in platform engineering.

While they are both needed in platform engineering, it is essential to understand the difference between them, primarily as a backend and a frontend, respectively. Table 10.3 summarizes these. Figure 10.5 shows a simplistic view of how IDPs and developer portals interact.

Table 10.3 Comparison of an IDP and a developer portal

Criteria	IDP	Developer portal
Purpose	Emphasizes operational aspects, enabling deployment and management of applications with ease and consistency	Focuses on information dissemination and collaboration, providing access to resources and facilitating communication
Usage pattern	Provides interfaces for performing actions such as deploying code, provisioning resources, and managing environments, directly affecting the development process	Serves as an information hub, often read-centric, offering access to documentation, APIs, tools, and resources to support developers in planning and decision-making
Key capabilities	Self-service deployment	Centralized documentation
	Automated provisioning	API catalog
	Infrastructure abstraction	Knowledge base
	CI/CD integration	Collaboration tools
	Environment management	Project templates
Delivery workflow	Directly streamlines and automates the development process, reducing manual tasks and speeding up deployment cycles	Supports planning and decision-making
Developer workflow	Directly affects the development workflow by automating repetitive tasks, enabling faster deployments, and managing application lifecycles	Supports the developer workflow by providing the necessary information and context, aiding in planning, decision-making, and learning processes

Table 10.3   Comparison of an IDP and a developer portal (*continued*)

Criteria	IDP	Developer portal
Focus	Operational efficiency and developer productivity are achieved by simplifying deployment, resource management, and infrastructure complexities	Knowledge sharing, discoverability, and collaboration by centralizing documentation, APIs, and tools for developers
Organizational effects	It offers actionability, allowing developers to deploy, configure, and manage applications effectively.	It acts as an access point to the IDP's capabilities, providing information and context about the actions available within the IDP.
Collaboration	Supports collaboration through shared tooling for deployment and operations, allowing cross-functional teams to work well together	Facilitates collaboration by providing a centralized clearing house for documentation, knowledge sharing, and communication among developers
Developer Experience	Enhances the developer experience by reducing complexity and providing self-service capabilities, making it easier to manage applications and environments	Enhances the developer experience by centralizing resources and reducing the effort needed to find information, promoting best practices and consistency
Integrations	Often integrates with CI/CD pipelines, monitoring tools, and infrastructure providers to automate and streamline operations	Integrates with various tools and platforms, such as source code repositories, API gateways, and project management systems, to provide a holistic view of available resources
Context switching	Minimizes context switching by providing an integrated deployment and resource management platform	Reduces context switching by serving as a single access point for documentation, tools, and resources, enhancing discoverability
Outcome	Streamlined deployment processes, reduced infrastructure complexity, and accelerated delivery cycles	Improved knowledge sharing, better documentation accessibility, and enhanced collaboration across teams
Example use cases	A developer uses the IDP to deploy a new microservice, automatically provisioning the necessary infrastructure and setting up monitoring.	A developer accesses the portal to find the API documentation and best practices for integrating a new feature into the microservice.
Example industry logos	Humanitec, Mia-Platform, Kratix	Backstage, Cortex, Port

Epetech integrated its LaunchPad IDP with a developer portal to create a unified platform that maximized the benefits of both systems. This integration provided a unified interface, allowing developers to access deployment tools and documentation from a single location, simplifying navigation and usage. It also enhanced collaboration by incorporating forums and knowledge bases, facilitating team interactions, and promoting a culture of shared learning and community support. By combining these resources, Epetech streamlined workflows and minimized context switching, reducing

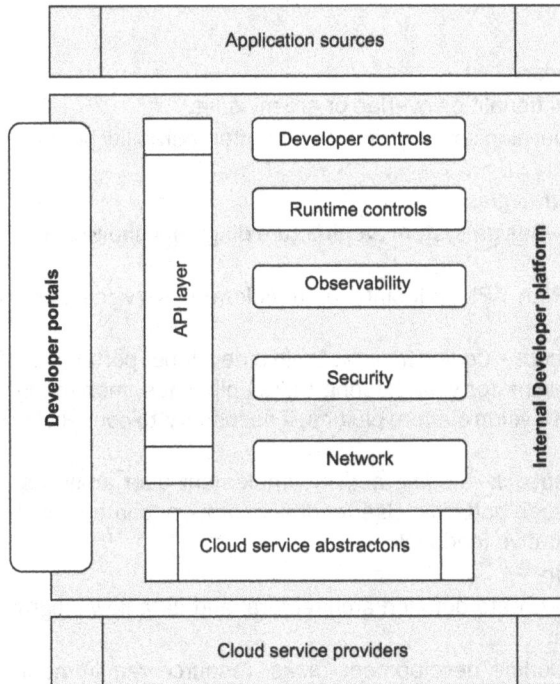

Figure 10.5 A simplistic view of how IDPs and developer portals interact in a platform-engineering-centric organizational construct

cognitive load and enabling developers to focus on delivering value more efficiently. This cohesive ecosystem supported developers throughout the entire software development lifecycle, driving productivity and innovation.

Exercise 10.8   Compare and Integrate IDPs and developer portals

Objective: Analyze the differences between IDPs and developer portals and develop a plan to integrate them for an improved developer experience, including building a coded proof-of-concept.

The recommended steps for this exercise are

1 *Research existing solutions—*
   a *Coding activity*—Set up local instances of open-source developer portals like Backstage. Explore their codebases to understand architecture and extensibility.
   b *Modeling activity*—Create comparison matrices highlighting features and capabilities.
2 *Assess your current environment—*
   a *Modeling activity*—Diagram your current tools and workflows using UML diagrams.
   b *Coding activity*—Write scripts to extract metadata from existing tools (e.g., services registered in a service registry).

(continued)

3 *Identify gaps and overlaps*—
   a Analyze where functionalities overlap or are missing.
   b *Coding activity*—Develop small scripts to test interoperability between tools via APIs.

4 *Develop integration strategies*—
   a *Modeling activity*—Design system architecture diagrams showing integrated components.
   b *Coding activity*—Plan API endpoints or middleware services needed for integration.

5 *Create a proof-of-concept*—*Coding activity*: Build a developer portal using Backstage, integrating plugins for your existing CI/CD pipelines, monitoring tools, and documentation. Develop custom plugins, if necessary, to connect to proprietary systems.

6 *Gather developer feedback*—*Coding activity*: Implement user analytics within the portal to track usage patterns. Use feedback forms or chatbots within the portal to collect qualitative feedback.

7 *Plan for full integration*—
   a *Modeling activity*—Create detailed architectural and data flow diagrams for the full integration.
   b *Coding activity*—Outline development tasks, resource requirements, and timelines using project management tools.

The deliverables are as follows:

- Comparative analysis report with findings from hands-on exploration
- Diagrams of current and proposed integrated environments
- Source code of the proof-of-concept with installation and usage documentation
- Developer feedback summary, including usage analytics and survey results
- Integration plan detailing coding tasks, dependencies, and schedules

10.7   *Outcomes from building the platform products*

Epetech's experience offers valuable lessons for organizations seeking to evolve their platform products. Each aspect of its journey highlights critical strategies and best practices that can drive successful platform evolution. In this section, we look at the technology benefits the engineering teams enjoyed, followed by the business benefits the organization as a whole achieved through its platform journey.

10.7.1 *Key takeaways from Epetech's journey*

Epetech's platform journey, as we covered throughout the book, demonstrated several key benefits for their engineering organization. The following are the six key takeaways.

IMPROVED DEVELOPER SATISFACTION BY ADOPTING A PLATFORM-AS-A-PRODUCT MINDSET

One of the foundational steps in Epetech's transformation was embracing the platform-as-a-product mindset. Instead of viewing the platform merely as a set of tools or infrastructure components, Epetech treated it as a product designed to meet its users' (developers and operators) specific needs. This shift in perspective meant prioritizing user-centric design and focusing on delivering real value. The platform team gained deep insights into their users' challenges and requirements by conducting thorough user research. They defined the platform's clear vision and mission, aligning it with user needs and business objectives. Based on this understanding, they planned features and enhancements, ensuring each addition addressed genuine pain points and improved the developer experience.

This approach drove adoption and satisfaction because users felt heard and saw tangible workflow improvements. Developers could focus more on writing code and delivering features rather than grappling with infrastructure complexities, and treating the platform as a product led to a more engaged user base and a platform that evolved in step with the organization's needs.

CLEARLY UNDERSTOOD THE SCOPE OF INVESTMENTS ALIGNED WITH QUANTIFIABLE SUCCESS MEASUREMENTS

Epetech recognized that it needed to measure success effectively to ensure the platform's effect was tangible and to guide continuous improvement. It established KPIs aligned with business goals, providing objective data to assess the platform's performance. By integrating both lagging and leading metrics, including the four key metrics from the DORA framework (deployment frequency, lead time for changes, change failure rate, and MTTR), Epetech could track operational efficiency and reliability. It complemented these with leading indicators like code quality metrics, test coverage, and developer satisfaction scores.

Regularly reviewing these metrics enabled the platform team to identify areas of strength and opportunities for improvement promptly. This data-driven approach ensured that efforts were focused where they would have the most significant effect.

REDUCED ORGANIZATIONAL FRICTION BY EMBRACING CULTURAL CHANGE

Understanding that technology changes alone were insufficient, Epetech focused on embracing cultural change. It broke down silos, enhancing collaboration. By adopting DevOps principles and reorganizing teams based on concepts from team topologies, Epetech accelerated delivery and innovation. Cross-functional teams were formed, integrating developers, operations, QA, and security professionals. This restructuring improved communication, reduced misunderstandings, and promoted a sense of ownership among team members.

The cultural shift also involved promoting transparency and trust, encouraging teams to share knowledge and support each other. This collaborative environment led to a more agile organization capable of adapting quickly to changing market demands and technological advancements.

USED UNIFIED AND CONSISTENT PLATFORM PRACTICES THAT REDUCED DUPLICATION OF WORK AND IMPROVED END-USER EXPERIENCE

To balance rapid innovation with the need for reliable systems, Epetech implemented SRE practices. It defined clear SLOs and monitored SLIs to set measurable system performance and availability targets. Epetech managed the tradeoff between deploying new features and maintaining system stability by establishing error budgets. If the error budget was exhausted due to incidents, efforts were shifted toward improving reliability before introducing additional changes. All these new capabilities were built as part of the platform engineering team's charter with clear inputs and contributions from the SRE team.

Embedding SRE practices enhanced customer trust by delivering consistent and dependable services. It also improved operational stability by proactively identifying and addressing potential problems before they affected users. This approach ensured that reliability was not an afterthought but an integral part of the development and deployment process.

USED INTELLIGENT TOOLS

Epetech recognized the value of technology in enhancing efficiency and quality. By using intelligent tools like automation and AI, it reduced complexity and improved the overall quality of their software delivery.

Automation tools streamlined repetitive tasks such as testing, deployment, and infrastructure provisioning, increasing speed and minimizing human errors associated with manual processes. AI-driven monitoring and analytics provided more profound insights into system performance, enabling proactive issue detection and resolution. These intelligent tools freed teams to focus on strategic initiatives and innovation rather than getting bogged down in routine operations. The result was a more efficient organization capable of delivering higher-quality products in less time.

INTEGRATED IDPS AND DEVELOPER PORTALS

To optimize the developer experience, Epetech integrated IDPs and developer portals. By combining operational capabilities with accessible information resources, it created a unified platform that empowered developers.

The IDP provided self-service capabilities for deploying applications and managing environments, reducing dependency on other teams and accelerating the development process. The developer portal offered a centralized hub for documentation, APIs, tooling, and collaboration resources.

This integration minimized context switching and made it easier for developers to find what they needed when they needed it. As a result, developers could focus on building features rather than navigating complex systems or searching for information, enhancing productivity and satisfaction.

10.7.2 *Benefits realized by Epetech*

In the previous section, we looked at all the benefits realized by the engineering organization at Epetech. However, none of those things matter if the business as a whole is unable to scale and increase its revenues and reduce its operational costs. Through its comprehensive approach, Epetech achieved significant and quantifiable outcomes that propelled the organization forward. These included the following:

ACCELERATED TIME-TO-MARKET

Epetech transformed its delivery capability from slow, periodic releases to a rapid, continuous deployment model. This shift meant the organization could respond swiftly to market demands and customer feedback, turning ideas into production-ready features in a fraction of the time it once took. The shorter lead time from code commit to release not only enabled faster delivery of new features and fixes but also gave Epetech the agility to seize emerging opportunities ahead of competitors.

IMPROVED RELIABILITY

By embedding SRE practices and enhancing monitoring, Epetech significantly reduced downtime and improved system stability. Critical incidents became less frequent, service availability increased, and operational resilience improved. Even when problems did arise, faster recovery times minimized the effect on customers and reduced the operational costs associated with outages. This reliability became a foundation for customer trust and long-term retention.

IMPROVED EMPLOYEE RETENTION

Developer experience improvements ranging from streamlined processes to better tooling and greater automation boosted morale and job satisfaction. Repetitive manual tasks were replaced with self-service capabilities and automation, enabling developers to focus on innovation and value-adding work. Empowered teams were able to deliver more significant features, fostering a sense of ownership and accomplishment.

ENHANCED COMPETITIVE ADVANTAGE

The combination of faster delivery, higher reliability, and improved developer experience directly translated into stronger customer satisfaction and loyalty. With a reputation for innovation and operational excellence, Epetech was able to differentiate itself in the market, attract new customers, and appeal to top engineering talent. This not only drove growth but also positioned the company as an employer of choice in the tech industry.

ACHIEVED TANGIBLE BUSINESS OUTCOMES

Epetech's comprehensive approach to evolving its platform product delivered measurable business gains. Increased efficiency and reduced downtime translated into substantial cost savings, while faster time-to-market fueled revenue growth. The company's ability to innovate rapidly and reliably opened new market opportunities and strengthened its competitive positioning. Culturally, a collaborative, empowered workforce fostered a continuous improvement mindset, ensuring these gains were sustainable well into the future.

As Epetech continues to evolve, it recognizes that platform development is an ongoing journey. Continuous improvement, adapting to new technologies, and aligning with organizational goals are essential for sustained success. Epetech remains committed to investing in its platform, culture, and people to meet future challenges and opportunities.

Summary

- Measure what matters by establishing clear, business-aligned metrics early to track platform success, using both lagging indicators like the DORA four key metrics and leading indicators such as code quality, test coverage, and developer satisfaction to guide continuous improvement.

- Adopt a platform-as-a-product mindset by treating the platform not just as a tool-kit but as a product with defined users, problems to solve, and measurable value propositions to ensure relevance, adoption, and strategic alignment.

- Define a clear vision and mission that capture long-term goals and the developer experience you want to create, anchoring all platform decisions to prevent scope drift and keep stakeholders aligned.

- Build and maintain a strategic roadmap that translates vision into actionable steps, prioritized through user feedback and business objectives, and use it as both a planning guide and a stakeholder communication tool.

- Iterate with agile practices, delivering platform capabilities in small, validated increments and incorporating continuous feedback loops.

- Empower the platform with the right roles, using a platform product manager to bridge technical execution and business outcomes through user research, stakeholder engagement, and tracking platform KPIs.

- Focus on developer experience by simplifying infrastructure complexity, providing robust self-service capabilities, and enforcing consistency and compliance to reduce cognitive load and speed up delivery.

- Foster a collaborative culture by breaking down silos, adopting DevOps principles, forming cross-functional teams, and applying team topologies to improve speed, quality, and team morale.

- Integrate reliability into the platform by applying SRE practices to balance change velocity with stability, using SLOs, SLIs, and error budgets to ensure reliability is a built-in feature.

- Use intelligent tools such as automation, AI, and orchestration platforms to reduce manual work, improve decision-making, and accelerate delivery cycles.

- Unify IDPs and developer portals to combine operational strengths with discoverability and collaboration benefits, reducing context switching and boosting productivity.

- Deliver tangible business outcomes by accelerating time-to-market, improving reliability, increasing developer satisfaction, strengthening competitive differentiation, and achieving measurable cost savings.

appendix
Solutions to the exercises

For readers working through the exercises in this book, we want to make sure you have access to all the supporting material, whether you are reading the digital edition or holding the printed book in your hands. Throughout the chapters, we mention that the "answers" or extended walkthroughs for exercises can be found in the appendix. In practice, we have chosen to make these materials available in two reliable locations:

- The official GitHub companion repository: github.com/effective-platform -engineering/companion-code
- The Manning book page: manning.com/books/effective-platform-engineering

This shift from a static printed appendix to online resources reflects a more modern approach to learning. Instead of flipping to the back of the book and working through fixed examples, you now have direct access to a searchable, indexed, and continuously updated set of solutions and examples. The GitHub repository provides runnable code, reference implementations, and evolving samples that mirror real-world platform engineering practices. These are not just "answers" but working artifacts you can clone, run, and adapt in your environments. The Manning site complements this by hosting downloadable PDFs for exercise solutions, as well as updates and errata, ensuring readers have a curated, official source of supporting material.

By pointing you to these locations instead of a printed appendix, we can ensure you always have the most current and practical resources. Code evolves quickly, and platform practices are never truly finished; they improve with feedback and iteration. This digital-first approach makes it easier for you to find what you need, revisit examples later, and stay aligned with updates to tools and practices. Whether you bought the digital edition or the printed book, both links are open and available to you. We encourage you to treat them as your living appendix, where you'll find not just "answers" but an ongoing companion to your platform engineering journey.

references

CHAPTER 1

[1] Doerrfeld, Bill (2023, January 18). State of DevOps report finds a rise in platform engineering. DevOps.com. https://devops.com/state-of-devops-report-finds-a-rise-in-platform-engineering/

[2] Ge, Ning, and Bartoletti, Dave (2025, January 23). Is your platform ready for 2025? New research on platform engineering reveals the secret to success. Google Cloud Blog. https://cloud.google.com/blog/products/application-modernization/new-platform-engineering-research-report

[3] Weiss, Todd R. (2025, May 30). Google study: 65% of developer time wasted without platforms. The New Stack. https://thenewstack.io/google-study-65-of-developer-time-wasted-without-platforms/

[4] Fowler, Martin (2020, April 22). Domain driven design. https://martinfowler.com/bliki/DomainDrivenDesign.html

[5] Ford, Neal, Parsons, Rebeccas, and Kua, Patrick (2017). *Building Evolutionary Architectures*. O'Reilly Media.

CHAPTER 2

[1] Engeström, Yrjö (1987). *Learning by Expanding. An Activity–Theoretical Approach to Developmental Research*. Orienta konsultit.

[2] Tan, David, Schulze, Keith, and Lisle, Mitchell (n.d.). Three delivery planning principles for iterating towards the right data product. In *Modern Data Engineering Playbook*. https://www.thoughtworks.com/en-us/insights/e-books/modern-data-engineering-playbook/delivery-planning-principles

[3] Gall, John (2002). *The Systems Bible*. 3rd ed. General Systemantics Press.

[4] Fowler, Martin (2020, April 22). Domain driven design. https://martinfowler.com/bliki/DomainDrivenDesign.html

[5] Evans, Eric (2003). *Domain-Driven Design: Tackling Complexity in the Heart of Software*. Addison-Wesley.

[6] Juhls, Hauke, and Morales, Luis (2021, July 22). Using cloud fitness functions to drive evolutionary architecture. AWS Architecture Blog. https://aws.amazon.com/blogs/architecture/using-cloud-fitness-functions-to-drive-evolutionary-architecture/

[7] Ford, Neal, and Richards, Mark (2020). *Fundamentals of Software Architecture*. O'Reilly Media.

[8] Evans, Eric (2004). *Domain-Driven Design*. Addison-Wesley.

[9] Nygard, Michael (2021, November 15). Documenting architecture decisions. Cognitect Blog. https://cognitect.com/blog/2011/11/15/documenting-architecture-decisions

[10] Thomas, Andrew, and Hunt, David (1999). *The Pragmatic Programmer*. Addison-Wesley.

[11] Gilbert, Seth, and Lynch, Nancy (2002). Brewer's conjecture and the feasibility of consistent, available, partition-tolerant web services. *ACM SIGACT News*, 33(2), 51–59.

[12] Rotem-Gal-Oz, Arnon (2008, January). Fallacies of distributed computing explained. https://www.se.rit.edu/~se442/doc/fallacies.pdf

CHAPTER 3

[1] Skelton, Matthew, and Pais, Manuel (2019). *Team Topologies*. IT Revolution.

[2] Martin, Karen, and Osterling, Mike (2013). *Value Stream Mapping*. McGraw-Hill. https://tkmg.com/books/value-stream-mapping/

[3] Kotagiri, Sridhar, and Chankramath, Ajay (2024). *Measuring the Value of Your Internal Developer Platform Investments*. IT Revolution. https://itrevolution.com/product/value-internal-developer-platform-investments/

CHAPTER 4

[1] Peña, Adolfo (2010). The Dreyfus model of clinical problem-solving skills acquisition: A critical perspective. *Medical Education Online, 15*. https://www.doi.org/10.3402/meo.v15i0.4846

[2] Dreyfus, Stuart E., and Dreyfus, Hubert L. (1980, February). A five-stage model of the mental activities involved in directed skill acquisition. Defense Technical Information Center. Report ADA084551. https://doi.org/10.21236/ADA084551

[3] Open Policy Agent. Option 5: Pull data during evaluation. In External Data. https://www.openpolicyagent.org/docs/latest/external-data/#option-5-pull-data-during-evaluation-paltform

[4] Lambert, John (2020, December 13). Important steps for customers to protect themselves from recent nation-state cyberattacks. Microsoft Blog. https://blogs.microsoft.com/on-the-issues/2020/12/13/customers-protect-nation-state-cyberattacks/

CHAPTER 6

[1] Gall, John (1975). *Systemantics: How Systems Really Work and How They Fail*. Crown.

CHAPTER 7

[1] AWS Security Hub. User's guide (2025). https://docs.aws.amazon.com/securityhub/latest/userguide/cis-aws-foundations-benchmark.html

[2] Internet Engineering Task Force (2012, October). The OAuth 2.0 Authorization Framework. RFC 6749. https://datatracker.ietf.org/doc/html/rfc6749

[3] Denniss, W., et al. (2019, August). OAuth 2.0 Device Authorization Grant. RFC 6828. https://datatracker.ietf.org/doc/html/rfc8628

index